FROMME[...] to

SAN ANTONIO & AUSTIN

1st Edition

By Edie Jarolim

FROMMER'S STAR RATINGS SYSTEM

Every hotel, restaurant, and attraction listed in this guide has been ranked for quality and value. Here's what the stars mean:

★	Recommended
★★	Highly Recommended
★★★	A must! Don't miss!

AN IMPORTANT NOTE

The world is a dynamic place. Hotels change ownership, restaurants hike their prices, museums alter their opening hours, and buses and trains change their routings. And all of this can occur in the several months after our authors have visited, inspected, and written about, these hotels, restaurants, museums, and transportation services. Though we have made valiant efforts to keep all our information fresh and up-to-date, some few changes can inevitably occur in the periods before a revised edition of this guidebook is published. So please bear with us if a tiny number of the details in this book have changed. Please also note that we have no responsibility or liability for any inaccuracy or errors or omissions, or for inconvenience, loss, damage, or expenses suffered by anyone as a result of assertions in this guide.

Mission Concepción, one of five historic Spanish missions open to visitors in San Antonio.

PREVIOUS PAGE: **Wine-tasting in the Pedernales River wine country, near Fredericksburg.**

CONTENTS

A modern cowboy keeps the spirit of the West alive in the Hill Country.

A LOOK AT SAN ANTONIO & AUSTIN

Two cities, a mere 80 miles apart, a straight shoot along I-35. At one end lies historic San Antonio, with its gracious River Walk and string of fine old Spanish missions, where the battle for Texas' independence began at the Alamo. At the other end lies the Texas state capital, Austin, which has burnished its hipster credentials with an influx of tech industry and arts festivals like South×Southwest. San Antonio is rich in museums, emphatically family-friendly, and wears its Hispanic heritage proudly, while Austin is less about sight-seeing and more about getting outdoors, listening to music, strolling around vibrant neighborhoods. Then there are the delights of the countryside between the two cities, where natural beauty, immigrant heritage, country music, and barbecue beckon visitors. Can't figure out which city to visit? Why make a choice? Come here and you can enjoy two very different cities in one glorious trip.

San Antonio's calendar is full of events celebrating its Hispanic heritage.

SAN ANTONIO

Originally a flood control project, River Walk (p. 80) has transformed downtown San Antonio with its lively waterside walkways, shops, and cafes.

Once a mission, then a fort, then a rallying cry for Texas independence, the Alamo (p. 77) evokes the spirit of Texas' colonial era.

San Fernando Cathedral (p. 88), in downtown San Antonio, is the oldest parish church in Texas.

Mission San Francisco de Espada is one of four early Franciscan missions comprising San Antonio Missions National Historic Park (p. 84).

The vast greenhouse complex at the San Antonio Botanical Garden (p. 82) displays thriving tropical and desert environments.

The Batman roller coaster thrills riders at Six Flags Fiesta Texas (p. 94), one of three amusement parks in San Antonio.

The repurposed Pearl Brewery (p. 81) is now a complex of shops and trendy restaurants that has kickstarted nightlife north of San Antonio's downtown.

Hispanic food remains an important element of San Antonio's culinary scene. One popular street food item is the gordita, a savory filled pastry from Mexico.

In Western wear shops in San Antonio (p. 116), high-end items boast fanciful, attention-grabbing decorative details.

Bike paths along the San Antonio River burst into color in spring, when the famous Texas bluebonnets bloom.

At numerous cultural festivals throughout the year, traditional Latin musicians such as these mariachi singers take the stage in San Antonio. See p. 34 for a calendar of events.

For 11 days in late April, Fiesta San Antonio (p. 35) takes over the city with a wide range of events, such as this *charreada*, or Mexican-style rodeo.

Adjacent to the River Walk, the circa-1926 Tobin Center for the Performing Arts (p. 119) was remodeled and expanded in 2014 to become a world-class venue, hosting everything from Ballet San Antonio and the San Antonio Symphony to touring rock acts.

Zilker Park is more or less Austin's outdoor living room, 347 acres of green space straddling the Colorado River across from downtown. On the river bank stands this statue of Austin guitar legend Stevie Ray Vaughan. See p. 231.

The state-of-the-art LBJ Library and Museum (p. 229), on the University of Texas campus, illuminates the life and times of native son Lyndon Baines Johnson, 36th President of the United States.

A huge bronze star, symbol of the Lone Star State, stands proud outside the Bullock Texas State History Museum (p. 228), full of intriguing exhibits celebrating Texas heritage.

The outstanding collection at the Blanton Museum of Art (p. 226), also on the University of Texas campus, ranges from Greek sculpture to impressive pieces of modern art.

ABOVE: Huge Barton Springs Pool (p. 237), in Zilker Park, has been refreshing residents of this area since early Native Americans first settled beside its flowing springs. BELOW: From March through November, Austinites gather every evening at sunset to watch millions of Mexican free-tail bats swarm from their roosts beneath the Congress Avenue Bridge. See p. 237.

To see Texas politics in action, hang out in the lobby of the Driskill Hotel (p. 178), just 5 blocks from the State Capitol, a time-honored gathering spot for legislators and lobbyists.

Austin has fallen in love with the kitschy-punk sport of roller derby. An avid fan base supports the hometown pros, the Texas Rollergirls (p. 283).

In hipster Austin, food trucks are a vital part of the culinary scene, with over 2,000 in business. Many of the city's most popular restaurants began as food trucks. See p. 213.

The Pub Crawler, a mobile bar propelled by pedaling customers, adds to the after-dark buzz of the South Congress Street nightlife scene.

The Elephant Room (p. 278), an intimate downtown jazz club, books top-drawer contemporary jazz artists.

A fixture among Austin's rock clubs, Emo's (p. 274) tends to book edgy alternative acts, drawing a young crowd as well as fellow musicians.

A self-styled "dive bar" in the Market Distract, Mean Eyed Cat (p. 277) has a strong local following and a loose, raucous vibe.

THE HILL COUNTRY

Just north of Boerne, Sister Creek Vineyards (p. 135) is one of several excellent wineries operating in what is increasingly being referred to as Texas Wine Country.

In downtown Boerne (p. 132), a life-size statue of iconic frontier gunfighter Wild Bill Hickok lounges on a bench amid Main Street's antiques stores and boutiques.

Around the town of Bandera, several guest ranches, like the Dixie Dude Ranch (p. 139), offer visitors a chance to get a taste of the cowboy lifestyle.

Outside of Fredericksburg, Enchanted Rock State Natural Area (p. 146) rises on a dome of pink granite above the surrounding Hill Country. Native Americans believed this beautiful spot was inhabited by evil spirits.

Surprisingly sophisticated Fredericksburg (p. 143) has plentiful shopping and a handful of art galleries.

Made famous by a Willie Nelson and Waylon Jennings song, quirky Luckenbach, Texas (p. 151), presents live music 7 days a week on its outdoor stage.

Known in its day as the "Texas White House," Lyndon B. Johnson's ranch outside Fredericksburg is now the LBJ National Historical Park (p. 147).

Texans take their barbecue seriously and endlessly debate which country town has the best. Many would vote for the tiny town of Lockhart, home to the famous Kreuz Market (p. 287), where the smoky meat is served in classic fashion on brown butcher paper.

The open stone pit at the Salt Lick (p. 289), in rural Driftwood, Texas, slow-cooks brisket, sausage, and ribs in what is sometimes called "cowboy style" barbecue.

Parklands along the pristine spring-fed San Marcos River, which begins in the town of San Marcos (p. 291), provide some excellent hiking trails.

German immigrants settled much of this part of Texas, and many small towns in the Hill Country proudly preserve that heritage. At a wurst festival in New Braunfels (p. 296), lederhosen and an oompah band are essential parts of the fun.

ABOVE: The rapids of the Guadalupe River near New Braunfels create ideal conditions in summer for rafting and tubing (p. 300). The water can be bracingly cold, refreshing in the heat of a Texas summer. BELOW: Just outside New Braunfels, the historic small town of Gruene is perhaps best known for Gruene Hall (p. 299), the state's oldest continually operating dance hall and beer garden, with a great line-up of live music year-round.

THE BEST OF SAN ANTONIO & AUSTIN

1

Composing best-of lists is a subjective exercise, but it can lead to some objective truths. In this case, the process reveals just how many entertaining—and distinctive—activities, sights, and experiences San Antonio and Austin offer their visitors.

No question: The River Walk is San Antonio's major tourist draw. The downtown stretch of this leafy linear park is packed with visitors hailing river taxis and sipping cold drinks by day; the light-draped trees and bustling patio restaurants lend it a festive, romantic atmosphere after dark. But with its expansion north to the trendy Pearl entertainment district and south to the older Hispanic neighborhoods that are home to the historic missions, the River Walk can no longer be distinguished from the "real" San Antonio. Locals frequent the paved banks of their famed waterway almost as much as visitors do—perhaps more on the southern stretch, where throngs of strollers and bicyclists gather on the weekends.

San Antonio is not only good at bringing back neglected rivers (the San Pedro's resurrection is now a work in progress). The city also has a penchant for revitalizing old neighborhoods, including King William, Southtown, and Monte Vista near downtown, and for converting derelict buildings into hotels, restaurants, museums, and even shopping centers (the posh Alamo Quarry Market was once a cement factory). As a result, the city is studded with historic treasures in everyday settings, well beyond such famous sights as the Alamo.

History is alive in other ways in San Antonio. The only major city in the state founded before Texas won its independence from Mexico, San Antonio was populated from early on by diverse groups with distinct goals: Spanish missionaries and militiamen, German merchants, Southern plantation owners, Western cattle ranchers. All left their mark on the city's rich culture and cuisine and festivals—including the 10-day-long Fiesta.

Austin has historic heft too—it is, after all, Texas's capital, with a massive state capitol building to prove it. Overall, however, it has a younger, hipper vibe, both as the "Live Music Capital of the

World" for its many music venues, and as "Silicon Hills" for its many tech companies. Austin's major festivals tell the same story: The 10-day-long SXSW started out as a tech conference and expanded into film and music components, while the Austin City Limits Music Festival takes over Zilker Park for 2 consecutive 3-day weekends.

Austin's dominance in the tech and music sectors—not to mention its youthful orientation—owes a great deal to the presence of the University of Texas (UT). The campus is a key source of the city's cultural savvy, including a presidential library; theater, dance, and concert venues; and a major art collection. But UT's original funding came from oil money, and even the most sophisticated Austinites revert to typical Texan fervor when it comes to rooting for the Longhorns.

Perhaps what most defines Austin is its love of the outdoors. Despite downtown's rapid development and the unbridled growth of the tech corridor in the Northwest, Austin's heart is green. The city has a vast municipal system of parks and preserves, and a string of lakes for water recreation. Downtown's Hike and Bike Trail, looping around Lady Bird Lake, is proof of this fresh-air obsession. There's no better place to mingle with Austinites of all ages, incomes, and abilities than on this tree-fringed thoroughfare.

THE most UNFORGETTABLE EXPERIENCES

- **Walking on Water** (San Antonio): Sure, the River Walk is overhyped, but you won't be disappointed by this landscaped waterway that threads through the heart of downtown. Few who come here leave without a memory of some moment—quiet or heart-quickening, sunlit or sparkling with tiny tree-draped lights—when the river somehow worked its magic on them. See p. 80.
- **Walking up Congress Avenue to the Texas Capitol** (Austin): The shops, restaurants, and hotels lining the grand boulevard that leads to the legislative hub of Texas may be different, but the sweeping approach to the grand historic capitol is the same as it was a century ago—as is the awe-inspiring first look up at the giant rotunda. See p. 224.
- **Lazing in the Courtyard at the Marion Koogler McNay Art Museum** (San Antonio): As fine as many of the paintings here are, when it comes to transcendent experiences, you can't beat sitting out on the lovely tree-shaded patio of the McNay, a converted mansion. Looking out at the well-manicured lawns and gardens, it's easy to imagine being part of a kinder, gentler era. See p. 81.
- **Checking Out the Talent at the Continental Club** (Austin): Whenever you visit, there will be some act at the Continental Club that you can't miss. It might be happy hour jazz; it might be an evening blues band; it might be somebody you haven't even heard of—yet. But there's no place like the

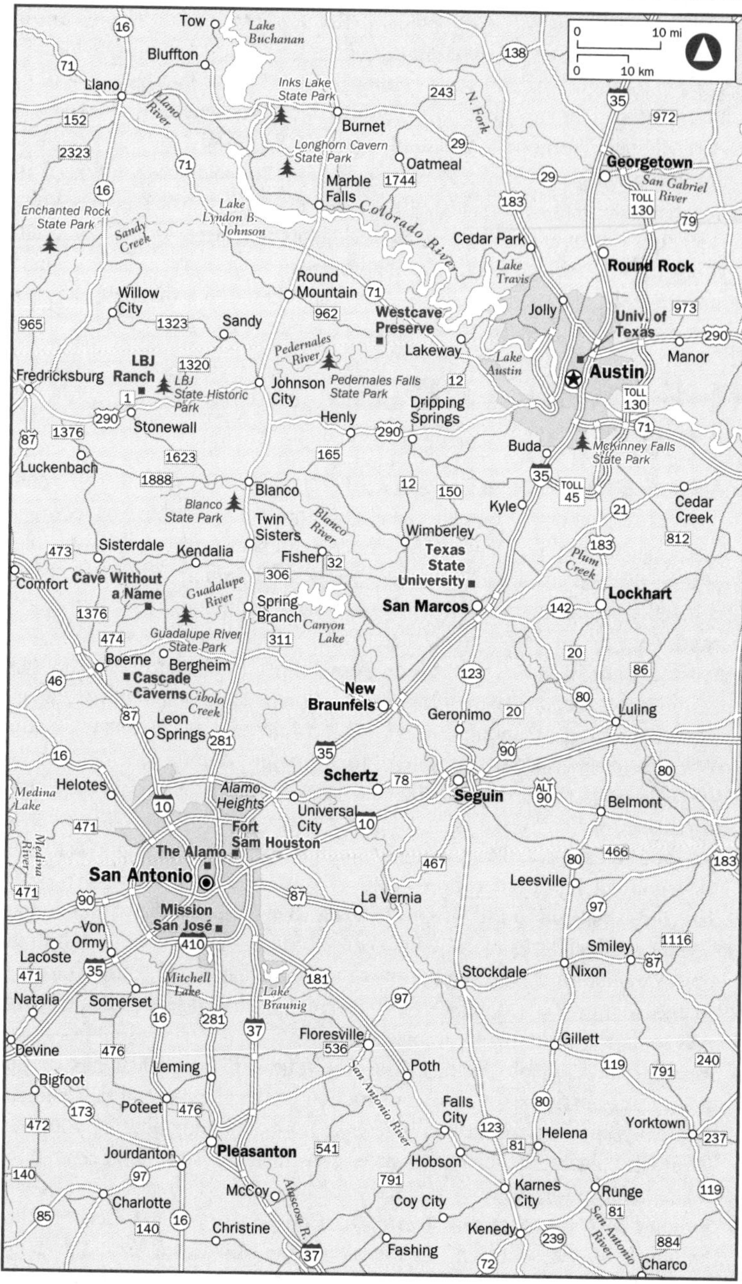
0
10 mi
0
10 km
Tow
Lake Buchanan
Bluffton
Llano
Llano River
Inks Lake State Park
Burnet
Longhorn Cavern State Park
Oatmeal
Marble Falls
Lake Lyndon B. Johnson
Colorado River
N. Fork
Georgetown
San Gabriel River
Cedar Park
Round Rock
Lake Travis
Jolly
Enchanted Rock State Park
Sandy Creek
Willow City
Round Mountain
Westcave Preserve
Sandy
Pedernales River
Lakeway
Lake Austin
Univ. of Texas
Manor
Austin
LBJ Ranch
LBJ State Historic Park
Fredricksburg
Johnson City
Pedernales Falls State Park
Dripping Springs
Stonewall
Henly
Luckenbach
Buda
McKinney Falls State Park
Blanco
Blanco State Park
Kyle
Cedar Creek
Twin Sisters
Blanco River
Wimberley
Sisterdale
Kendalia
Fisher
Texas State University
Plum Creek
Comfort
Cave Without a Name
Guadalupe River
Spring Branch
San Marcos
Lockhart
Canyon Lake
Guadalupe River State Park
Boerne
Bergheim
Cascade Caverns
Cibolo Creek
New Braunfels
Luling
Leon Springs
Geronimo
Schertz
Seguin
Helotes
Medina Lake
Alamo Heights
Universal City
Belmont
Fort Sam Houston
The Alamo
Medina River
San Antonio
Leesville
La Vernia
Mission San José
Von Ormy
Lacoste
Smiley
Nixon
Stockdale
Mitchell Lake
Natalia
Somerset
Lake Braunig
Floresville
Gillett
Devine
Poth
San Antonio River
Leming
Bigfoot
Poteet
Falls City
Yorktown
Helena
Pleasanton
Jourdanton
Hobson
Charlotte
McCoy
Atascosa R.
Coy City
Karnes City
Runge
Christine
Kenedy
Fashing
Charco
San Antonio River
16
71
152
2323
16
71
138
243
35
972
29
29
1744
183
TOLL 130
79
71
962
973
965
1323
290
1320
12
1
290
290
TOLL 130
71
87
1376
1623
165
1888
35
TOLL 45
12
150
21
183
812
473
32
306
142
1376
474
311
20
86
46
123
80
87
20
281
16
35
90
78
80
10
ALT 90
471
10
466
183
467
471
90
87
97
1116
410
87
471
35
181
97
16
281
37
476
536
119
240
791
173
476
80
472
123
237
81
541
140
97
791
119
85
16
81
140
37
239
884
72

little club on South Congress Avenue to indulge or expand your musical tastes. See p. 274.

- **Strolling Through the King William Historic District and Upper South Side** (San Antonio): Meandering through this area just south of downtown is a trip through time and across cultures, from the opulent homes built by 19th-century German merchants to the vibrant galleries and cafes of the Hispanic neighborhood to the south and east. See p. 91.
- **Sipping a Margarita While Watching the Sun Set over Lake Travis** (Austin): Relax at the Oasis on one of the many decks that stretch across a hillside high above Lake Travis, order a large margarita, and congratulate yourself on living the good life. Laid out before you are miles of watery landscape. If conditions are right, a soft redness will tint the view and help create a sense of oneness with the universe. See p. 242.

THE best THINGS TO DO FOR (ALMOST) FREE

- **Attending Mariachi Mass at San José** (San Antonio): With the hike-and-bike path completed, you can make a visit to this venerable Spanish mission—part of the San Antonio Missions National Historical Park—as part of a 12-mile physical and religious exercise. On Sundays at noon, a Mass is held by the community of San José to the accompaniment of a mariachi band. That's *puro* San Antonio. See p. 85.
- **Touring Central Market or Whole Foods** (Austin): According to the Visit Austin tourism board, these two gourmet supermarkets—and they really are SUPER-sized—are among the top five most popular attractions in Austin. You'll be mesmerized by the rows of fresh produce, the cooking demonstrations, the ethnic food stations, the cold cases bearing prepared foods. Entering the stores themselves is free, but here's the "almost" catch: There's no way you'll walk out of here without wanting to buy something to eat. Plan to visit at lunch or dinner time. See p. 258.
- **Scouting the Alamo and the River Walk** (San Antonio): How many other cities have freebies as their two major attractions? Even if you didn't think you'd be interested in seeing the site of a church and an old battle, you have no excuse for not checking it out. Odds are, you'll be fascinated, and spend a lot more time here than you imagined. See p. 77.
- **Touring the Capitol** (Austin): The free tour will give you loads of fun insider information about the construction of the Capitol and the colorful political goings-on inside. You'll have an easy time remembering you're in Texas; the place is loaded with state icons, and the size—bigger than all other state capitols—says it all. See p. 224.
- **Soaking in Culture at the Blue Star Contemporary Art Center** (San Antonio): At the south end of San Antonio's downtown area, this huge warehouse offers thousands of square feet of studio and gallery space. In

the thick of it all, the artist-run Contemporary Arts Center incubates all that's new in San Antonio's local art scene. See p. 91.

- **Enjoying Free Outdoor Concerts (and Theater)** (Austin): There are so many free outdoor performances in Austin, sponsored by both public and private money, that you'll almost certainly have a chance to catch one during your visit. Check the local entertainment listings for information. See p. 272.

THE best SAN ANTONIO HOTEL BETS

- **Best Splurge:** Visitors in the know eschew River Walk lodgings for the **Hotel Emma,** a converted brewery in the happening Pearl complex. Wonderful architectural detail, a great location near some of the best restaurants in town, and excellent service all add to the experience. Sportscaster Charles Barkley—not known for being a San Antonio fan—professed his love of this hotel on ESPN. You're likely to encounter other A-listers in the lobby, too. See p. 48.
- **Best-Kept Lodging Secret:** Not until you get past the shabby red-carpeted steps out front and ascend to the second floor of a narrow building in the heart of downtown do you see the treasure that is the **Riverwalk Vista.** It's independently owned, reasonably priced, and centrally located, and its rooms are spacious and beautifully furnished. See p. 46.
- **The Best Place to See (or Feel) a Ghost:** San Antonio's got plenty of historic hotels—the kind where haunts tend to linger—but only the **Menger** claims to have 32 ghosts. You can take your pick of the spirits you want to sleep with—or drink with. The bar where Teddy Roosevelt recruited his Rough Riders is in this hotel, too. See p. 46.
- **Best for People Traveling with Pets:** You might not expect the swanky **St. Anthony** to be amenable to the four-legged, but its no-fee, no-size restriction policy (with the usual waivers, of course) plus proximity to Travis Park make this a prime spot to bunk with a furry companion or two. See p. 42.
- **Best Downtown Bargain:** Low room rates, lots of freebies, attractive rooms in a converted historic building, and a convenient location near downtown all make the **Best Western Sunset Suites** a super deal. See p. 47.
- **Best One-Stop Bunk:** You never have to wander far from the **Marriott Rivercenter,** with its excellent health club (on the same floor as the hotel's free washers and dryers), its proximity to the Shops at Rivercenter and the River Walk, and its abundant on-site eateries. See p. 40.
- **Best Resort:** Whether you're visiting San Antonio with family, looking to play great golf, or seeking a spa getaway with friends, **La Cantera** has your number. The facilities are top-notch, the grounds are spectacular, the dining is outstanding (one of the best chefs in town presides over Signature), and you'll be near the posh Shops at La Cantera. See p. 50.

THE best AUSTIN HOTEL BETS

- **Best Splurge:** The **Four Seasons Austin** is better than ever after a multi-million dollar revamp. Settle into one of the airy guest rooms overlooking the lake, have the front desk schedule you a massage at the highly regarded spa, press the margarita button on your phone to have the drinks cart brought to your room, and then pinch yourself to make sure you're not dreaming. The only thing that could make a stay at this hotel any more special would be billing someone else for it. See p. 180.
- **Best For Music Lovers:** Several hotels in town offer live music on-site now and then, but only the **Kimpton Hotel Van Zandt** has a Director of Music, who programs the sounds that waft throughout the building (including in the pool), displays music art in the lobby, and books live performances nightly in Geraldine's restaurant. See p. 181.
- **Best Place to Play Cattle Baron:** If you want to imagine you've acquired your fortune in an earlier era, bed down at the **Driskill,** Austin's hotel jewel. In the original building, where big cattle baron Jesse Driskill still surveys the scene in stone bust effigy, you'll find suites that ooze character. See p. 178.
- **Hippest Budget Hotel:** Look for the classic neon sign for the **Austin Motel,** in the trendy SoCo district. Rooms done in bright primary colors, a kidney-shaped pool, and a tropical-themed reception area/gift shop give the place retro-chic cachet at (almost) retro prices. See p. 188.
- **Best View of Lady Bird Lake:** Lots of downtown properties have nice water views, but the **Hyatt Regency's** location on the lake's south shore gives it the edge. You get a panoramic spread of the city with the capitol as a backdrop. See p. 185.
- **Greenest Hotel:** Almost all hotels in Austin are eco-conscious to some degree, but no one takes earth-friendly policies nearly as far as **Habitat Suites,** which from its opening day has relied on solar electricity, practiced water conservation, and used all-natural cleaning products. Not only is this place ecofriendly, it's also pocketbook friendly. Each large hypo-allergenic room has cooking facilities, and breakfast is included in the room rate. See p. 191.
- **Best for Forgetting Your Troubles:** Stress? That's a dirty word at the **Lake Austin Spa Resort.** After a few days at this lovely, ultra-relaxing spot about 20 minutes from central Austin, you'll be ready to face the world again, even if you don't especially want to. See p. 195.

THE best SAN ANTONIO DINING BETS

- **Best Place to Rub Shoulders with Locals: Paesanos** in Alamo Heights has long been San Antonio's go-to spot for special occasions, family gatherings, and anytime hankerings for great Italian food. Don't miss the signature Shrimp Paesano's. There's a branch on the River Walk, but locals mostly stick to the original. See p. 72.

- **Best Movable Feast:** It used to be that you could dine on the water only if you were with a group, but among the restaurants that now offer dinner cruise reservations to individuals and couples, **Boudro's** tops the meals-on-river-barge-wheels list. See p. 58.
- **Best Place for Fat Expense Accounts:** If you need to wine and dine someone in San Antonio, whether for business or personal reasons, **Bohanan's** is there for you. Not only is it one of the best steakhouses in Texas, but it completely looks the part—soft lights, white tablecloths, lots of dark woodwork, and a serious wine list. See p. 58.
- **Best Place to Dine with Music:** Savor creative South American, Mexican, and Caribbean fare at Southtown's **Azuca,** while tapping your feet to salsa, merengue, and other Latin sounds. See p. 63.
- **Best Blast from the Past: Schilo's** not only serves up German deli in portions that date back to pre-cholesterol-conscious days, but also maintains prices from that era. See p. 62.
- **Best Fine Dining Kept Simple:** It's a tie: Both **Silo** (p. 73), one of the first New American restaurants in town, and **Bliss** (p. 62), a Southtown favorite run by Silo's first executive chef, pull off upscale dining without ostentation or unnecessary fuss. This is creative cooking at its finest, with enough variety to please just about everyone, while steering clear of weirdly worded descriptions and one-upmanship.
- **Best Cross-Cultural Experience:** Peru and Asia may not strike you as a natural culinary coupling, but **Botika** makes it seems like a match made in food heaven. Chef/owner Geronimo Lopez, a former instructor at San Antonio's Culinary Institute of America, is adept at combinations that complement the flavors and textures of both cultures. See p. 66.

THE best AUSTIN DINING BETS

- **Best, Full Stop:** If I had to choose one place to have dinner in Austin, it would be **Olamaie.** The restaurant's superb contemporary Southern cooking is in-depth without being fussy or self-conscious. The setting, in an old house in a residential neighborhood near the university, is charming, the service is attentive but not overbearing, and the cocktails are as creative as the food. And did I mention the biscuits? See p. 218.
- **Best Asian Food:** There are a lot of terrific Asian restaurants in town, but **Uchi,** which wowed Austinites when it first burst on the dining scene in 2003, is still number one. The sushi is as fresh as ever, the cooked Japanese dishes as creative. See p. 205.
- **Best Vegetarian Cuisine:** Not only are the locally sourced vegetarian and vegan dishes served at **Bouldin Creek** artfully prepared and tasty, the dining experience is just plain fun. Carnivores will not encounter anti-meat pamphlets or holier-than-thou attitudes, just excellent food and drink in a friendly atmosphere. See p. 208.

THE best OF SAN ANTONIO & AUSTIN ONLINE

Texas

- **The Handbook of Texas Online** (www.tsha.utexas.edu/handbook/online): This encyclopedic site offers concise entries that explain who's who, what's what, and where's where in Texas. It's easy to use and has information on just about everything, from the locations of towns and counties to explanations of some of the state's legends, plus biographical data on the many characters who left their mark on Texas history.
- **Travel Texas** (www.traveltex.com): The state's official tourism website provides a good general overview of everything you want to know about the state—divided by region, city, geography, interests such as food or art, lodging types . . . you name it. Under the "Travel Tools" tab, click on "Travel Deals" to find the featured discount coupons, primarily for attractions.
- **Texas Monthly** (www.texasmonthly.com): You won't necessarily find San Antonio or Austin stories on the *Texas Monthly* site, but the state's best magazine—and one of the best geographically focused publications in the country—offers in-depth treatments of lots of interesting topics. And the site often highlights hot new San Antonio and Austin dining spots.
- **Drive Texas** (www.drivetexas.org): Created by the Texas Department of Transportation, this site is devoted to traffic conditions all over the state. It's an invaluable resource to check before you hit the road.

San Antonio

- **www.MySanAntonio.com**: The website of the city's only mainstream newspaper, the *San Antonio Express-News*, not only provides the daily news but also links to dining reviews and entertainment listings.
- **www.SACurrent.com**: The *San Antonio Current* isn't very impressive in its paper version, but its website is a good source of information on restaurants, nightlife, and other local events.

- **Best Quintessentially Austin:** Its casual Texas menu, huge outdoor patio, and "unplugged" music series all make **Shady Grove** a good representative of Austin dining at its most kicked-back. See p. 209.
- **Best Brunch:** Austinites do love going out for brunch, and the title is evenly split between two old-timers: **Fonda San Miguel** (p. 217) where you can sample Mexican regional cuisine and cocktails in a stunning hacienda-style setting, and **Mattie's at Green Pastures** (p. 204), a gracious mansion where you can sip a peach julep and savor the likes of fried chicken eggs Benedict.
- **Best for Carnivores:** Austin is renowned for its barbecue, but I'm not entering the smoked meat fray here. However, **Salt & Time,** in the back of an East Austin butcher shop, is the place to come for cooked-to-your-liking burgers and steaks sourced from local ranches and for meats cured in house. See p. 212.
- **Best Seafood:** From its raw oyster bar and meaty lobster rolls to its rich bouillabaisse and oak-grilled Gulf redfish, **Perla's** rocks the seafood scene.

- **www.SanAntonio.gov**: The City of San Antonio's website offers timely information on such topics as traffic and street closures, accessibility, and so on. The "Visitors" section is a good place to find out about city-sponsored arts events, public parks, and such city-run cultural attractions as La Villita, Market Square, and the Spanish Governor's Palace.
- **www.VisitSanAntonio.com**: You're not going to get honest critiques of hotels and attractions on the tourism bureau's comprehensive website; you are going to get useful links to many of them, however, plus an excellent overview of what the city has to offer. Easy to navigate and comprehensive, this is one of the best visitor information sites around.

Austin

- **www.Austin360.com**: Movie times, traffic reports, restaurant picks, homes, jobs, cars. . . . This site, sponsored in part by the *Austin American-Statesman*, the city's main newspaper, is a one-stop clicking center for a variety of essentials. It's easy to navigate, too.
- **www.AustinChronicle.com**: The free weekly indie paper, the *Austin Chronicle*, has so many local stories, events, and dining listings that some information is only available online. The site is a bit overwhelming but very useful.
- **www.Austin.Eater.com**: Not all cities get equal play on the national Eater.com dining sites, but the one devoted to Austin is one of the best in the country, with regular restaurant reviews and constant updates on dining news.
- **www.AustinTexas.gov**: Because so many attractions, from parks to museums and theaters, fall under the City of Austin's aegis, this website provides invaluable information to visitors.
- **www.AustinTexas.org**: The website for Visit Austin, the city's tourism bureau, is not the easiest to navigate but you'll eventually find a great deal of useful information.

Being able to enjoy your meal on one of the best outdoor patios in SoCo is a bonus. See p. 205.

THE best SHOPPING EXPERIENCES

- **Browsing South Congress Avenue** (Austin): You never know what you're going to find when you stroll along the row of shops and galleries on South Congress Avenue, just beyond Oltdorf; it's the most concentrated strip of independent retailers in town. Some have been around since SoCo became trendy in the late 1990s, but new boutiques keep cropping up too. See p. 253.
- **Checking Out the Headgear at Paris Hatters** (San Antonio): Even if you're not in the market for a Stetson, wander over to this San Antonio institution that has sold hats to everyone from Queen Elizabeth to Pope

John Paul II ("We 'hatted' a saint," said one of the owners). See how big your head is compared to those of the stars. See p. 117.

- **Shopping for Handmade Boots at Lucchese** (San Antonio): For many adult male Texans, getting fitted for Lucchese (pronounced Loo-*kaiz*-ee) boots is a sign that one has made it in the world. A symbol of Texas roots, they're worn both with suits and jeans. The boots are also a fashion statement for sassy Texas women, who love the pointy sh*t-kicking toes. See p. 117.
- **Buying Folk Art at Tesoros** (Austin): Tesoros means "treasure" and for anyone who loves colorful crafts from around the world, this shop definitely qualifies. Textiles, ceramics, tinwork, paper cut-outs from across the globe are among the many types of folk art featured. There's plenty to capture the eye across a wide range of prices. See p. 262.
- **Looking for Reading Matter at BookPeople** (Austin): One of the largest independent bookstores in the country, BookPeople caters to all reading tastes, from graphic novels to historic tomes, from middlebrow to cutting-edge. Check the website for the many author events. See p. 260.
- **Buying "Easy-Life" Potion from a Neighborhood Botanica** (San Antonio): Okay, you might prefer the standard love potion, but for my money, getting the easy-life mojo up and running is far more important. And there's a lot more to explore in these places than folk remedies. Stores like **Papa Jim's** are fertile grounds for the amateur urban anthropologist. See p. 115.
- **Picking Up Tacky Souvenirs at Alamo Plaza** (San Antonio): Seeking souvenirs with no redeeming aesthetic value, the perfect something to staunch all pesky requests to bring something back from your trips? Souvenir stores are scattered throughout the touristy areas of downtown, but the west side of Alamo Plaza is especially fertile hunting ground. Take your pick of such gems as an Alamo ashtray, a beer can wind chime, or a barbed wire candle, to name a few.
- **Picking Up Tacky Souvenirs at Wild About Music** (Austin). You'll find Keep Austin Weird mugs, bumper stickers, and T-shirts all over town (even in the Capitol Complex bookstore), but the concentration of music-related schlock (think boom-box lunchboxes or light-up key chains shaped like turntables) is unsurpassed at the famed gift and art gallery on Congress Avenue. See p. 263.

THE best PLUNGES INTO TEXAS EXCESS

- **Best Stereotype Wrapped Up in a Caricature** (San Antonio): A visit to the **Buckhorn Saloon & Museum** makes you ponder some of life's deeper questions, such as "Why don't more museums let you walk around with a beer in hand?" There are no easy answers. This is the Old West on a platter, with exhibits on blood-thirsty desperadoes and lots of taxidermied animal heads. Definitely not for everyone. See p. 86.

- **Best Sensory Overload** (San Antonio): Excess, thy name is mariachi. To set the scene, you need a table by the river, a large platter of nachos in front of you, a frozen margarita, and strolling musicians wearing large sombreros and belting out a standard like "Guadalajara, no te rajes," with great bravado. You will be expected to tip, but the music is rousing and authentic, and you be comfortable in the knowledge that you have reached the promised land of travel brochures.
- **Best State Jingoism** (Austin): It's far from tasteless or badly done, but the huge star that fronts the **Bullock Texas State History Museum** announces that you're entering a temple to the Lone Star State. The exhibits are laser focused on Texas's many accomplishments, and a film in the Spirit Theater proudly proclaims, "We're all Texans." I defy you to walk away from here without hankering for a pair of cowboy boots. See p. 228.
- **Best Evidence of Barbecue Addiction** (Austin): The arguments over who has the best barbecue in town and whether the Austin branches meet the standards of the originals in rural Texas are endless—and sometimes rancorous. But the true sign of serious addiction is the willingness to line up for hours to buy the brisket at Franklin Barbecue. Lots of people bring chairs and coolers with drinks and settle in. It's a way to make friends with fellow members of the city's smoked meat cult. See p. 214.

2

SUGGESTED SAN ANTONIO ITINERARIES

There's so much to see and do in San Antonio that organizing your time can be tough. You won't be able to cover everything if you only have a day or two to spend, but the following itineraries will at least give you a good taste for what the city has to offer. I've geared the following touring plans toward travelers with various schedules and different interests, as well as a tour for families traveling with kids. ***Note:*** The longer you stay, the more likely you'll need wheels, but for the first day you're better off leaving the car behind. See chapter 18 for more details about parking and getting around San Antonio.

THE BEST OF SAN ANTONIO IN 1 DAY

This first day of highlights is pretty much set in stone for everyone. If you're not sleeping downtown, the smartest thing is to leave your car in a downtown lot and retrieve it after dinner. It's easy to visit the downtown attractions (#1, #2, #3) in the morning on foot if the weather's nice (it usually is in the early morning), then take a river taxi to #4, after that using ride-shares or (much slower) public transportation. You'll be going from downtown to the Broadway Cultural Corridor, then circling back downtown.

---

1 Mi Tierra ★★ & Market Square

San Antonio's ties with Mexico may have been mightily tested at the Alamo (see #2), but a century and a half later, all seems friendly as can be—especially when it comes to food. Fortify yourself for a long day of sightseeing with *desayuno* at **Mi Tierra** (p. 61). Come as early as you want—the restaurant is open 24 hours a day. This is the quintessential San Antonio restaurant, where everyone from *abuelas* with grandkids to power brokers to tourists gathers, while strains of strolling

San Antonio in 1, 2 & 3 Days

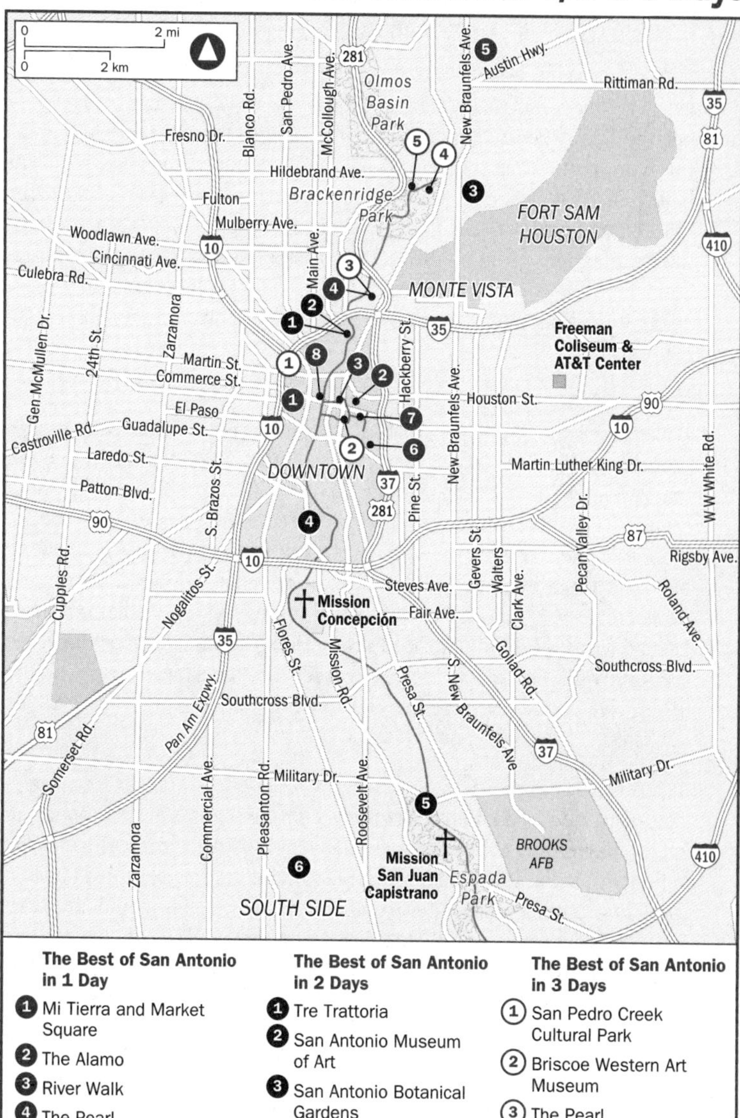

The Best of San Antonio in 1 Day

1. Mi Tierra and Market Square
2. The Alamo
3. River Walk
4. The Pearl
5. Marion Koogler McNay Art Museum
6. Tower of the Americas
7. Return to River Walk
8. *San Antonio: The Saga*

The Best of San Antonio in 2 Days

1. Tre Trattoria
2. San Antonio Museum of Art
3. San Antonio Botanical Gardens
4. King William Historic District
5. The San Antonio Missions
6. Southtown

The Best of San Antonio in 3 Days

1. San Pedro Creek Cultural Park
2. Briscoe Western Art Museum
3. The Pearl
4. Witte Museum
5. The San Antonio Zoo

mariachi music drift by your table—yes, even in the morning. If the stalls at **Market Square** are open when you're finished, give them a glance for future reference but keep on moving.

2 The Alamo ★★★

Even if you're not interested in military history, you can't say you've been to San Antonio and didn't see the **Alamo** (p. 77), the 18th-century mission that became the site of one of the country's best-known losing battles in 1736. The church and long barrack are good examples of frontier colonial Spanish architecture, typical of the region. It's a stretch of the imagination, given all the tacky tourist attractions that are now there, but Alamo Plaza was the original *atrio* of the church—a walled plaza for celebrating Mass when there were too many celebrants to fit into the church.

3 River Walk ★★★

Because it kept flooding its banks, the San Antonio River was once the problem child of the city's center. The solution was a feat of engineering that became the ever-expanding **River Walk** (p. 80). From Alamo Square, take the entrance on Losoya Street, which descends to the first section of the River Walk to be developed; it's still the prettiest, with its old-growth tall cypress and palms and ornamental flowers, but also the most congested, because of the many restaurants and hotel entrances. Escape from the loop and head north along the newer Museum Reach section. Walk a little way to get a feel for the storied waterway, and then take a river taxi—look for the GO Rio Shuttle signs (p. 104)—to your next stop.

4 The Pearl ★★★

The converted 1883 **Pearl Brewery complex** (p. 81), a shopping and entertainment hub centered by the happening Hotel Emma, is the hottest culinary ticket in town, gathering some of the best restaurants in a single sprawling public space. (See p. 48 in chapter 4). For a quicker, more casual meal, head for the **Bottling Dept. Food Hall.** If you're lucky enough to visit on a weekend, don't miss the farmers market in all its grazing glory.

5 Marion Koogler McNay Art Museum ★★★

About a 10-minute drive northeast of the Pearl, the **Marion Koogler McNay Art Museum** (p. 81) has its main collections housed in a lovely Spanish Colonial Revival mansion set on 23 landscaped acres (don't miss the Japanese garden). The museum is especially strong in 19th- and 20th-century American and European art, along with contemporary art in the Stieren Center wing and a trove of theatrical set designs in the Tobin Collection.

6 Tower of the Americas ★

In this longest transportation leg of the day (about 20 min. by car), you'll be heading to the southern part of downtown. Here, the 750-foot-tall **Tower of the Americas** (p. 90), built for the HemisFair world exposition of 1968, is the tallest building in San Antonio. It has an observation deck, but to get the same glorious sunset views without an entrance fee, go for a cocktail in **Bar 601** at dusk. (Weekday happy hours from 4:30 to 7pm offer bargain prices.)

7 Return to River Walk

After you've had your drink, stroll a few blocks north to the nearest entrance to the River Walk. Sure, you saw it in the morning, but it looks entirely different at night when the trees are softly illuminated by strings of tiny fairy lights. There are lots of excellent restaurants along the river in all price ranges and noise levels; see p. 56 in chapter 5.

8 *San Antonio: The Saga*

If you're in town on Tuesday, Friday, Saturday, or Sunday evening—and have any energy left after this long day of sightseeing—emerge from the River Walk and head over to Main Plaza to see *San Antonio—The Saga,* a delightful 24-minute show by French artist Xavier de Richemont, with video clips exploring the city's history projected onto the facade of the **San Fernando Cathedral** ★★ (p. 88) at 9, 9:30, and 10pm.

THE BEST OF SAN ANTONIO: DAY 2

Driving is probably the easiest way to get from one place to the next on this second day, and parking should be easy for the most part: You'll start out a bit north of downtown, head farther north to the Broadway Cultural Corridor, and then move south of the city's hub. The neighborhoods closest to downtown, King William and Southtown, are the only stops where you might have a little difficulty finding a space for your car.

---

1 Tre Trattoria ★★

Kickstart your day with caprese avocado toast or house-made gnocchi and mushrooms—or Nutella pancakes if you prefer—at **Tre Trattoria** (p. 68); it's in a historic building on the grounds of the San Antonio Museum of Art, but not in the museum itself. If the weather permits, dine on the patio overlooking the river.

2 San Antonio Museum of Art ★★

You didn't think I'd send you to the **San Antonio Museum of Art** (p. 82) for breakfast and not suggest you look at the art, did you? Housed in the old Lone Star Brewery, the museum is best known for its Rockefeller Center of Latin American Art, but smaller Asian, Egyptian, and Greek collections are definitely worth browsing.

3 San Antonio Botanical Garden ★★

A short walk west of the museum, a 2018 expansion of the **San Antonio Botanical Garden** (p. 82) not only added kid-friendly attractions to one of the best botanical gardens in the Southwest, representing landscapes from all over the region; it also provided adults with new points of interest like the Culinary Garden, featuring an outdoor chef's teaching kitchen and exploration station. Tapping into San Antonio's awareness of its potential water shortage, the gardens offer useful ideas about xeriscaping as well as other tips for home gardeners. For lunch, try **Rosella,** the cafe in the botanical gardens, set in a landmark 1896 carriage house.

4 King William Historic District ★★

It's about a 15-minute drive south to the **King William Historic District** (p. 91), just beyond downtown. Declared the most beautiful historic neighborhood in Texas by *Thrillist,* which praised its Greek Revival, Victorian, and Italianate architecture, the area was settled by prosperous German merchants in the 1870s. To explore the 25 blocks in the designated historic neighborhood, you can pick up a self-guided tour booklet outside the offices of the San Antonio Conservation Society at 107 King William St.; or just wander along King William Street, where most of the grandest houses reside. The King William district occupies land that once belonged to Mission San Antonio de Valero (aka the Alamo); you're now near the Mission Reach section of the River Walk.

5 The San Antonio Missions ★★★

Drive farther south for another 6 minutes to reach the first of the five historic religious complexes that comprise the **San Antonio Missions National Historical Park** (p. 84). They're only 2 or 3 miles apart from each other, and never far from the life-sustaining San Antonio River. With so much focus on the Alamo as a battle site, it's easy to forget that the missions were farming communities founded by Franciscan missionaries to bring religion to the natives; the other four missions are still active parishes. Make your first stop **San José,** the largest, best known, and most beautiful of the Texas missions, which has been reconstructed to give visitors a complete picture of daily life in a mission community. If you have time for a second mission, check out **San Juan Capistrano,** where, in a unique partnership with the National Park Service, the San Antonio Food Bank farms 50 acres, with all crops going to feed the hungry. It has a short nature trail, too.

6 Southtown

Head back north toward the King William District, stopping just before you get there to reach one of the city's hottest restaurant districts, Southtown (see p. 62 in Chapter 5 for specific recommendations). If you want only alcohol and ice cream—no judgment!—Boozy's Creamery (p. 74) is another option.

THE BEST OF SAN ANTONIO: DAY 3

This itinerary may not be the most logical from a geographical perspective—it has you heading from northwest downtown to the center and then back north again—but this is necessary to work around the fact that, although it's smart to get an early start to beat the hot weather, many shops and attractions open comparatively late, at 10am. (That's one of the few frustrating things about visitor-friendly San Antonio.) That said, this route lets you enjoy the outdoors in the cool of the morning, which is often a very good thing.

---

1 San Pedro Creek Culture Park ★★

Grab a light breakfast near your hotel and head for **San Pedro Creek Culture Park** (p. 102), which completed its first phase in 2018, to enjoy its public artworks and the restored ecosystem of one of San Antonio's key waterways. (Download a free app at www.spculturpark.com to get in-depth information about what you're seeing.) By the end of the route, you'll have worked up an appetite for a hearty breakfast at **Schilo's** ★★ (p. 62), billed as the oldest restaurant in town; it's been in its current location since 1942. On the way, stop in to see the even older—and far grander—**San Fernando Cathedral** ★★ (p. 88); parts of it date back to 1738.

2 Briscoe Western Art Museum ★★★

In the heart of downtown, the **Briscoe Western Art Museum** (p. 78) is the perfect size for an hour or so of browsing. Even if you don't think you like Western art, you're likely to be pleasantly surprised; special exhibitions in 2018 included one with a Cowboys and Indians series by Andy Warhol.

3 The Pearl ★★★

Take a river taxi north to the **Pearl** (see Day 1, #4) and spend some time visiting the boutiques you didn't have time to check out earlier. Peer into the pricy **Hotel Emma** (p. 48) as an aspirational place to stay, then have a relaxed lunch at another one of the complex's trendy restaurants.

4 Witte Museum ★★

In the afternoon, head north from the Pearl through Brackenridge Park to the **Witte Museum** (p. 84), at the park's north end, to learn more about the natural history of the area, including dinosaurs that roamed here millennia ago.

5 The San Antonio Zoo ★★

Not far from the Witte, you can spend the cooler late afternoon hours ogling non-extinct animals at the **San Antonio Zoo** (p. 93). Finish the day with dinner at one of the local favorite restaurants in the Alamo Heights, Monte Vista, or Olmos Park areas; see Chapter 5 for suggestions.

SAN ANTONIO WITH KIDS

Because of its comparatively low costs for lodging and activities, its casual attitudes, and its general family friendliness, San Antonio is a major destination for those traveling with children. Many come and stay at one of the large resorts on the outskirts of town (see chapter 4), where there are so many kid-friendly activities that there's little need to leave the property—except to go to one of the city's three major play lands: **Six Flags Fiesta Texas** (p. 94), **Sea World** (p. 96), or **Morgan's Wonderland and Inspiration Island** (p. 94). That's especially true if you're visiting during the summer, when they're open every day for long hours. I'm going to assume you'll allot one full day to visit whichever of these theme parks you chose. The following itinerary suggests ways to spend your other days in San Antonio.

DAY 1

1 The Alamo ★★★

To make sure your kids get the most out of visiting San Antonio's top historic landmark, consider watching the 3D film *The Alamo,* playing at the nearby Shops at Rivercenter, before going to see the real thing. The **Alamo** itself (p. 77) has tours geared for kids of all ages, which bring into perspective the dramatic 1736 battle that made this 18th-century Spanish Colonial mission famous. The grounds themselves are lovely, with live oak trees, gnarled mesquites, fronded palms, and prickly cacti and ocotillo all growing within the mission walls.

2 River Walk ★★★

Kids tend to love secret paths and underground places, so once they've found their way down to **River Walk** (p. 80), they'll be intrigued by its lush landscaping, underpasses, cunningly tucked-in restaurants, and back hotel entrances. There are lots of maps mounted on the railings so they can get the whole picture. Getting to the next stop is part of the fun: You'll be riding a river taxi.

3 The Pearl ★★★

Northeast of downtown, **The Pearl** dining-and-shopping complex (p. 81) has plenty of kid-friendly food and lawns on which to picnic. You can buy the fixings for a picnic in the Hotel Emma's **Larder,** an upscale grocer, or go to the **Bottling Department Food Hall,** which has several fast-casual choices for kids.

4 The DoSeum ★★★

About a mile north of the Pearl (a 20-min. walk up Broadway, if your kids are good walkers), you'll find the **DoSeum** (p. 90), the city's world-class children's museum, full of interactive exhibits and hands-on activities. If your children are ages 10 or younger, it may be hard to get them

San Antonio with Kids

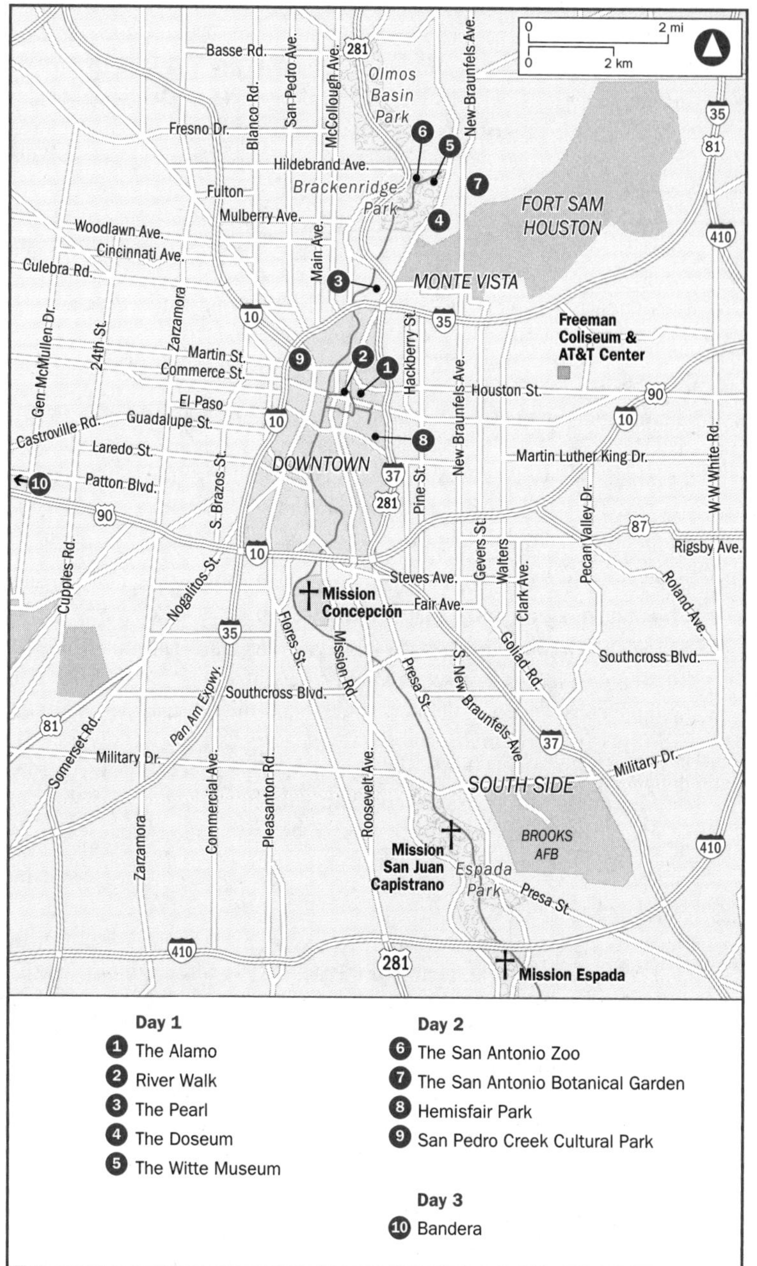

Day 1

1. The Alamo
2. River Walk
3. The Pearl
4. The Doseum
5. The Witte Museum

Day 2

6. The San Antonio Zoo
7. The San Antonio Botanical Garden
8. Hemisfair Park
9. San Pedro Creek Cultural Park

Day 3

10. Bandera

out of this place. Plan your visit for a weekday if you can—local families keep it busy on Saturday and Sunday.

5 The Witte Museum ★★

Another 15 minutes' walk up Broadway, the **Witte Museum** (p. 84) will intrigue older kids, with its dinosaur gallery exploring the huge inhabitants of Texas's prehistoric eras. The H-E-B Body Adventure takes participants on a virtual tour of San Antonio through a series of fun activity stations.

DAY 2

This is essentially a reversal of Day 1. You'll be starting out in Brackenridge Park and, after lunch, heading south to downtown.

1 The San Antonio Zoo ★★

The morning is a good time to visit the **San Antonio Zoo** (p. 93): Animals are friskier in the cool part of the day—and it's more comfortable for humans to walk around. You can choose your exotic environment for creature ogling—giraffes and zebras in the savannah area, say, or rope-swinging gibbons in a forest setting—and then interact with domestic goats and pigs in a petting zoo.

2 The San Antonio Botanical Garden ★★

About a 10-minute drive east of the zoo, the **San Antonio Botanical Garden** debuted its interactive Family Adventure Garden in 2018. Education about local ecosystems is made fun with such features as Tumble Hill (the name says it all), and the Retama Recharge, a wading area that demonstrates how the city's aquifers work. There's a cafe at the garden, but you might also consider the nearby (15-min. walk or 3-min. drive) **Smoke Shack barbecue** (p. 65) food truck, with its kid friendly Pig Pen playground/beer garden out back.

3 Hemisfair Park ★

On the southern edge of downtown, less than 15 minutes south of the botanical garden by car, **Hemisfair Park** (p. 87) was originally built for San Antonio's 1968 world expo. Head for the **UTSA Institute of Texan Cultures** ★ (p. 90), where interactive displays and a film detail the 26 ethnic groups that contribute to the state of Texas. It's a fun way to pick up some social history. Also in Hemisfair Park, the **Tower of the Americas** ★—the tallest building in San Antonio at 750 feet—has an observation deck with views of the entire city.

4 San Pedro Creek Culture Park ★★

After an early dinner in the downtown area—**Schilo's** ★★ (p. 62) is a good option—head to the northwest corner of downtown and **San Pedro Creek Culture Park** ★★ (p. 102), where something really cool happens after dark. At the head of the project, on Camaron Street, an enormous steel plate box designed to filter the creek water doubles as a piece of art and a free outdoor planetarium. Holes punched in the metal, backlit at night, re-create the constellations of the night sky on May 5, 1718, when the Spanish founded the area.

DAY 3

Take a Hill Country excursion to **Bandera** (p. 136), where you can visit the **Bandera Natural History Museum,** with its replicas of dinosaurs and Ice Age animals on an 8-acre spread; stop by the small **Frontier Times Museum;** enjoy a casual lunch at **Brick's Restaurant,** overlooking the Medina River; and even go horseback riding in the **Hill Country State Natural Area** (p. 138). In fact, I suggest you plan to spend 2 or 3 nights here, bunking with the family at a guest ranch in Bandera. It's a great way to experience Texas and the cowboy lifestyle.

CITY LAYOUT

Although it lies at the southern edge of the Texas Hill Country, San Antonio itself is mostly flat. Streets are jumbled, especially in the old parts of town, while a number of the thoroughfares leading in and out of town wind along old Spanish trails or 19th-century wagon trails. For detailed information about how to get around the city, see Chapter 18.

MAIN ARTERIES & STREETS Most of the major roads in Texas meet in San Antonio, where they form a rough wheel-and-spoke pattern. There are two loops: I-410 circles around the main part of the city, while Hwy. 1604 forms an even larger circle outside of that, with a 13-mile radius. You may hear locals referring to something as being "in the loop"—that doesn't mean it's privy to insider information, but rather, that it lies within the circumference of I-410 (or as locals call it, Loop 410), and is therefore in central San Antonio. The spokes of the wheel are formed by highways I-35, I-10, I-37, U.S. 281, U.S. 90, and U.S. 87, although occasionally two or three of these merge together on their ways in or out of town.

Within the city, **Broadway Street, McCullough Avenue, San Pedro Avenue,** and **Blanco Road** are all major thoroughfares leading north from downtown into the most popular shopping and restaurant areas of town. **Fredericksburg Road** goes northwest out to the Medical Center from just northwest of downtown. **St. Mary's Street,** which turns into **Roosevelt Avenue,** and **South Presa Street,** work as arteries to the south.

LOCATING AN ADDRESS Few locals are aware that there's any method to the madness of finding downtown addresses, but in fact, directions are based on the layout of the first Spanish settlements—back when the San Fernando cathedral was at the center of town. Market Street is the north-south divider, and Flores separates east from west. Thus, South St. Mary's becomes

North St. Mary's when it crosses Market, with addresses starting from zero at Market going in both directions. North of downtown, San Pedro is the east-west dividing line, although not every street sign reflects this fact.

There are few clear-cut rules like this in Loop land, but on its northernmost stretch, Loop 410 divides into east and west at Broadway, and at Bandera Road, it splits into Loop 410 north and south. Keep going far enough south, and I-35 marks yet another boundary between east and west. Knowing this will help you a little in locating an address, and explains why, when you go in a circle around town, you'll notice that the directions marked on overhead signs have suddenly completely shifted.

San Antonio Neighborhoods in Brief

Like other Sunbelt cities, San Antonio has a relatively compact downtown nucleus, encircled by old neighborhoods and commercial areas, which then give way to wide stretches of suburbia. The older areas described here, from downtown through Alamo Heights, are all "in the loop" (I-410). The Medical Center area in the Northwest lies just outside it, and the rest of the Northwest, as well as North Central, is now expanding even beyond Loop 1604.

I've used the designations most locals use to refer to the neighborhoods, though they're not necessarily reflected on maps. For example, though the Pearl Brewery is technically in the area called Tobin Hill, few locals use that neighborhood's name anymore. Rather, they just say "I'm going to the Pearl" or "it's just north of the Pearl." Similarly, areas that are commonly used as reference points might overlap two neighborhoods. For example, the Broadway Cultural Corridor—which is a Chamber of Commerce-type designation, but one that's often used—straddles both the Monte Vista and Alamo Heights neighborhoods.

Bottom line: You're in the sprawling Southwest, which doesn't do neighborhoods like East Coast cities do.

DOWNTOWN

Site of San Antonio's original Spanish settlements, this vibrant tourist hub includes the Alamo, Market Square, La Villita, the San Fernando Cathedral . . . really, almost all the major historic sights. It's also home to the newer River Walk, the convention center, theaters, and the hotels, restaurants, and shops that rose in their wake. In 2019, the 23-story Frost Bank tower will be the first skyscraper to be built here in more than a quarter of a century, which many see as a sign of downtown's rebound as a banking and business center. The area lags in residential development, and many homeless still roam the streets, but mixed-use housing is promised as part of the ongoing Hemisfair Park development. The area is bounded by I-37 to the east, I-35 to the north and west, and U.S. 90 (which merges with I-10) to the south. ***Note:*** The Alamodome and the adjacent Sunset Station, a restored 1902 train depot, along with the AT&T Center, home to the Spurs, are generally considered to be downtown, even though they are east of I-35.

KING WILLIAM

The city's first suburb, this historic district directly south of downtown alongside the San Antonio River was settled in the mid- to late 1800s by wealthy German merchants who built some of the most beautiful mansions in town. It began to be gentrified in the 1970s, and, at this point, you'd never guess it had ever been allowed to deteriorate. A few of the area's impeccably restored homes are open to the public—the Guenther House, the Steves Homestead Museum, and Villa Finale—and others have become bed-and-breakfasts. It can be a good, quiet base for exploring downtown and Southtown, but it has few restaurants or large hotels.

SOUTHTOWN

Alamo Street marks the border between King William and adjoining Southtown, which is often considered King William's business district. Depressed for years, it became trendy by the start of the 21st century, when its Main Street was refurbished and the Blue Star Arts complex opened; the 2019 completion of the Ruby City contemporary art museum adds to its artistic clout. It's now a hot neighborhood, where rising real estate values have almost driven out older Hispanic businesses in favor of hip restaurants and shops (although many of those properties are still owned by Hispanic landlords, who carry plenty of political weight in this city).

SOUTHSIDE

Home to four of the five of the historic missions, the city's earliest settlements, the old, largely Hispanic southeast section of town begins where Southtown ends (there's no agreed-upon boundary, but it's roughly a few blocks south of the Blue Star Arts complex). Once a string of quiet working-class neighborhoods, it's begun to be developed as the Mission Reach section of the River Walk draws increasing numbers of visitors. The area near the decommissioned Brooks Air Force Base is developing especially fast; other recent conversion projects include the remodeled South Park Mall and the Mission Marquee Plaza, formerly the Mission Drive-In Theater.

PEARL/BROADWAY CULTURAL CORRIDOR

Directly north of downtown, the older Tobin Hill neighborhood has regained new life with the development of the wildly popular **Pearl** culinary and entertainment campus, which is where most locals go for fun these days rather than to downtown. The old **St. Mary's Strip** entertainment drag has been revived by proximity to the Pearl as well. This part of town is full of cranes and scaffolding these days, evidence that it's become a hot place to live as well as play. At the north end of the Museum Reach section of the River Walk, the Pearl is also adjacent to the **Broadway Cultural Corridor,** so named because of the attractions clustered here—the San Antonio Museum of Art, the San Antonio Botanical Garden, the Witte Museum, and the DoSeum. If you take it to its northernmost point, you'll be in Alamo Heights.

MONTE VISTA/OLMOS PARK

Further north, above the Pearl, **Monte Vista** was established at the turn of the 20th century by a conglomeration of wealthy cattlemen, politicos, and generals who moved "on to the hill." The Monte Vista Historic District, more architecturally eclectic than King William, is the largest historic district in the U.S. and home to Trinity University (est. 1869). A number of the area's large houses have been split into student apartments, but many others have been restored. North of Monte Vista, high-end **Olmos Park** was developed in the mid-1920s by oilman/real estate mogul H. C. Thorman. In both neighborhoods you'll find several bed-and-breakfasts, located on quiet streets within easy reach of downtown, and a number of good dining spots.

ALAMO HEIGHTS

In the 1890s, when construction began in this area northeast of downtown, Alamo Heights was at the far reaches of San Antonio. It's now a ritzy residential neighborhood, with many fashionable shops and restaurants. Here you'll find the upscale Alamo Quarry shopping mall, as well as shop-lined Broadway and New Braunfels Avenue. Most of this section of town shares the 78209 zip code—thus the local term "09ers," shorthand for the area's affluent residents. The McNay Museum of Art is in this neighborhood, and Brackenridge Park, which contains the San Antonio Zoo and the Japanese Tea Garden.

NORTH CENTRAL/NORTHEAST

San Antonio is inching toward Bulverde and other Hill Country towns via this major northside corridor, between Loop 410 and Loop 1604, east of I-10 and west of I-35; it's bisected by U.S. 281. This is where you'll find the San Antonio airport as well as Morgan's Wonderland and Inspiration Island theme park. Lots of high-end homes have been built in the posh Stone Oaks area, which also has great shopping and restaurants (although too far from the city center to be covered in this book). The down side of all this growth? Terrible traffic at U.S. 281 and Loop 1604, especially in the afternoons.

NORTHWEST

Mostly characterless neighborhoods surround the South Texas Medical Center (always referred to as just the Medical Center), where most of San Antonio's hospitals and health care facilities are located. But the farther north you go in this prime growth area, which includes Six Flags and Friederich Park, the nicer the housing complexes get. Several high-end resorts and golf courses have cropped up just beyond Loop 1604, along with the Shops at La Cantera (San Antonio's fanciest retail center) and the RIM mall and entertainment complex.

FAR WEST

Although SeaWorld has been out here since the late 1980s, the former ranches and farms along Loop 1604 between I-10 and Hwy. 90 weren't developed until comparatively recently. Now the West is booming with mid-price housing developments, strip malls, schools, and businesses. As with other areas on the outskirts of town, road building hasn't kept pace with growth, so traffic can be a bear—be prepared for congestion.

SAN ANTONIO IN CONTEXT

3

San Antonio is a rich, complex, and BIG city—the seventh-largest in the United States and the fastest-growing—and you'll learn a lot more about it in the next several chapters. This brief overview is just to give you a taste for what's to come, distilling the city's past and present into a few brief pages so you'll have some insight into what you'll be seeing when you arrive.

Home to Spanish missions and the vibe-changing River Walk, San Antonio has more character than any other big city in Texas. It's one of the oldest cities in the country, celebrating the 300th anniversary of its founding in 2018. It's often ranked with New Orleans, Boston, and San Francisco as one of America's most distinctive cities; that recognition became official in 2014, when San Antonio's missions were declared a UNESCO World Heritage Site, and in 2017, when the entire city was deemed a UNESCO Creative City of Gastronomy.

SAN ANTONIO TODAY

Visitors today will encounter a city with a strong sense of community, a city whose downtown shows its age and its respect for the past. At the same time, the city is moving forward, and at a rapid pace. With a population of approximately 1.5 million, fast-growing San Antonio has also seen a commensurate growth in tourism, which is the city's second biggest industry, with an annual economic impact of more than $14 billion.

Outlying theme parks and attractions are benefiting from increased visitation, but downtown is by far the most affected section. The city's Henry B. Gonzalez Convention Center completed its second major expansion in 2016, followed by strong growth in downtown hotels. An even bigger trend in the past few decades has been recovering the past: Historic has become hot. It started with the renovation of the Majestic Theatre, which was reopened in the late 1980s after many years of neglect. This proved a great success

The Fiesta City

San Antonio's nickname refers to its huge April bash, but it also touches on the city's tendency to party at the drop of a sombrero. It's only natural that a place with strong Southern, Western, and Hispanic roots would know how to have a good time. Elaborately costumed festival queens, wild-and-woolly rodeos, and parades and mariachis are rolled out year-round.

and a point of civic pride, and resulted in the birth of several projects.

Hotel and theater transformations have continued apace in the first decades of the new century—the Empire and Aztec theaters have been refurbished and reopened for performances and the Alamada is next—and more and more old buildings have been turned into hotels, including links in lower-end chains. The three reclamation projects with the largest impact are the expansion of the River Walk into the northern **Museum Reach** and southern **Mission Reach** portions, and the transformation of the old **Pearl Brewery** (p. 81), just north of downtown, into a multi-use complex. In addition to apartment buildings, the Pearl hosts a branch of the Culinary Institute of America; some of the top restaurants in town; a popular farmers market; and the Hotel Emma, the city's poshest lodging. This development, in turn, has spurred a spate of building—and higher real estate prices—in the adjacent neighborhoods.

What's next for downtown? Phase One in the reclamation of the **San Pedro Creek** has been completed on the northwest side (p. 102). Long covered by concrete, the waterway is being restored to its natural flow, allowing for the concomitant return of the natural ecosystem along its banks. On the south side, Hemisfair Park, home to the convention center, is undergoing a major redevelopment. Several restaurants have already opened in new **Yanaguana Park** (p. 87), and a hotel and residential housing are planned. In addition, Frost Tower, headquarters for the Frost Bank, is rising in downtown's center. The first new skyscraper in the area in more than a quarter century, it's a heartening sign that business is returning to the old heart of the city.

Of course, the outlook isn't entirely rosy. Not all the new building projects are infill; more people are moving to the outskirts of the city than are settling in its center. San Antonio and Austin are 80 miles apart, but the two cities are spreading ever closer. Although they haven't yet melded to form the single metropolis that futurists predict, increasing suburban sprawl and the growth of New Braunfels and San Marcos, two small cities lying between San Antonio and Austin, are causing a great deal of congestion on I-35.

An even more serious concern is the city's water supply. For a long time, the city was reliant on direct and steady pumping from the Edwards Aquifer, but no one knew exactly how long that resource would last. In the early 1990s the centralized San Antonio Water System (SAWS) was created to address the problem, and it has made progress over the subsequent decades. Solutions include better management of groundwater withdrawal from the Edwards

Did You Know?

- San Antonio is the home of top-selling Pace Picante Sauce, and more jars of salsa than ketchup are consumed in the United States today.
- The first military flight by an American took place at Fort Sam Houston in 1910; in 1915, the entire U.S. Air Force—six reconnaissance planes—resided at the fort.
- Barbed wire was first used in San Antonio's Military Plaza for cattle holding pens by inventor-manufacturer Joseph F. Glidden.

Aquifer; the creation of the nation's largest direct recycling system, with three wastewater retreatment plants; and the construction of a huge desalinization plant. SAWS is also turning to other aquifers as water sources; the largest project, the 142-mile-long Vista Ridge pipeline, is slated to bring water to San Antonio taps as soon as 2020.

LOOKING BACK: SAN ANTONIO HISTORY

San Antonio's past is the stuff of legend—if it were a movie, the story of the city would be an epic with an improbable plot, encompassing the end of a great empire, the rise of a republic, and the rescue of the river with which the story began. For most of its history, San Antonio was the largest city in Texas and the "cosmopolitan" center, where multiple cultures came together and coexisted—the native Indians, called Coahuiltecans; Spanish settlers, soldiers, and priests; and German settlers, fleeing the revolutions in Europe. Through the following decades, these different immigrant groups would accommodate each other and forge a unique local culture.

MISSION SAN ANTONIO

In the late 17th century, the Spanish Empire in America stretched from Texas to Tierra del Fuego. Administering such a vast territory was difficult. Spain divided the continent into viceroyalties; the viceroyalty of New Spain included all of Mexico, Guatemala, and large stretches of the southwestern United States, where Spanish presence was still minimal.

In 1691, an early reconnaissance party passing through what is now San Antonio found a wooded plain watered by a clear river, called Yanaguana by the native Coahuiltecan Indians. The explorers named it San Antonio de Padua, after the saint's day on which they arrived. The Coahuiltecans, at that time suffering the depredations of the Apaches, regarded the Spaniards as protectors. They soon converted to Christianity and invited the Spanish to establish missions. In 1718, **Mission San Antonio de Valero**—later known as the Alamo—was founded by Franciscan priests. To protect the religious complex from Apache attack, the *presidio* (fortress) of San Antonio de Béxar went up a few days later. In 1719, a second mission was built nearby, and in 1731 three ill-fated East Texas missions that had been nearly destroyed by French and Indian attacks were moved from hundreds of miles away to the safer banks of the San Antonio River.

In March of that same year, 15 families from the Canary Islands arrived, sent by order of the King of Spain, and established the village of San Fernando de Béxar close by the garrison. Within little more than a decade, what is now downtown San Antonio became home to three distinct, though related, settlements: a mission complex, the military garrison designed to protect it, and the civilian town of Béxar (it wasn't officially renamed San Antonio until 1837). To make crop irrigation easier, the early settlers were given narrow strips of land stretching away from the river and nearby San Pedro Creek; centuries later, the winding paths connecting these strips were paved and became the city's streets.

As the 18th century wore on, bands of Apache Indians frequently attacked the village, but far more devastating to the Coahuiltecans were the diseases brought from Europe, for which they had little resistance. By the beginning of the 19th century, the Spanish missions were sorely depopulated. In 1794, Mission San Antonio de Valero was secularized and its farmlands redistributed, but in 1810, Spanish authorities turned the former San Antonio mission into a garrison, recognizing the military potential of its thick walls. Because the men recruited to serve here all hailed from the Mexican town of San José y Santiago del Alamo de Parras, the name of their station was soon shortened to the Alamo, Spanish for "cottonwood tree."

THE ALAMO

By 1824, all five missions in the San Antonio area had been secularized. Mexico had gained its independence from Spain, yet so long as Apache and

SAN ANTONIO: DATELINE

- **1691** On June 13, feast day of St. Anthony of Padua, San Antonio River is discovered by the Spanish; governor of Spanish colonial province of Texas makes contact with the resident natives, the Coahuiltecan Indians.
- **1718** Mission San Antonio de Valero founded; presidio San Antonio de Béxar established to protect it.
- **1720** Mission San José founded.
- **1731** Missions Concepción, San Juan Capistrano, and Espada relocated from East Texas to San Antonio area; 15 Canary Island families, sent by Spain to help populate Texas, establish first civil settlement in San Antonio.
- **1793–94** The missions are secularized by order of the Spanish crown.
- **1820** Moses Austin petitions Spanish governor in San Antonio for permission to settle Americans in Texas.
- **1821** Mexico wins independence from Spain.
- **1835** Siege of Béxar: first battle for Texas independence from Mexico.
- **1836** The Alamo falls after 13-day siege by Mexican general Santa Anna;

Comanche freely roamed the territory, it was next to impossible to persuade more Spaniards to move there. Mexico's political leaders—rightly suspicious of Anglo-American designs on their land—entered into an agreement with Moses Austin to settle some 300 Anglo-American families in the region east of San Antonio. Austin died before he could carry out his plan, but his son Stephen prevailed to bring the settlers into Texas. Shortly afterward, others (now called *empresarios*) made similar agreements with the Mexican government.

Mexicans wanted a buffer between the Indians and their settlements in northern Mexico, but eventually grew nervous about the large numbers of Anglos entering their country. They'd already repealed many of the tax breaks they'd initially granted the settlers; now they moved in to prohibit all further U.S. immigration to the territory.

Then historical events prevailed. In 1835, General Antonio López de Santa Anna abolished Mexico's democratic 1824 constitution, and Tejanos (Mexican Texans) and Anglos alike balked at his dictatorship. A cry rose up for a separate Texas republic. One of the first battles for Texas independence was fought in 1835 in San Antonio when insurgents attacked the garrison there. The battle was intensely fought, much of it door-to-door combat. Eventually, Mexican general Martín Perfecto de Cós surrendered on December 9, 1835. Under terms of the surrender, Mexicans were allowed to leave, as no one had food for so many prisoners.

But the Mexican army, under General Santa Anna, would return in force the next year to retake **the Alamo,** in a lopsided battle that would fire the American imagination (p. 77). The siege lasted from February 23 through March 6, 1836. Some 180 volunteers under the command of William Travis —among them Davy Crockett and Jim Bowie—died in the final attack, defending the Alamo against a force that was 10 times their number. Though the Americans ultimately lost the Alamo, the delay allowed the Texian army's leader, Sam

using "Remember the Alamo!" as a rallying cry, Sam Houston defeats Santa Anna at San Jacinto. Republic of Texas established.

1845 Texas annexed to the United States.

1861 Texas secedes from the Union.

1876 Fort Sam Houston established as new quartermaster depot.

1877 The railroad arrives in San Antonio.

1880s King William, first residential suburb, is developed by German immigrants.

1939–40 Works Project Administration builds River Walk, based on plans drawn up in 1929 by architect Robert H. H. Hugman.

1968 HemisFair exposition.

1975 The University of Texas at San Antonio (UTSA) opens campus in north San Antonio.

1994 North American Free Trade Agreement (NAFTA) signed in San Antonio

1998 Opening of the Nelson A. Rockefeller Center for Latin American Art, a three-story, $11-million addition to the San Antonio Museum of Art.

continues

Houston, to muster his forces and eventually defeat the Mexican army at San Jacinto with the battle cry "Remember the Alamo!"

As early as 1849, the Alamo was designated a quartermaster depot for the U.S. Army; in 1876, the much larger **Fort Sam Houston** (p. 93) was built to take over those duties. Apache chief Geronimo was held in the fort's Quadrangle for six weeks in 1886, en route to exile in Florida, and 12 years later Teddy Roosevelt outfitted his Rough Riders—some of whom he recruited in San Antonio bars—at Fort Sam.

AFTER THE FALL

During Texas' brief stint as a republic (1836–45), few Americans came to live in San Antonio, but settlers came from overseas in droves: By 1850, Tejanos and Americans were outnumbered by European, mostly German, immigrants. (Fun fact: By 1860, German speakers in San Antonio outnumbered both Spanish and English speakers.) The Civil War put a temporary halt to the city's growth (while Texas joined the Confederacy, many new settlers were Union sympathizers), but expansion picked up again soon afterward. As elsewhere in the West, the coming of the railroad in 1877 set off a new wave of immigration. Riding hard on its crest, the **King William district** of the city (p. 91), a residential suburb named for Kaiser Wilhelm, was developed by prosperous German merchants.

Some immigrants set up Southern-style plantations, others opened factories and shops, and more and more who arrived after the Civil War earned their keep by driving cattle. The Spanish had brought Longhorn cattle and *vaqueros* (cowboys) from Mexico into the area, and now Texas cowboys drove herds north on the Chisholm Trail from San Antonio to Kansas City, where they were shipped east. Others moved cattle west, for use as seed stock in the fledgling ranching industry.

1999 San Antonio Spurs outgrow the Alamodome; funding approved for the new SBC Center. Spurs win the first of many NBA championships.

2002 Opening of SBC Center, new home to the Spurs, the rodeo, and more; now called AT&T Center.

Silver Ventures purchases the shuttered Pearl Brewery property and begins its renovation and adaptive reuse projects.

2008 The Culinary Institute of America's third campus opens in the Pearl Brewery complex.

2009 Museum Reach stretch of the River Walk completed.

2013 Mission Reach section of the River Walk completed.

2015 San Antonio Missions declared a UNESCO World Heritage site.

2017 San Antonio designated a UNESCO Creative City of Gastronomy.

2018 300th anniversary of the city's founding. Citywide celebrations and projects include the completion of Phase One of the San Pedro Creek Culture Park.

As the city marched into the 20th century, Fort Sam Houston continued to expand. In 1910, it witnessed the first military flight by an American, and early aviation stars such as Charles Lindbergh honed their flying skills here. From 1917 to 1941, four Army air bases—Kelly Field, Brooks Field, Randolph Field, and Lackland Army Air Base—shot up, making San Antonio the largest military complex in the United States outside the Washington, D.C., area. The military remains one of the city's largest employers; it's now home to Joint Base San Antonio-Randolph, JBSA-Fort Sam Houston, JBSA-Lackland, and JBSA-Camp Bullis. San Antonio trademarked Military City, USA, as an official designation in 2017.

> **Impressions**
>
> *From all manner of people, business men, consumptive men, curious men, and wealthy men, there came an exhibition of profound affection for San Antonio. It seemed to symbolize for them the poetry of life in Texas.*
>
> —Stephen Crane, *Patriot Shrine of Texas*, 1895

But, with all due deference to the Alamo's memory, San Antonio has also forged strong ties with Mexico. With its large Hispanic population, regular flights to Mexico City, and cultural attractions such as the Latin American wing of the San Antonio Museum of Art, San Antonio has a lot of reasons to maintain strong business relations with our southern neighbors. The North American Free Trade Agreement (NAFTA), signed in San Antonio in 1994, has been a boon for the city, which hosts the North American Development Bank— NAFTA's financial arm—in its downtown International Center, where representatives from the various states of Mexico have offices. The 2018 rebranding of NAFTA as the United States-Mexico-Canada Agreement (USMCA) suggests that "build a wall" rhetoric is not going to significantly change the balance of economic self-interest on both sides of the border.

A RIVER RUNS THROUGH IT

The city continued to grow. In the early 1900s, it showcased the first skyscraper in Texas. But San Antonio wasn't growing fast enough to keep up with Houston or Dallas. By the 1920s, it had become Texas' third-largest city and had arrived at a crossroads. Was it to follow Houston and Dallas in their bull-rush toward growth and modernism? Or was it to go its own way, preserving what it thought most valuable? This dilemma took the form of a political dispute over the meandering San Antonio River. In 1921, during a violent storm, the river overflowed its banks and flooded the downtown area, killing 50 people and destroying many businesses. A city commission recommended draining the riverbed and channeling the water through underground culverts to remove the flood threat and free up space for more downtown buildings. This outraged many locals. A group of women's clubs formed to save the river and create an urban green space along its banks, decades before anyone in Texas had ever heard of urban planning. Mounting a multipronged campaign

The Lay of the Land

Frederick Law Olmsted's description in his 1853 *A Journey Through Texas* is poetic. San Antonio, he writes, "lies basking on the edge of a vast plain, through which the river winds slowly off beyond where the eye can reach. To the east are gentle slopes toward it; to the north a long gradual sweep upward to the mountain country, which comes down within 5 or 6 miles; to the south and west, the open prairies, extending almost level to the coast, a hundred and fifty miles away."

(even including a puppet-show dramatization), the women's group won the battle, and the river was saved.

In 1927, Robert H. H. Hugman, an architect who'd lived in New Orleans and studied that city's Vieux Carré district, came up with a detailed design for improving the waterway. His proposed **River Walk** (p. 80), with shops, restaurants, and entertainment areas buttressed by a series of floodgates, would render the river profitable as well as safe, and also preserve its natural beauty. The Depression intervened, but in 1941, with the help of a federal Works Project Administration (WPA) grant, Hugman's vision became a reality.

For some decades more, the River Walk remained just another pretty space. Then, in 1968, when the city celebrated its 250th anniversary by mounting the **HemisFair** exposition (p. 87), record crowds were drawn to the rescued waterway. (San Antonio's convention center was also built for the exposition, putting the city on the trade show and convention map.) From then on, the city really began banking on its banks—and it hasn't looked back since. New cultural attractions opened in rapid succession: The **San Antonio Botanical Garden** (p. 82) in 1980; the **San Antonio Museum of Art** (p. 82) in 1981; the Rivercenter Mall (now **Shops at Rivercenter,** p. 110) and **SeaWorld San Antonio** (p. 96) in 1988; the Fiesta Texas theme park (now **Six Flags Fiesta Texas,** p. 94) in 1992; and the **Alamodome** (p. 120) in 1993. San Antonio had come into its own as a world-class visitor destination.

SAN ANTONIO IN POP CULTURE

Before **Frederick Law Olmsted** became a landscape architect—New York's Central Park is among his famous creations—he was a successful journalist, and his 1853 *A Journey Through Texas* includes a delightful section on his impressions of early San Antonio. William Sidney Porter, better known as **O. Henry,** had a newspaper office in San Antonio for a while. Two collections of his short stories, *Texas Stories* and *Time to Write,* include a number of pieces set in the city, among them "A Fog in Santone," "The Higher Abdication," "Hygeia at the Solito," "Seats of the Haughty," and "The Missing Chord."

O. Henry wasn't very successful at promoting his newspaper *Rolling Stone* (no, not *that* one) in San Antonio during the 1890s, but there's a lively literary scene in town today. Resident writers include **Jay Brandon,** whose *Loose Among the Lambs* kept San Antonians busy trying to guess the identities of the local figures they (erroneously) thought had been fictionalized therein. His most San Antonio-centric work is *Milagro Lane,* which the author describes as "part mystery, part insider's guide." **Rick Riordan's** *Tequila Red* kicked off his Tres Navarre series, hard-boiled detective novels set in a seamy San Antonio. A finalist for the National Book Award, **John Phillip Santos's** memoir, *Places Left Unfinished at the Time of Creation,* traces the San Antonio author's roots back to Mexico through dreams, myths, and other poetic devices. (Look for Santos's words on the art installations in San Pedro Creek Culture Park.) The poet laureate of San Antonio from 2012 to 2014 and of Texas from 2015 to 2016, **Carmen Tafolla** focuses on Chicana culture in books such as the early *Get Your Tortillas Together* to the more recent *This River Here: Poems of San Antonio.*

For in depth, nonfictional takes on the city, consider works by **Lewis F. Fisher** such as *Saving San Antonio: The Precarious Preservation of a Heritage*; *Crown Jewel of Texas: Story of San Antonio's River*; and *Chili Queens, Hay Wagons, and Fandangos: The Spanish Plazas in Frontier San Antonio.*

WHEN TO GO

Most tourists visit San Antonio in summer, though it's not the ideal season. The weather is hot, and restaurants and attractions tend to be crowded. That said, there are plenty of places to cool off around town, and hotel rates are slightly lower (conventioneers come in the fall, winter, and spring). Also consider that some of the most popular family-oriented attractions, such as SeaWorld and Six Flags Fiesta Texas, keep far longer hours when school's out.

In fall and spring, temperatures are comfortable for exploring. If there's a large convention in town, downtown hotels will have high occupancy rates and, consequently, higher prices. ***Tip:*** Check out the "Meeting Professionals" calendar on the Visit San Antonio website (http://meetings.visitsanantonio.com) to see what meetings are planned for the time you're planning to visit.

Winter is a slow season for San Antonio hotels, and good deals can be had. December, in particular, is a great time to see San Antonio, if you don't mind running the risk of cold weather (see below). The River Walk is all lit up with lights, and piñatas are hung everywhere.

San Antonio is the most popular in-state destination for Texans, many of whom come for the weekend. This, too, can raise room rates for hotels on the River Walk, but not necessarily for downtown business hotels or hotels in the vicinity of the airport. Try these options on weekends for discount rates.

Weather

From late May through September, expect regular high temperatures and often high humidity.

Fall and spring are prime times to visit; the days are pleasantly warm and, at least in late March or early April, the wildflowers in the nearby Hill Country will be in glorious bloom. Temperate weather combined with lively Christmas celebrations make November and December also good months to visit. Sometimes a "Norther" wind blows in, dropping daytime temperatures to between 40 and 50 degrees Fahrenheit (4°–10°C). January and February can be colder, but not necessarily—it's a matter of luck.

San Antonio/Austin Average Daytime Temperature (°F & °C) & Monthly Rainfall (Inches)

	JAN	FEB	MAR	APR	MAY	JUNE	JULY	AUG	SEPT	OCT	NOV	DEC
AVG. TEMP. (°F)	51	55	62	70	76	82	85	85	80	71	60	53
AVG. TEMP. (°C)	11	13	17	21	24	28	29	29	27	22	16	12
RAINFALL (IN.)	1.7	1.9	1.6	2.6	4.2	3.6	1.9	2.5	3.2	3.2	2.1	1.7

Holidays

Banks, government offices, post offices, and many stores, restaurants, and museums are closed on the following legal national holidays: January 1 (New Year's Day), Martin Luther King, Jr., Day (3rd Monday in January), Presidents' Day (3rd Monday in February), Memorial Day (last Monday in May), July 4 (Independence Day), Labor Day (1st Monday in September), Columbus Day (2nd Monday in October), Veterans Day/Armistice Day (November 11), Thanksgiving Day (4th Thursday in November), and December 25 (Christmas). The Tuesday after the first Monday in November is Election Day, a federal government holiday in presidential-election years (held every 4 years, the next in 2020).

San Antonio Calendar of Events

Please note that the information contained below is always subject to change. For the most up-to-date information on these events, call the number provided, or check with **Visit San Antonio** (www.visitsanantonio.com; ✆ **210-244-2000**).

JANUARY

Martin Luther King, Jr., March and Rally and **Dreamweek,** various venues. Started in 1987, this has become the country's largest march in honor of Dr. Martin Luther King, Jr., a nearly 3-mile walk through San Antonio's east side. It's the centerpiece of activities for DreamWeek San Antonio, a 16-day series of events designed to foster diversity dialogues (www.sanantonio.gov/mlk, ✆ **210/207-7084;** and www.dreamweek.org). Mid-January.

FEBRUARY

Stock Show and Rodeo, AT&T Center. San Antonio hosts more than 2 weeks of rodeo events, including music, a farmers market, and carnivals. It's been running since 1949 (www.sarodeo.com; ✆ **210/225-5851**). Early February.

MARCH

Bud Light St. Patrick's Day Festival. Are leprechauns responsible for turning the San Antonio River green—and for turning the beer emerald? Irish dance and music fill the Arneson River Theatre from the afternoon on; kid-friendly events include face-painting and gold coin hunting (www.thesanantonio riverwalk.com/events; ✆ **210/227-4262**). St. Patrick's Day weekend.

Contemporary Art Month, various venues. More than 400 exhibitions at more than 50 venues make this month a contemporary art lover's heaven (www.contemporaryartmonth.com; ✆ **210/630-0235)**. Throughout March.

APRIL

Crafts Day/Starving Artist Show, River Walk and La Villita. Nearly 900 artists from throughout Texas sell their works, with proceeds going to benefit the Little Church of La Villita's program to feed the hungry (www.lavillita.com; ✆ **210/226-3593**). First weekend in April.

Fiesta San Antonio, various venues. What started as a modest marking of Texas' independence in 1891 is now a huge 11-day event, with an elaborately costumed royal court, parades, balls, foodfests, sports events, concerts, and art shows (www.fiesta-sa.org; ✆ **210/227-5191**). Late April (always includes Apr 21, San Jacinto Day).

MAY

Tejano Conjunto Festival, Rosedale Park and Guadalupe Theater. Sponsored by the Guadalupe Cultural Arts Center, this annual event celebrates south Texas' lively blend of Mexican and German music (www.guadalupeculturalarts.org; ✆ **210/271-3151**). Mid-May.

Culinaria Festival, various venues. This multi-day food extravaganza includes wine tastings and seminars, haute cuisine sampling, and food truck grazing (www.culinaria sa.org; ✆ **210/822-9565**). Mid-May.

JUNE

Texas Folklife Festival, UTSA Institute of Texas Cultures. Ethnic foods, dances, crafts demonstrations, and games celebrate the diversity of Texas' heritage (www.texan cultures.com; ✆ **210/458-2300**). Early June.

Juneteenth, various venues. The anniversary of the 1865 announcement of the Emancipation Proclamation is the occasion for a series of African-American celebrations, including an outdoor jazz concert, gospelfest, parade, picnic, and more (www.june teenthsanantonio.com; ✆ **210/843-7805**). June 14 and 15.

JULY

San Antonio CineFestival, Guadalupe Cultural Arts Center. The nation's oldest and largest Chicano/Latino film festival screens more than 70 films and videos over 4 days (www.guadalupeculturalarts.org; ✆ **210/271-3151**). Second weekend in July.

AUGUST

Restaurant Week, various venues. Special tasting menus and other incentives draw food-lovers to sample the fare at many of the city's dining spots (www.culinariasa.org; ✆ **210/822-9565**). Late August.

SEPTEMBER

World Heritage Festival, San Antonio Missions. Five days of celebration at San Antonio's missions include biking and walking tours, art exhibits, picnics, food trucks, and music (www.sanantonio.gov/WorldHeritage; ✆ **210/207-2111**). First weekend in September.

Diez y Seis, various venues. Mexican independence from Spain is feted at several spots around the city, including La Villita, Market Square, the Arneson River Theatre, Guadalupe Plaza, and the Pearl complex (www.getcreativesanantonio.com). Weekend nearest September 16.

Jazz'SAlive, Travis Park. Bands from around the world come together for a weekend of hot jazz (www.saparksfoundation.org; ✆ **210/212-8423**). Third weekend in September.

OCTOBER

Oktoberfest, Beethoven Halle and Garten. San Antonio's German roots show at this festival with food, dance, oompah bands, and beer (www.beethovenmaennerchor.com; ✆ **210/222-1521**). Early October.

Mala Luna Music Festival, Nelson Wolff Stadium. Headliners in hip-hop, EDM (electronic dance music), and Latin music join local musicians and artists at this 2-day festival benefitting the Miracle League of San Antonio (www.malalunafestival.com). Halloween weekend.

NOVEMBER

Ford Holiday River Parade and Lighting Ceremony. With trees and bridges illuminated by some 122,000 lights, this floating river parade kicks off the Paseo del Rio Holiday Festival (www.thesanantonioriverwalk.com; ✆ **210/227-4262**). Day after Thanksgiving.

DECEMBER

Humana Rock 'n' Roll San Antonio Marathon & ½ Marathon, downtown and south. Looping from Market Square past the historic missions and ending up at the Alamodome, this marathon features rocking bands along the route to inspire participants to keep their feet moving (www.runrocknroll.com/en/events/san-antonio). Early December.

WHERE TO STAY IN SAN ANTONIO

4

You don't have to leave your lodgings to sightsee in San Antonio: This city has the highest concentration of historic hotels in Texas. Even low-end hotel chains are reclaiming old buildings—many examples in all price ranges are covered in this chapter, from a converted seminary to a revamped brewery. Most visitors to San Antonio want to stay downtown so they can be close to the River Walk and many other major tourist attractions. As a result, that's where you'll find the greatest number of hotel rooms, many of them high-end. The most convenient of the lower-priced chain hotels and motels are clustered in the northwest near the Medical Center, as well as in the north central area around the airport.

If your main objective is a family vacation, consider staying at a resort or hotel on the west/northwest side of town, near the two big theme parks, SeaWorld (p. 96) and Six Flags Fiesta Texas (p. 94)—you can combine days at the parks with swimming, golfing, shopping, and spa treatments, making the drive into San Antonio when you're ready for a change of pace. On the northeast side, Morgan's Wonderland theme park (p. 94) is close enough to the airport to make lodgings there a good bet.

Want to get a feel for the city outside the tourist zones? Consider a B&B or inn in the historic King William and Monte Vista neighborhoods—both close to downtown and interesting in their own right, with lots of dining and entertainment options. The **San Antonio Bed & Breakfast Association** (www.SanAntonioBB.org; **© 888-272-6700**) lists several places that are vetted by the organization; keep in mind, however, that they're rarely kid- or pet-friendly. Travelers who prefer crowd-vetted arrangements like **Airbnb** (www.airbnb.com) and **VRBO** (Vacation Rental by Owner; www.vrbo.com)—see below—will have plenty of choices all around the city.

GETTING AN online deal

Before going online, it's important that you know what "flavor" of discount you're seeking. Currently, there are three types of online reductions:

1. **Extreme discounts on sites where you bid for lodgings without knowing which hotel you'll get.** You'll find these on such sites as **Priceline.com** and **Hotwire.com**, and they can be money-savers, particularly if you're booking within a week of travel (that's when the hotels resort to deep discounts to get beds filled). As these companies use only major chains, you can rest assured that you won't be put up in a dump. For more reassurance, visit the website **BiddingTraveler.com**. On it, actual travelers spill the beans about what they bid on Priceline.com and which hotels they got. I think you'll be pleasantly surprised by the quality of many of the hotels that are offering these "secret" discounts.
2. **Discounts on chain hotel websites.** In 2016, all of the major chains announced they'd be reserving special discounts for travelers who booked directly through the hotels' websites (usually in the portion of the site reserved for loyalty members). They weren't lying: These are always the lowest rates at the hotels in question, though discounts can range widely, from as little as $1 to as much as $50. ***Our advice:*** Search for a hotel that's in your price range and ideal location (see below for where to do that) and then, if it is a chain property, book directly through the online loyalty portal.
3. **Use the right hotel search engine.** They're not all equal, as we at Frommers.com learned in the spring of 2018 after putting the top 20 sites to the test in 20 cities around the globe. We discovered that **Booking.com** listed the lowest rates for hotels in the city center, and in the under $200 range, 16 out of 20 times—the best record, by far, of all the sites we tested. And Booking.com includes all taxes and fees in its results (not all do, which can make for a frustrating shopping experience). For top-end properties, again in the city center only, both Priceline.com and HotelsCombined.com came up with the best rates, tying at 14 wins each.
4. **Or skip hotels altogether.** Nowadays, on such sites as Airbnb.com, Wimdu.com, Homeaway.com, VRBO.com, and others, it is often possible to get a room in someone's home for half of what you'd spend for a hotel. Or a complete apartment for the usual cost of a hotel room. The key to making this sort of option work is to look at all the fees involved. Sometimes "cleaning fees" and user fees can wipe out the savings.
5. **Last-minute discounts.** Booking last minute can be a great savings strategy, as prices sometimes drop in the week before travel as hoteliers scramble to fill their rooms. But you won't necessarily find the best savings through companies that claim to specialize in last-minute bookings. Instead, use the sites recommended in #3 of this list.

Most importantly these days: Go to the last page of the booking widget before hitting "pay." Some hotels now tack on "resort fees" to the nightly costs, a fee you won't usually see right away. The average fee is now $21, not an insignificant amount, and it can go up from there.

It's a lot of surfing, I know, but in the hothouse world of lodgings pricing, this sort of diligence can pay off.

For a full alphabetical listing of the city's accommodations, mapped by area and including rate ranges as well as basic amenities, phone **Visit San Antonio** (✆ 210/244-2000) to request a lodging guide, or go to **www.visitsanantonio.com** and click on the Lodging section, which is linked with TripAdvisor.com, so you can book directly online.

A few words about the listing info: Rates included here are those that prevail for most of the year, before taxes (16.75%); some resorts also tack on a daily fee. They can go higher or lower, depending on occupancy. By now, almost all large hotels are **nonsmoking;** when smoking rooms are available, it's noted in the review. **Parking fees** are always per day, before taxes (and the fact that they're often exorbitant in the downtown area helps make the case for forgoing a rental car in favor of using ride services). **Pet fees** are per visit, unless the listing specifies otherwise. Rates for **Internet use** are noted, but many hotels will waive the fee if you sign on to their member's club. You can decide whether the savings are worth adding to your glut of emails.

A final note: The details of the merger of the Marriott and Starwood hotel groups (including the Westin brand) continue to be hammered out. As a result, booking websites are in flux. In theory, changes were to have been finalized by the end of 2018. In fact, you might still notice differences in listed websites. With luck, what is now the world's largest hotel conglomerate will have perfected its electronic redirects by the time you read this.

DOWNTOWN

Expensive

Hotel Contessa ★★★ Tall twin palm trees wrapped in glittering white lights center a soaring atrium in the grand lobby of this welcoming River Walk hotel, set along a quiet bend in the river but just steps from the jazzy active areas. Because the hotel was originally supposed to be an Embassy Suites (before being sold mid-build), all rooms have a large sitting area and separate bedrooms with king-size bed or two double beds, making them ideal for business travelers and families alike. Done in saucy red, black, and earth hues, with exposed brick walls and lots of bright Picasso-esque art, all rooms offer either a river or city view. The best river views are those on lower levels overlooking the cypress tree–lined pathways, while the prime city views are from higher floors—including those from the chic rooftop pool. ***Other pluses:*** a stylish lobby bar; the full-service **Ramblas** restaurant, with dining indoors and outdoors on a quiet spot of the River Walk; a small on-site spa (a rarity in downtown San Antonio hotels); a well-equipped fitness room; and an off-street porte-cochere that gives car services a convenient place to wait for you (and vice versa).

306 W. Market St. (at Navarro St.). www.thehotelcontessa.com. ✆ **866/435-0900** or 210/229-9222. 265 units. $249–$319 suite; from $329 executive suite. Valet parking $38. Pets 50 lb. and under accepted, $50 per pet per night. **Amenities:** Restaurant/bar; fitness center; pool; room service; spa; Wi-Fi (free).

Hotel Valencia Riverwalk ★★★ One of the most stylish hotels on the River Walk was made more wow-worthy by a $10-million renovation in 2017. Rooms still look contemporary Mediterranean, with clean lines and soft lighting, but the public areas are now more in tune with the hotel's Iberian name. Lots of dark wood, leather, and wrought-iron accents lend a Spanish Colonial heft to the decor, but the service is friendly, not formal. The excellent Buenos Aires–inspired **Dorrego** restaurant and adjoining **Naranja** bar, both opened with the renovation, are hot local gathering spots in an area of downtown that has no shortage of them; another such spot, Ácenar (p. 60), though not affiliated with the hotel, is right downstairs on the River Walk. ***A nice bonus:*** complimentary coffee and freshly baked pastries served in the lobby each morning.

150 E. Houston St. (at St. Mary's St.). www.hotelvalencia-riverwalk.com. ✆ **855/596-3387** or 210/227-9700. 213 units. $189–$239 double; from $350 suite. Valet parking $38. **Amenities:** Restaurant; bar; concierge; exercise room; room service; in-room spa services; Wi-Fi (free).

Hyatt Regency San Antonio River Walk ★ With its soaring atrium and lush greenery in the lobby, its glass elevators ascending and descending in perpetual motion, this is your classic Hyatt. The guest rooms are sleek and modern too, done in classic earth tones with the luxury heft of rich dark wood. Such touches as lights under the bed that go on when you put your feet down at night add to the sense of being cossetted. This is a conference hotel, but leisure travelers also enjoy its prime location on the River Walk at the point where it passes closest to the Alamo—not to mention the rooftop pool and **Q Restaurant/Bar,** which offers an excellent selection of microbrews and a lunch buffet with done-to-order pasta bowls. Interior rooms are the least expensive; you'll pay more for Alamo views and (the priciest but not worth it) river views.

123 Losoya St. (at College St.). www.hyatt.com. ✆ **800/233-1234** or 210/222-1234. 629 units. $259–$349 double; $328–$768 suite. Self-parking $32; valet parking $43. **Amenities:** Restaurant; bar; concierge; club-level rooms; 24-hr. health club; outdoor heated pool; room service; business center; spa, Wi-Fi (free).

Marriott Rivercenter San Antonio ★ This massive hotel rising high above the Rivercenter Mall is mainly a convention hotel, but its location in the heart of the tourist hub means it also works well for shoppers and sightseers, who can get good rates when no big convention is in town. Guest rooms are attractive and comfortable, and most afford views of the city. Convenience is definitely a plus here; for example, free washers and dryers on the same floor as the top-notch health club allow you to bicycle while your clothes cycle.

101 Bowie St. (at Commerce St.). www.marriott.com. ✆ **800/648-4462** or 210/223-1000. 1,001 units. $219–$349 double; $419 and up suite. Self-parking $37; valet parking $43. **Amenities:** 3 restaurants; concierge; club-level rooms; fitness room; Jacuzzi; indoor pool; outdoor pool; room service; Wi-Fi ($15/day).

Central San Antonio Hotels

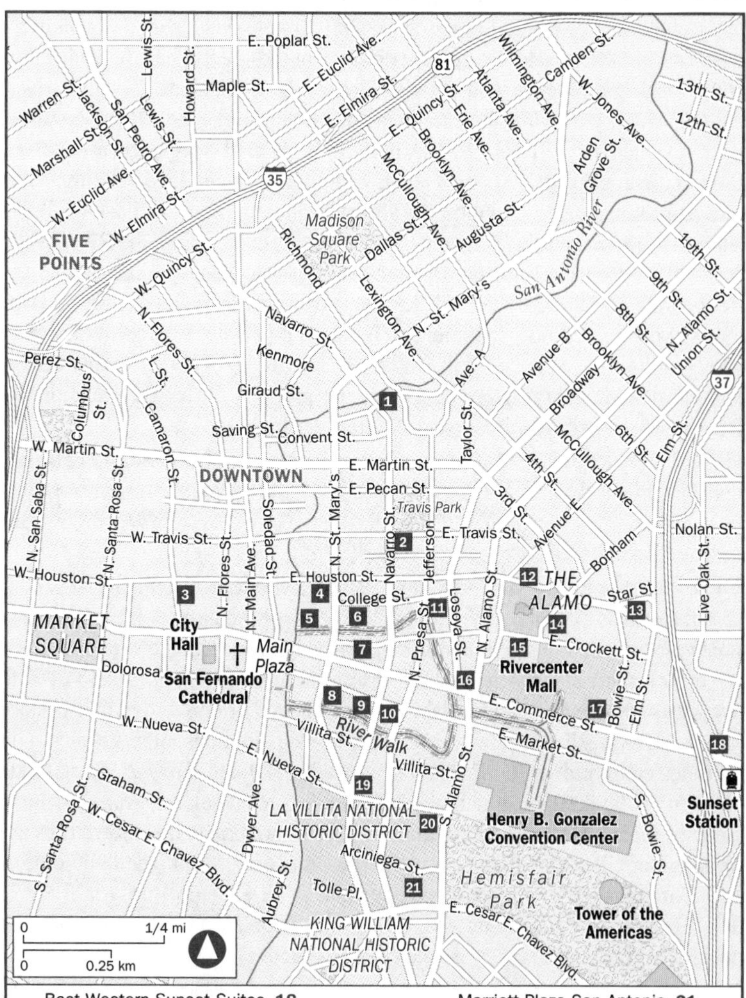

Best Western Sunset Suites **18**
Crockett Hotel **14**
Drury Inn & Suites San Antonio Riverwalk **5**
Emily Morgan **12**
The Fairmount **20**
Holiday Inn Express—Riverwalk **3**
Homewood Suites by Hilton **8**
Hotel Contessa **10**
Hotel Havana **1**
Hotel Valencia Riverwalk **4**
Hyatt Regency San Antonio River Walk **11**
Marriott Plaza San Antonio **21**
Marriott Rivercenter **17**
Menger Hotel **15**
Mokara Hotel & Spa **7**
O'Brien Hotel **19**
Omni La Mansión del Río **6**
Riverwalk Vista **16**
St. Anthony Hotel **2**
Tru by Hilton San Antonio **13**
Westin Riverwalk Inn **9**

Mokara Hotel & Spa ★★★ Downtown San Antonio hotels tend to be short on nice spas, but Mokara has one of the best in the area. In fact, everything about this centrally located River Walk hotel—it's close to downtown's three major theaters and several fine dining venues—feels peaceful and restorative: From the moment you enter the lobby, the soft palette of vanilla hues, natural wood, and white limestone creates a sense of calm. An overstuffed leather couch pays tribute to the building's past: It was once a saddlery. Rooms are comfortably sophisticated, with high ceilings, luxe bedding, oversize bathrooms with jetted tubs and separate showers, and touches of a Texan leather-and-wood aesthetic; many have balconies overlooking the River Walk. A small rooftop cafe and pool is another pleasant place to relax, while the state-of-the art fitness room will let you work off any residual stress. **Ostra** offers excellent seafood, including an oyster bar, in a sleek modern room with some outdoor tables overlooking the river. One of the perks of staying here is that guests have charging privileges at sister property **Omni La Mansión del Río** hotel (see below), directly across the river from Mokara.

212 W. Crockett St. (at St. Mary's St.). www.omnihotels.com. ✆ **866/605-1212** or 210/396-5800. 99 units. $279–$559 double; from $800 suite. Valet parking $39. Pets 25 lb. and under accepted, $50 fee. **Amenities:** Restaurant; cafe; concierge; health club; outdoor pool; room service; sauna; spa; Wi-Fi (free).

Omni La Mansión del Río ★★ Built in 1892 as a seminary, this converted Spanish Colonial structure exudes old-world charm. With arched passageways, terra-cotta tile floors, wrought-iron balconies, and beamed ceilings, it's quintessential San Antonio. Rooms are simple, cool, and spacious, with oversize hand-hewn wood furnishings and subdued Southwestern hues. Those facing the river stand level with tall cypress and palm trees; others look out on an inner courtyard or (less desirable) on a busy street. ***Caveat:*** An upgrade planned for late 2019 is much-needed—public areas look a bit run-down and some of the modern electronics guests expect from pricey downtown digs are missing here. But excellent service helps compensate. And when you dine at **Las Canarias** (p. 59) or sip a craft cocktail at **El Colegio Bar,** you'll forget that you ever wanted to plug your laptop into your TV. Guests have charging privileges at the Mokara across the river (see above).

112 College St. (btw. St. Mary's and Navarro sts.). www.omnilamansion.com. ✆ **800/292-7300** or 210/518-1000. 338 units. $189–$349 double; $329–$599 junior suite; $750–$2,000 suite. Valet parking $39. Pets 25 lb. and under accepted, $50 fee. **Amenities:** Restaurant; 2 bars; coffee shop/snack bar; children's programs; concierge; outdoor pool; room service; Wi-Fi (free).

The St. Anthony Hotel ★★★ For years this downtown hotel was *the* place to stay in San Antonio (or get married or have Fiesta balls), and a recent impeccable renovation has restored its reputation as the crown jewel of Alamo City. Although the lobby is formally elegant, with glittering chandeliers, plush peacock-green carpet, and white marble walls, guest rooms and restaurants are sleekly contemporary and even a tad trendy. **Rebelle** feels almost *too* hip;

its mod furniture and changing colored lights work great at dinner, but the glam decor can seem a bit much at breakfast. The chic rooftop infinity pool and well-equipped fitness center contrast with the **Haunt** bar, where cocktails are named after the purported resident ghosts (who wouldn't be caught dead on an elliptical trainer). Another plus: A prime location on Travis Park—far from the crowds, but close to the River Walk and state-of-the-art **Tobin Theater** (p. 119).

300 E. Travis St. (at Navarro St.). www.thestanthonyhotel.com. ✆ **855/811-0218** or 210/227-4392. 277 units. $299–$450 double; $500–$5,000 suite. Valet parking $39. Pets accepted, no fee. **Amenities:** Restaurant; 4 bars; breakfast cafe; 24-hr. business center; concierge; fitness center; Jacuzzi; outdoor pool; room service; Wi-Fi (free).

Westin Riverwalk Inn ★★ Designed to blend in architecturally with its older neighbors on this (relatively) quiet section of the river bend, this property's clean lines reflect a modern aesthetic. Rooms, however, are furnished in a traditional style and are large and comfortable. All the "riverview" rooms (more peek-a-boo than full view) have balconies. Nice details for the business traveler include an ample desk with stone countertop and convenient connections, and of course the signature "Heavenly Beds." This Westin has also nicely incorporated several kid-pleasing features and is exceptionally pet-friendly.

420 W. Market St. (at Navarro St.). www.westin.com/riverwalk. ✆ **888/627-8396** or 210/224-6500. 474 units. $289–$429 double; $419 and up suite. Off-site parking $25; valet parking $39. Pets under 40 lb. (max. 2) accepted, no fee. **Amenities:** Restaurant; bar; kids' program; concierge; fitness room; outdoor pool; room service; spa; Wi-Fi ($15).

Moderate

Crockett Hotel ★★ Many hotels in downtown San Antonio are in converted historic buildings; this one has been operating as a lodging for more than 100 years. Location, location, location—it's a few steps from the Alamo—and lots of local character make this an excellent choice. Fresh-looking rooms are attractive and airy, with work by local artists. An outdoor pool with tropical landscaping is another asset, as is a bar featuring Texas brews and spirits. A complimentary hot breakfast includes waffles shaped like the state of Texas—perhaps not unexpected in a hotel named for Alamo defender Davy Crockett. Check for online deals; already value-priced rooms are discounted for every imaginable reason.

320 Bonham St. (at Crockett St.). www.crocketthotel.com. ✆ **877/958-6030** or 210/225-6500. 138 units. $129–$157 double; $345 and up suite. Pets (max. 2) accepted, $60 fee. Parking (self- or valet) $25. **Amenities:** Restaurant; bar; outdoor pool; room service; use of fitness center at nearby Menger Hotel; Wi-Fi (free).

Drury Inn & Suites San Antonio Riverwalk ★★ Built in the days when the municipal gas and electric company merited a headquarters constructed by a top architecture firm, the 1921 City Public Service building was also the first commercial structure to take advantage of a river location. Both the grand high-ceilinged design and the prime location are not what you'd expect from moderately priced digs, where a hot breakfast and happy-hour snacks and drinks are included in the room rate. The rooftop pool affords views of the San Fernando Cathedral; on the nights when *Saga—San Antonio* (p. 88) is projected on the cathedral's side, you get a free sound-and-light show without having to leave your hotel.

201 N. St. Mary's St. (at Commerce St.). www.druryhotels.com. ✆ **800/DRURY-INN** (378-7946) or 210/212-5200. 150 units. $129–$220 double; $210 and up suite. Rates include breakfast. Self-parking $16. Pets (max. 2 with combined weight 80 lb.) accepted, $35 fee. **Amenities:** Restaurant; fitness room; Jacuzzi; outdoor pool; Wi-Fi (free).

Emily Morgan—A Double Tree by Hilton ★★ Located just a musket shot from the Alamo and overlooking it from many rooms, the Emily Morgan resides in a 1924 Gothic Revival-style medical arts center, replete with gargoyles, said to have been placed there to help the doctors ward off diseases. But there's little to suggest either battlefields or anything medicinal inside: Rooms are colorful and stylish, with salmon walls and leather accents. This historic—and reputedly haunted—hotel is a fun place to stay, and the lobby bar during happy hour is a lively local scene. A variety of specials also make it an economical choice.

705 E. Houston St. (at Ave. E). www.emilymorganhotel.com. ✆ **210/225-5100**. 177 units. $169–$329 double; $191–$379 suite. Valet parking $39. Pets accepted, $50 fee. **Amenities:** Restaurant; bar; concierge; fitness center; business center; outdoor pool; room service; Wi-Fi (free).

The Fairmount ★★ Not to be confused with the Fairmont luxury hotels, this is a small San Antonio original, independently owned and one of a kind. Built in 1906 for the benefit of railroad passengers, in 1985 the entire three-story, redbrick Victorian was moved 6 blocks (in one piece) to its present site near Hemisfair Park and La Villita. The move made headlines and the *Guinness Book of World Records*. Elaborate decorative details in the hotel's interior were thus preserved and add to the charm of staying here. The rooms, decorated in period style and furnished with antiques, vary a great deal, but most are of comfortable size and have lovely marble bathrooms. The junior suites are a good bargain and worth an upgrade. The hotel's restaurants are top-notch: The swanky **Silo Prime** steakhouse (part of the Silo group; p. 73) and the rustic Italian **Nonna Osteria.**

401 S. Alamo St. (at E. Nueva St.). www.thefairmounthotel-sanantonio.com. ✆ **877/229-8808** or 210/224-8800. 37 units. $179–$249 double; $189–$409 suite. Valet parking $39. Pets under 35 lb. accepted, $75 fee. **Amenities:** Restaurant; bar; concierge; fitness room; business center; room service; Wi-Fi (free).

Homewood Suites by Hilton Riverwalk ★ Occupying the former San Antonio Drug Company building (built in 1919), this all-suites hotel is a good downtown deal, especially for families. Located on a central stretch of the river, it's convenient to most downtown attractions. Rooms don't have much flash, but they are large, comfortable, and furnished with microwaves, refrigerators with icemakers, and dishwashers. On Monday through Thursday in the early evening/late afternoon, the hotel offers free refreshments; breakfast is always included in the room rate. Despite being on the river, there are no rooms with river views, but the rooftop pool area compensates.

432 W. Market St. (at St. Mary's St.). www.homewood-suites.com. ✆ **866/238-4218** or 210/222-1515. 146 units. $169–$199 suite; $309–$339 2-bedroom suite. Rates include breakfast and afternoon snacks (Mon–Thurs). Valet parking $29. **Amenities:** Fitness room; concierge; laundry; business center; outdoor pool; Wi-Fi (free).

Hotel Havana ★★ Built as a hotel in 1914 in Mediterranean Revival-style, this was one of the first lodgings in town to adopt a retro-chic aesthetic when it started welcoming guests again in the early 2000s; it's now part of the Bunkhouse group, with uber-hip properties in Austin, Marfa, San Francisco, and Todos Santos, Mexico. (See "The Boutique Hotel Queen" box, p. 186.) Each room is individually, and quirkily, furnished with a mix of antique and midcentury modern pieces (including dressers and bureaus, which compensate for a lack of closets). Style doesn't, however, compensate for creaky wood floors and occasional glitches in electronics (including, crucially, the A/C). **Ocho** terrace restaurant, set in a high-ceilinged glass conservatory overlooking a quiet River Walk path, is a hot spot with locals and visitors alike—great for a late Sunday breakfast or a romantic dinner. Likewise, the **Havana Bar,** hidden below street level, is as cozy and clandestine as they come—the perfect cool hideaway after a sizzling San Antonio day.

1015 Navarro St. (btw. St. Mary's and Martin sts.). www.havanasanantonio.com. ✆ **210/222-2008.** 27 units. $158–$199 double; $209–$599 suite. Self-parking $17. Pets accepted, $25 fee. **Amenities:** Restaurant; bar; concierge; gym passes; room service; Wi-Fi (free).

Marriott Plaza San Antonio ★ Tucked away at the south end of downtown and set on 6 palm-studded acres, this hotel feels like an island of tranquillity, though it's convenient to the convention center and River Walk attractions. It incorporates four 19th-century buildings, saved from the bulldozer in 1968 during the creation of nearby Hemisfair Park; one houses the hotel's health club and spa, the others are offices and conference centers. The hotel is scheduled for a remodel—the guest quarters and public areas look a little tired—but rooms are larger than the norm and most come with a balcony overlooking the hotel's manicured grounds, including a croquet lawn.

555 S. Alamo St. (at Chávez Blvd.). www.plazasa.com. ✆ **800/228-9290** or 210/229-1000. 251 units. $169–$274 double. Self-parking $37; valet parking $43. **Amenities:** Restaurant; bar; concierge; club-level floor; fitness room; Jacuzzi; outdoor pool; room service; Wi-Fi (free).

Menger Hotel ★★ In the late 19th century, no one who was anyone would consider staying anywhere but the Menger, which opened its doors in 1859 and has never closed them. Ulysses S. Grant, Sarah Bernhardt, and Oscar Wilde were among those who walked—or, rumor has it, in the case of Robert E. Lee, rode a horse—through the halls, ballrooms, and gardens. Successfully combining the original, restored building with myriad additions, the Menger now takes up an entire city block. The hotel's location is terrific—between the Alamo and the Shops at Rivercenter, a block from the River Walk. And its public areas, particularly the Victorian lobby, are gorgeous. The **Menger Bar** (p. 129) is one of San Antonio's historic taverns, and while nearly every vintage hotel in town boasts a ghost, this one claims to have no fewer than 32. Rooms in the modern sections tend to be a bit plain. Those in the original Victorian section, furnished with period pieces, are much more entertaining, though more costly. These tend to fill up first, so if you intend to book one, book well in advance.

204 Alamo Plaza (at Crockett St.). www.mengerhotel.com. ✆ **800/345-9285** or 210/223-4361. 316 units. $169–$229 double; $250–$495 suite. Valet parking $28. Pets (1 per room) accepted, $125 fee. **Amenities:** Restaurant; bar; fitness room; Jacuzzi; outdoor pool; room service; spa; Wi-Fi (free).

Riverwalk Vista ★★ A worn set of carpeted stairs on a busy downtown block leads to this surprise gem of an inn, its 17 huge, beautifully furnished rooms tucked away on the upper floors of an 1883 mercantile building. All offer long-leaf-pine floors, leather chairs, exposed-brick walls, and handsome Arts and Crafts–style furnishings. Luxe touches such as robes, high-quality bath products, and free high-speed Internet are nice, but what makes this place really stand out are such sweet, homey details as afternoon lemonade and cookies and a teddy bear in every room. The location, near the River Walk, Alamo, and other key attractions, can't be beat. The downsides: In spite of attempts at sound proofing, noise from the street below, including the busy late-night McDonald's next door, filters up to some rooms. And if you're driving, you're on your own trying to find parking. It's worth bringing ear plugs, just in case—and it's one more reason to go carless if you're bunking downtown.

262 Losoya St. (at Commerce St.). www.riverwalkvista.com. ✆ **866/898-4782** or 210/223-3200. 17 units. $175–295 double; $199–$315 suite. Rates include breakfast. **Amenities:** Business center/conference room; fitness center; pool access at sister property; Wi-Fi (free).

Tru by Hilton San Antonio Downtown River Walk ★ Opened in 2018 on downtown's east side, this representative of Hilton's burgeoning youth-oriented brand has all the touchstone amenities—a huge lobby-cum-gathering spot with games like foosball; a 24/7 market selling snacks, beer, and wine; and tablets and work stations for guest use. Also encouraging guests to hang in the public areas—as opposed to lingering upstairs—are the no-frills rooms, without closets or desks (although they do have 55-inch TVs). A counterpoint to all this contemporary chic is Tru's location in a historic building, a car dealership built in the 1930s. This, and the fact that there's an AARP discount on an already low rate, make the hotel appealing also to budget-conscious travelers who aren't millennial age.

901 E. Houston St. (at Bowie St.). www.tru3hilton.com. ✆ **210/348-2924.** 95 units. $157–$184 double. Rates include breakfast. Parking $24. **Amenities:** Business center; outdoor pool; fitness room; market; coin laundry; Wi-Fi (free).

Inexpensive

Best Western Sunset Suites–Riverwalk ★★ A rare combination of economy and location, this hotel sits east of the freeway from the rest of downtown, in an up-and-coming area near the Sunset Station entertainment complex, just a few blocks east of the River Walk and other attractions. The hotel has plenty of character: The reception and lobby area are in an 1896 brick building that once hosted a speakeasy (among other businesses), while spacious suites, in a newer building next door, feature custom-made Arts and Crafts–style furnishings. Accommodations are also equipped with sleeper sofas, microwaves, and minifridges. Despite the proximity of the freeway, rooms are surprisingly quiet.

1103 E. Commerce St. (at Hwy. 281). www.bestwesternsunsetsuites.com. ✆ **866/560-6000** or 210/223-4400. 64 suites. $109–$165 double. Rates include breakfast buffet. Parking $13. **Amenities:** Fitness room; Wi-Fi (free).

Holiday Inn Express San Antonio—River Walk ★★ Don't expect cell-like rooms in this five-story landmark, even though the 1879 building was once the Bexar County Jail. A total gut of the structure created spacious rooms—even the bathrooms are larger than those you might normally see in this price range. All offer microwaves and refrigerators; a complimentary hot

family-friendly HOTELS

Homewood Suites (p. 44) This reasonably priced all-suites hotel near the River Walk, with in-room kitchen facilities and two TVs per suite—not to mention a guest laundry—is extremely convenient for families.

Hyatt Regency Hill Country Resort and Spa (p. 50) In addition to its 5-acre water park and proximity to SeaWorld, this hotel offers a Camp Hyatt program for ages 3 to 12. Kids who are up early in some seasons can even help staff members feed the birds and squirrels.

Omni San Antonio (p. 51) This hotel's location near the major theme parks, including Morgan's Wonderland, as well as in-room games and other Omni Kids features, helps keep all family members entertained.

Tru by Hilton (p. 46) Low rates, available board games, an outdoor pool, foosball in the lobby, fun snacks, and (for teenagers) a social media wall are among the features that make this a good bet for all ages.

breakfast adds to the value. The hotel is in the western part of downtown, close to Market Square, the San Fernando Cathedral, and the Spanish Governor's Palace. ***Note:*** The fact that many prisoners were executed in this building makes it a stop on several ghost tours.

120 Camaron St. (btw. Houston and Commerce sts.). www.holidayexpressriverwalk.com. ✆ **877/545-7015** or 210/281-1400. 82 units. $89–$160 double. Parking $17/day. **Amenities:** Business center; exercise room; outdoor pool; Wi-Fi (free).

O'Brien Hotel ★★ Though this small hotel occupies a three-story brick building dating back to the turn of the 20th century, nothing remains of the past except for the facade—and the style of the rooms. Some have wrought-iron balconies and/or whirlpool tubs; others have high ceilings and clawfoot bathtubs. The friendly staff is old-style hospitable too. The hotel works for both business and leisure travelers; it's in a quiet section of downtown near the convention center, not far from the River Walk and the King William district.

116 Navarro St. (at St. Mary's St.). www.obrienhotel.com. ✆ **800/257-6058** or 210/527-1111. 39 units. $99–$159 double. Rates include breakfast. Self-parking $15. **Amenities:** Laundry; Wi-Fi (free).

THE PEARL

Expensive

Hotel Emma ★★★ The term "industrial chic" has become a cliché, but Hotel Emma embodies it—and rescues it from its ho-hum connotations. It isn't hard to fathom the success of San Antonio's hottest (and priciest) lodging, a converted 19th-century brewery. Attention to detail makes the hotel a delight on every level, especially historic and aesthetic. Even if you don't take advantage of the many on-site programs (cooking classes, say, or readings by visiting authors), you feel like just staying here raises your IQ a few points. Welcome cocktails are served in a library lined with carefully chosen books of local interest, all available for guests to peruse; rooms display a smart blend of the contemporary and the nostalgic—pedestal sinks, black-and-white tile floors in the bathroom, seersucker robes. And once you've sunk a fortune into your stay, you're not nickeled and dimed for extras: A fresh pot of coffee is brought to your room every morning and your bottled water is replenished daily, gratis. The nightly turndown of French macarons from Pearl's world-class Bakery Lorraine is a sweet reminder that, while the Emma has its own excellent restaurant (**Supper**) and bar/club (**Sternewirth**), the hotel is the hub of a complex with some of the best shops, restaurants, and entertainment in town (**Cured, Botika,** and **La Gloria** are covered in chapter 5, while **Jazz, TX** is detailed in chapter 8). If you stay here you'll be at the heart of the action, while remaining cossetted and relaxed.

136 E. Grayson St. www.thehotelemma.com. ✆ **844/845-7384** or 210/448-8300. 146 units. $445–$795 double; $795–$3,000 suite. Valet parking $15. **Amenities:** 3 restaurants; bar/lounge; bikes; concierge; fitness center; in-room spa treatments; rooftop pool; Wi-Fi (free).

Greater San Antonio Hotels

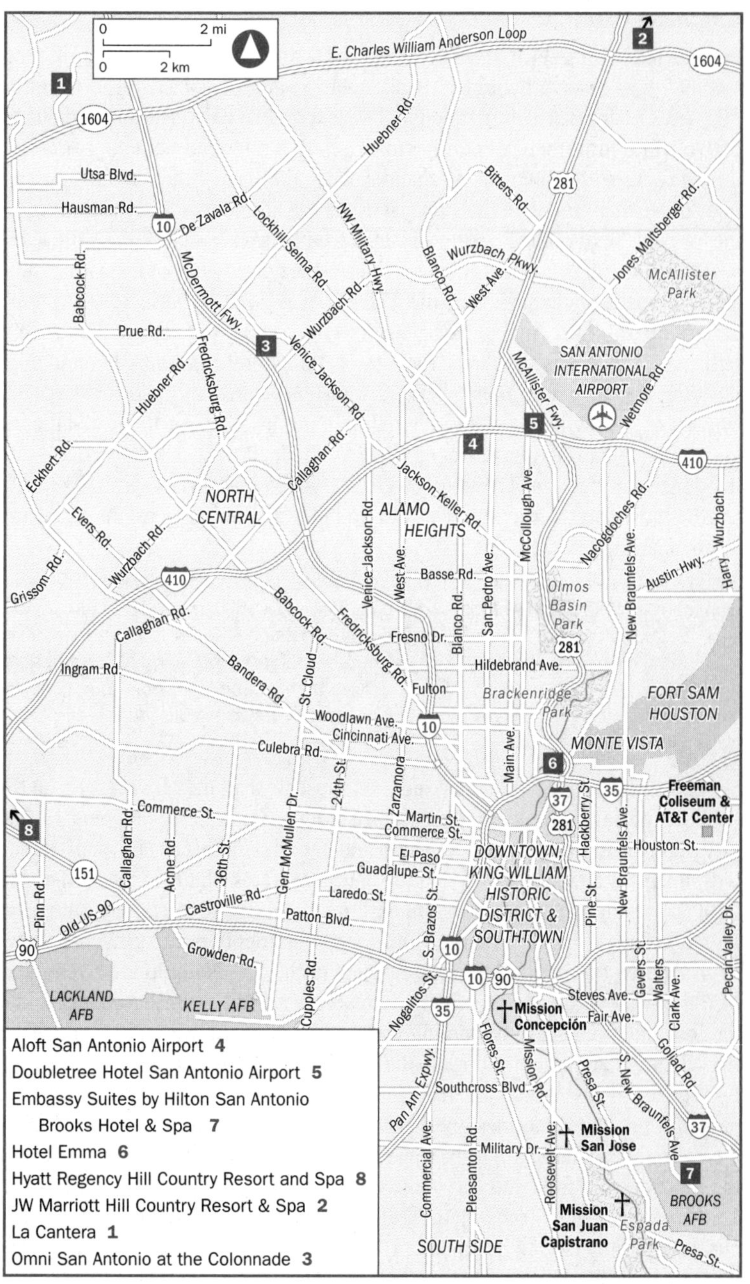

WEST/NORTHWEST

Expensive

Hyatt Regency Hill Country Resort and Spa ★★ The quintessential Texas resort, the kicked back, splashy, and oversized Hyatt is set on 300 acres of former rolling ranchland lush with live oaks. Buildings made of native white limestone, a country store, a long bar topped with copper, a fine dining room with a huge antler chandelier . . . these and other details never let you forget that you're in the Lone Star state. And the nearby Hill Country is the part of Texas that's green and laced with lakes and streams—thus the 950-foot-long man-made Ramblin' River, where you can float in an inner tube along a shallow channel, and the **Windflower Spa,** set around a soothing natural pond. The 27-hole championship golf course was designed by Arthur Hills and Associates to take advantage of the natural terrain. All sound a bit too tame for your teenagers? The 22-foot-long waterslide and Flow Riding Wave machine will keep their adrenaline pumping. One of the specialties at the rustic-elegant **Antlers Lodge** is game—think elk with dried cherries—and it's done to perfection. The hotel celebrated its 25th anniversary in 2018, and, for the most part, it has not only held up but improved. The rooms could use a refresher, however.

9800 Hyatt Resort Dr. (off Hwy. 151, btw. Westover Hills Blvd. and Potranco Rd.). www.hyatt.com. ✆ **800/55-HYATT** [554-9288] or 210/647-1234. 500 units. $189–$440 double; $450–$3,000 suite or villa. Free self-parking; valet parking $30. Pets 50 lb. and under (2 max., with combined weight of 75 lb.) accepted, $150 fee (up to 6 nights). **Amenities:** 4 restaurants; 2 bars; grocery; bikes; kids' programs; concierge; golf course; health club; Jacuzzis; jogging trails; 4 outdoor pools; room service; sauna; spa; tennis court; waterpark; Wi-Fi (free).

La Cantera ★★★ Grander and more upscale than the other resorts on the outskirts of San Antonio, La Cantera is a magnet for golfers, shoppers, lovers, girlfriends seeking a luxe getaway—and families who can afford it (along with a variety of kid-friendly features and programs, the resort's partnership with BabyQuip means you can rent high-quality cribs, strollers, and other gear on-site). The setting is stunning, with rocky outcroppings and gorgeous views from a perch on one of the highest points in the San Antonio area; remnants of the limestone quarry on which the resort was built were incorporated into the four interconnected swimming pools and a dramatic waterfall. On-site are two championship golf courses—the PGA-tour favorite La Cantera course, a joint effort of Jay Moorish and Tom Weiskopf, and the newer Palmer course, named for its legendary designer—plus a golf academy. **Signature** restaurant, a creation of acclaimed San Antonio chef Andrew Weissman, offers some of the most elegant food and service in town (p. 75), while the nearby **Shops at La Cantera** (p. 110) runs the upscale gamut, counting Apple, Neiman Marcus, and Tiffany among its tenants. The **Loma de Vida Spa and Wellness** has won awards galore for its natural settings and array of treatments and activities. With all that to enjoy, rooms are almost superfluous—but of course, they're large and luxurious and understatedly elegant. For a full-out splurge, go for a casita with a private pool and patio.

16641 La Cantera Pkwy. (La Cantera Pkwy. exit off I-10). www.destinationhotels.com/la-cantera-resort-and-spa. ✆ **855/499-2960** or 210/558-6500. 496 units. $259–$369 double; $380 and up suite; $420 and up villa. Free self-parking; valet parking $30. **Amenities:** 7 restaurants; 2 bars; kids' program; concierge; 2 18-hole golf courses; spa; fitness center; 5 outdoor pools; room service; tennis court; complimentary shuttle to nearby attractions, including the Shops at La Cantera and SeaWorld; Wi-Fi (free).

Moderate

Omni San Antonio at the Colonnade ★★ Location, location, location. This polished granite high-rise off I-10 is convenient to SeaWorld, Six Flags Fiesta Texas, Morgan's Wonderland, the airport, and the Hill Country, while the shops and restaurants of the Colonnade shopping/restaurant complex are even closer. Guest rooms are luxe with polished dark woods, rich earth-toned fabrics, and Southwest accents. The hotel gets a lot of business travelers, but its proximity to the theme parks, various Omni Kids features (including a kids' fantasy suite), and a large pool make it a good choice for families. Fitness facilities, including a hydrotherapy pool and sauna along with state-of-the-art workout equipment, are excellent. Guests can get an in-room workout package as part of the Omni "Get Fit" program—or just say the heck with it and opt for an in-room massage.

9821 Colonnade Blvd. (at Wurzbach). www.omnihotels.com. ✆ **800/843-6664** or 210/691-8888. 326 units. $169–$249 double; $289 and up suite. Free self-parking; valet parking $15. Pets under 25 lb. accepted, $50 fee. **Amenities:** Restaurant; bar; free airport transfer and local shuttle; concierge; business center; health club; Jacuzzi; indoor pool; outdoor pool; room service; Wi-Fi ($10).

AIRPORT/NORTH CENTRAL

Expensive

JW Marriott Hill Country Resort & Spa ★★ This huge (600-acre, 1,000-room) link in Marriott's luxury brand chain really earns its "Hill Country" designation: It's farther from the city center than the other resorts. That's okay: You never have to go anywhere if you settle in here. On-site ways to get wet include a 9-acre waterpark with a lazy river; a River Bluff Water Experience, with seven water slides; and four swimming pools, one for adults only. Among other grownup-oriented features are two 18-hole championship golf courses, designed by Greg Norman and Pete Dye; and the **Lantana Spa,** which embraces the Latin American curandero tradition—a nice touch, given the city's Hispanic roots. In addition to the **Replenish Spa Bistro,** dining options include the **High Velocity** bar, with craft beers and wall-to-wall TVs;

18 Oaks, a swank steakhouse with an excellent list of Hill Country wines; and **Cibolo Moon,** raising Tex-Mex to a gourmet level.

23808 Resort Pkwy. www.marriott.com/sanantonio. ✆ **210/276-2500.** 1,002 units. $369–$449 double; $699–$1,569 suite. Free self-parking; valet parking $37. **Amenities:** 5 restaurants; coffee shop; game room; waterpark; 2 golf courses; health club; 4 pools; spa; room service; Wi-Fi (free).

Moderate

Aloft San Antonio Airport ★★ Marriott's burgeoning Aloft brand of trendy, business-friendly lodgings provides pared-down decor and industrial-chic public spaces at good prices. This link in the chain has a pool, lounge, bar with lighting that changes to set the mood, and a snack area that allows guests to pick out treats on the go and charge them to their rooms. The hotel also features a 24/7 gym, fun little Fido-friendly amenities, and room service provided by a local pub. Like many airport hotels, this one offers free parking and a complimentary airport shuttle. ***Note:*** The terminals aren't exactly next door, so leave plenty of time to make your flight.

838 NW Loop 410. www.aloftsanantonioairport.com. ✆ **800/716-8143** or 210/541-8881. 141 units. $134–$169 double. Rates include breakfast buffet. Free self-parking. Pets under 40 lb. accepted, no fee. **Amenities:** Exercise room; outdoor splash pool; Wi-Fi (free).

Doubletree Hotel San Antonio Airport ★★ For an airport hotel, the Doubletree is surprisingly serene and stylish. Moorish arches, potted plants, stone fountains, and colorful tiles create a Mediterranean mood in the public areas. Intricate wrought-iron elevators descend from the guest floors to the lushly landscaped pool patio, eliminating the need to tramp through the lobby in a swimsuit. Guest rooms are equally appealing, many with brick walls, wood-beamed ceilings, and draped French doors. And because this hotel gets a large business clientele from Mexico, most of the staff is bilingual. The hotel offers free shuttles to the airport and other destinations within 2 miles.

37 NE Loop 410 (McCullough exit). www.doubletree.com. ✆ **800/535-1980** or 210/366-2424. 290 units. $126–$229 double; $209–$350 suite. Free self-parking. **Amenities:** Restaurant; 2 bars; concierge; business center; coin-op laundry; exercise room; Jacuzzi; outdoor pool; Wi-Fi (free).

SOUTHSIDE

Moderate

Embassy Suites by Hilton San Antonio Brooks Hotel & Spa ★★★ Opened in 2017 in a fast-growing southside neighborhood, this $40-million hotel kicks up the Embassy Suites image a few notches. Highlights include the swanky **Nineteen17** lobby bar/restaurant, showcasing organic fare, including honey from an on-site hive; a gourmet-to-go lobby shop; and the full-service

PurSol spa, with treatments that include the city's first salt cave for inhalation therapy. The hotel draws on the area's rich history in a variety of ways: Its conference rooms are named for the nearby chain of missions, for example, and its event space is the converted airplane Hangar 9 from Brooks AFB. Add all the usual Embassy Suites features—well-equipped accommodations designed for business travelers and families, made-to-order breakfasts, and an afternoon reception—and you've got an exceptional place to stay. It's just about a 10-min. trip by car to downtown, and you don't have to worry about finding (or paying for) parking here.

7610 S. New Braunfels Ave. www.embassysuites3.hilton.com. ✆ **210/534-1000**. 156 suites. $129–$236 suite. Rates include breakfast and afternoon snacks. Free self-parking. **Amenities:** Fitness room; outdoor pool; business center; room service; Wi-fi (free).

WHERE TO EAT IN SAN ANTONIO

5

San Antonio has long been synonymous with Tex-Mex cooking. Perfected over the centuries, the rich array of dishes created by this adaption of south-of-the-border fare relies on heaping helpings of tradition. But these days, the dining scene's sizzle comes from far more than fajitas. San Antonio's designation as a UNESCO Creative City of Gastronomy (see "A Gastronomical Honor," p. 56) recognizes both the unique contribution and evolution of Tex-Mex and the fact that a wider culinary revolution has been slowly simmering. The Mexican influence is still key, but now chef-driven restaurants come in all flavors—French, Italian, New American, vegetarian, fusion—as do the more modest dining rooms that locals flock to. You can also find lots of down-home barbecue shacks, local *taquerías,* and popular neighborhood dives.

Downtown restaurants, especially those along the River Walk, still draw the most visitors—often deservedly so. Because most out-of-towners either sleep downtown or spend the day there, I devote a good deal of space to dining in this area. (To locate restaurants downtown, see the map on p. 57.) But the two epicenters of San Antonio's serious food scene reside in adjacent neighborhoods. To the north of downtown, along the Museum Reach stretch of the San Antonio River, **The Pearl** multi-use complex is the city's newest foodie magnet, anchored by the **Culinary Institute of America** (CIA) (www.ciachef.edu/cia-texas; ✆ **210/554-6400**), with its student-run cafe, and the **Hotel Emma** (p. 48). Some of the city's best-loved chefs as well as up-and-comers operate restaurants in the Pearl (several reviewed below), where you'll also find a farmers market on Saturdays and Sundays year-round and the **Bottling Department** (www.bottlingdept.com), a food hall with five fast-casual eateries and a bar. Just downstream from the city center, the

Categories of Cuisine

Rather than trying to make fine distinctions between overlapping labels such as Regional American, New Southwestern, and American Fusion, which generally identify the kind of cooking that tweaks classic American dishes using out-of-the-ordinary ingredients—roast chicken with tamale stuffing, say, or blue cheese fritters with pesto dipping sauce—I lump them all into the category of **New American. Tex-Mex** is, of course, Tex-Mex, and should not be confused with the cooking south of the border, which is labeled **Mexican.**

eclectic, vivacious **Southtown** area became popular a couple of decades ago with artists, gallery owners, and innovative restaurateurs; the neighborhood and food scene are still predominantly Mexican-American, but now creative south-of-the-border dining rooms and holdover *taquerías* mix with fine dining spots of all ethnicities.

There's also no shortage of restaurants, new and well-established, farther afield, especially in such prosperous northside neighborhoods as **Monte Vista, Olmos Park,** and **Alamo Heights.** (To locate restaurants outside of downtown, see the map on p. 67.)

Practical Information

RESERVATIONS San Antonio's serious foodie scene is still a bit under the radar, which is good news for visitors. You'll rarely find yourself unable to get a table at the restaurant of your choice if you book a few days in advance; even if you turn up without a reservation, you might have to wait but you'll eventually get seated. Willingness to sit in the bar speeds up the process.

DRESS CODE San Antonio is a very casual town—in part dictated by the warm weather. I can't think of any place where men would be required to wear a jacket or tie. Even the fanciest steakhouses are fine with business casual—khakis, say, or intact jeans, and a nice short-sleeved shirt. That said, a lot of San Antonians, especially younger women, like to get gussied up for a night out. Don't hesitate to strut your fashion stuff.

SMOKING San Antonio was one of the first cities in Texas to ban indoor smoking, so diners are guaranteed smoke-free indoor environments. Smoking is permitted in designated areas on most restaurant patios. San Antonio's "Tobacco 21" ordinance, which went into effect in September 2018, bans the sale of tobacco products, including e-cigarettes, to anyone under 21. It's hard to predict, but that seems likely to inhibit patio smoking by a younger crowd.

DINING TIMES Typically of dwellers in warm weather cities, San Antonians are early risers—and early diners. Most kitchens close by 10pm. The most popular time to eat is from 6:30 to 7:30pm.

A GASTRONOMICAL honor

Designated in 2017 as a UNESCO Creative City of Gastronomy, San Antonio is now officially an international culinary treasure. But the honor did more than just acknowledge the city's world-class restaurants and its many food education programs, including the program at the prestigious Culinary Institute of America. It also paid tribute to the city's role as a culinary crossroads, a gateway to Mexico positioned between the coastal plains and fertile hill country of south Texas. The region's waterways, especially the San Antonio River, gave rise to indigenous settlements dating back some 13,000 years. In the 1700s the Spanish and Canary Islanders arrived, many of whom established vast cattle ranches, and they were followed by other waves of European immigrants, including the Germans. The Texas Mexican, or Tex-Mex, cuisine that resulted was heralded by the UNESCO committee as the product of the confluence of local game, beef, fish, produce, herbs, and spices with ingredients, recipes, and cooking techniques imported from a wide array of cultures.

While the award celebrated humble Tex-Mex as the original fusion cuisine of the Southwest, it also recognized sophisticated attempts to rediscover its roots in what has been dubbed Tex-Next cuisine. A prime example of a restaurant embodying this ethos is tiny **Mixtli,** 5251 McCullough Ave. (www.restaurantmixtli.com; ✆ **210/338-0746**), where nationally acclaimed chefs Rico Torres and Diego Galicia turn to indigenous ingredients and pre-Hispanic techniques for their innovative fare.

Future developments include a plan to meld history with gastronomy at a new restaurant complex in **La Villita** (p. 87). The city of San Antonio will collaborate in this project with three top chefs: Stephen McHugh of Cured, Elizabeth Johnson of Pharm Table, and Johnny Hernandez of . . . many things, including La Gloria, all covered below. In addition, the city will also develop a series of culinary trails connecting the four historic missions. It will take several years to accomplish these goals, but there's no question that the days of automatically dismissing San Antonio's homegrown cuisine are in the rearview mirror.

DOWNTOWN

Expensive

Along with the restaurants listed below, you may also want to consider **Paesanos Riverwalk,** 111 W. Crockett St., #101 (✆ **210/227-2782**), a downtown branch of the beloved Alamo Heights restaurant Paesanos (p. 72).

Biga on the Banks ★★ NEW AMERICAN Bruce Auden is a household name in San Antonio, a multiple-time James Beard "Best Chef" nominee whose restaurant on the River Walk is a fine-dining favorite. Because it's on the ground floor of the International Center building and guests enter at St. Mary's Street (not at River Walk) level, the modern high-ceilinged dining room has river and city-lights views from its picture windows, but it rests above the din of crowds on the bustling pathways below. Auden's fresh menu

Central San Antonio Restaurants

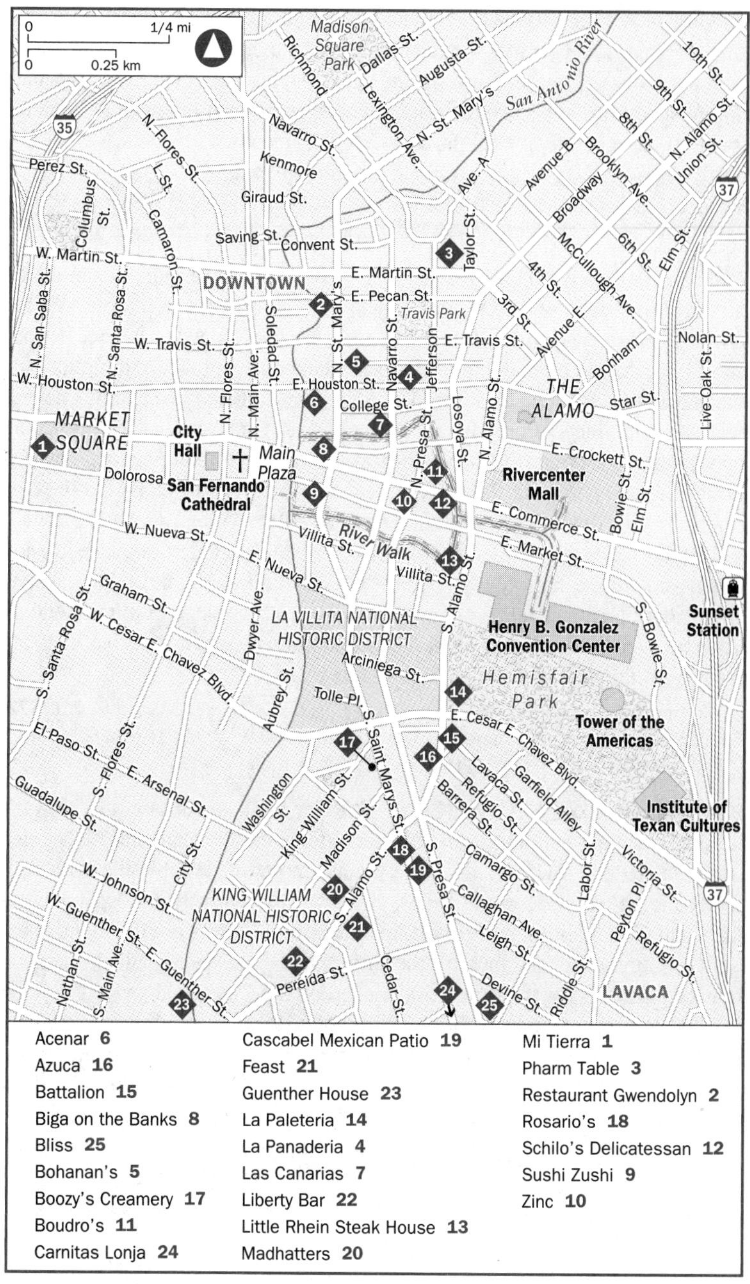

changes daily and stays true to the season, although year-round you're likely to find a juicy Angus rib-eye served with Shiner Bock–battered onion rings. Snapper is stuffed with Gulf crab, and Hill Country venison and quail come with 11 spices and juniper sauce. For dessert, Auden's popular sticky toffee pudding rocks the house. For a special occasion, reserve Table 31, an intimate dining space for five to eight people, where guests can enjoy Chef Auden's specially designed five- to eight-course tasting menus.

203 S. St. Mary's St./River Walk. www.biga.com. ✆ **210/225-0722.** Reservations recommended. Main courses $25–$40. 3-course prix-fixe menu $39 (before 6:30pm and after 9pm). Sun–Thurs 5:30–10pm; Fri–Sat 5:30–11pm.

Bohanan's ★★★ STEAK/SEAFOOD What could be more Texan than a big, gleaming high-end steakhouse—and a home-grown one to boot? With a prime location on Houston Street, not far from the Majestic Theatre, Bohanan's is considered by many to be the best steakhouse in town. It definitely fits the decor stereotype, all dark wood, creamy white tablecloths, clubby cocktail bar, and humidor stuffed with expensive cigars. Chef/owner Mark Bohanan opened this restaurant in 2002 in a historic building with long-beam pinewood floors and has perfected the cooking and service over the years. On the first floor, a pianist tickles the ivories in **Bohanan's Bar,** with a banquette of tufted leather and a long, slender bar. Upstairs, in the dining room, the kitchen pumps out prime mesquite-grilled steaks, seafood flown in daily, and a la carte sides. The waitstaff is well-trained, knowledgeable, and ultra-attentive. You can't smoke inside any San Antonio building, but you can buy that big cigar from the humidor and enjoy it on the patio.

219 E. Houston St. (btw. St. Mary's and Navarro sts.). www.bohanans.com. ✆ **210/472-2600.** Reservations recommended. Main courses $27–$60; steaks $42-$126. Mon–Sat 11am–2pm and 5–10pm (until 11pm Fri–Sat); Sun 5–10pm.

Boudro's ★★ NEW AMERICAN A River Walk standby set in a turn-of-the-20th-century building with a handcrafted mesquite bar, this self-styled Texas bistro is known for its chunky guacamole, made tableside with fire-roasted tomatoes and serrano chiles, as well as for its lively atmosphere. Tex-Mex and Gulf seafood made with fresh local ingredients are the menu stars. Start with the guac, and then try the shrimp and grits, made with chorizo and roasted poblanos; or the prime rib, cooked on a pecan-wood grill. If you get the lighter herb-crusted fish fillet you might have room for dessert: whiskey-soaked bread pudding, say, or Key lime chess pie. For the ultimate San Antonio experience, book a Boudro's Dinner Cruise 2 weeks in advance, and for $60 per person (not including tax, tip, and spirits) you can dine on a delicious prix-fixe menu on a barge floating on the river.

421 E. Commerce St./River Walk. www.boudros.com. ✆ **210/224-8484.** Reservations recommended. Main courses $22–$42. Sun–Thurs 11am–11pm; Fri–Sat 11am–midnight.

Las Canarias ★ NEW AMERICAN The fine dining room at the **Omni La Mansión del Río** (p. 42) has a couple of things going for it: the setting and the food. You have a choice of dining on well-prepared, beautifully presented cuisine on a lovely riverside veranda; a palm-decked, Mexican tiled patio; or inside in one of several antiques-filled interior rooms, The menu changes seasonally and tweaks traditional dishes—the chicken pot pie might include truffles, for example—but most of the fare is comfortingly familiar; go for the chef tasting menu ($65; $95 with wine) if you're feeling adventurous. While this is a special-occasion and visitor-oriented restaurant at dinnertime, the copious Sunday champagne brunch buffet is a local favorite; be sure to reserve.

112 College St./River Walk. www.omnihotels.com. ✆ **210/518-1063.** Reservations recommended. Main courses $25–$42; Sun brunch (10:30am–2:30pm) $43 adults, $23 children. Daily 6:30am–10:30pm.

Little Rhein Steak House ★ STEAKS/SEAFOOD Built in 1847 in what was then the German Little Rhein district, one of the oldest two-story structures in San Antonio has hosted a steakhouse abutting the river and La Villita since 1967. Antiques deck the indoor main dining room and a miniature train surrounded by historic photos runs overhead. Little sparkling lights drape tree branches overhanging the River Walk patio, which is elevated slightly and railed off for privacy. This is the place to come if you're looking for a good steak—all are prime beef and grilled over hardwood—in a homier, more romantic setting than your typical sleek meat emporium.

231 S. Alamo St. at Market St. www.dine.littlerheinsteakhouse.com. ✆ **210/225-2111.** Reservations recommended. Entrees $26–$29; steaks $28–$56; children's menu $7–$20. Daily 5–10pm.

Restaurant Gwendolyn ★★★ AMERICAN REGIONAL Gwendolyn chef/owner Michael Sohocki is a soft-spoken man with a tiny, whisper-quiet restaurant, its kitchen the size of a closet. His unassuming eatery on a near-forgotten bend in the River Walk would be a surprising find—except that it's been lauded by the major food press. Named for Sohocki's grandmother, the restaurant hearkens back to an era when food was prepared without electrical equipment: Its cooks use no blenders, mixers, deep fryers, or anything with a motor (other than the fridge, which the health department insists upon). Sample fresh-made po'boys at lunch; at dinner, the changing tasting menu might include a venison tartare, Caesar salad with charred broccoli, or barbecued quail with stewed collard greens. Sohocki buys whole animals from nearby farms and he butchers, dry-ages, and preserves them; he smokes his own bacon, grinds his own sausage. Restaurant Gwendolyn is no stunt; it's a labor of love, cooking unplugged.

152 E. Pecan St. (at N. St. Mary's St.). www.restaurantgwendolyn.com. ✆ **210/222-1849.** Reservations required. Main courses lunch $8–$12; dinner (chef's tasting menu only) $75 or $95. Tues–Fri 11am–1:30pm; Tues–Thurs 5:30–9pm; Fri–Sat 5:30–10pm.

Moderate

Ácenar ★★ MEXICAN/TEX-MEX This high-energy spot downstairs from the Hotel Valencia (p. 40) features updated Tex-Mex fare, including tacos with such nontraditional fillings as chicken-fried oysters or guajillo-braised short ribs, alongside more elaborate dishes like crepes with duck in a tamarind–cherry–grilled onion sauce or *camarones al Diablo* (grilled shrimp in chipotle-butter). Decorated in bold Mexican hues with midcentury modern tables and banquettes, the multi-level dining room is bright and inviting. Sip drinks in the **Balcony Lounge** with views of the river, or dine outside on an elevated shaded patio, which overlooks the River Walk but isn't in the thick of the touristy crowds. It's also a lively, bright place for Mexican brunch on the weekend.

146 E. Houston St. at River Walk. www.acenar.com. ✆ **210/222-2362.** Reservations not accepted (priority seating for large parties). Main courses $9–$14 lunch, $13–$35 dinner. Sun–Thurs 11am–10pm; Fri–Sat 11am–11pm (bar open until midnight).

Sushi Zushi ★ JAPANESE/SEAFOOD For a Japanese food fix in a congenial atmosphere, you can't beat this clean, well-lit place. You'll find sushi in all its variety, including a My Spurs roll—yellowtail, cilantro, avocado, chives, and serrano chiles—but far more is on the menu. Choose from rice bowls, soba noodle bowls, soups, teppanyakis, tempuras—a mind-boggling array of food options, not to mention a long list of sakes. This spot is popular with downtown office workers. Other branches are in the Northwest, at the Colonnade Shopping Center, 9867 I-10 W. (✆ **210/691-3332**); in the Northeast, at Stone Oak Plaza II, 18720 Stone Oak Pkwy., at Loop 1604 (✆ **210/545-6100**); and in Lincoln Heights, at 999 E. Bosse Rd., near Broadway (✆ **210/826-8500**).

203 S. St. Mary's St. (The International Center). www.new.sushizushi.com. ✆ **210/472-2900.** Reservations recommended Sat–Sun. Sushi rolls and sashimi $7–$17; other entrees $8–$28. Mon–Thurs 11am–10pm; Fri 11am–11pm; Sat 11:30am–11pm; Sun 11:30am–10pm.

Zinc ★★ AMERICAN Ask locals about this intimate restaurant and wine bar and they're bound to mention the addictive Zinc burger: smoked cheddar, bibb lettuce, and spicy tomato aioli. Just as many come back time after time for the steak and frites, where the meat is pan-seared and finished with a cognac pan sauce. Zinc occupies an old brick building near the River Walk but not on it; a small patio in the back provides romantic atmosphere without the bustle—or the raised prices. In the evening many patrons come just for the wine.

209 N. Presa St. (btw. Market and Commerce sts.). www.zincwine.com. ✆ **210/224-2900.** Reservations recommended. Pizzas, burgers, sandwiches $10–$12; main courses $10–$28. Mon–Fri 11am–2am; Sat–Sun 3pm–2am.

IT'S ALWAYS chili IN SAN ANTONIO

It ranks up there with apple pie in the American culinary pantheon, but nobody's mom invented chili. The iconic stew of meat, chiles, onions, and a variety of spices was likely conceived around the 1840s by Texas cowboys who needed to make tough meat palatable while covering up the taste as it began to go bad. The name is a Texas corruption of the Spanish *chile* (*chee*-leh), after the peppers—which are not really peppers at all, but that's another story—most conventionally used in the stew.

The appellation chili *con carne* is really redundant in Texas, where chili without meat isn't considered chili at all. Indeed, most Texans think that adding beans is only for wimps. Beef is the most common base, but everything from armadillo to venison is acceptable.

While no one really knows exactly where chili originated, San Antonio is the prime candidate for the distinction. Written accounts from the mid–19th century describe the town's "chili queens," women who ladled steaming bowls of the concoction in open-air markets and on street corners. They were dishing out chili in front of the Alamo as late as the 1940s.

William Gebhardt helped strengthen San Antonio's claim to chili fame when he began producing chili powder in the city in 1896. His Original Mexican Dinner package, which came out around 20 years later, included a can each of chili con carne, beans, and tamales, among other things, and fed five for $1. This precursor of the TV dinner proved so popular that it earned San Antonio the nickname "Tamaleville."

Oddly enough, chili isn't generally found on San Antonio restaurant menus. But modern-day chili queens come out in force for special events at Market Square, as well as for the Chili Queens Cook-off at the Bonham Exchange, one of the most popular bashes of the city's huge Fiesta celebration. And there's not a weekend that goes by without a chili cook-off somewhere in the city.

Inexpensive

Mi Tierra ★★ TEX-MEX A Tex-Mex tradition since 1941, this family-owned restaurant in Market Square is not to be missed. Sure, tourists flock here, but local families and businesspeople love it, too. Strolling mariachis pluck big guitars and pour their hearts out singing traditional Mexican ballads—even at breakfast. (The place is open 24/7). At the front of the restaurant, a traditional *panederia* showcases a variety of Mexican pastries and candies; just beyond the bakery are three dining rooms—check out the one in the back for its mural of San Antonio notables and a Selena shrine. Start with a bowl of hot queso and crispy tortilla chips, then move on to traditional Tex-Mex fare like *enchiladas verdes* and *chile rellenos*. If you can't decide what to order, go with a *botanas* platter, a generous sampler of *antojitos* (appetizers).

218 Produce Row (Market Sq.). www.mitierracafe.com. ✆ **210/225-1262.** Reservations for groups of 25 or more only. Breakfast $2.50–$15; lunch & dinner $8–$45. Open 24 hr.

Schilo's Delicatessen ★★ GERMAN/DELI You can't leave town without stopping into this San Antonio institution, if only for a hearty bowl of split-pea soup or a slice of the signature cherry cheesecake. This old-fashioned German deli started as a saloon in Beeville, Texas, in the early 1900s, moved to San Antonio in 1914, and settled at its current location in a former mercantile building in 1942. Career waitresses who look like they were born to sling strudels in a *biergarten* patrol the large open room with high-partitioned wooden booths and hexagon-patterned tile floors. This is a great refueling station near Alamo Plaza for the entire family, with a large kid-friendly selection and retro low prices. For less than $10, an overstuffed Reuben or a kielbasa plate should keep you going for most of the day.

424 E. Commerce St. (btw. Presa and Losoya sts.). www.schilos.com. ✆ **210/223-6692.** Reservations for large groups at breakfast and dinner only. Sandwiches $6.50–$9.50; main dishes $8–$11. Sun–Thurs 7:30am–2:30pm; Fri–Sat 7:30am—10pm.

KING WILLIAM/SOUTHTOWN

Expensive

Bliss ★★★ NEW AMERICAN This stylish dining room in a converted gas station is the creation of Mark Bliss and his wife and business partner, Lisa. Bliss earned a loyal local following from working in several kitchens under another beloved San Antonio chef, Bruce Auden (see **Biga on the Banks,** p. 56), helping him open **Silo** (p. 73) in 1997. Now as the owner/chef of this off-the-beaten-path Southtown restaurant, Bliss brings contemporary American cuisine to new heights. Like the high-ceilinged room with exposed brick walls, the dishes, large and small, are elegantly simple, fresh, and masterfully plated. You could sate yourself with a big arugula salad and sharable plates: a charcuterie board of house-cured meats, artisanal cheeses, and breads, or oysters on the half-shell. Or go a little heartier with small dishes like maple-glazed Kurobuta pork belly, the oyster sliders, or roasted bone marrow with beef tenderloin tartare. Main courses include Arctic char with wild mushrooms, and red snapper over a bed of shrimp risotto. Reserve the chef's table for 10 in the kitchen for an unforgettable culinary experience.

926 S. Presa St. (at Sadie St.). www.foodisbliss.com. ✆ **210/225-2547.** Reservations recommended. Shared/small plates $11–$18; main courses $27–$58. Tues–Thurs 5:30–10pm; Fri–Sat 5:30–11pm.

Moderate

Also in this neighborhood, check out two other restaurants by chef Johnny Hernandez (see La Gloria in the Pearl section, p. 69): **Burgerteca,** 403 Blue Star #105 (www.chefjohnnyhernandez.com/restaurants/burgerteca; ✆ **210/635-0016**), and **La Fruiteria,** 1401 S. Flores St. #102, (www.chefjohnnyhernandez.com/restaurants/fruiteria-southtown; ✆ **210/251-3104**).

Azuca ★★ NUEVO LATINO Chef/owner Rene Fernandez takes diners to Central and South America, with stops in the Caribbean, with his recipes: The menu includes refined versions of Brazilian curry, Cuban *ropa vieja* (a stew of shredded beef and veggies), Argentine-style steaks, and plantain fritters from the islands. The boldly decorated restaurant is fun and creative, with colorful folk-art chandeliers (from its neighbors at Garcia Art Glass), and casual indoor/outdoor spaces. On weekends, live music from 10pm to 2am gets everyone moving ($5 cover), and margaritas, mojitos, and more start flowing.

709 S. Alamo St. (btw. Refugio and Barrera sts.). www.azuca.net. ✆ **210/225-5550.** Reservations recommended. Main courses $9–$12 lunch, $16–$30 dinner. Mon–Thurs 11am–9:30pm; Fri–Sat 11am–10pm; Sun 4–9:30pm.

Battalion ★★ ITALIAN If you arrive before dark in this converted historic firehouse at the head of Southtown's main drag, you'll witness the gradual transformation of a fairly restrained, austere room into a red-lit, buzzy hub—if your attention isn't riveted on your food, that is. Main courses are well-prepared versions of Italian classics like herb-crusted lamb chops and braised pork shanks, but the house-made pastas are where the kitchen really shines. Done with a light touch, they feature slightly nontraditional ingredients: A sweet corn ravioli comes with goat cheese, say, while the ricotta gnocchi is topped with squash ragu. If the food rather than the scene is your interest, come early; the buzz is literal as more and more fashionably dressed young people pour in to see and be seen at the swanky bar. ***Bonus:*** This restaurant has the rare large parking lot. The earlier you come, the easier it is to nab a spot.

604 S. Alamo St. (at Lavaca St.). www.battalionsa.com. ✆ **210/816-0088.** Reservations recommended. Pastas $10; main courses $18–$26. Mon–Thurs 5–10pm; Fri–Sat 5–11pm.

Feast ★★ NEW AMERICAN Yes, it's a tad trendy, from the austere-chic decor in different shades of white to the tongue-in-cheek menu categories—"Oceanic," "Heat," "Chilled," "Grilled," "Crispy," and "Hearty"—but chef Stefan Bowers' masterful New American cuisine goes a long way to compensate. This is the perfect place to go with fellow food lovers who like to share small plates and try lots of different textures and tastes—think cornmeal-fried oysters with watermelon radish slaw, or ground lamb kebabs with serrano feta dip. Traditionalists will be happy with such comfort food favorites as burgers (you can choose one patty or two) or a jack-cheese-and-mac casserole. ***Best bet:*** Sit on the patio, sip a well-crafted cocktail, and watch the King William/Southtown street action.

1024 S. Alamo St. (btw. Cedar and Mission sts.). www.feastsa.com. ✆ **210/354-1024.** Reservations recommended. Small/shared plates $7–$12; main courses $12–$22. Tues–Thurs 5–10pm; Fri–Sat 5–11pm; Sun 10:30am–2:30pm.

Liberty Bar ★★ NEW AMERICAN Ask a long-time San Antonian about the Liberty Bar and you're likely to get an earful. Some say, "It was better before it moved from its old location"—in a ramshackle 1890 brothel/saloon with a decided lean on Josephine Street. Mind you, that was in 2010, but this local institution had been around for 25 years before that, and old loyalties die hard. The former convent where it now resides doesn't have as much character during the day—both the upstairs and downstairs dining room are open and sunny—but at night live music brings back the soul. More important: The born-again hippie fare remains largely the same, served in generous portions at reasonable prices. You'll find everything from comfort food (pot roast sandwich) to regional Mexican cuisine (the chile relleno *en nogada*). Lovers of exotic meats like venison and wild boar sausage mingle happily with vegetarians, who all find plenty to like on the menu.

1111 S. Alamo St. (btw. Sheridan and Pereida sts.). www.liberty-bar.com. ✆ **210/227-1187.** Reservations accepted. Main courses $11–$29; sandwiches $10–$16. Mon–Fri 11am–midnight; Sat–Sun 9am–midnight (brunch 9am–2pm).

Rosario's ★★ TEX-MEX/REGIONAL MEXICAN Lisa Wong, chef/owner of Rosario's, was one of the first local restaurateurs to raise Tex-Mex to a higher culinary standard by using fresh local ingredients and updated recipes. She was also one of the first to open an upscale Mexican spot in Southtown. Rosario's remains as vital as ever to the local dining scene—and it remains as good as ever, too. The wildly colorful room comes alive at night, its walls lit by neon strips and blown glass chandeliers refracting the light. Tex-Mex staples like nachos, fajitas, and gorditas mingle on the menu with such interior Mexican dishes as *enchiladas suiza*, chicken enchiladas topped with a sweet white wine cream sauce; Veracruz-style tilapia, basking in a sauce of tomato, olives, and onions; or pork tips in a cascabel chile sauce. The dining rooms are large, which means you generally don't have to wait long for a table—but it also means that the noise level can make conversation difficult. On Friday and Saturday nights, there's live music starting at 8 or 9pm. There's another location in the north, 9715 San Pedro Ave. (✆ **201/481-4100**), but it lacks the neighborhood feel of the Southtown original.

910 S. Alamo St. (at St. Mary's St.). www.rosariossa.com. ✆ **210/223-1806.** Reservations not accepted. Lunch $7–$11; dinner main courses $9–$25. Mon–Thurs 11am–10pm; Fri–Sat 11am–11pm (bar open until midnight); Sun 11am–9pm.

Inexpensive

Carnitas Lonja ★ MEXICAN Texans love their barbecue, and it makes not a whit of difference that one of the city's hottest, most celebrated barbecue spots—it made the Eater.com list of one of the best new restaurants of 2018—is a Mexican version. The pork for the carnitas is slow-cooked for hours for both tenderness and to remove all traces of fat, while corn tortillas are made on the premises and finished on the grill. Cheese quesadillas and steak tacos are also good picks. Close to Mission Concepcion, this glorified shack with a large back yard is the perfect spot to savor some local food along with some local history. Thursday through Sunday evenings from 7 to 11pm, this place turns into a *taquería*—great for a pre- or post-drinks snack.

1107 Roosevelt Ave. (at Steves Ave.). www.facebook.com/Lonja17. ✆ **210/612-3626.** Reservations not accepted. Tacos from $2.50; combination plates from $7. Tues–Sun 7am–5pm.

Cascabel Mexican Patio ★★ MEXICAN Inside a brightly colored modest frame house that's slightly off square, a small kitchen turns out excellent versions of central and southern Mexico classics—such dishes as chicken *pipián verde* (with ground tomatillos, herbs, and pumpkin seeds) and *cochinita pibil* (pulled pork rubbed with achiote). You'll also find more casual tacos, tostadas, and *huaraches* (large masa cakes topped with a variety of ingredients). Don't miss the signature *puerco a la cascabel* (pork in a *chile cascabel* sauce). ***Two things to note:*** Hours are limited, and this is different from the similarly named restaurant at the DoubleTree San Antonio hotel.

1000 S. St. Mary's St. (btw. S. Alamo and Pereida sts.). ✆ **210/212-6456.** Reservations accepted. Main courses $7–$12. Mon–Fri 10am–4pm; Sat 10am–3pm.

WHERE TO queue for 'cue IN SAN ANTONIO

Although its barbecue scene is not as well-known as those in Austin and other Texas cities, San Antonio is no slouch when it comes to slow-cooked meat. Here are a few of the town's top spots.

A no-frills joint just north of downtown, **Augie's Alamo City BBQ,** 909 Broadway (www.augiesbbq.com; ✆ **210/314-3596**), is known for its brisket, jalapeño sausage, and creamed corn. There's also a second location, in Brackenridge Park next to the Sunken Gardens and the San Antonio Zoo—look for the large pink pig out front.

The Granary, 602 Avenue A in the Pearl complex (www.thegranarysa.com; ✆ **210/228-0124**), was heralded by *Texas Monthly* as one of the "50 best bbq joints . . . in the world!" It's too upscale for some—at dinner time you'll find the likes of Moroccan lamb—but at lunch the pulled pork and ribs taste like they come straight from a country pit.

Part of the charm of the original **Rudy's Country Store,** 24152 I-10 West at the Leon Springs/Boerne Stage exit (www.rudysbbq.com; ✆ **210/698-2141**), is its location next to a combination gas station, garage, and grocery store that dates back decades. The other part is the fall-off-the-bone tender meat and tangy sauces, which have been replicated at numerous Rudy's branches all around Texas and, lately, other parts of the Southwest.

For a fun experience for the entire family, you can't beat the **Smoke Shack** food truck, parked up by I-410 near the airport at 2347 Nacogdoches Rd. (www.smokeshacksa.com; ✆ **210/829-8448**), and affiliated **Pig Pen** pub out back. A bar, playground, and brisket mac and cheese . . . what's not to like? It's cross-cultural too, including brisket nachos and pulled pork tacos among the hearty offerings. The same menu is available in-town at a Smoke Shack restaurant near the Witte Museum (p. 84).

Guenther House ★ AMERICAN You don't have to stay in a King William B&B to step inside a Victorian mansion filled with exquisite turn-of-the-20th-century furnishings: Simply have lunch or brunch at Guenther House. Set in the home of the owners of San Antonio's Pioneer Flour Company—the crenellated castle-like tower of the flour mill just across the river is a San Antonio icon—the restaurant is a charming spot for a hearty breakfast or a light lunch. Biscuits and gravy and other baked goods (using Pioneer flour) are popular here, as are the waffles and pancakes, served 'til closing time at 3pm. At lunch, the Tex-Mex taco salad is a local favorite. When the weather is fine, dine alfresco on the trellised patio. A small museum and gift shop selling Pioneer products like pancake mix are adjacent to the restaurant.

205 E. Guenther St. at the San Antonio River. www.guentherhouse.com. © **210/227-1061.** Reservations not accepted. Breakfast $6–$13; lunch $8.50–$10. Daily 7am–3pm. House and mill store Mon–Sat 8am–4pm; Sun 8am–3pm.

Madhatters ★ DELI/ECLECTIC This colorful storefront attracts everyone from nouveau hippies to buttoned-down office workers. They come for Age-of-Aquarius-meets-south-of-the-border food: granola bowls and breakfast burritos in the morning, veggie and deli sandwiches for lunch, and a variety of high teas, including one for kids. The rambling house has several indoor and outdoor dining areas, all with a comfortable lived-in feel. The main dining area, where you place your order, has cold cases full of reasonably priced wines and beers.

320 Beauregard St. (at S. Alamo St.). www.madhatterstea.com. © **210/212-4832.** Reservations not accepted. Breakfast $4–$10; sandwiches and salad plates $7–$11; tea party for 2 $20. Mon–Fri 7am–3pm; Sat 8am–9pm; Sun 9am–3pm.

PEARL/BROADWAY CULTURAL CORRIDOR

Expensive

Botika ★★★ PERUVIAN-ASIAN Latin America and Asia might sound like an odd culinary couple, but Geronimo Lopez, Botika's owner and chef, ensures the success of this international marriage. A former instructor and executive chef at the Pearl's Culinary Institute of America, Lopez uses creative techniques with traditional ingredients—and knows how to complement textures and flavors. Opt for a bento box so you can sample an array of such dishes as pork and cabbage gyoza; chicken and waffles breaded with panko and dipped in mesquite honey and ginger; and *lomo salteado*, slices of tenderloin served with a sunny side egg, plantains, and Peruvian sweetie drop peppers. The restaurant in the Pearl complex is large and colorful with lots of seating choices, including a sushi-ceviche bar, indoor tables, and an outdoor patio. Along with more familiar cocktails, you'll find several made with sakes,

Greater San Antonio Restaurants

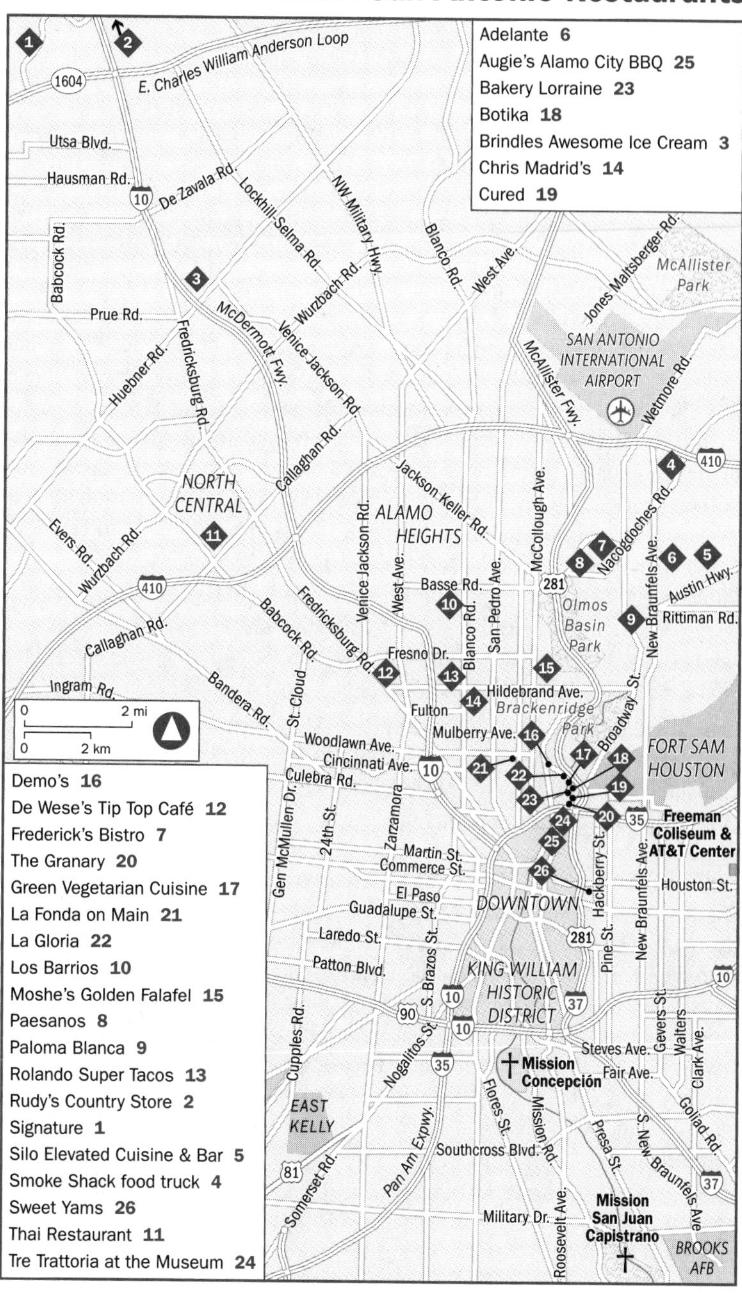

piscos, and *cachaças.* A late-night happy hour Fridays and Saturdays from 10pm to midnight is a hit with weekend revelers.

303 Pearl Pkwy. www.botikapearl.com. ✆ **210/670-7684.** Reservations advised. Main courses $16–$36. Mon 3–9pm; Tues–Thurs 11:30am–10pm; Fri–Sat 11:30am–10:30pm; Sun 11:30am–3pm.

Cured ★★★ GASTROPUB/CHARCUTERIE Embodying the nose-to-tail, artisanal approach, this restaurant in the Pearl complex cures the meat for its charcuterie boards, jars its own mustards, pickles cauliflower from nearby farms . . . and does it all with consummate skill (and without the pretentiousness that sometimes accompanies such efforts). This place works on many levels—from the excellent food to the bright, inviting space (it's the former administrative building of the Pearl Brewery), to the friendly, electric atmosphere, which makes Cured a happy-hour and late-night favorite. The restaurant's name is a double entendre, referring not only to the processing of ingredients but to the fact that chef/owner Steve McHugh won his battle against non-Hodgkin's lymphoma a few years ago. Today McHugh is active in the community, giving back to causes that look for a cure. He spent years in the kitchens of several John Besh restaurants, and the menu's subtle nods to New Orleans cuisine show it. (Don't miss the smoked pork gumbo.) Among the powerful craft cocktails, the Bees Knees is made with a local farmers market honey.

306 Pearl Pkwy. www.curedatpearl.com. ✆ **210/314-3929.** Reservations advised. Main courses lunch $12–$29 (charcuterie plates $20–$36); dinner $20–$40. Mon–Fri 11am–3pm and 5–11pm; Sat 10am–3pm and 5–11pm.

Tre Trattoria at the Museum ★★ ITALIAN With its move to the grounds of the San Antonio Museum of Art in 2018, Tre Trattoria has found a fit showcase for the talents of chef Jason Dady—morning, noon, and night. Not part of the main museum complex, but in a separate building that was originally the hops house of the old Lone Star Brewery, the restaurant fronts a quiet section of the River Walk. Kickstart your day with house-made gnocchi with mushrooms and fried eggs, or a Caprese version of avocado toast, using fresh hand-pulled mozzarella, San Marzano tomatoes, and basil. Those ingredients also work well on the small handcrafted pizzas, a good bet for lunch. The dinner menu is organized in typical Italian style with first and second courses, designed to be shared. A primo combination: Smoked gouda *radiatore* with brown butter cauliflower and hazelnuts, followed by grilled rainbow trout with crispy skin. The two small interior dining rooms, flanking an open kitchen and bar, can be noisy, so outdoors is your best bet, weather permitting.

200 W. Jones Ave. at the River Walk. www.tretrattoria.com. ✆ **210/805-0333.** Reservations accepted. Pizza $15–$17; pastas $16–$28; main courses $24–$38. Tues–Sat 8am–10pm; Sun 8am–8pm.

MORE THAN A meat-and-burritos KIND OF TOWN

San Antonio has long been celebrated for its superb steaks, chimis, and other hearty, artery-clogging fare, but now there are plenty of places to satisfy healthier cravings, some created by top chefs. All of the following cater to the taste-conscious as well as to the budget-conscious:

In Alamo Heights, **Adelante,** 21 Brees Blvd. (www.adelanterestaurant.com; ✆ **210/822-7681**), has been dishing up savory Health Mex fare—no lard, plenty of veggie and vegan options—in a cheerful folk-art-filled room for more than three decades. Cash only.

Green Vegetarian Cuisine, in the Pearl Brewery, 200 E. Grayson St., Ste. 120 (www.eatatgreen.com; ✆ **210/320-5865**), features some faux-meat dishes (for example, Chik'N Marsala, or veggie cheeseburgers with fakin' bacon), but mostly celebrates its plant-based fare. The dairy is kosher certified, and all dishes can be made vegan. There's another location in the northwest part of town, at the Alon Town Center, 10003 NW Military Hwy.

Known best for his upscale dining rooms (see **Signature,** p. 75), Chef Andrew Weissman applies equal care to **Moshe's Golden Falafel,** 3910 McCullough St. (✆ **210/994-9838**), his fast-casual Middle Eastern spot in Olmos Park. Everything is spiced to perfection. The falafel are never dry—and neither is the pita. On weekdays, it's breakfast and lunch only; Friday and Saturday nights it's also open 5–9pm (closed Sundays).

Practicing her "culinary medicine" at **Pharm Table,** 106 Auditorium Circle (www.pharmtable.com; ✆ **210/802-1860**), nationally acclaimed chef Elizabeth Johnson creates Ayurvedic-inspired fare that's as pleasing to the eye as it is to the palate. Practically on the steps of the Tobin Center for the Performing Arts (p. 119) in the north end of downtown, it would be perfect for a pre- or post-performance bite, but it's only open from 11am–3pm.

Using local, organic ingredients for its soul food-oriented eatery on downtown's east side, **Sweet Yams,** 218 N. Cherry St. (www.facebook.com/sweetyamsorganic; ✆ **210/229-9267**), serves brown rice with its gumbo, features all-natural turkey in its chili, and bakes gluten-free sweet potato cupcakes.

Moderate

La Gloria ★★ MEXICAN La Gloria celebrates the street foods of Mexico: casual, affordable, and (often) eaten with your hands. Here, however, you can be sure that all the simple, zesty south-of-the-border fare is made-to-order fresh. (Chef Johnny Hernandez gets much of his produce from the Pearl's weekend farmers market.) Corn tortillas for the tacos, *queso fundido* (savory melted cheese), and quesadillas are all handmade. In season, don't miss the roasted corn, rich with white cotija (farmer's cheese) and a drizzle of Mexican cream. Adding to the casual atmosphere: Garage doors transform the restaurant into an indoor-outdoor space, weather permitting, and you can grab your Mexican soda or cold Corona out of an ice box as you walk in. One of the hottest chefs in town and getting an international reputation, Hernandez has several other popular eateries in town, including at the airport, and in other cities (see his website for details). He's nevertheless meticulously involved in everything, down to plates designed by Mexican artists.

100 E. Grayson St., Pearl complex. www.chefjohnnyhernandez.com. ✆ **210/267-9094.** Reservations not accepted. Main courses $6–$26. Sun–Thurs 11am–10pm; Fri–Sat 11am–midnight.

MONTE VISTA/OLMOS PARK

Moderate

Demo's ★ GREEK Located across the street from a Greek Orthodox church, Demo's is a little bit of Greece in San Antonio, and a favorite among members of the local Greek community. Occasionally you might see a belly-dancing show (not only here, but in its other two locations as well, see below). You can dine on the airy patio or in the dining room, decorated with murals of Greek island scenes. The menu includes gyros, Greek burgers, *dolmas, spanakopita,* and other Mediterranean specialties. If you go for the Dieter's Special—a Greek salad with your choice of gyros or souvlaki—you might be able to justify the baklava. The original (but more characterless) restaurant is at 7115 Blanco Rd. #120 (✆ **210/342-2772**), near Loop 410, across from what used to be Central Park Mall. A third location is farther out at 1205 N. Loop 1604 at Blanco (✆ **210/798-3840**).

2501 N. St. Mary's St. www.demosgreekfood.com. ✆ **210/732-7777.** Reservations accepted for parties of 10 or more. Sandwiches $6–$15; main courses and plates $9–$18. Mon–Thurs 11am–9pm; Fri–Sat 11am–10pm; Sun noon-8pm.

La Fonda on Main ★★ MEXICAN/REGIONAL MEXICAN One of San Antonio's oldest continuously operating restaurants, established in 1932 in a handsome residence with a red-tiled roof, La Fonda never went the way of many culinary institutions that rest on their laurels and grow tired. That's thanks to restaurateur Cappy Lawton, whose Alamo Heights restaurant, **Cappy's** (5011 Broadway St.; www.cappysrestaurant.com; ✆ **210/828-9669**), is also a longstanding local favorite for its excellent New American dishes. Lawton acquired La Fonda in the late 1990s and spiffed up both the menu and the premises; he's kept everything fresh and up-to-date ever since, while maintaining the best San Antonio traditions. The adobe-walled main dining room is cheerful and bright—almost as inviting as the garden-fringed outdoor patio, one of the rare ones in town that's shady and breezy enough to be comfortable in summer. The menu has retained some Tex-Mex staples such as the La Fonda special: two cheese enchiladas, a beef taco, a pork tamale with chile con queso and chile con carne, guacamole, Mexican rice, and refried beans. Most of the menu, however, is on the lighter side: fish tacos with blackened mahi mahi in a chipotle sauce sided by a salad of *nopalitos* (cactus pads), for example. Many celebrities dined here in the old days, including Franklin

Roosevelt, John Wayne, and Yul Brenner, and tasty, generous specialties dished up daily still attract power lunch types and local families alike.

2415 N. Main Ave. at W. Woodlawn Ave. www.lafondaonmain. ✆ **210/733-0621.** Reservations recommended for 6 or more. Main courses $13–$18 lunch, $14–$20 dinner. Mon–Thurs 11am-9:30pm; Fri 11am–10:30pm; Sat 3-10:30pm; Sun 3-9:30pm.

Los Barrios ★ TEX-MEX Dishing out hearty portions of excellent Tex-Mex fare since 1979 in a former Dairy Queen, this is the type of unpretentious, friendly spot San Antonians love. The enchiladas are made of red tortillas and cheese bathed in hearty chile gravy; a classic assortment plate lets you try all five varieties. Departures from Tex-Mex include *cabrito* (goat) in salsa and the *milanesa con papas,* described on the menu (accurately) as a Mexican-style chicken-fried steak. If you're really hungry, try the Los Barrios deluxe special platter, which includes two beef tacos, two cheese enchiladas, a strip of steak, rice, beans, and guacamole. Portions are large. You can easily satisfy hunger pangs with a *chalupa Vallarta* a la carte ($4), a large red tortilla stacked with chicken, lettuce, tomato, guacamole, carrot strips, jalapeños, cheese, and sour cream.

4223 Blanco Rd. at San Angelo. www.losbarriosrestaurant.com. ✆ **210/732-6017.** Reservations accepted for large groups only. Main courses $10–$21. Mon–Thurs 10am–10pm; Fri–Sat 10am–11pm; Sun 9am–10pm.

Inexpensive

Chris Madrid's ★★ AMERICAN/TEX-MEX Tex-Mex meets Americana at this fun, down-home joint known for its extra-large "macho" burger, a supersize version of the standard burger. The ever-popular tostada burger comes with crushed tortilla chips, refried beans, and real cheddar. In its macho variety, the "cheddar cheesy" burger is intimidating, with cheddar oozing out over the large patty, engulfing even the platter. The kid-friendly menu also includes chicken sandwiches, nachos, and *chalupas* (tostadas). After a fire in 2017, the business started operating out of its food truck, and pitched a tent

family-friendly RESTAURANTS

Chris Madrid's (see above) With its kid-friendly menu including burgers, nachos, fries, and various combinations thereof, this restaurant's casual atmosphere and down-home cooking make it popular with families.

Madhatters (p. 66) Even if your kids aren't up for an entire children's tea, they'll be happy to find their faves on the menu, from PB&J to plain turkey or cheese sandwiches. The chocolate-chip cookies and brownies won't be sneezed at, either.

Schilo's (p. 62) A high noise level, a convenient location near the River Walk (but with prices far lower than anything else you'll find there), and a wide selection of familiar food make this German deli a good choice for the family.

with a bathroom in back for seating. A return to the original space is planned, but building is going slowly. Check the website for updates.

830 W. Hollywood Ave. (at Blanco Rd). www.chrismadrids.com. ✆ **210/735-3552.** Reservations not accepted. Burgers $7–$11. Mon–Thurs 11am–9pm; Fri–Sat 11am–10pm.

Rolando's Super Tacos ★ TEX-MEX One of the many small businesses that pack both sides of West Hildebrand Avenue between I-10 and Trinity University, Rolando's is a good example of the dining bargains you'll find outside of the downtown tourist zone. Don't be put off by the setting, a rambling shack painted in vivid red and green next door to a Chevron station. It's worth coming here for the extra-large tacos (corn or flour tortillas) with fillings like chorizo and eggs, beans and bacon, steak and guacamole . . . the variations seem endless. You can also get small (as in normal size) versions. Also popular, especially for Saturday and Sunday breakfast or brunch, are the huge combination plates.

919 W. Hildebrand Ave. (just west of Blanco Rd.). www.facebook.com/rolandossuper tacos1. ✆ **210/549-5950.** Reservations not accepted. Super tacos $6; plates $7–$12. Mon–Tues and Thurs–Fri 8am–2pm; Sat 7am–3pm; Sun 8am–3pm.

ALAMO HEIGHTS AREA

Expensive

Paesanos ★★★ ITALIAN "A thousand people on a Friday night can't all be wrong," wrote one San Antonio food critic about Paesanos some 20 years ago. That hasn't changed—the volume, if not the specific number—though somehow there's rarely a wait. This place isn't fancy or fussy (there are no white tablecloths and it can get noisy), but the food has been consistently wonderful for more than 4 decades. Most notable: the signature shrimp Paesano, lightly breaded and dredged in a buttery lemon sauce whose recipe is often copied but never quite mastered. Little-known fact: The center-cut tenderloin served here is better and less expensive than that at any of the city's pricey premier steakhouses. Start with the house salad (the dressing is delectable—what is it? They'll never tell.) and have an appetizer sampling of the shrimp Paesano, followed by a steak or excellent red snapper. All main courses come with a side of pasta (stick with the butter garlic or you'll feel like you've ordered a second meal). The Alamo Heights crowd treats this place like it's their personal dining room; you never know who you'll run into, from a Spurs player to a local pol. The kitchen stays open late—a rarity in this town. Paesanos has two other San Antonio locations: **Paesanos 1604,** 3622 Paesanos Pkwy. (✆ **210/493-1604**), and **Paesanos Riverwalk,** 111 W. Crockett St., #101 (✆ **210/227-2782**), both of which will satisfy but neither of which has the same panache.

555 E. Basse Rd. (Lincoln Heights). www.paesanos.com. ✆ **210/828-5191.** Reservations accepted for large groups only. Main courses $20–$35. Mon–Sat 11am–11pm; Sun 11am–10pm.

Silo Elevated Cuisine & Bar ★★★ NEW AMERICAN An early adopter of the shared plates concept, this culinary pioneer has never lost its touch, continuing year after year to fashion simple, pleasing dishes that are understated yet "elevated." The constantly changing menu offers a three-course prix-fixe menu, along with a la carte and main dish offerings like cider-braised Kurobuta pork shank, green chile orzo mac and cheese, and vegetarian risotto with grilled portobello mushrooms. Lunchtime stars include crispy duck spring rolls or Silo's signature chicken-fried oysters with mustard hollandaise. Downstairs, at sister restaurant **Nosh,** guests snack on small-plate fare and fun items like pizza, chicken wings, and wild-boar sliders. At the Silo bar, also downstairs, guests may order from the full Silo menu. Now called Silo Alamo Heights to distinguish it from the newer Silo arrivals (one in Stone Oak at Loop 1604, another downtown in the Fairmont Hotel, 401 S. Alamo St.), this first still shines.

1133 Austin Hwy. at Mt. Calvary Dr. www.siloelevatedcuisine.com. ✆ **210/824-8686.** Reservations recommended. Main courses $18–$40; 3-course prix fixe $29. Mon–Sat 11am–2:30pm and 5:30–10pm.

Moderate

Paloma Blanca ★★ MEXICAN With its warm but stylish eating areas—a light-filled main dining room, a pretty tiled patio with a fountain, a bar with modern leather couches—and a menu that ranges all over the map of Mexico, this is the place to come for a sophisticated, Mexico City–type experience. You might start with any of the distinctive selection of soups, such as *poblano crema,* pozole, or a non-Americanized version of tortilla soup (among other things, it comes with crispy *chicharron* rather than chicken). Interior menu mainstays include Veracruz-style red snapper, steak *a la tampiqueña*, and "divorced" chicken enchiladas, one covered with salsa verde, the other with ranchero sauce. Tex-Mex standards are available, too, as are dishes catering to other dietary preferences such as vegetarian, paleo, and gluten-free. The margarita menu is comprehensive and, if you stick to the 100% agave tequila, gluten-free as well.

5800 Broadway St. (just north of Austin Hwy.). www.palomablanca.net. ✆ **210/822-6151.** Reservations recommended for large groups only. Main courses $12–$25. Mon–Wed 11am–9pm; Thurs–Fri 11am–10pm; Sat 10am–10pm; Sun 10am–9pm.

NORTH CENTRAL

Expensive

Frederick's Bistro ★★ FRENCH/FUSION Year in and year out, this restaurant serves outstanding food with admirable consistency. Not as well-known as many of San Antonio's glitzier establishments, it has a large body of loyal customers who know its semi-hidden location at the back of a Broadway strip mall. The focus in this low-lit, comfortable dining room is on the

SAN ANTONIO'S sweet spot(s)

From locally made Mexican ice pops to Paris-worthy pastries, San Antonio has plenty of ways to satisfy a sweet tooth. Here are five favorites, ranging all over the map.

After the first branch of **Bakery Lorraine,** 306 Pearl Pkwy, #110 (www.bakerylorraine.com, ✆ **210/862-5582**), opened in the Pearl, the clamor for its French-inspired desserts and breads grew so loud that branches soon opened in several spots around town, including in the DoSeum (p. 90). Come for a light breakfast or lunch, but don't even think of leaving without trying a melt-in-your-mouth macaron. (Bet you'll buy half a dozen.)

The only ice cream parlor in town where you might get carded, **Boozy's Creamery and Craft,** 711 S. St. Mary's St. (www.facebook.com/boozyscreameryandcraft; ✆ **210/ 919-3552**), in Southtown, adds alcohol to its cold confections, made in house. The booze-infused flavors change every day—for example, Groom's Cake with Kahlua, On the Rocks featuring tequila—and you can add a shot for an extra kick. Not all the varieties include alcohol, so it's a fun place for the whole family.

At **Brindles Awesome Ice Cream,** 11255 Huebner Rd. (www.brindlesicecream.com; ✆ **210/641-5222**), an espresso and ice cream emporium in the northwest, you've got more than 200 flavors to choose from (about 45 on any given day)—anything from white chocolate Frangelico to spiced apple brandy. Gelato (candied ginger, say) and sorbets (perhaps champagne or cranberry) are offered too. Many of San Antonio's most popular restaurants serve this brand.

The delicious Mexican ice-and-fruit pops known as *paletas*, usually tucked away in the freezer cases of Hispanic convenience shops and supermarkets, are now available fresh in Southtown at **La Paleteria,** 510 S. Alamo St., Ste. 104 (www.paleteriasanantonio.com; ✆ **210/ 954-8753**). They come in water- and milk-based varieties, with flavors depending on what produce is in season; the goodness is year round.

Artisan breads and *pan dulce* (Mexican pastries) are the main draws at **La Panaderia,** 301 E. Houston St. (www.lapanaderia.com; ✆ **210/592-6264**), a Mexican cafe downtown. Come in for a sweet roll and *cafe con leche* in the morning or for a glass of wine and an open-faced *torta* (sandwich) in the evening—though by dinnertime, the sweets are likely to be sold out. There's a second location in Alamo Heights at 8305 Broadway.

cuisine rather than on the show. Chef-owner Frederick Costa was born in Vietnam but moved to France early on, and his cooking combines elements from both cultures. For starters, consider delicate and crispy spring rolls of shrimp, pork, and mushrooms; or escargots with Spanish chorizo. Entrees might include baked sea bass in truffle oil with artichoke hearts, or duck breast cooked in a sauce of green peppercorns and cognac. Save room—and time—for rich chocolate lava cake, served with fondant and cherry ice cream.

7701 Broadway, Ste. 20 (in Dijon Plaza). www.frederickssa.com. ✆ **210/828-9050.** Weekend reservations recommended. Main courses $27–$43. Mon–Fri 11:30am–2:30pm and 5–10pm; Sat 5–10 pm.

NORTHWEST

Expensive

Signature ★★★ NEW AMERICAN Chef Andrew Weissman burst onto the local dining scene some 25 years ago with Le Reve, earning raves in the national press for his world-class cooking, knockout presentations, and impeccable service. The latest showcase for Weissman's talents is this fine dining room at La Cantera resort, and it doesn't disappoint. An elegant two-tier room with brocaded banquettes, a wrought-iron chandelier, and windows overlooking the rolling greens of the golf course is the stage for rotating menus that apply French cooking techniques to the best quality seasonal ingredients. Appetizers might include a superb French onion tart—a holdover from Le Reve, it's a must if available—or a delicate lobster risotto. For the main courses, you might find roasted Branzino (a Mediterranean sea bass) with a zingy ginger-chile glaze or tender pheasant with crispy skin. Service is Texas friendly but also more elaborate than is typical for San Antonio. Probably no other restaurant in town offers a choice of citrus, cucumber, and mint for your water, or punctuates your meal with an amuse bouche, a palate cleanser, and post-prandial truffles. All in all, this is perfect for a romantic occasion splurge or for hosting a client you'd like to impress.

La Cantera Resort, 16401 La Cantera Pkwy. www.destinationhotels.com/signature-restaurant. ✆ **210/247-0176.** Reservations recommended. Main courses $24–$48. Tues–Sat 5:30–10pm; Sun 10:30am–2pm and 5:30–9pm.

Moderate

In addition to these restaurants, consider the branch of **Sushi Zushi** (p. 60) in the Colonnade Shopping Center, 9867 I-10 W.

De Wese's Tip Top Café ★ AMERICAN Opened in 1938 and passed down through three generations of the same family, the Tip Top was brought to national attention in 2008 by the Food Network's *Diners, Drive Ins and Dives*. Its 15 minutes of fame never went to the restaurant's head, however—it's still the same down-home spot, serving generous portions of dishes like roast pork, chicken and dumplings, and—the most praised—chicken-fried steak. The house-made pies are a big hit too. ***Note:*** This isn't an after-hours diner. The locals come early, and the place closes by 8pm on Saturday night.

2814 Fredericksburg Rd. (btw. Santa Anna and Santa Monica). ✆ **210/735-2222.** Reservations not accepted. Sandwiches $5–$10; main courses $9–$16. Mon–Sat 11am–9pm; Sun 11am–8pm.

Thai Restaurant ★ THAI Sure, the name and location—a small strip center just outside Loop 410—are generic, but the cooking at this intimate family-owned restaurant is anything but. Many of Thailand's most famous dishes are prepared here with great care and with fresh ingredients: pad thai (not too sweet, noodles cooked to the perfect texture, crunchy bean sprouts), pad kra pao (generous with the basil leaves), and panang curry (nicely scented, with just the right hint of lime and shrimp paste). The fried tofu appetizer comes with a delicious peanut and cilantro dipping sauce, while *yum nua,* a cold beef salad with fresh butter lettuce, red onion, tomato, and cucumber, has a light, tangy citrus dressing. Attentive service, low prices, and a quiet dining room (at least until 9pm, when music from the bar next door begins to seep through the wall) also make this an attractive choice.

1709 Babcock Rd. (at Callaghan Rd.). www.thairestaurant-sa.com. ✆ **210/341-0606.** Reservations accepted. Main courses $10–$14. Mon–Sat 11am–3pm and 5–9:30pm.

EXPLORING SAN ANTONIO

6

San Antonio's dogged preservation of its past and avid development of its future—two goals that often overlap—guarantee that there's something in town to satisfy every visitor's taste. The biggest problem with sightseeing here is figuring out how to get it all in; you can spend days in the downtown area alone and still not cover everything (see Chapter 2 for suggestions about how to organize your time). Along with some of the state's most storied historic sites, cultural attractions, and a splashy multi-use River Walk that keeps expanding its reach, the city offers plenty of family destinations, including three major theme parks on the outskirts of town.

A smart first stop would be at Visit San Antonio's **Official San Antonio Visitor Information Center,** 317 Alamo Plaza (www.visitsanantonio.com; ✆ **800/447-3372**), across the street from the Alamo, where you can pick up a helpful coupon book for discounts on everything from theme parks to city tours to museums. Many hotels also have a stash of discount coupons for their guests.

THE TOP ATTRACTIONS

Downtown

The Alamo ★★★ HISTORIC SITE It's not just the most famous of San Antonio's five missions, it's Texas's most-visited attraction, drawing 2.5 million people annually. So yes, the Alamo is a must-see, but don't expect anything dramatic at first glance—sitting smack in the heart of a touristy downtown plaza, the site looks surprisingly small. That said, you'll immediately recognize the graceful mission church where, for 13 days in March 1836, a band of 188 "Texian" volunteers turned back the much larger army of Mexican dictator Santa Anna. Eventually all the men, including pioneers Davy Crockett, William Travis, and Jim Bowie, were killed, but a month later Sam Houston's cry "Remember the Alamo!" used their deaths to rally his troops and defeat the Mexican army at the Battle of San Jacinto, thus securing Texas's independence.

the alamo: THE MOVIE(S)

At least one weighty tome, Frank Thompson's *Alamo Movies*, has been devoted to the plethora of films featuring San Antonio's most famous site. Some outtakes:

Most famous movie about the Alamo not actually shot at the Alamo: *The Alamo* (1959), starring John Wayne as Davy Crockett. Although it has no San Antonio presence, it was shot in Texas. Wayne considered shooting the film in Mexico, but was told it wouldn't be distributed in Texas if he did.

Latest controversy-ridden attempt to tell the Alamo story: A 2004 Disney version, also called *The Alamo*, starring Dennis Quaid, Billy Bob Thornton, and Jason Patric. Ron Howard was originally slated to direct, but eventually he only co-produced, turning directing duties over to John Lee Hancock. The resulting film was not a success in any shape or form, though it wasn't an embarrassment, either.

Most accurate (and largest) celluloid depiction of the Alamo story: *Alamo—The Price of Freedom*, which you can see at the AMC Rivercenter 11 IMAX Theater, just across the plaza from the actual Alamo. According to writer and historian Stephen Harrigan in an interview on National Public Radio, it's "90 percent accurate."

Least controversial film featuring the Alamo: *Miss Congeniality* (2000), starring Sandra Bullock and Benjamin Bratt. A beauty pageant presided over by William Shatner takes place in front of the shrine to the Texas martyrs.

Built by the Spanish in 1744 as Mission San Antonio de Valero, in 1905 the compound was saved by the Daughters of the Republic of Texas from becoming a hotel. Since 2011 it has been managed by the General Land Office (GLO)—which has brought many of its displays and events, not to mention its website, into the 21st century. The three main buildings are the **Shrine** (church), which hosts artifacts like Travis's ring, Crockett's buckskin vest, and a period Bowie knife; the **Long Barrack Museum,** where videos provide an overview of the Texas revolution and the Alamo Siege; and the **Alamo Gift Shop and Museum.** Visitors can also stroll the pecan oak–shaded **Alamo Gardens** behind the church. The exhibits and many interpretive talks and videos are free; it's definitely worth shelling out extra for the tours, which include a self-guided audio tour and one geared toward kids.

Because the first impression of this key historic site is less than inspiring, the GLO is working on a variety of solutions, including the possibility of closing Alamo Street to vehicular traffic. Click the "Master Plan" link on the website to check on the progress of these plans.

300 Alamo Plaza. www.thealamo.org. ✆ **210/225-1391.** Free admission (donations welcome). Basic tour $15; Young Texans Tour $12; self-guided audio tour $7. May 25–Sept 3 daily 9am–7pm; rest of year daily 9am–5:30pm. Last entry 15 min. before closing. Closed Christmas Day. Bus: VIVA lines 11, 40, 301.

The Briscoe Western Art Museum ★★★ MUSEUM This intimate museum on the River Walk bend is a delightful place to spend an hour or two

Central San Antonio Attractions

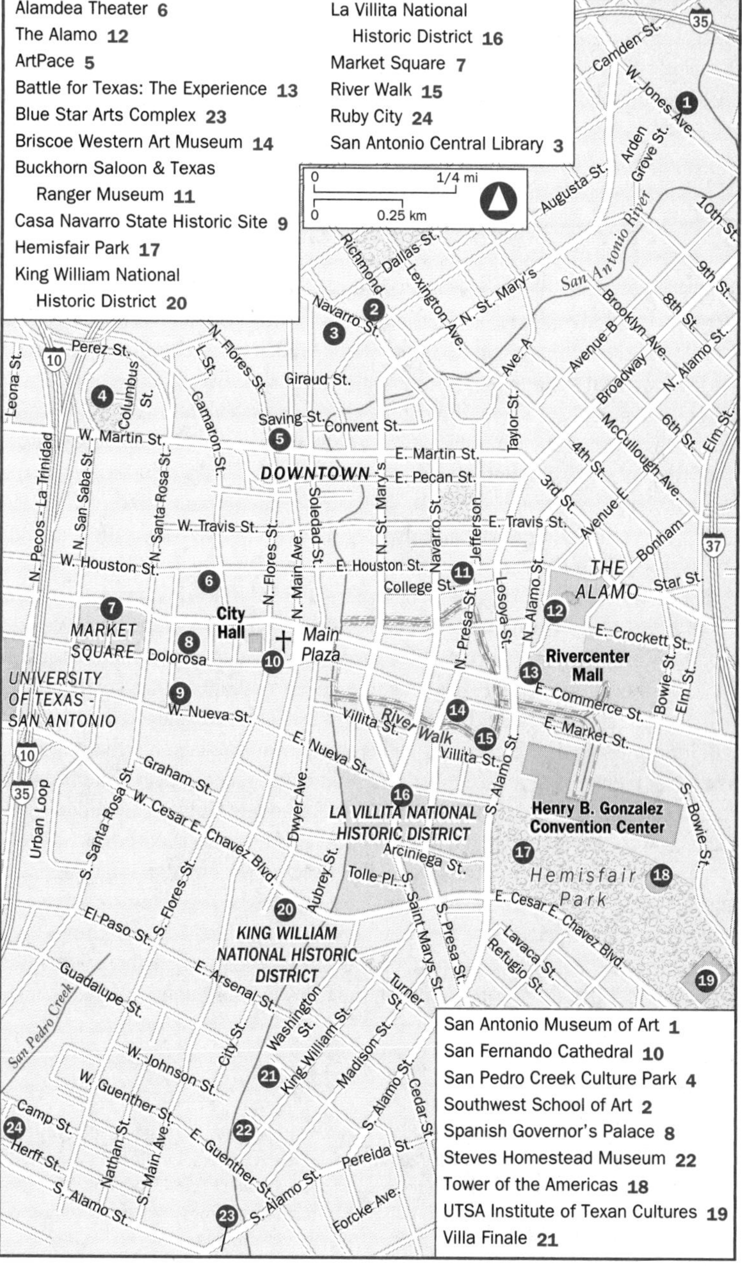

in the Wild West, both the real and romanticized versions. The collection includes everything from ornate saddles to a wall of shiny spurs, from a re-created Wells Fargo stagecoach to cowboy-and-Indian–themed art. There's a small sculpture garden at river level. The building alone is a stunner; it was the city's first public library and once housed a circus museum. You may spend a good deal of time gazing up at the ornate ceilings and Art Deco light fixtures.

210 W. Market St. www.briscoemuseum.org. ✆ **210/299-4499.** $10 adults; $8 seniors (65+), students, and retired military; free for ages 12 and younger and active military with families (show ID). Free admission Tues 4–9pm. Daily 10am–5pm (Tues until 9pm); check for holiday closings. Bus: VIVA line 301.

The River Walk (Paseo del Río) ★★★ ATTRACTION Hidden below street level in downtown San Antonio, a romantic riverside world awaits. The Old World–style "Paseo del Rio," or "River Walk," is a series of pathways and bridges wending along a 15-mile-long stretch of the San Antonio River, roughly 5 miles of which flow through downtown. Hotels, outdoor cafes, shops, and restaurants line the bustling downtown tourist areas, but you can also find places of quiet along the curving riverbanks, shaded by cedar, cypress, oak, pecan, and willows, with an occasional palm tree or two. Rio taxis, river-cruise tour boats, and floating dinner barges slowly follow a circular section of the Downtown Reach.

The River Walk was originally part of a 1939 federal WPA project designed by architect Robert Hugman, with cobblestone pathways, arched bridges, and entrances steps from street-level locations; its development expanded just in time for the 1968 HemisFair exposition. In the decades since, many feared that the River Walk would become so overdeveloped and crowded that it would lose its charm. But subsequent expansions have ensured that the River Walk has plenty of quiet stretches and revitalized green spaces. The Museum Reach section (p. 81) extends up the Pearl/Broadway Cultural Corridor, while the Mission Reach section (p. 84) runs down through the South Side.

There are numerous entrances to the River Walk by stair or ramp, with about 50 ADA-accessible spots along the way, as well as elevators that take you to river level. Maps line the route, so it's hard to get lost. Mornings are a good time to visit the main part of the River Walk, when there are fewer crowds and light filters softly through the trees. At night the River Walk takes

A Taxi No One Can Grab from You

Hop on board a GO RIO river-taxi shuttle (www.goriocruises.com; ✆ **210/227-4746**) to locations along the Downtown Reach and Museum Reach sections of the River Walk. Rio taxis run daily from 10am to 9pm. Tickets cost $12 for 1 day of unlimited rides on either the Downtown Reach or Museum Reach sections, $16 for a ticket to both sections. You can buy tickets from boat drivers—just wave from one of the marked stops—or at various hotels along the River Walk.

on a different character, with sparkling lights reflected on the water. **The San Antonio River Authority** (SARA) offers downloadable maps and information on the natural attractions and associated sports; the **San Antonio Riverwalk Association** covers the more commercial aspects of this multi-use thoroughfare.

San Antonio Riverwalk Association; www.thesanantonioriverwalk.com; ✆ **210/227-4262.** San Antonio River Authority; 100 E. Guenther St.; www.sara-tx.org; ✆ **866/345-7272.** All Via VIVA bus lines stop somewhere along the river's route.

Pearl/Broadway Cultural Corridor

With the completion of the 1.3-mile-long Museum Reach section of the River Walk, the continuing development of the Pearl Brewery complex, and South Broadway's transformation into a pedestrian-friendly thoroughfare, this section of San Antonio lying just north of downtown has become as tourist-friendly (but not yet as tourist-heavy) as the original River Walk area. With so many museums, it's now known as the Broadway Cultural Corridor, and the Museum Reach section of the River Walk is an attraction in itself, with lush landscaped terraces and lots of artwork decorating the bridges of the lock-and-dam system.

Marion Koogler McNay Art Museum ★★★ MUSEUM If you only have time for one San Antonio museum, make it the McNay. Perched atop a hill with panoramic urban views, this Spanish Colonial Revival mansion (ca. 1929), once the home of a wealthy art collector, is so picturesque that it's often used as a backdrop for photo shoots. The focus of the holdings, comprising 20,000 works, is modern art, but Medieval and Renaissance works are represented too. You'll spot big names like Van Gogh, Manet, Gauguin, O'Keeffe, Hopper, Modigliani, Cézanne, and Picasso, while being introduced to many lesser known masters. Southwestern prints and drawings, a collection of art glass, and the **Tobin Collection of Theatre Arts** are also draws for art lovers. Attached to the original mansion is a contemporary wing, designed by French architect Jean Paul Viguier to house temporary exhibitions. I find the contrast with the original building jarring—kind of like the glass pyramid in front of the Louvre—but the modern structure's innovative roof and ceiling allow it to adjust the lighting according to the needs of a particular exhibit, many of which are interactive and oriented toward kids. It'll take you 2 hours to go through this place at a leisurely pace, longer if it's cool enough for you to stroll the beautiful 23 acres of landscaped grounds dotted with sculpture.

6000 N. New Braunfels Ave. www.mcnayart.org. ✆ **210/824-5368.** $10 adults; $5 seniors, students with ID, and active military; free for ages 19 and under; free admission Thurs 4–9pm. Wed and Fri 10am–6pm; Thurs 10am–9pm; Sat 10am–5pm; Sun noon–5pm. Closed Mon–Tues (except for tours). Closed Jan 1, July 4, Thanksgiving, Dec 25. Bus: VIVA line 11A.

Pearl Brewery ★★★ ENTERTAINMENT/DINING COMPLEX Praised far and wide as an example of infill done right, this eco-friendly development just north of downtown has been described as San Antonio's leading urbanist destination. I can't emphasize enough how this 22-acre multi-use complex—incorporating apartment buildings, the city's poshest hotel, top restaurants, and elegant boutiques—has changed the face of San Antonio since around 2010, and it just keeps getting better. Different aspects of the Pearl are described in other chapters—its hotels (p. 48), restaurants (p. 66), and shops (p. 110)–but the whole is greater than the sum of its parts. Pearl's public spaces include an amphitheater where you can take outdoor yoga classes; a pocket park where First Thursdays feature live music and crafts vendors; and an array of free seasonal events.

Bounded by Newell St., E. Elmira St., E. Josephine St., and Avenue B. 303 Pearl Pkwy. www.atpearl.com. ✆ **210/212-7260.**

San Antonio Botanical Garden ★★★ GARDEN With the debut of the $5-million Family Adventure Garden in 2018, the city's premier 38-acre green space just got a little livelier. Playscapes include the aptly named Tumble Hill and a shallow stream that invites splashing. Looking for a more serene experience? The lovely grounds include a sensory garden, a rose garden, a Japanese garden, and an herb garden. Interested in the culinary aspects of plants? Cooking classes are offered at the Goldsbury Foundation Pavilion. Outdoor areas highlight Texas landscapes, but the vast Lucile Halsell Conservatory complex replicates tropical and desert environments as well. The garden's entryway, the Sullivan Carriage House—built in 1896 by Alfred Giles and later moved stone-by-stone from its original downtown site—houses a gift shop and **Rosella at the Garden,** a cafe offering salads, quiches, sandwiches, and outrageously rich desserts.

555 Funston Place (at N. New Braunfels Ave.). www.sabot.org. ✆ **210/207-3250.** $12 adults; $9 seniors, students, and military; $10 ages 3–13; free for children 2 and under. Daily 9am–5pm. Closed Thanksgiving, Dec 25, Jan 1. Bus: VIVA line 11.

San Antonio Museum of Art ★★★ MUSEUM In 2017, the San Antonio Museum of Art (SAMA) completed a $10-million overhaul, making this excellent museum better than it ever was. Its core consists of several castle-like buildings of the 1904 Lone Star Brewery, which in 1981 were gutted, connected, and transformed into a visually exciting exhibition space (enjoy terrific views of downtown from the crosswalk between the two main structures). Exhibits range from early Egyptian, Greek, and Asian collections to 19th- and 20th-century American artworks, but the jewel of the collection is the **Nelson A. Rockefeller Center for Latin American Art,** a 30,000-square-foot wing that has one of the U.S.'s most comprehensive collections of Latin American art, from pre-Columbian, folk, and Spanish colonial pieces to contemporary works—everything from elaborate altarpieces to a whimsical Day of the Dead tableau. The contemporary art in this collection is particularly strong, and computer stations help make this a nationwide resource for Latinx culture. The **Lenora and Walter F. Brown Asian Art Wing** represents

Greater San Antonio Attractions

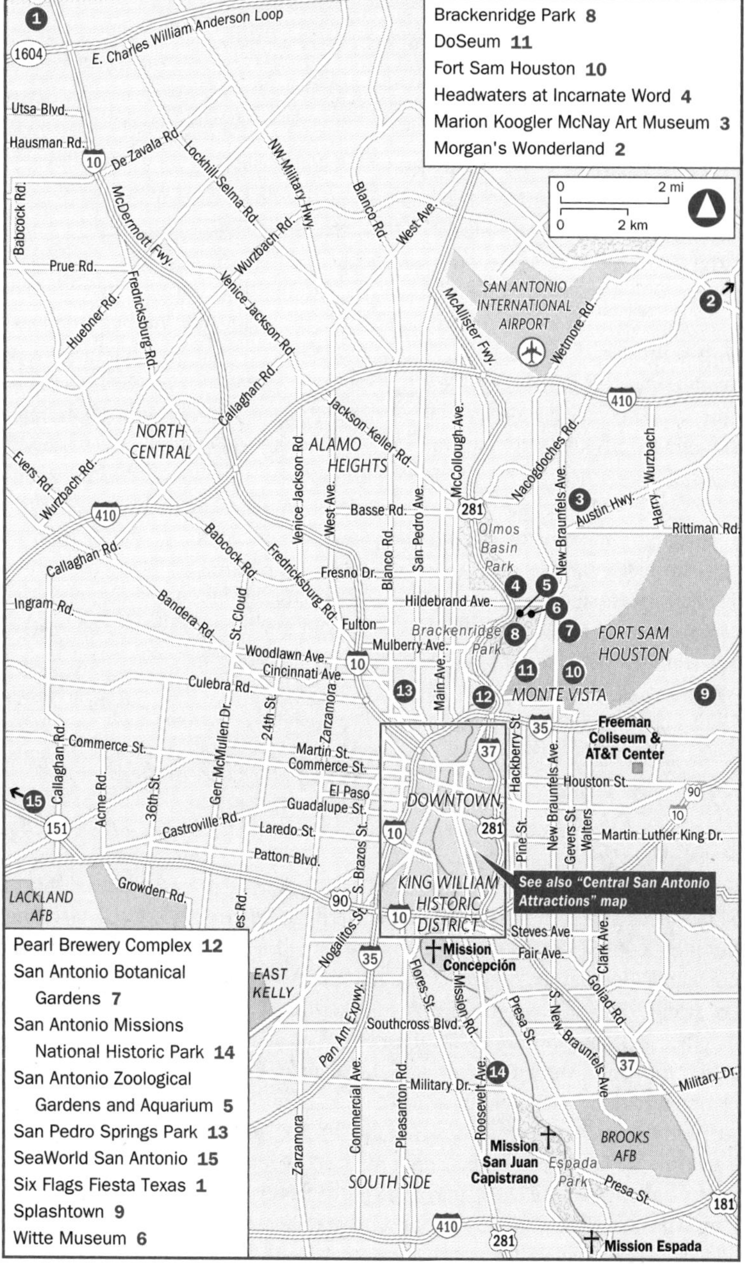

another major collection, the largest Asian art collection in Texas and one of the largest in the Southwest. ***Bonus:*** The museum can now be reached by river taxi.

200 W. Jones Ave. www.samuseum.org. ✆ **210/978-8100.** $20 adults, $17 seniors, $12 students with ID, free ages 12 and younger; free admission Tues 4–9pm and Sun 10am–noon (fee for some special exhibits). Tues 10am–9pm; Wed–Sun 10am–5pm. Closed Thanksgiving, Dec 25, Jan 1, Easter, Fiesta Friday. Bus: VIVA line 11.

Witte Museum ★★★ NATURAL HISTORY MUSEUM For more than 90 years, this Smithsonian affiliate has been San Antonio's top family-friendly museum, with a focus on the story of Texas as well as on nature and science. After the DoSeum kids' museum opened down the road (p. 90), some lamented that the Witte might be relegated to the back burner. Not to worry: In spring 2017, after two years of extensive renovation, the museum reopened with refurbished exhibits and some 170,000 square feet of new space to explore. Among the New Witte's innovations: **The Zachry Family Acequia Garden,** showcasing a man-made irrigation canal and diversion dam hand-dug on the museum's grounds in 1719; the **Texas Wild** exhibit, with expanded dioramas underneath a big Texas sky; and the massive **Naylor Family Dinosaur Gallery,** a sure family draw, with dinosaur skeletons in fearsome poses. A narrative called **Texas Deep Time** weaves together three important periods in Texas history: millions of years ago when dinosaurs roamed the land; thousands of years ago when prehistoric Indians studied the night sky; and hundreds of years ago when cattle was king and cowboys in the saddle worked Texas prairie lands.

3801 Broadway (adjacent to Brackenridge Park). www.wittemuseum.org. ✆ **210/357-1900.** $12 adults, $11 seniors and active military with ID, $9 ages 4–11, free for children 3 and under; free admission Tues 3–8pm. Mon–Sat 10am–5pm (Tues until 8pm); Sun noon–5pm. Closed Easter, 3rd Mon in Oct, Thanksgiving, Christmas Day. Bus: VIVA line 11A.

South Side

San Antonio Missions National Historical Park ★★★ HISTORIC SITE Designated a UNESCO World Heritage Site in 2015, the five frontier mission complexes in San Antonio—including the Alamo—afford an unmatched look at the Spanish Colonial influence in North America. You can see strings of missions in California and Arizona, but none are as easily visited together as San Antonio's set of missions, established by the Franciscans along the San Antonio River to Christianize the native population. The National Park Service now runs the other four missions besides the Alamo, all still active parishes, run in cooperation with the Archdiocese of San Antonio. The Park Service has assigned each mission an interpretive theme to educate visitors about the roles they played in early San Antonio society. The 8-mile-long Mission Reach section of the River Walk, which opened in 2012, has added recreational trails, picnic areas, pedestrian bridges, and portals to the missions; an ongoing effort has been restoring the riparian woodland ecosystem and reintroducing native plants. In 2018, the $13.7-million **Confluence Park**—so named because it's at the intersection of the San Antonio River and the San Pedro Creek—was dedicated as a gateway to the trail, which begins near the Blue Star Arts complex and ends near Mission Espada; see **www.confluencepark.sariverfound.org** for more information on this architecturally stunning space.

The missions are about 3 miles apart from each other; Via VIVA bus line Mission route No. 40 stops at all of them, but it's easier to bike here or drive. Each mission has an information office with free maps and can give you driving instructions to the next mission. The main information office is at Mission San José.

The first of the missions you'll come to heading south is **Concepción,** 807 Mission Rd., at Felisa Street. Built in 1731, it's the oldest unrestored Texas mission, looking much as it did 200 years ago. We tend to think of these old missions as somber and austere places, but traces of color on the facade and restored wall paintings inside show how vibrant this one originally was.

San José ★★ (6701 San José Dr., at Mission Rd.), established in 1720, was the largest, best known, and most beautiful of the Texas missions. It has been reconstructed to give visitors a complete picture of life in a mission community—right down to the granary, mill, and Indian quarters. The beautiful rose window is a big attraction, and popular mariachi Masses are held here every Sunday at noon (come early if you want a seat). This is also the site of the missions' excellent visitor center; the film about the mission system offered here is worth viewing. If you're going to visit only one of the missions, this is it.

Moved in 1731 from an earlier site in east Texas, **San Juan Capistrano** (9101 Graf Rd., at Ashley Rd.), doesn't have the grandeur of the missions to the north—the larger church intended for it was never completed—but the original simple chapel and the wilder setting give it a peaceful air. A 3-mile interpretive trail, with a number of overlook platforms, winds through the woods to the banks of the old river channel.

The southernmost mission in the San Antonio chain, **San Francisco de la Espada,** 10040 Espada Rd., also has an ancient, isolated feel, although the beautifully maintained church shows just how vital it still is to the local community. Be sure to visit the Espada Aqueduct, part of the mission's original *acequia* (irrigation ditch) system, about a mile north of the mission. Dating from 1740, it's one of the oldest Spanish aqueducts in the United States.

Headquarters: 2202 Roosevelt Ave. Visitor Center: 6701 San José Dr. at Mission Rd. www.nps.gov/saan. ✆ **210/932-1001.** Free admission (donations accepted). Daily 9am–5pm. National Park Ranger tours daily (5 tours daily at Mission San José, check with rangers at other missions for tour times). Closed Thanksgiving, Dec 25, Jan 1. Bus: VIVA line 40 stops at all the missions (including the Alamo).

OTHER ATTRACTIONS

Downtown

ArtPace ★ GALLERY San Antonio's premier art incubator features rotating shows, displaying the work of three artists selected by a guest curator for two-month residencies: One artist must be from Texas, one from anywhere else in the United States, and one from anywhere else in the world. The result has been a fascinating mélange, with everything from twists on the traditional to cutting-edge conceptual. It's a very stimulating art space, with lecture series by the artists as well as public forums to discuss the work.

445 N. Main Ave. www.artpace.org. ✆ **210/212-4900.** Free admission. Wed–Sun noon–5pm. Check local listings or call for lectures and other special events. Bus: 2, 3, or 9.

Battle for Texas: The Experience ★★ MUSEUM I wouldn't ordinarily recommend a simulation over the real historic deal, but this re-creation of the Alamo personalities and battle enhances a visit to the famous mission and battle ground, about half a block away. It also helps that genuine artifacts from the Alamo—250 pieces, including some belonging to Mexican General Santa Anna—are on display here. You get the idea of how the immersion works if you've seen the movie *Night at the Museum*—and, indeed, a rousing nighttime adventure at Battle for Texas is named for the film.

Alamo Plaza at Blum St. (inside Shops at Rivercenter). www.battlefortexas.com. ✆ **210/592-6825.** $19.50 adults; $17.50 seniors, military, students; $14.50 ages 6–12; free for ages 5 and under. Daily noon–5pm (opens 10am Sat). Night at the Museum times vary; call ahead or check the website. Bus: VIVA line 11, 40, and 301.

Buckhorn Saloon & Texas Ranger Museum ★ MUSEUM For pure Texas kitsch, it's hard to beat a museum you can browse with a cold brew in hand. Stop by the bar for a longneck, cocktail, or root beer on your way to check out the extensive collection of taxidermied wild animals from all over the globe in the **Hall of Horns,** or the Old West memorabilia displayed at the **Texas Ranger Museum.** Founded in 1890 by a bellhop from the Southern Hotel on Main Plaza, the Buckhorn also houses other quirky exhibits as well as a small cafe and a gift shop featuring tons of Texana and souvenirs.

318 E. Houston St. www.buckhornmuseum.com. ✆ **210/247-4000.** $20 adults, $18 seniors (55+) and military, $15 ages 4–12. Memorial Day–Labor Day daily 10am–6pm; rest of year daily 10am–5pm. Closed Thanksgiving and Dec 25. Bus: VIVA 11, 40, and 301.

Casa Navarro State Historic Site ★ HISTORIC SITE A key player in Texas's transition from Spanish territory to American state, merchant and landholder José Antonio Navarro participated in several legislatures and assemblies, and was a signer of the 1836 Texas Declaration of Independence, one of only two native Texans to do so. He also participated in the convention that ratified the annexation of Texas to the United States in 1845. He bought this property in the 1830s and made it his residence in the 1850s, which is when the three buildings you see were all probably built. The single-story main house with attic (to which additions were later constructed) is typical of San Antonio houses of the period. Designated a National Historic Landmark in 2017, the house hosts many special events—everything from altar-making to historic recipe displays.

228 S. Laredo St. www.thc.texas.gov/historic-sites/casa-navarro-state-historic-site. ✆ **210/226-4801.** $4 adults, $3 ages 6–12, free for children 5 and under. Tues–Sat 10am–5pm; Sun noon–5pm. Bus: VIVA line 301.

Hemisfair Park ★ PARK Built for the 1968 HemisFair, a World's Fair exposition celebrating the 250th anniversary of San Antonio's founding, this 92-acre urban space at the southern boundary of downtown has been undergoing a massive revitalization. The goal: to bring back the vibrant neighborhood that was destroyed to . . . well, build Hemisfair Park. Older structures such as the **Institute of Texan Cultures** and the **Tower of the Americas** (p. 90) and the **Magik Theatre** (p. 122) have long been popular with tourists, and more recently the Henry B. Gonzales Convention Center has brought even more activity to the park. In 2015 the **Yanaguana Garden** opened, a fanciful playscape with a wading pool and colorful beach chairs abutted by a cheerful restaurant complex, which has drawn a great many locals as well as visitors. Plans for mixed-income housing, a boutique hotel, and more retail are in the works; if these materialize, Hemisfair Park is bound to become a major hub.

Bounded by S. Alamo St., E. Market St., E. Cesar Chavez Blvd., and Tower of the Americas Way. www.hemisfair.org. ✆ **210/709-4750.** Daily 5am–midnight. Bus: VIVA lines 11, 40, and 301.

La Villita National Historic District ★★ NEIGHBORHOOD Developed by European settlers along the east bank of the San Antonio River in the late 18th and early 19th centuries, La Villita (the Little Village) was on the proverbial wrong side of the tracks until natural flooding of the west-bank settlements made it fashionable again. It fell back into poverty at the beginning of the 20th century, then was revitalized in the late 1930s by artists and craftspeople and the San Antonio Conservation Society. Now boutiques, crafts shops, and restaurants occupy this historic district, which resembles a Spanish/Mexican village, replete with shaded patios, plazas, brick-and-tile streets, and some of the settlement's original adobe structures. You can see (but not enter, unless you rent it for an event) the house of General Cós, the Mexican military leader who surrendered to the Texas revolutionary army in 1835, or attend a performance at the **Arneson River Theatre** (p. 120). Walking tour maps of these and other historical structures are available throughout the site. It'll take you only about 20 minutes to do a quick walk-through, unless you're an inveterate shopper—in which case, all bets are off.

Bounded by Durango, Navarro, and Alamo sts. and River Walk. www.lavillitasantonio.com. ✆ **210/207-8614.** Free admission. Shops Mon–Sat 10am–6pm; Sun 11am–4pm. Closed Thanksgiving, Dec 25, and Jan 1. Bus: VIVA lines 11 and 40.

Market Square ★★ MARKET Colorful Market Square has the feel of a small Mexican downtown plaza, where food booths, retail kiosks, artist stalls, street performers, and musicians gather on weekends or pleasant spring and summer days. *Ballet folklórico* dancers or mariachi bands at local festivals are held here throughout the year. Inside the adjacent El Mercado building, a mall of Mexican import vendors re-creates an authentic border-style marketplace where you can buy everything from huge sombreros and Mexican vanilla to scorpion-inlaid paperweights; you'll find a few high-quality stores, including **Galería Ortiz,** here too. In addition to food stalls, two popular Mexican restaurants edge Market Square, including **Mi Tierra** (p. 61).

Bounded by Commerce, Santa Rosa, and Dolorosa sts. and I-35. www.sanantonio.com/places/el-mercado. ✆ **210/207-8600.** Free admission. El Mercado and Farmers' Market Plaza summer daily 10am–8pm; winter daily 10am–6pm; restaurants and some shops open later. Closed Thanksgiving, Dec 25, Jan 1, and Easter. Bus: VIVA line 301.

San Antonio Public Library ★ ARCHITECTURE San Antonio's main library, opened in the mid-1990s at a cost of $38 million, has a number of important holdings, including the Latino Collection and Resource Center (p. 95). It is perhaps most notable for its architecture, a wildly colorful and whimsical public space designed by Ricardo Legorreta, renowned for his buildings throughout Mexico. People apparently love to enter this space—by the second month after the library opened, circulation had gone up 95 percent. The boxy building, painted what has been called "enchilada red," is designed like a hacienda around an internal courtyard. A variety of skylights, windows, and wall colors (including bright purples and yellows) afford a different perspective from each of the six floors.

600 Soledad St. www.mysapl.org. ✆ **210/207-2500.** Free admission. Mon–Thurs 9am–9pm; Fri–Sat 9am–5pm; Sun 11am–5pm. Bus: VIVA lines 11, 40, and 301.

San Fernando Cathedral ★★ CHURCH Although tourists probably think of the Alamo as the centerpiece of downtown San Antonio, historians consider the heart of the city this handsome Spanish cathedral, portions of it dating back to 1738–1759 when it was first built by Canary Island settlers. Overlooking the town's historic Main Plaza, San Fernando Cathedral was

Did You Know?

- Elmer Doolin, the original manufacturer of Fritos corn chips, bought the original recipe from a San Antonio restaurant in 1932 for $100. He sold the first batch from the back of his Model T Ford.
- *Wings,* a silent World War I epic that won the first Academy Award for best picture in 1927, was filmed in San Antonio. The film marked the debut of Gary Cooper, who was on screen for a total of 102 seconds.
- Lyndon and Lady Bird Johnson were married in San Antonio's St. Mark's Episcopal Church.

completed in 1749, and the original parts of the structure make it the oldest cathedral sanctuary in the United States and the oldest parish church in Texas. Between 1840 and 1873, the church fell into disrepair until it was rebuilt and consecrated in October 1873. Alamo defender James "Jim" Bowie married his wife, Ursula, at the cathedral in 1831, before he was killed during the 1836 siege of the Alamo. The cathedral has undergone major renovations over the centuries, including the addition of a 24-foot-high gilded altarpiece or *retablo*. It's the mother church of the Archdiocese of San Antonio and the seat of its archbishop, and a very active parish, with weekend Masses, weddings, and funerals, as well as concerts and other special events, held regularly. ***Note:*** Four nights a week, the spectacular ***San Antonio—The Saga*** (www.mainplaza.org/san-antoniothe-saga), a video collage by French artist Xavier de Richemont, is projected on the church facade.

115 Main Plaza. ✆ **210/227-1297.** Free admission. Mon–Thurs 9am–8pm; Fri 9am–5pm; Sat–Sun 9am–6:30pm. Free shows Tues and Fri–Sun at 9, 9:30, and 10pm. Bus: 9, 10, 43.

Southwest School of Art ★ ARCHITECTURE/ART GALLERY A stroll along the River Walk to the northern corner of downtown will lead you into another world: a rare French-designed cloister where contemporary crafts blossom. An exhibition gallery and artist studios–cum–classrooms (not open to visitors) occupy the garden-filled grounds of the first girls' school in San Antonio, established by the Ursuline order in the mid–19th century. Learn about both the school and the historic site at the Visitors Center Museum in the First Academy Building. You can enjoy a nice, light lunch in the **Copper Kitchen Restaurant** (Mon–Fri 11:30am–2pm, closed national holidays). See also p. 112 in chapter 7.

300 Augusta St. www.swschool.org. ✆ **210/224-1848.** Free admission. Mon–Sat 9am–5pm, Sun 11am–4pm (adjacent Navarro Campus gallery only); Mon–Fri 10am–5pm (museum). Bus: VIVA lines 11, 40, and 301.

Spanish Governor's Palace ★ HISTORIC SITE The name makes it sound like a mansion, so you may be surprised when you see this one-story adobe barracks. It's impressive nonetheless, one of the oldest, best-preserved residential buildings in Texas—thus its National Historic Landmark status. It was built as a one-room house in 1722 and, in 1749, three other rooms were added (along with the insignia of Spanish King Ferdinand VI; the date is shown on one of the doorways,). The house served as the headquarters and residence for the captain of the Spanish garrison and was the capital of the Spanish province of Texas from 1772 to 1821, when Mexico gained its independence. San Antonio's last captain, Juan Ignacio Pérez, and his descendants remained in the house until the 1860s. The house lived many lives—from a saloon to a pawn shop to a tailor's shop—until the city purchased it in 1928. Today its rooms are filled with period furnishings. Like most Spanish-style dwellings of its time, the house has a shaded garden and a patio with a stone fountain and mosaic flooring.

105 Plaza de Armas. www.getcreativesanantonio.com/Explore-San-Antonio/Spanish-Governors-Palace. ✆ **210/224-0601.** $5 adults, $3 seniors, $3 ages 7–13, free for children 6 and under. Tues–Sat 9am–5pm; Sun 10am–5pm. Closed Jan 1, Easter, for 2 days around San Jacinto Day (Apr 21), Thanksgiving, and Dec 25. Bus: VIVA line 30.

Tower of the Americas ★ VIEW For a good take on the lay of the land, just circle the eight panoramic panels on the observation deck of the Tower of the Americas, a 750-foot-high tower built for the HemisFair in 1968. Sitting at the equivalent of 59 stories, the deck is lit for spectacular night viewing. Also included in the price of admission: A 4D helicopter simulation "Skies Over Texas" ride. The tower also hosts the rotating Chart House restaurant with surprisingly decent food (for the revolving genre), as well as a thankfully stationary cocktail lounge.

Impressions

We have no city, except, perhaps, New Orleans, that can vie, in point of picturesque interest that attaches to odd and antiquated foreignness, with San Antonio.

—Frederick Law Olmsted, *A Journey Through Texas*, 1853

739 E. Cesar Chavez Blvd. www.toweroftheamericas.com. ✆ **210/223-3101.** $13 adults, $11 seniors 55+, $10 ages 4–11, free for children 3 and under. Sun–Thurs 10am–10pm; Fri–Sat 10am–11pm. Bus: VIVA lines 11, 40, and 301.

UTSA Institute of Texan Cultures ★ HISTORIC SITE It's the rare visitor who won't discover that his or her ethnic group has contributed to the history of Texas: 26 different ethnic and cultural groups are represented in the imaginative, hands-on displays of this educational center, one of three campuses of the University of Texas at San Antonio (it's also a Smithsonian affiliate). Outbuildings include a one-room schoolhouse, an adobe home, a windmill, and the multimedia Dome Theater, which presents images of Texas on multiple screens. A variety of heritage festivals and kid-friendly shows and events, such as pioneer life reenactments, holography exhibits, and ghost-tale storytellers at Halloween are always on tap; phone or check the institute's website for a current schedule.

801 E. Cesar E. Chavez Blvd. (at Chavez and Tower of the Americas Way, in Hemisfair Park). www.texancultures.com. ✆ **210/458-2300.** $10 adults; $8 seniors, ages 6–17, and active military (with ID); free for children 5 and under. Mon–Sat 9am–5pm; Sun noon–5pm. Closed Thanksgiving, Dec 24–25, Jan 1, and for 3 days during June's Texas Folklife Festival. Bus: VIVA line 301.

Pearl/Broadway Cultural Corridor

The DoSeum ★★ CHILDREN'S MUSEUM Opened in 2015 on a 5½-acre park at the edge of Alamo Heights' busy stretch of Broadway, this stellar facility for children features two-story exhibit halls designed to foster creativity in the arts and sciences through interactive exhibits. Entirely solar powered, and relying solely on recycled water, the DoSeum practices as well as preaches sustainability. Kids are crazy about the DoSeum's interactive robot, Baxter, and its clever **Spy Academy** filled with math challenges. There's also an interactive puppet parade and a musical staircase. The **Big Outdoors,** a 39,000-square-foot outdoor play space, has a lazy stream, climbing structures, and an ADA-accessible treehouse. Although all ages enjoy it, the museum is specially geared for kids up to about 10 years old.

2800 Broadway St. www.thedoseum.org. ✆ **210/212-4453.** Ages 1 and older $14. Free family night 1st Tues of month 5:30pm–7:30pm. Mon–Fri 10am–5pm; Sat 9am–5pm; Sun noon–5pm. Bus: VIVA line 11a.

Southtown/King William

Blue Star Arts Complex ★★ GALLERY This huge former warehouse in Southtown hosts a collection of working studios and galleries, as well as several shops, dining spots, artist studios, and apartments. A one-stop entertainment center, offering everything from gelato and pub fare to a hair salon and bike rentals, it's anchored by the 11,000-square-foot artist-run **Contemporary Art Center.** The style of work varies from gallery to gallery—you'll see everything from primitive-style folk art to feminist photography—but the level of professionalism is generally high. A number of galleries sell arty gift items such as jewelry, picture frames, and crafts.

116 Blue Star St. (bordered by Probandt, Blue Star, and S. Alamo sts. and the San Antonio River). www.bluestarartscomplex.com. ✆ **210/227-6960.** Free admission (suggested donation for art center). Gallery hours vary; most are open Wed–Sun noon–6pm, some open at 10am. Bus: VIVA line 40.

King William Historic District ★★ NEIGHBORHOOD San Antonio's first suburb, King William was settled in the 19th century by prosperous German merchants who displayed their wealth through extravagant homes and named the 25-block area after Kaiser Wilhelm of Prussia. (Other residents of San Antonio were less complimentary, dubbing this German area "Sauerkraut Bend.") The neighborhood fell into decline in the middle of the 20th century, as the affluent abandoned the inner city for prosperous neighborhoods and suburbs to the north, but you'd never know it today, as tour buses ply its revived streets. If the weather's agreeable, I suggest skipping the bus tour in favor of strolling around the tree-lined streets, gawking at beautifully landscaped mansions in a variety of architectural styles. Outside the gate of the **San Antonio Conservation Society,** 107 King William St. (www.saconservation.org; ✆ **210/224-6163**), you can pick up self-guided tour pamphlets covering three separate historic districts within the neighborhood. To see some of the homes' interiors, you can tour **Villa Finale** (see below) and the **Steves Homestead Museum** (see below), or have a meal at the **Guenther House** (p. 66). The neighborhood is a pleasant 15-minute hike from downtown, following the Mission Reach extension of the River Walk.

East bank of the river, just south of downtown. Bus: VIVA line 11.

Ruby City ★ ARCHITECTURE/GALLERY Before she died in 2007, Linda Pace, the artist and philanthropist whose foundation created ArtPace

(p. 86), worked with world-renowned architect David Adjaye on plans for a clean-lined, crimson-hued building to house her extensive contemporary art collection (as befits a complex called Ruby City, Pace envisioned it in a dream). When completed in 2019, the striking structure will be the centerpiece of an arts campus extending from South Flores Street to the San Pedro Creek Culture Park (p. 102). Two parts of the campus are already open: **Chris Park,** at 150 Camp St., a one-acre sculpture garden dedicated to (and named for) Pace's late son; and the adjacent **Studio,** an auxiliary exhibition space focused on feminist works.

Camp St. www.lindapacefoundation.org. ✆ **210/227-8400.** Free admission. Chris Park open Tues–Sun 9am–5pm; Studio open Wed–Sat noon–5pm. Bus: VIVA line 11.

Steves Homestead Museum ★ MUSEUM Don't be misled by the word "homestead"—this is a Victorian mansion, built in 1876 for lumber magnate Edward Steves, and most likely designed by prominent San Antonio architect Alfred Giles. Steves' granddaughter bequeathed it to the San Antonio Conservation Society, who then restored it. One of the few houses in the King William Historic District open to the public, it gives a fascinating glimpse into the life of the local upper class in the late 19th century. You can opt for a self-guided tour, but if you have time, wait for a 45-minute-long docent tour—the guides' knowledge of local color and gossip make these quite entertaining.

509 King William St. www.saconservation.org. ✆ **210/227-9160.** Self-guided tours $7.50 adults; $5 seniors, students, and active-duty military with ID; ages 11 and under free. Guided tours $10 adults; $7.50 seniors, students, and active military; ages 11 and under free. Daily 10am–4:15pm (last tour 3:30pm). Closed major holidays. Bus: VIVA line 40.

Villa Finale ★ HISTORIC SITE The house of Walter Mathis, now a property of the National Trust, is a Italian villa–style mansion dating from 1876. Because the National Trust mandated that all the items in the home had to stay in the same place as they were when Mathis died, few of the eclectic assortment of artifacts are in display cases (perhaps that's why all visitors' bags must be stored in lockers before entering). A rare and very valuable death mask of Napoleon, for example, sits out in the open. The eccentric Mathis was a great collector of fine and decorative arts, from the quirky to the sublime—everything from cattle-themed cutlery to the works of artist Mary Bonner. The collection is especially strong on French furniture and art objects. You can see the first floor on a self-guided tour; to go upstairs you'll have to take a guided tour (reservations recommended). The beautifully landscaped 1½-acre grounds are open free to the public.

401 King William St. (visitor center 122 Madison St.). www.villafinale.org. ✆ **210/223-9800.** Self-guided tours $10 adults; $8 seniors, students, and active-duty military with ID. Guided tours $12 adults; $10 seniors, students, and active-duty military. Self-guided tours Tues–Sat 10am–1pm; guided tours Tues–Sat at 1:30pm and 3pm. Grounds open Tues–Sat 9:30am–4pm. Bus: VIVA line 40.

Alamo Heights Area

Headwaters at Incarnate Word ★ PARK On the campus of the University of the Incarnate Word, you'll find a 53-acre nature sanctuary run by the Sisters of Charity of the Incarnate Word, who came to San Antonio in 1869 to help with a cholera outbreak and founded the university in 1881. Members of the order also provide educational programs about conservation. This serene spot is popular for its trails, and locals throng here around the holidays, when the campus twinkles with thousands of Christmas lights. Its centerpiece is the San Antonio Springs Blue Hole, the recognized source of the San Antonio River.

Off Hwy. 281, just north of W. Hildebrand Ave. (see website for directions). www.headwaters-iw.org/visit. ✆ **210/828-2224.** Free admission. Open 24 hours. Bus: 11 or 14.

San Antonio Zoological Gardens and Aquarium ★★ ZOO Home to more than 700 species, this zoo has one of the largest animal collections in the United States, and it's considered one of the country's top facilities for its conservation efforts and successful breeding programs (it produced the first white rhino in the U.S.). Kids will get a kick out of many of the critters; Lory Landing, featuring close encounters with lorikeets (small parrots), is especially popular. Parents will appreciate the fact that they won't run into an expensive gift shop around every corner.

3903 N. St. Mary's St., in Brackenridge Park. www.sazoo.org. ✆ **210/734-7183.** $17 adults, $13 ages 3–11, free for children 2 and under. Daily 9am–5pm (until 6pm in summer). Bus: 7 or 8.

Fort Sam Houston Area

Fort Sam Houston (Joint Base San Antonio) ★ HISTORIC SITE Since 1718, when the armed Presidio de Béxar was established to defend the Spanish missions, the military has played a key role in San Antonio's development, and it remains one of the largest employers in town today. The 3,434-acre Fort Sam Houston, which currently hosts the Army Medical Command and the headquarters of the Fifth Army, affords visitors an unusual opportunity to view the city's military past; the first military flight in history took off from the fort's spacious parade grounds, for example. Most of the historic buildings are still in use and thus off-limits, but two are open to the public. Located in the **Quadrangle**—an impressive 1876 limestone structure centered on a brick clock tower and enclosing a grassy square where peacocks and deer roam freely—is the **Fort Sam Houston Museum,** Building 16 (✆ **210/221-1886;** free admission; Mon–Fri 10am–4pm, Sat noon–4pm). Its six rooms, containing some 8,200 artifacts, highlight the history of the armed forces in Texas, with a special focus on San Antonio. On 7 acres, the **U.S. Army Medical Department Museum,** 2310 Stanley Rd., Building 1046 (www.ameddmuseum.amedd.army.mil/visit.html; ✆ **210/221-6358** or

210/221-0015; free admission; Mon–Sat 10am–4pm), displays army medical equipment and American prisoner-of-war memorabilia. The main building is a restored hospital train car. ***Note:*** Anyone wishing to visit the fort must get written permission from or be accompanied by a member of the DOD, whether active or retired, and come with a government-issued photo ID (such as a driver's license). See the Joint Base San Antonio website (www.jbsa.af.mil/library/visitorinformation.asp) for the most up-to-date base entry requirements.

Grayson St. and New Braunfels Ave., about 2½ miles NE of downtown. ✆ **210/221-1151** (public affairs). No public transportation to the Quadrangle.

Far Northwest

Six Flags Fiesta Texas ★★ AMUSEMENT PARK This popular 200-acre theme and water park has always drawn crowds with its state-of-the-art rides, and the thrills just keep on coming. In 2018, Six Flags debuted the **WONDER WOMAN: Golden Lasso Coaster,** where riders sit single file on interlaced monorail tracks, the better to give them unobstructed views of the 100-foot-high quarry walls (if you can pay attention while dropping 90 degrees straight down). As you queue, you'll move through the tropical landscaping and ancient architecture of Themyscira, Wonder Woman's fictional

A theme park FOR EVERYONE

Inspired by the special needs of his daughter, who was unable to participate in most activities in traditional theme parks, Gordon Hartman created the $36-million **Morgan's Wonderland** (www.morganswonderland.com; ✆ **210-495-5888** or 210-637-3486 TDD), the world's first fully accessible theme park. Spread over 25 acres in a former limestone quarry, it features rides, playgrounds, gardens, a catch-and-release fishing lake, an events center, and an amphitheater, all of which accommodate wheelchairs and other aids. The word got out about this unique playscape among the communities that most benefited from it—the park has welcomed more than 1.3 million guests from all 50 states and 69 other countries—but it wasn't until the debut of the companion waterpark, **Morgan's Inspiration Island,** in 2017, that it received wider notice: Morgan's was named one of *Time* magazine's World's Greatest Places in 2018. For guests to enjoy such activities as splash pads and a River Boat Adventure ride, the tropically-themed waterpark offers support facilities such as access to waterproof wheelchairs and temperature-controlled areas for those sensitive to the heat and cold. Morgan's was also designed to be more affordable to families than most mega-play lands (admission to both parks is $27 adults; $21 ages 3–17, seniors, and military—and kids with special needs enter free). It's located in northeast San Antonio, 5223 David Edwards Dr., a half-mile west of I-35 at the intersection of Wurzbach Parkway and Thousand Oaks Drive. Opening days and hours vary by season (it's closed Jan–Feb); check website for current schedule.

EXPLORING SAN ANTONIO'S hispanic HERITAGE

A Hispanic heritage tour is almost redundant in San Antonio, which is a living testament to the role Hispanics have played in shaping the city. **Casa Navarro State Historic Site** (p. 86), **La Villita** (p. 87), **Market Square** (p. 88), **San Antonio Missions National Historical Park** (p. 84), and the **Spanish Governor's Palace** (p. 89) all give visitors a feel for the city's Spanish colonial past, while the Nelson A. Rockefeller wing of the **San Antonio Museum of Art** (p. 82) hosts this country's largest collection of Latin American art.

Perhaps the jewel of the city's Hispanic culture is the old **Alameda Theater** (310 W. Houston St.) on downtown's west side. A grand movie palace built in 1949, the Alameda was the largest ever dedicated to Spanish-language entertainment; it's been described as being to U.S. Latinos what Harlem's Apollo Theater is to African Americans. Features include a spectacular 86-foot-high sign on the marquee that's lit by rare cold cathode technology, not neon. A major restoration scheduled to begin in 2019 is a joint effort of several local groups, including the city of San Antonio and Texas Public Radio, which will broadcast from there when the renovation is complete.

Cultural events and blowout festivals abound, many of them held at Market Square. The **Guadalupe Cultural Arts Center** (p. 121) organizes many of them. In Hemisfair Park, the **Instituto Cultural Mexicano/Casa Mexicana,** 600 HemisFair Plaza Way (www.hemisfair.org/destinations/mexican-cultural-institute; ✆ **210/227-0123**), sponsored by the Mexican Ministry of Foreign Affairs, hosts Latin American film series, concerts, conferences, performances, contests, and workshops—including ones on art, language, literature, and folklore. The institute also hosts shifting displays of art and artifacts relating to Mexican history and culture, from pre-Columbian to contemporary (free admission; Tues–Fri 10am–5pm, Sat–Sun noon–5pm).

In 2017, the 6,000-square-foot **Latino Collection and Resource Center** opened on the first floor of the San Antonio Public Library (p. 88). In addition to an excellent non-circulating collection of 10,000+ books about the Mexican-American experience in Texas and the Southwest, the center hosts an art gallery highlighting local and international Latino artists. Events include presentations by local authors (for example, on the history of Tejana writing and the role of newspapers) and writing workshops. This is also the place to come to do genealogical research into your family's Hispanic roots.

home island. America's first rocket-blast water coaster, **Thunder Rapids,** introduced in 2017 in the splashy White Water Bay waterpark, shoots riders uphill at lightning speeds and then thrills them with sudden high drops. Other rides include the **Superman Krypton Coaster,** with nearly a mile of twists and turns and two big inversions; the **Iron Rattler,** a wooden coaster with modern steel rails and track; the 60+-mph **Poltergeist** roller coaster; and **Scream!,** a 20-story "space shot and turbo drop," to name just a few. Virtual-reality simulators and laser games keep the theme park just tech-y enough to thrill millennials. Wet-'n'-wild attractions (especially popular in hot Texas summers) include the **Lone Star Lagoon,** the state's largest wave pool, and the **Texas Treehouse,** a five-story "drenchfest" with a 1,000-gallon cowboy hat that tips over to pour water on unsuspecting passersby. Some traces of local character date back to the days when this park was plain old Fiesta Texas. Themed areas include **Los Festivales,** a Hispanic village where every day feels like Fiesta; a German village called **Spassburg** with a large Sangerfest Halle theater; an old-fashioned Texas town called **Crackaxle Canyon;** the **Fiesta Bay Boardwalk** with its Midway vibe and Ferris wheel; and a 1950s town center called **Rockville** with a retro-style Frostee Freeze ice cream shop.

17000 I-10 W. (take exit 555 off I-10 W. and go west on La Cantera Pkwy.). www.sixflags.com/parks/fiestatexas. ✆ **800/473-4378** or 210/697-5050. $83 adults, $68 children 48 in. and under, free for ages 2 and under. Online discounts often available. Daily late May–mid-Aug; Mar–late May and mid-Aug–Oct Sat–Sun only. Park opens 10am, closing times vary depending on season (as late as 10pm in summer). Bus: 64 or 660.

West Side

SeaWorld San Antonio ★★ AMUSEMENT PARK The largest of the brand's three marine life adventure parks in the United States, 250-acre SeaWorld San Antonio keeps adding to its wet-'n'-wild attractions, which include an enormous wave pool, a "loco" river, and a variety of watery roller coasters. The biggest draw continues to be the marine mammals, from penguins and sea lions to dolphins and orcas, whether you prefer to watch them perform, view them from underwater, or swim with them. Negative press slowed down attendance for a while but SeaWorld's focus on its conservation efforts—not to mention the public's short memory—have made this place more popular than ever.

10500 SeaWorld Dr., 16 miles NW of downtown San Antonio at Ellison Dr. and Westover Hills Blvd. (just off Hwy. 151 W.). www.seaworld.com/san-antonio. ✆ **800/700-7786.** 1-day passes start at $69 for ages 3 and up; free for children 2 and under. Online discounts available. Parking $20 per day. Early Mar–late Nov; days of operation vary seasonally. Park open at 10am, closing times vary. Bus: 64.

DOWNTOWN SAN ANTONIO: A WALKING TOUR

One of downtown San Antonio's gifts to visitors on foot is its wonderfully meandering early pathways—they were not laid out by drunken cattle drivers as has been wryly suggested, but formed by the course of the San Antonio River and the various settlements that grew up around it. Turn any corner in this area and you'll come across some fascinating testament to the city's historically rich past.

Walking Tour: Downtown San Antonio

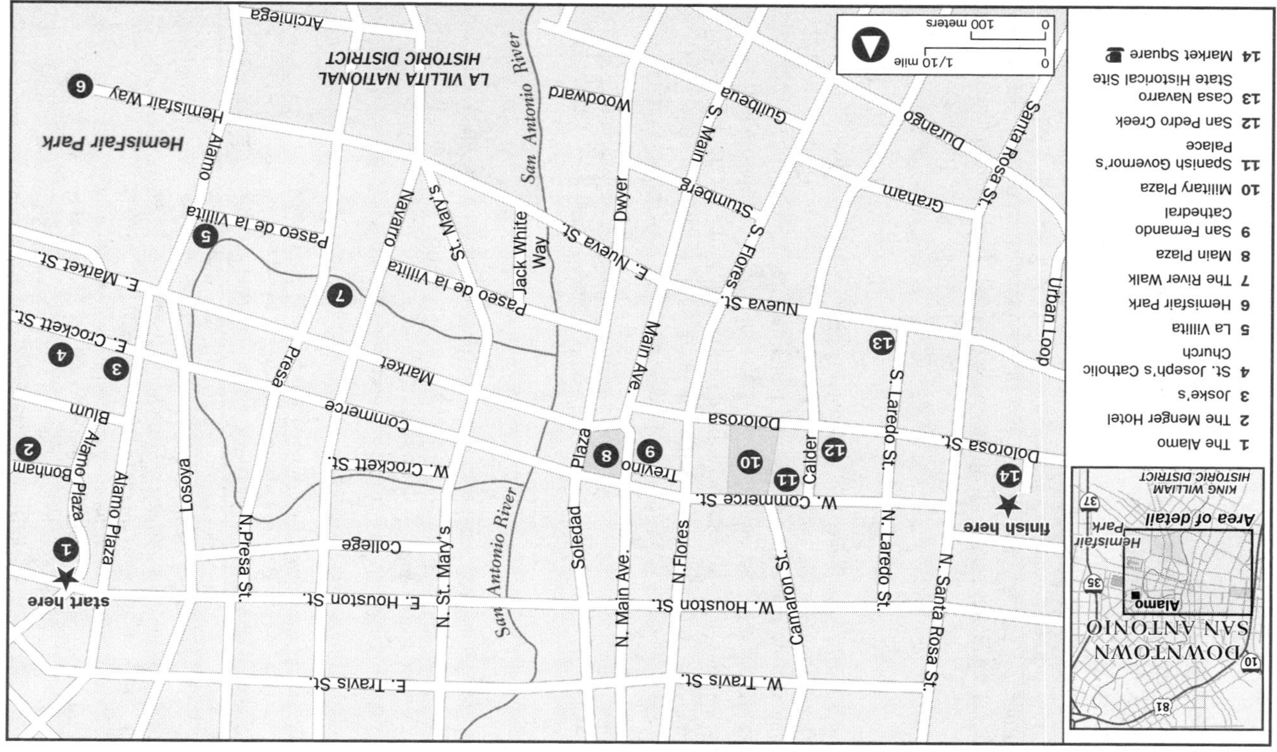

WALKING TOUR: DOWNTOWN

START: **The Alamo.**

FINISH: **Market Square.**

TIME: **Approximately 1½ hours, not including stops at shops, restaurants, or attractions.**

BEST TIMES: **Early morning during the week, when the streets and attractions are less crowded. If you're willing to tour the Alamo museums and shrine another time, consider starting out before they open (9am).**

WORST TIMES: **Weekend afternoons, especially in summer, when the crowds and the heat render this long stroll uncomfortable. (If you do get tired, you can always pick up a streetcar within a block or two of most parts of this route.)**

Built to be within easy reach of each other, San Antonio's earliest military, religious, and civil settlements are concentrated in the downtown area. The city spread out quite a bit in the subsequent 300 years, but downtown still functions as the seat of the municipal and county government, as well as the hub of tourist activities.

Start your tour at Alamo Plaza (bounded by E. Houston St. on the north); at the plaza's northeast corner, you'll come to the entrance for:

1 The Alamo

Originally established in 1718 as the Mission San Antonio de Valero, the first of the city's five missions, the Alamo (p. 77) was moved twice before settling at this site. The heavy limestone walls of the church and its adjacent compound later proved to make an excellent fortress. In 1836, fighters for Texas' independence from Mexico took a heroic, if ultimately unsuccessful, stand against Mexican general Santa Anna here.

Walk south along the plaza to:

2 The Menger Hotel

German immigrant William Menger built this hotel in 1859 on the site of Texas' first brewery, which he opened with partner Charles Deegan in 1855. Legend has it that Menger wanted a place to lodge hard-drinking friends who used to spend the night sleeping on his long bar. Far more prestigious guests—presidents, Civil War generals, writers, stage actors, you name it—stayed here over the years, and the hotel turns up in several short stories by frequent guest William Sidney Porter (O. Henry). The Menger has been much expanded since it first opened but retains its gorgeous three-story Victorian lobby.

On the south side of the hotel, Alamo Plaza becomes N. Alamo Street. Take it south 1 block to Commerce Street, where you'll spot:

3 Joske's (now Shops at Rivercenter)

After lying empty for several years, in 2016 the building that once hosted San Antonio's first department store was restored to its former glory. Opened by the Joske Brothers in 1889, the modest retail emporium was enlarged in successive stages until, in 1939, it became the large Art Deco building you see now, distinctive for its intricate Spanish Renaissance–style details. This was the first department store in Texas to be fully air-conditioned. The interior was gutted to incorporate the building into the Shops at Rivercenter mall complex, but the exterior is as impressive as ever.

Walk a short way along the Commerce Street side of the building to:

4 St. Joseph's Catholic Church

Built for San Antonio's German community in 1876, this Gothic revival–style house of worship is as notable for the intransigence of its congregation as for its beautiful stained-glass windows. The worshipers' refusal to move from the site when Joske's department store was rising up all around it earned the church the affectionate moniker "St. Joske's."

Head back to Alamo Street and continue south 2 blocks past Market Street to reach:

5 La Villita

Once the site of a Coahuiltecan Indian village, La Villita (p. 87) was settled over the centuries by Spanish, Germans, and, in the 1930s and '40s, a community of artists. A number of the buildings have been continuously occupied for more than 200 years. The "Little Village" on the river was restored by a joint effort of the city and the San Antonio Conservation Society, and now hosts a number of crafts shops and two upscale restaurants in addition to the historic General Cós House and the Arneson River Theatre.

Just south of La Villita, you'll see HemisFair Way and the large iron gates of:

6 Hemisfair Park

This park (p. 87) was built for the 1968 exposition held to celebrate the 250th anniversary of San Antonio's founding. The expansive former fairgrounds are home to two museums, a German heritage park, an observation tower—the tallest structure in the city and a great reference point if you get lost downtown—as well as the new Yanaguana Garden complex, with several restaurants. To explore the entire park would take several hours, so for the purposes of this tour, you might want to confine yourself to the observation tower and the German heritage park.

Retrace your steps to Paseo de la Villita and walk 1 block west to Presa Street. Take it north for about half a block until you see the Presa Street Bridge, and descend from it to:

7 The River Walk

You'll find yourself on a quiet section of this 2.6-mile paved walkway (p. 80) that lines the banks of the San Antonio River through a large part of downtown and the King William Historic District. The bustling cafe, restaurant, and hotel action is just behind you on the stretch of the river that winds north of La Villita.

Stroll west to the St. Mary's Street Bridge (along the way you'll pass under the Navarro St. Bridge). Ascend at St. Mary's Street and walk north 1 block to Market Street. Walk west across the Market Street Bridge to:

8 Main Plaza (Plaza de Las Islas)

This is the heart of the city, established in 1731 by 15 Canary Island families sent by King Philip V of Spain to settle his remote New World outpost. Much of the history of San Antonio—and of Texas—unfolded on this modest square. A peace treaty with the Apaches was signed on the plaza in 1749 (and later broken). In 1835, the Texan forces battled Santa Anna's troops here before barricading themselves in the Alamo across the river. Much calmer these days, the plaza still sees some action as home to the Romanesque-style Bexar County Courthouse.

Walk along the south side of Main Plaza to the corner of Main Avenue. Across the street and just to the north you'll find:

9 San Fernando Cathedral

The oldest parish church building in Texas (p. 88), this is also the site of the earliest marked graves in San Antonio. Three walls of the original church started by the Canary Island settlers in 1738 can still be seen in the rear of the 1868 Gothic revival cathedral, which recently underwent a massive renovation. Among those buried within the sanctuary walls are Eugenio Navarro, brother of José Antonio Navarro (see stop #13, below), and Don Manuel Muñoz, first governor of Texas when it was a province of a newly independent Mexico.

On the north side of the cathedral is Trevino Street; take it west to the next corner and cross the street to reach:

10 Military Plaza (Plaza de Armas)

This used to be the parade grounds for the Spanish garrison charged with guarding San Antonio de Béxar. The garrison was stationed here in 1718, the same year the mission San Antonio de Valero (the Alamo) was established. After Texas won its independence, Military Plaza became one of the liveliest spots in Texas, where cowboys, rangers, and anyone passing through would come to obtain local news. In the 1860s, it was the site of vigilante lynchings, and after the Civil War, it hosted a bustling outdoor market. At night, the townsfolk would come to its open-air booths to buy chili con carne from their favorite chili queen. The plaza remained completely open until 1889, when the ornate City Hall was built at its center.

The one-story white building you'll see directly across the street from the west side of the plaza is the:

11 Spanish Governor's Palace

Despite the name, this building (p. 89) was the residence and headquarters of the captain of the Presidio de Béxar, not of any Spanish governors. From here, the commander could watch his troops drilling across the street.

From the front of the Governor's Palace, walk south to Dolorosa Street and turn right (west). One block further is a drainage ditch, the sad remains of:

12 San Pedro Creek

The west bank of this body of water—once lovely and flowing, but now usually dry—was the original site of both Mission San Antonio de Valero and the Presidio de Béxar. In the first phase of the San Pedro Creek Culture Park (see below), a stretch of the creek half a mile north of here has already been restored; this section, between Houston and Nueva streets, is currently under construction as phase 2 of the project.

Continue west on Dolorosa Street to Laredo Street, and take it south 1 block to:

13 Casa Navarro State Historic Site

The life of José Antonio Navarro, whose lived in this single-story house (p. 86), traces the history of Texas itself: He was born in Spanish territory, fought for Mexico's independence from Spain, and then worked to achieve Texas's freedom from Mexico. (He was one of only two Texas-born signatories to the 1836 Texas Declaration of Independence.) In 1845, Navarro voted for Texas's annexation to the United States, and a year later, he became a senator in the new Texas State Legislature. He died here in 1871, at the age of 76.

Trace your steps up Laredo to Dolorosa, and go west on Dolorosa Street. When you reach Santa Rosa, you'll be facing:

14 Market Square

Home to the city's Market House at the turn of the 20th century, this low, arcaded structure (p. 88) was converted to El Mercado in 1973, and switched from selling household goods and personal items to crafts, clothing, and other more tourist-oriented Mexican wares. Directly behind and west of this lively square, the former Haymarket Plaza is now called the Farmers' Market, although it currently sells souvenirs instead of produce. You can enjoy a well-deserved lunch here at Mi Tierra (p. 61).

PARKS & GARDENS

Brackenridge Park ★★ PARK With its rustic stone bridges and winding walkways, the city's main park has a charming, old-fashioned feel. It's a popular center for such recreational activities as golf (p. 105), polo, biking, and picnicking. Especially notable is the **Japanese Tea Garden** (also known as the Japanese Sunken Garden), created in 1917 by prison labor to beautify an abandoned cement quarry. (The same quarry furnished cement rock for the state capitol in Austin.) You can still see a brick smokestack and a number of the old lime kilns among the beautiful flower arrangements—lusher than those in most Japanese gardens. The on-site **Jingu House Café** (www.jingu housesa.com/cafe, ✆ **210-559-3148**) is a serene spot to enjoy creative Asian fare or sip a cup of green tea. After the Pearl Harbor attack in 1941, the garden was officially renamed the Chinese Sunken Garden, and a Chinese-style entryway was added; the original name wasn't restored until 1983. Just to the southwest, a bowl of limestone cliffs found to have natural acoustic properties was turned into the **Sunken Garden Theater** (p. 121), with a 60-foot-high waterfall and water lily–laced ponds. Across from the entrance to the **San Antonio Zoological Gardens** (p. 93), you can buy tickets for the **San Antonio Zoo Eagle train** (www.sazoo.org/experiences/zoo-train; ✆ **210/734-7184**), a miniature train replicating an 1863 model, for a pleasant 2-mile ride through the park that takes about 20 minutes (tickets $4, children 2 and under ride free; daily 9:30am, weather permitting, until zoo gate closes).

3700 N. St. Mary's St. www.brackenridgepark.org. ✆ **210/826-1412.** Daily 5am–11pm. Bus: VIVA line 11.

San Pedro Creek Culture Park ★★ PARK Celebrated by Native Americans and, later, Spanish explorers for the lush beauty of its surroundings, the San Pedro Creek was channeled and diverted underground in the 20th century—much like its more famous counterpart, the San Antonio River. Judging from the first phase of this project, completed in 2018, the restoration of this body of water to its natural flow will be a major contribution to the ongoing beautification of downtown. Aquatic plants, shade trees, and perennials planted on the creek's shores have already begun to attract ducks and other native wildlife, while the new walkways that overlook them draw locals and visitors alike with such features as interpretive signs, benches, and local artwork. A free mobile app, downloadable from the website, provides an interactive audio walking tour of this remarkable linear park.

705 Camaron St. (Plaza de Fundacion), off I-35. www.spcculturepark.com. ✆ **210/302-3652**. Daily 5am–11pm. Bus: 44 or 82.

San Pedro Springs Park ★ PARK Established in 1729 by a grant from the king of Spain, this park built around the headwaters of San Pedro Creek is often said to be the second-oldest municipal park in the United States (the oldest being Boston Common). Located at the south end of the Alta Vista neighborhood, just north of downtown, it has a spring-fed swimming pool, tennis courts, a playground, entertainment gazebo, and the **Public Theater of San Antonio** (p. 122).

1315 N. San Pedro Ave. www.sanantonio.gov. Bus: 44 or 82.

ESPECIALLY FOR KIDS

The prime attractions for kids in San Antonio are **Six Flags Fiesta Texas** (p. 94), **SeaWorld** (p. 96), and **Morgan's** (p. 94). On the Broadway Cultural Corridor, the **DoSeum** (p. 90) provides a wonderful introduction to the city for pint-size folks, while the **Witte Museum** (p. 84) focuses on nature, science, and history; the **San Antonio Botanical Garden** (p. 82) is also very kid-friendly, with areas specifically designed to engage youngsters. **Battle for Texas: The Experience** (p. 86) is also a kid magnet, especially the Night at the Museum feature. By the time you read this, both the **Legoland Discovery Center** (https://sanantonio.legolanddiscoverycenter.com) and the **Sea Life Aquarium** (www.visitsealife.com/san-antonio) should be open in downtown's Shops at Rivercenter; they're slated for 2019.

Live-theater adaptations of beloved children's books are a specialty at **Magik Theatre ★**, 420 S. Alamo, in Hemisfair Park (www.magiktheatre.org; ✆ **210/227-2751**), which also hosts classes and camps for creative kids. The professional troupe performs a full season of plays; past shows have included *Dr. Seuss's The Cat in the Hat* and Roald Dahl's *Willy Wonka and the Chocolate Factory*. See p. 122.

In addition to these sights, there's a pair of three-fer commercial attractions on Alamo Plaza—Louis Tussaud's Waxworks, Ripley's Believe It or Not Odditorium, and Ripley's 4D Moving Theater (301 Alamo Plaza; www.ripleys.com/sanantonio; ✆ **210/224-9299**) and **Ripley's Haunted Adventure, Guinness World Records Museum, and Tomb Rider 3D** (329 Alamo Plaza; www.ripleys.com/phillips; ✆ **210/226-2828**). Their admission prices are relatively high, and they won't add anything to your knowledge of San Antonio. In fact, when their leases are up, they're likely to fall victim to local attempts to make the area adjacent to the Alamo less cheesy, more historically oriented. In the meantime, they're convenient places to keep bored kids occupied for a while—and guilty pleasures for grownups.

Splashtown ★ ATTRACTION Cool off at this 20-acre waterpark, which includes a huge wave pool, hydro tubes nearly 300 feet long, a Texas-size water bobsled, more than a dozen water slides, and a two-story playhouse for the smaller children. A variety of concerts, contests, and special events are held here.

3600 I-35 N. (exit 160, Splashtown Dr.). www.splashtownsa.com. ✆ **210/227-1400.** $34 adults, $29 children under 48 in., seniors 65+ and children under 2 free. Online discounts available; reduced admission after 4pm. Check website for exact dates and closing times, which change seasonally. Bus: 21.

ORGANIZED TOURS

In addition to the tours listed below, you can always opt for a carriage ride around downtown ($25 per person per 20 minutes). You can find carriages lined up around Alamo Plaza. You'll also see pedicabs (bicycle rickshaws) circulating. These don't have set routes or prices, but are generally inexpensive.

City Tours ★ This company serves up a mix-and-match menu of long and short guided bus and trolley tours, with a hop-on, hop-off option for the trolleys. Trolleys—among them a double-decker—focus on the city's key sights for shorter tours, while the larger buses travel farther to such destinations as the Hill Country for an 8-hour day.

101 Alamo Plaza (ticket office). www.citytoursinc.com. ✆ **210/492-4144.** Trolley tours start at $22 adults, $10 children. Full-day tours start at $79 adults, $62.50 seniors, $30 children 6–12. Tours run daily; earliest tours depart 9am, latest return is 4:30pm.

GO RIO Cruises ★ Maybe you've sat in a River Walk cafe looking out at people riding by in open, flat-bottom barges. Go ahead—give in and join 'em. The barges are colorful and eco-friendly, and the 35-minute tours are narrated by city experts, who will tell you about the history of the river. There are three spots on the river where you can buy a ticket and board a boat.

Ticket offices: Shops at Rivercenter, 849 E. River Walk; Historia, 706 River Walk; Aztec Theatre, 731 River Walk. www.goriocruises.com. ✆ **210/244-5700.** (Tickets can also be purchased online.) $12 adults, $9 seniors and active-duty military with ID, $6 children 5 and under. Boats depart daily every 15–20 min., from 9am–10pm.

San Antonio Bike Tours ★ These personalized guided excursions on recumbent tricycles are hard to beat for combining relaxation with education. You get to enjoy the fresh air, have a bit of exercise, and learn a great deal about the city without having to focus on keeping your balance as you would on a regular bicycle. Indeed, most of the trikes are tandem, so you share the pedaling. You're connected by radio intercom to company owner and certified guide Steve Wood, whose sense of humor and insider knowledge about the art, architecture, history, and personalities of the city make the tours an all-around delight.

875 E. Ashby Pl. www.sanantoniobiketours.cm. ✆ **210/823-2200.** 2-hr tours $75 per person, 4-hr tours $125 (includes a snack), 6-hr tours $200 (including a meal at a local restaurant), discount if you bring your own trike. Departure times depend on weather.

SegCity Tours ★ See some of downtown San Antonio while trying to master using one of these horseless chariots. Before the tour there's a little teaching session. Tours vary in length and price. ***Exercise caution:*** Sidewalks in San Antonio can be narrow, and pedestrians don't always lift their heads up from their phones.

124 Losoya St. www.segcity.com/sanantonio. ✆ **210/224-0773.** Tours start at $65 adults. Earliest tours depart 6:30am.

SPORTS & OUTDOOR ACTIVITIES

Many San Antonians head for the hills—that is, nearby Hill Country—for outdoor recreation; see chapter 9.

BIKING In the San Antonio Missions National Historical Park (p. 84), 8 miles of paved pathways are laid out as the **Mission Hike and Bike Trail** (www.nps.gov/saan/planyourvisit/hikebike), which has become extremely popular with cyclists as well as trekkers. The trail is not a loop, so the round-trip path is 16 miles long. It's about 3 miles between each of the five missions (the trail starts at the Alamo), however, so you can park at one of the southern four missions and tailor the length of your ride. Other options within San Antonio itself include: **Brackenridge Park** (p. 102); **McAllister Park** on the city's north side, 13102 Jones Maltsberger Rd. (✆ **210/207-7275** or 207-3120); and the area near **SeaWorld** (p. 96). If you didn't bring your own bike, San Antonio's **SWell bike share bicycles** (https://sanantonio.bcycle.com) are available all over town. Download the SWell Cycle app and it's as easy as using a credit or debit card to pick up a bike at any SWell Cycle station. Hourly, daily, weekly, monthly, and even annual rates are available. If you'd rather rent from a local who can give you personalized advice, **Blue Star Bike Shop,** in Southtown at 1414 S. Alamo St. (www.bluestarbikeshop.com; ✆ **210/858-0331**), will rent cruisers and other bikes.

FISHING For good angling close to town, try **Braunig Lake,** a 1,350-acre city-owned reservoir, a few miles southeast of San Antonio off I-37; and **Calaveras Lake,** one of Texas's great bass lakes, a few miles southeast of San Antonio off U.S. 181 S. and Loop 1604. A bit farther afield but still easy to reach from San Antonio are **Canyon Lake,** about 20 miles north of New Braunfels, and **Medina Lake,** just south of Bandera. Fishing licenses—sold at most sporting-goods and tackle stores and sporting-goods departments of large stores such as Wal-Mart or H-E-B, as well as at county courthouses and Parks and Wildlife Department offices—are required for all nonresidents; for current information, go to www.tpwd.texas.gov/business/licenses/online_sales or call ✆ **512/389-4800,** ext. 3. **Tackle Box Outfitters,** 6330 N. New Braunfels (www.tackleboxoutfitters.com; ✆ **210/821-5806**) can refer you to private guides for fishing trips on area rivers and on the Gulf coast ($500–$800 per person).

GOLF Golf is a big deal in San Antonio, with many visitors coming to town expressly to tee off. Of the city's municipal golf courses, two of the most notable are northwest San Antonio's **Cedar Creek,** 8250 Vista Colina (✆ **210/695-5050**), repeatedly ranked as south Texas's best municipal course; and **Brackenridge,** 2315 Ave. B (✆ **210/226-5612**), which is the oldest 18-hole public course in Texas (laid out in 1816), featuring oak- and pecan-shaded fairways. For details on these and other municipal courses, go to www.alamocitygolftrail.com. Other options for unaffiliated golfers include the high-end **Quarry,** 444 E. Basse Rd. (www.quarrygolf.com; ✆ **210/824-4500**), one of the city's most popular public courses; and **Canyon Springs,** 24405 Wilderness Oak Rd. (www.canyonspringsgc.com; ✆ **210/497-1770**), at the north edge of town in the Texas Hill Country, lush with live oaks and dotted with historic rock formations.

Top-notch resort courses in San Antonio include the two at **La Cantera Golf Club,** 16641 La Cantera Pkwy. (www.lacanteragolfclub.com; ✆ **210/558-4653**)—one designed by Jay Morish and Tom Weiskopf, the other by Arnold Palmer—with knockout designs and dramatic hill-and-rock outcroppings. Equally nice are the resort courses of the **JW Marriott Hill Country Resort & Spa,** 23808 Resort Pkwy. (www.marriott.com/hotels/travel/satjw-jw-marriott-san-antonio-hill-country-resort-and-spa; ✆ **210/491-5806**). Its AT&T Canyons Course was designed by Pete Dye and PGA Tour Player Consultant Bruce Lietzke; its AT&T Oaks Course was designed by Greg Norman and PGA Tour Player Consultant Sergio Garcia. Both are built with the infrastructure to host PGA tour tournaments. The JW Marriott resort offers a nice "Stay and Play" golf vacation package, too.

Expect to pay $50 to $80 per person for an 18-hole round at a municipal course, plus a $16 (not including tax) fee for a cart, and from $70 up to $205 (Sat–Sun) per person at a private resort course. Twilight (afternoon) rates are often cheaper.

HIKING The 600-acre nature preserve **Friedrich Wilderness Park,** 21480 Milsa St. (www.sanantonio.gov/parksandrec; ✆ **210/207-3780**), operated by the city of San Antonio, is crisscrossed by 5.5 miles of trails that attract birdwatchers as well as hikers; some stretches are accessible to people with disabilities. The **Mission Hike and Bike Trail** along the River Walk Mission Reach has 8 miles of dedicated paved pathways for hikers and bikers (see "Biking," above). **Enchanted Rock State Natural Area,** near Fredericksburg, is the most popular spot for trekking out of town (p. 146).

RIVER SPORTS For tubing, rafting, or canoeing along a cypress-lined river, San Antonio river rats head 35 miles northwest of downtown to the 2,000-acre **Guadalupe River State Park,** 3350 Park Rd. 31 (www.tpwd.texas.gov/state-parks/guadalupe-river; ✆ **830/438-2656**), near Boerne. About 5 miles north of Hwy. 46, just outside the park, you can rent tubes, rafts, and canoes at the **Bergheim Campground,** 103 White Water Rd. (www.bergheimcampground.com; ✆ **830/336-2235**).

SWIMMING/WATERPARKS Most hotels have swimming pools, but if yours doesn't, the Parks and Recreation Department (www.sanantonio.gov/sapar/swimming.asp; ✆ **210/207-3113**) can direct you to the nearest municipal pool. **Morgan's Wonderland** (p. 94), **SeaWorld** (p. 96), and **Six Flags** (p. 94), all have water park sections; **Splashtown** (p. 103) is another prime place to get wet. Many San Antonians head out to New Braunfels to get wet at the huge **Schlitterbahn** (p. 301).

TENNIS With a reservation, you can play at the 22 lighted hard courts at San Pedro Springs Park's **McFarlin Tennis Center,** 1503 San Pedro Ave. (www.sanantonio.gov/ParksAndRec/Home/tennis; ✆ **210/207-5357**), for the very reasonable fee of $6.25 per adult per hour before 5pm, $7.25 per adult per hour after 5pm ($3.25 per hour for students/seniors before 5pm, $4.25 after 5pm). For more about this court and others in the area, as well as details about tournaments, contact the **San Antonio Tennis Association** (www.satennis.com; ✆ **210/735-3069**).

SHOPPING IN SAN ANTONIO

7

San Antonio offers shoppers a nice balance of large malls and little enclaves of specialized shops, along with one-off boutiques scattered around the city. You'll find everything here from the utilitarian to the unusual: a Saks Fifth Avenue fronted by a 40-foot pair of cowboy boots, a mall with a river running through it, and some lively Mexican markets.

Most shops around town are open from 9 or 10am to 5:30 or 6pm Monday through Saturday, with shorter hours on Sunday. Malls are generally open Monday through Saturday 10am to 9pm and on Sunday noon to 6pm. Sales tax in San Antonio is 8.25%.

THE SHOPPING SCENE

Most out-of-town shoppers will find all they need **downtown,** between the boutiques and crafts shops of La Villita, the colorful Mexican wares of Market Square, and the large Shops at Rivercenter, near the Alamo. More avant-garde boutiques and galleries can be found in the adjacent area known as **Southtown.** Just north of downtown, the **Pearl complex** is the latest hip retail hub. Most San Antonians prefer to shop in the suburban malls along Loop 410 and Loop 1604. A number of upmarket retail outlets can also be found in the fancy strip centers that line Broadway, where it passes through Alamo Heights.

Between Austin and San Antonio along I-35, two adjacent outlet malls form one of south Texas's largest tourist destinations: the **Tanger Factory Outlet Center** and **Premium Outlets,** with more than 350 stores and more than 1,000,000 square feet of shopping (p. 294).

Malls/Shopping Complexes

Alamo Quarry Market ★★ Alamo Quarry Market may be its official name, but no one ever calls this popular mall anything but "The Quarry" (from the early 1900s until 1985, the property was in fact a cement quarry). Its four smokestacks, lit up dramatically at night, now signal play, not work. There are no department store anchors, just a series of large emporiums (Old Navy, Bed Bath

Central San Antonio Shopping

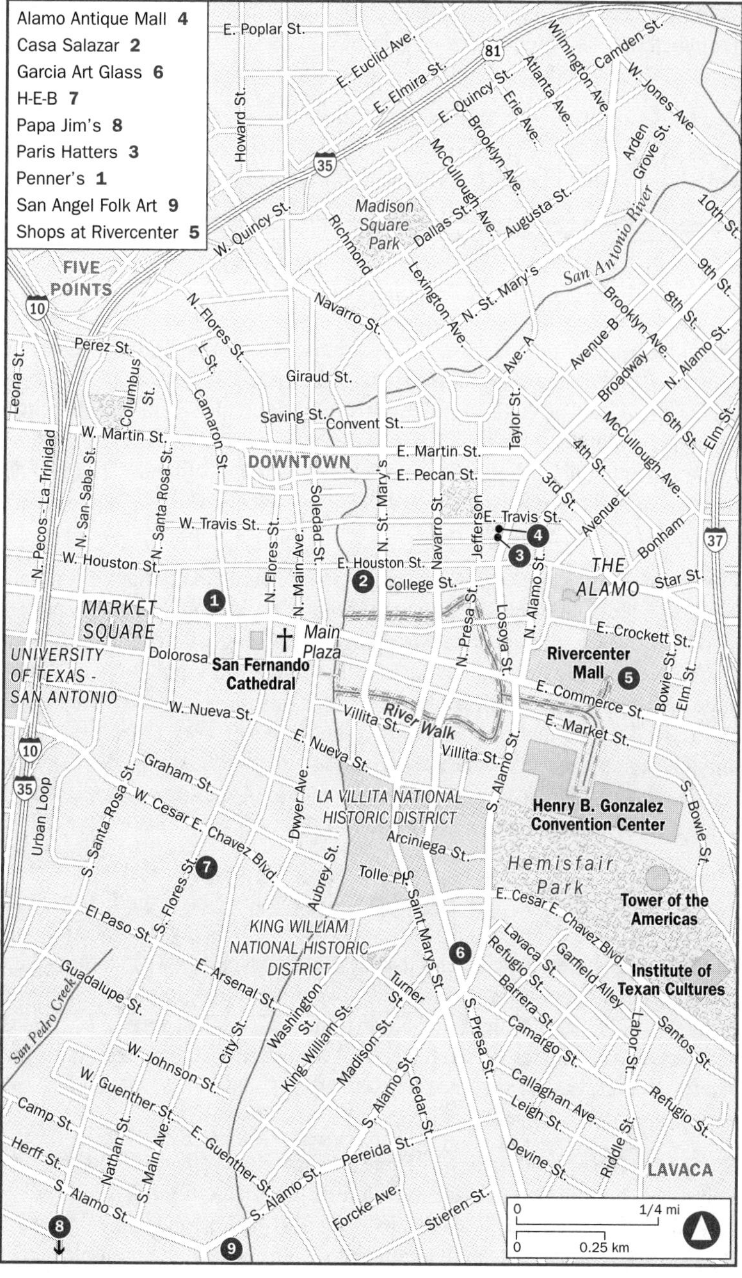

& Beyond, Pottery Barn, Gap) and smaller upscale boutiques (Ann Taylor, Jos. A. Bank, and Lucchese Gallery; see p. 117). Also on the premises: a multiplex cinema and an array of eateries, from Chili's to Fleming's to Piatti's, an Italian eatery well-liked by locals. 255 E. Basse Rd. www.quarrymarket.com. ✆ **210/824-8885.**

North Star Mall ★ Starring Saks Fifth Avenue and such upscale boutiques as Vera Bradley and Louis Vuitton, this is the crème de la crème of the San Antonio indoor malls. It also has highly desired outlets, such as an Apple Store. But there are many sensible shops here, too, including a JCPenney department store. Food choices climb up and down the scale, ranging from a Godiva Chocolatier to a Chick-Fil-A. Loop 410, btw. McCullough and San Pedro aves. www.northstarmall.com. ✆ **210/340-6627.**

Pearl ★★★ A popular weekend farmers market, 14 carefully selected boutiques, and a gourmet grocery store (The Larder, in the Hotel Emma) are among the draws of the 22-acre Pearl Brewery complex. Some of the city's best dining spots (see chapter 5, p. 66) are here as well. A splash pad, grassy spots for lounging, a shop that rents bikes, and the kid-friendly Twig bookstore make this a fun destination for the whole family. Grayson St. and Ave. A. www.atpearl.com. ✆ **210/212-7260.**

The RIM ★★ Right across I-10 from the more upmarket Shops at La Cantera (see below), this sprawling outdoor complex is as much an entertainment and dining destination as it is a shopping stop. Along with chain stores such as Old Navy, Bass Pro Shop, and Best Buy, there's a wide range of dining options (38 of them!), from IHOP to Texas chains like Hopdoddy Burger Bar and Lupe Tortilla, and San Antonio's homegrown Bakery Lorraine. It's the only place in town—maybe in the country—where you can go indoor skydiving, bowl, play miniature golf, and see a movie in the same place. 17703 La Cantera Pkwy. www.therimsa.com. ✆ **210/641-1777.**

The Shops at La Cantera ★★ The city's newest, fanciest mall is in far northwest San Antonio, off Loop 1604, beside the Six Flags Fiesta Texas theme park. Like the nearby RIM (see above), it's a nicely designed outdoor mall. All the stores face a central pedestrian concourse, with parking kept separate, behind the stores. Anchored by two of San Antonio's fanciest department stores, Neiman Marcus and Nordstrom, it also offers several boutiques, jewelers, and cosmetics stores. It's perfect for mixed-tech families: Apple and Microsoft both have a presence here. 15900 La Cantera Pkwy. www.theshopsatlacantera.com. ✆ **210/582-6255.**

Shops at Rivercenter ★★ There's a festive atmosphere at this bustling, light-filled mall located on an extension of the San Antonio River. You can pick up a river taxi from a downstairs dock or listen to bands play on a stage surrounded by water. Other entertainment options include the multiple-screen AMC (where the IMAX screens *The Alamo*) and the Rivercenter Comedy

Club. The shops—more than 100 of them, anchored by Macy's—run the price gamut, but tend toward upscale casual. Food picks range from Dairy Queen and Chipotle to Morton's of Chicago and Fogo de Chao. This can be a great place to shop, but remember that it's thronged with teens on Friday and Saturday nights. 849 E. Commerce, btw. S. Alamo and Bowie sts. www.shoprivercenter.com. ✆ **210/225-0000.**

Markets

There's a popular farmers market at the **Pearl** (see above) on Saturdays and Sundays; the First Thursday market in Pearl Park features lots of local vendors as well as free live music. See p. 88 for details on the lively Mexican Market at Market Square.

FLEA MARKETS

Bussey's Flea Market ★ Though it's a bit out of the way (unless you're heading to New Braunfels or Austin), Bussey's is definitely worth the half-hour drive from downtown, with 500-plus vendors selling goods from as far afield as Asia and Africa. Crafts, jewelry, antiques, incense—it's hard to imagine anything you couldn't find at this market. 18738 I-35 N. www.busseysfm.com. ✆ **210/651-6830.**

Eisenhauer Road Flea Market ★ This air-conditioned indoor flea market, complete with grill and bar, is a good site to hit at the height of summer. You'll see lots of new stuff here—purses, jewelry, furniture, toys, shoes—and everything from houseplants to kinky leatherwear. 3903 Eisenhauer Rd. www.eisenhauerfleamarketsa.net. ✆ **210/468-1081.** Closed Mon–Tues.

Flea Mart ★ On weekends, Mexican-American families make a day of this huge market, bringing the entire family to catch up, listen to live bands, and eat freshly made tacos. There are always fruits and vegetables, electronics, crafts, and new and used clothing—and you never know what else. 12280 Poteet Jourdanton Fwy. (about 1 mile S. of Loop 410). www.fleamarketsanantonio.com. ✆ **210/624-2666.**

SHOPPING A TO Z

Antiques

A number of antiques shops line Hildebrand Avenue between Blanco Road and San Pedro Avenue in Monte Vista, and along McCullough Avenue between Hildebrand and Basse Road in Olmos Park. Serious antiques hounds might head to the town of **Boerne,** about half an hour away, where many shops are concentrated along Main Street (p. 134).

Alamo Antique Mall ★ The easiest way for visitors to go antiques shopping is to try this downtown collection of 100 independent dealers distributed among three floors in the old Anderson Building. It's just a few blocks from the Alamo. Inside, you'll find for sale just about anything that is collected, from jewelry to furniture, from military memorabilia to glassware. 125 Broadway. www.alamoantiquemall.com. ✆ **210/224-4354.**

Art Galleries

ArtPace and the **Southwest School of Art,** both downtown, and **Blue Star Contemporary Arts Center** in Southtown (see chapter 6 for details on all three) have the city's highest concentrations of cutting-edge art by up-and-coming artists. For information on other galleries and the art scene in general, visit the **Office of Cultural Affairs** website (www.getcreativesanantonio.com). For events held during **Contemporary Art Month** every March, see www.contemporaryartmonth.com. The following galleries show more established artists.

NanEtte Richardson Fine Art ★ Come here for a wide array of oil paintings, watercolors, bronzes, ceramics, and handcrafted wood furnishings. 555 E. Basse Rd. www.nanetterichardsonfineart.com. ✆ **210/930-1343.**

Parchman Stremmel ★★ Specializing in contemporary work by regional, national, and international artists who have made it big (or come close), this gallery caters to well-heeled individuals and corporate clients. 7726 Broadway. www.psgart.com. ✆ **210/824-8990.**

Books

Cheever Books ★★ Just across the road from the Witte Museum, this San Antonio institution has a huge selection of used books of all kinds, along with the city's largest stock of rare antiquarian volumes. 2613 Broadway. ✆ **210/824-2665.**

The Twig ★★ The literary hub of the Pearl complex, this bright and cheerful bookstore showcases the latest reads for children and adults, as well as classic literature. A large Texana collection, author readings, and other special events make this the most popular indie bookstore in town. Pearl Brewery, 306 Pearl Pkwy., Ste. 106. www.thetwig.com. ✆ **210/826-6411.**

Crafts/Folk Art

As noted in the introduction, La Villita and Market Square, in the downtown historic area, are both good resources for crafts, especially Mexican imports and Mexican folk art. See also **Fiesta on Main** (p. 115) and **La Casa Frida** (p. 116).

Casa Salazar ★ This colorful store next door to the Majestic Theatre's box office has a wide selection of Mexican crafts, including crosses, jewelry, milagros, and a little furniture. 216 E. Houston St. www.themajestic.com/casa. ✆ **210/472-2272.**

Garcia Art Glass, Inc. ★★★ You'll see many of the wild and colorful glass bowls, wall sconces, and mobiles created in this Southtown shop at upscale hotels around town. Often, especially in the morning, you can watch glass blowers at work behind the store. The bracelets and other pretty baubles made out of glass beads are the most portable. 715 S. Alamo St. www.garciaartglass.com. ✆ **210/354-4681.**

San Angel Folk Art ★★★ One of the best folk art stores in Texas, San Angel has a sizable collection of pieces from Mexico and Latin America, along with the work of American folk artists, including some talented locals. Pottery, baskets, textiles, clothing, tinwork, wood carvings—there's much to look at. 110 Blue Star. www.sanangelfolkart.com. ✆ **210/226-6688.**

Fashion

The following stores offer clothing in a variety of styles; if you're keen on the cowpuncher look, see "Western Wear," p. 116.

CHILDREN'S

Bambinos Boutique ★ Whether your child goes for the English-country look or veers more toward punk rocker, you'll find clothing to suit his or her (okay, probably your) tastes at this delightful store, which also carries maternity clothes and a great selection of kiddie room furnishings and toys. The focus is on the younger set—infants to age 12. 999 E. Basse Rd., Ste. 196. bambinosboutique.com. ✆ **210/824-7676.**

MEN'S

Dos Carolinas ★★ Talk about specialization—this clothier has been known since the late 1980s for one thing: custom-tailored *guayaberas.* These men's shirts, worn throughout Latin America and the Caribbean for special occasions as well as for everyday comfort in the heat, come in several basic styles. Only natural fabrics are used here. Pearl Brewery, 303 Pearl Pkwy., Ste. 102. www.doscarolinas.com. ✆ **210/224-7000.**

Penner's ★★ You'd be hard pressed to find a man or boy's body type or style preference that this downtown institution (opened 1916) doesn't cater to, from head to toe. Panama hats and fedoras, Dockers and dress shoes, *guayaberas* and classic business shirts, custom-made suits . . . the store has them all. Goods of this quality don't come cheap, but alterations are free and the products will last for a long, long time. 311 W. Commerce. www.pennersinc.com. ✆ **210/239-0735.**

Satel's ★★ This family-run Alamo Heights store has been the place to shop for menswear in San Antonio since 1950; classic, high-quality clothing and personal service make it a standout. The staff is both helpful and knowledgeable about different clothing styles. 5100 Broadway. www.satels.com. ✆ **210/822-3376.**

WOMEN'S

Adelante Boutique ★ The focus here is on free-flowing clothes made with colorful, natural fabrics, embroidery, and hand weaving. You'll also find a good selection of artistic jewelry, leather belts, and other accessories. Pearl Brewery, 303 Pearl Pkwy., Ste. 107. www.adelanteboutique.com. ✆ **210/826-6770.**

Couleur + Blindé ★★ Opened in 2018 by *Project Runway*'s All-Star Winner, Anthony Ryan, this Alamo Heights boutique is for girls (and women) who just wanna have fun with fashion. Clothing lines by Ryan mingle with those of other Project Runway winners, as well as labels from New York, Los Angeles, and other fashion centers. The styles are not for everyone, but the prices are surprisingly accessible. And, yes, the name is tongue-in-cheek and is pronounced "color blind." Ryan has another store called **Anthill** in the Stone Oak area, north of Loop 1604. 4704 Broadway. www.couleurblinde.com. ✆ **210/480-1807.**

Kathleen Sommers ★ This small shop on the corner of Main and Woodlawn has been setting trends for San Antonio women for years. Kathleen Sommers, who works mainly in linen and other natural fabrics, designs all the clothes that bear her label. The store also carries eye-catching bags and purses, great jewelry, bath items, books, fun housewares, and a selection of unusual gifts. 2417 N. Main St. www.kathleensommers.com. ✆ **210/732-8437.**

Red Cat & Co. ★★ A retrofitted vintage bus is the perfect setting for clothing created by local Texas designers—everything from feminist T-shirts to little black dresses—along with handcrafted candles, jewelry, essential oils, art prints, and more. This is a treasure trove for those seeking to buy a distinctive gift or make a strong personal adornment statement. 2202 Broadway (in the Broadway News complex). www.redcatandco.com. ✆ **210/912-3955.**

Food

Central Market ★★ You'll feel as though you've died and gone to food heaven as you walk amid gorgeous mounds of produce, cheeses and other dairy products, sauces, pastas, and more in this branch of the Austin-born supermarket chain (it's now owned by H-E-B, headquartered in San Antonio). If you don't want to just graze, there are freshly prepared hot and cold gourmet foods, including a soup and salad bar, and a seating area in which to enjoy them. Wine tastings and cooking classes draw crowds in the evenings. 4821 Broadway. www.centralmarket.com. ✆ **210/368-8600.**

H-E-B South Flores ★★ You'll find H-E-B grocery stores all over San Antonio—the privately owned Texas chain originated in 1905—but this downtown branch, adjacent to H-E-B's new corporate headquarters, is more upscale than most. Among the highlights: plenty of fresh produce, fish, and meats (organic and grass-fed included); daily-made baked goods; a huge selection of wine and craft beer (some on tap); a pizzeria; and a coffee bar. Lots of natural light and colorful local art enhance the shopping experience, and you can enjoy your grab-and-go meals on a cheerful outdoor patio. A bike rack and a parking lot—as well as a gas station—make this location ultra-convenient. 516 S. Flores St. www.HEB.com. ✆ **210/444-1879.**

Gifts/Souvenirs

See also **La Casa Frida** (below) and **Red Cat & Co.** (above).

Felíz Modern ★★ This colorful store in Olmos Park stocks more than 5,000 items, ranging from art prints and home goods to party supplies and dog accessories. 110 W. Olmos Dr. www.felizmodern.com. ✆ **210/622-8364.**

Fiesta on Main ★★ Head just north of downtown to this two-level store near Monte Vista for a huge selection of Mexican folk art and handicrafts—everything from tinwork to colorful masks and piñatas—at extremely reasonable prices. Less touristy than most such shops, Fiesta on Main is geared to local Hispanic families looking to celebrate special occasions. The newer **Fiesta at North Star,** 102 W. Rector St. (✆ **210/738-1189**) has the same merchandise, easier parking. 2025 N. Main Ave. at Ashby Pl. www.alamofiesta.com. ✆ **210/738-1188.**

Sloan/Hall ★ A cross between the Body Shop, Sharper Image, and Barnes and Noble, only more concentrated and more upscale, this addictive boutique carries an assortment of toiletries, gadgets, books, and those uncategorizable items that you probably don't need but find you desperately want. 5424 Broadway. www.sloanhall.com. ✆ **210/828-7738.**

Ten Thousand Villages ★ If you're not familiar with the Ten Thousand Villages stores, created to distribute and sell handcrafts by artisans in developing countries at a fair price, this airy branch in the Pearl complex provides an

love potion NO. 9

Ask a proprietor of a **botanica,** "What kind of store is this?" and you'll hear anything from "a drugstore" to "a religious bookstore." But along with Christian artifacts (including glow-in-the-dark rosaries and dashboard icons), botanicas carry magic floor washes, candles designed to keep the law off your back, wolf skulls, amulets, herbal remedies, and, of course, love potions. The common theme is happiness enhancement, whether by self-improvement, prayer, or luck.

Many of San Antonio's small botanicas specialize in articles used by *curanderos,* traditional folk doctors or medicine men and women. Books directing laypersons in the use of medicinal herbs sit next to volumes that retell the lives of the saints. It's easy enough to figure out the use of the *santos* (saints), candles in tall glass jars bearing such labels as "Peaceful Home," "Find Work," and "Bingo." *Milagros* (miracles) are small charms that represent parts of the body—or mind—that a person wishes to have healed. Many of the labels are in Spanish; the person behind the counter will be happy to translate them for you if necessary.

San Antonio's best-known botanica is **Papa Jim's ★**, 5630 S. Flores (www.papajimsbotanica.com; ✆ **210/922-6665**). Although Papa Jim, who used to bless the various artifacts he sold, died a few years ago, the shop still thrives. Can't make it to the shop? Order online, or get a copy of Papa Jim's comprehensive print catalog by phoning or ordering through the website.

excellent introduction. Come here for feel-good-about-the-source gifts, jewelry, home decor, clothing, and more. You'll find everything from traditional baskets to more unusual items such as a tablet-charging stand made from recycled circuit boards. 302 Pearl Pkwy., Ste. 114. www.tenthousandvillages.com/sanantonio. ✆ **210/444-1393.**

Jewelry

La Casa Frida ★★ What would Frida Kahlo wear (or carry or have in her house)? That seems to be the guiding principle behind the bright, bold, and colorful items sold in this converted airstream trailer. The jewelry, including handmade earrings from Oaxaca, sacred heart pendants from Mexico City, and beaded bracelets made by Huichol people, is especially noteworthy. Everything is bought from artisans throughout Mexico at fair-trade prices. Shops at Broadway News, 2202 Broadway. www.lacasafrida.com. ✆ **210/920-1907.**

Gavin Metalsmith ★ For contemporary metal craft with a flair, come to this small gallery, where the exquisite original pieces range from wedding rings to salt-and-pepper shakers. The work sold here incorporates lots of unusual stones into silver and white-gold settings. 4024 McCullough Ave. www.patgavin.com. ✆ **210/82-5254.**

Shoes

SAS Shoemakers ★★ Men and women have been coming here to buy comfortable and handsome shoes and sandals since 1976. The brand is well known for making shoes without cutting corners, and you'll now find many SAS stores around the country. There are several branches in San Antonio, too, but the factory store, on the south side of town, is the one to visit. You can even take one of three daily factory tours Monday through Thursday; call ahead for reservations. 101 New Laredo Hwy. www.sasshoes.com. ✆ **210/921-7415** or 924-6507 (tour reservations).

Western Wear

D&D Farm and Ranch Superstore ★★★ For one of the best and most authentic Western shopping experiences in Texas, mosey on outside of town about 35 miles east to Seguin, where D&D sells everything from saddles, spurs, horse trailers, and firepits to cowboy boots, jeans, cowboy hats, home decor, and children's Western toys. If it's your first time in Texas, this place will wow you; it's worth the trip. 516 I-10 Frontage Rd. (exit 609 off I-10). www.ddtexasoutfitters.com. ✆ **830/379-7340.**

Little's Boots ★★★ Lucchese (see below) is better known, but this place—established in 1915—uses as many esoteric leathers and creates fancier footwear designs. You can get anything you like bespoke if you're willing to wait a while—possibly in line behind Reba McEntire or Tommy Lee Jones, both of whom have had boots handcrafted here. Purchase some just so you can tell your friends back home, "Oh, Lucchese is so commercial. Little's is still the real deal." 110 Division Ave. www.littlesboots.com. ✆ **210/923-2221.**

Lucchese Gallery ★★ The term "gallery" is apt indeed: Footwear is raised to the level of art at Lucchese. The store carries boots made of alligator, elephant, ostrich, pirarucu, shark, lizard—basically, if it ever crawled, ran, hopped, or swam, these folks can probably put it on your feet. Come here for everything from executive to special-occasion boots, all handmade and expensive, all serious Texas status symbols. Lucchese also carries jackets, belts, and sterling silver belt buckles. 255 E. Basse Rd., Ste. 800. www.lucchese.com. ✆ **210/828-9419.**

Paris Hatters ★★★ What do Pope John Paul II, Bob Dylan, Jimmy Smits, and Dwight Yoakam have in common? They've all had headgear made for them by Paris Hatters, in business since 1917 and still owned by the original family. About half of the sales are special orders, but the shelves are stocked with high-quality, ready-to-wear hats, including Kangol caps from Britain, Panama hats from Ecuador, Borsalino hats from Italy, and, of course, Stetson, Resistol, Dobbs, and other Western brands. A lot of them can be adjusted to your liking while you wait. Check out the pictures and newspaper articles in the back of the store to see which other famous heads have been covered here. 119 Broadway. www.parishatters.com. ✆ **210/223-3453.**

Wines and Spirits

See also **Central Market** and **H-E-B,** p. 114.

Gabriel's ★ A large, warehouse-style store, Gabriel's combines good selection with good prices. On any given day, you never know what bargains on wine, spirits, or beer you'll find. Opened in 1948 by the Gabriel family, the store now has 15 locations in the greater San Antonio area; you're bound to be near one, wherever you are. The Hildebrand store is slightly north of downtown; there's also a location downtown at 606 Broadway (✆ **210/858-9171**). 837 Hildebrand Ave. www.gabrielsliquor.com. ✆ **210/735-8329.**

JS Fine Wine & Spirits ★★ When Joe Saglimbenni and his brother Robert opened a wine store in San Antonio in 1990, it was the first in the area to provide temperature and humidity control for their bottles. The shop is not especially convenient to most visitor attractions, but oenophiles and neophytes alike might want to make the trip on Saturday when free afternoon tastings focus on a different wine (and sometimes a spirit) each week. There's outdoor seating and a food truck, the better to enjoy your purchases. 638 W. Rhapsody Dr. www.jsfinewines.com. ✆ **210/349-5149.**

8 SAN ANTONIO ARTS & NIGHTLIFE

San Antonio has its symphony and its Broadway shows and some of the most beautiful restored movie palaces in the country. But much of what the city has to offer is less mainstream. Latin influences, especially, lend sabor to some of the best local nightlife. San Antonio is the birthplace of Tejano music, a unique blend of German polka and northern Mexico ranchero sounds (with a dose of pop added for good measure). And Southtown, with its many Hispanic-oriented shops and galleries, celebrates its art scene with the monthly First Friday and Second Saturdays, extended block parties with a cultural kick.

First Friday, the original and still the largest of these mini-Fiestas, centers around the Blue Star complex (p. 91) and surrounding blocks. Its spinoff, **Second Saturday,** features less-established artists and galleries, with its hub the Freight gallery on South Flores Street and the surrounding area—which, predictably, has been rebranded as "SoFlo."

But the Fiesta City throws big public parties year-round: Fiestas Navideñas and Las Posadas around Christmastime, Fiesta San Antonio and Cinco de Mayo events in spring, the Texas Folklife Festival in summer, and Oktoberfest in autumn (see p. 34 for a calendar of events). Oktoberfest in particular is fun way to tap into San Antonio's German heritage with the city's renewed craft brewing scene.

For the most complete current listings for the time when you're visiting, pick up a free copy of the weekly alternative newspaper, the ***Current,*** or the Friday "Weekender" section of the ***San Antonio Express-News.*** You can also check out the website of **San Antonio Department of Arts & Culture:** www.getcreativesanantonio.com. There's no central office in town for tickets, discounted or otherwise; you'll need to reserve seats directly through the venues. Generally, box office hours are Monday to Friday 10am to 5pm, and 1 to 2 hours before performance time.

THE PERFORMING ARTS

The San Antonio Symphony is the city's only resident performing arts company of national stature, but smaller groups keep the local arts scene lively, and cultural organizations draw world-renowned artists. The city provides them with some unique venues—everything from standout historic structures such as the Majestic, Empire, Aztec, Arneson, and Sunken Garden theaters to the massive AT&T Center arena.

Major Arts Venues

The Aztec Theater ★★★ A paean to Meso-American architecture, this theater is much loved by San Antonians. When it opened in 1926, it was one of the most ornately decorated movie houses in the nation; the three-ton, two-story chandelier in the lobby was said to be the largest in Texas. Since reopening in 2015 it has featured concerts from national touring artists including Snoop Dogg, Los Lonely Boys, and Eagles of Death Metal. 104 N. St. Mary's St. www.theaztectheatre.com. ✆ **210/812-4355.**

Majestic and Empire Theatres ★★★ The Majestic Theatre introduced air-conditioning to San Antonio—the hall was billed as "an acre of cool, comfortable seats"—and society women wore fur coats to its opening, held on a warm June night in 1929 (see box below). The slightly smaller Charlene McComb Empire Theatre, just around the corner, is not far behind in swankiness. Nowadays, they are managed by the same company and host a variety of performances, including the occasional San Antonio Symphony concerts (p. 121), traveling Broadway shows, and a variety of musical and theater productions. 224 E. Houston St. (Majestic) & 226 N. St. Mary's St. (Empire). www.majesticempire.com. ✆ **210/226-5700.**

Tobin Center for the Performing Arts ★★★ Designed by famed Texas architect Atlee Ayres in 1926 as the San Antonio Municipal Auditorium, in 2014 the remodeled and expanded Tobin was re-opened as a

A Theater That Lives Up to Its Name

Everyone from Jack Benny to Mae West played the **Majestic ★★★**, one of the last "atmospheric" theaters to be built in America: The stock market crashed 4 months after its June 1929 debut, and after that no one could afford to build such expensive showplaces anymore. Designed in baroque Moorish/Spanish revival style by John Eberson, this former vaudeville and film palace features an elaborate village above the sides of the stage and, overhead, a magnificent night sky dome, replete with twinkling stars and scudding clouds. Designated a National Historic Landmark, the Majestic affords a rare glimpse into a gilded era (yes, there's genuine gold leaf detailing).

world-class performance venue. The main space, the 800-seat H-E-B Performance Hall, has a seemingly magical capacity to adjust stage and seat configurations; two smaller performance spaces were added in the redesign, one inside the building and one outside adjacent to the River Walk, which can be used independently and concurrently to the main hall. The Tobin functions as the main home for the San Antonio Symphony (p. 121), San Antonio Chamber Choir, OPERA San Antonio, and Ballet San Antonio, as well as smaller arts groups; it has hosted acts such as Paul McCartney, Wilco, and David Byrne in the past few years. 115 Auditorium Circle. www.tobincenter.org. ✆ **210/223-3333** or 210/223-8624 (box office).

Other Arts Venues

In addition to the **Alamodome,** 100 Montana St. (www.sanantonio.gov/dome; ✆ **210/207-3663**), which sits just east of Hemisfair park on the edge of downtown, San Antonio's major concert venues include **Verizon Wireless Amphitheater,** 16765 Lookout Rd., just north of Loop 1604 (www.vwatx.com; ✆ **210/657-8300**), and, when the Spurs aren't playing basketball there, downtown's **AT&T Center,** One AT&T Center Pkwy. (www.nba.com/spurs; ✆ **210/444-5000**). See p. 95 for information on the **Alameda Theater.**

Arneson River Theatre ★★★ If you're visiting San Antonio in the summer, try seeing something at the Arneson. Built by the Work Projects Administration (WPA) in 1939 as part of architect Robert Hugman's design for the River Walk, this unique theater has a stage on one side of a narrow section of the river, with seating on the opposite side. Most of the year, performance schedules are erratic and include everything from opera to Tejano, but summer brings a stricter calendar: The Fiesta Noche del Río takes the stage every Friday and Saturday from May through July, and the Fandango folkloric troupe performs on Tuesdays and Thursdays in June and July. Both offer lively music and dance with a south-of-the-border flair. La Villita, 418 Villita St. www.lavillitasanantonio.com/venues. ✆ **210/207-8614.**

Beethoven Halle and Garten ★★ San Antonio's German heritage is celebrated at this venue, a converted 1894 Victorian mansion in the King William area. The Garten is the site of various events celebrated with beer, with bands playing everything from oompah to rock, as well as regular performances by the Mannerchor (men's choir), which dates back to 1867. Lots of traditional German food, drink, and revelry make Oktoberfest an autumn high point. In December, a *Kristkrindle Markt* welcomes the holiday season with a European–style arts-and-crafts fair. 422 Pereida St. (at S. Alamo St.). www.beethovenmaennerchor.com. ✆ **210/222-1521.**

Carver Community Cultural Center ★★ Located just east of downtown, the Carver theater was built by the city's African-American community in 1929, and over the years hosted the likes of Ella Fitzgerald, Charlie "Bird"

Parker, and Dizzy Gillespie. It continues to serve the community while providing a widely popular venue for an international array of performers in various genres, including drama, music, and dance. 226 N. Hackberry. www.thecarver.org. ✆ **210/207-7211**.

Guadalupe Cultural Arts Center ★ There's always something happening at the Guadalupe Center, based in a 1942 Art Deco/Mission Revival movie house just southwest of downtown. Visiting and local directors put on six or seven plays a year; the resident Guadalupe Dance Company might collaborate with the San Antonio Symphony or invite modern masters up from Mexico City; the annual Tejano Conjunto Festival (see box p. 126) is the largest of its kind; and the CineFestival, running since 1977, is one of the town's major film events. Parties are often thrown to celebrate new installations at the theater's art gallery and its annex, around the corner at 723 S. Brazos St. 1301 Guadalupe St. www.guadalupeculturalarts.org. ✆ **210/271-3151.**

Laurie Auditorium ★ Some pretty high-powered people turn up at the Laurie Auditorium, on the Trinity University campus north of downtown. Everyone from Paul Krugman and Jane Goodall to Vicente Fox and Jimmy Carter have taken part in its Distinguished Lecture Series. The 2,700-seat hall also hosts major players in the popular and performing arts: Duran Duran and Alison Krauss were among those who took the stage in recent years. Dance recitals, jazz concerts, and plays, many with internationally renowned artists, are held here, too. Trinity University, 715 Stadium Dr. https://new.trinity.edu/visitors. ✆ **210/999-8117** (box office) or 210/999-7011.

Sunken Garden Theater ★★ Built by the WPA in 1936 in a natural acoustic bowl in Brackenridge Park, the Sunken Garden Theater features an open-air stage set against a wooded hillside; cut-limestone buildings in Greek Revival style hold the wings and the dressing rooms. This appealing outdoor arena offers a little bit of everything—rock, country, hip-hop, rap, jazz, Tejano, Cajun, and sometimes even the San Antonio Symphony. Annual events include Taste of New Orleans (a Fiesta event in April) and the Margarita Pour-Off in August. Check www.sanantonio.gov/ParksAndRec for current information. Brackenridge Park, 3875 N. St. Mary's St. (Mulberry Ave. entrance). ✆ **210/207-7275.**

Classical Music

San Antonio Symphony ★★ Founded in 1939, the city's symphony orchestra performs from September to May, usually with two concert series, one classical and the other pops. Current music director Sebastian Lang-Lessing is a German native who has conducted orchestras around the world, including the Tokyo Philharmonic and the Orchestre de Paris. He is particularly well known for his opera direction, including work with the opera companies of San Francisco, Houston, and Los Angeles, as well as the Washington National Opera. Tobin Center, 100 Auditorium Circle. www.sasymphony.org. ✆ **210/223-8644** (box office) or 210/554-1000 (administration). Tickets $10–$96.

Youth Orchestra of San Antonio ★ Around in one form or another since 1949, this company has been led since 2008 by musical director Troy Peters. Its nine orchestras—two full orchestras, a wind ensemble, a flute choir, and five string orchestras—put on multiple performances throughout the season, including their Classic Albums Live series, featuring dozens of local musicians and partnering with the "grownup" Symphony for a side-by-side concert each year. 106 Auditorium Circle, Ste. 130. www.yosa.org. ✆ **210/737-0097.**

SOLI Chamber Music Ensemble ★ Celebrating its 25th anniversary for the 2019 season, the well-regarded SOLI performs works by contemporary classical composers such as Steve Reich, Clarice Assad, and Robert X. Rodriguez at venues including the Tobin Center, Jazz, TX at the Pearl, and the Laurie Auditorium at Trinity University. Check website for events and venues, and to purchase tickets. www.solichamberensemble.com. ✆ **210/317-8816.**

Theater

Most of San Antonio's major road shows turn up at the Majestic, Empire, or Aztec theaters (p. 119), but several smaller houses are of interest too. The **Woodlawn Theatre ★**, 1920 Fredericksburg Rd. (www.woodlawntheatre.org; ✆ **210/267-8388**), uses local talent for its productions, which tend to be in the less commercial, off-Broadway tradition. Opened in 1946 as a movie house, in 1960 the Woodlawn premiered *The Alamo*, with star John Wayne hosting. The community-based **Josephine Theatre ★★**, 339 W. Josephine St. (www.josephinetheatre.org; ✆ **210/734-4646**), mounts an average of five productions a year—mostly musicals—at its Art Deco–style theater, only 5 minutes north of downtown.

Whether it's an original piece by a member of the company or a work by a guest artist, anything you see at the **Jump-Start Performance Company ★** (710 Fredericksburg Rd.; www.jump-start.org; ✆ **210/227-JUMP** [5867]) is likely to push the social and political envelope. This is the place to find performance artists such as Erik Bosse or Marisella Barerra.

Magik Theatre ★★★, Beethoven Hall, 420 S. Alamo St., in Hemisfair Park (www.magiktheatre.org; ✆ **210/227-2751**), puts on shows exclusively for children and families (one of very few such organizations with its own professional company and venue) in a 600-seat theater originally built in 1895 for an old German singing society. Shows are popular, so you need to reserve in advance, especially on weekends. Magik Theatre performs a full season of plays, mostly adaptations from children's books.

The Public Theater of San Antonio ★, 800 W. Ashby Pl. (www.thepublicsa.org; ✆ **210/733-7258**), established in 1912 as the San Antonio Dramatic Club, presents a wide range of plays in the neoclassical-style San Pedro Playhouse, built in 1930. **Teatro Audaz ★**, various locations (www.teatroaudaz.com), specializes in productions emphasizing groups that are traditionally under-represented in theater, including people of color, Latinx, and members of the LGBTQ community. Some productions are bilingual.

For information on other small theaters in San Antonio and links to many of those listed in this section, log on to the website of the **San Antonio Theatre Coalition** at www.satheatre.com.

THE CLUB & MUSIC SCENE

Rock venues in San Antonio are clustered for the most part on **The Strip,** the stretch of North St. Mary's Street between Mistletoe Avenue and Grayson Street, just north of downtown and south of Brackenridge Park. Though it went through a period of decline, proximity to the Pearl has recently helped bring the Strip back.

River Walk clubs tend to be touristy, and many close early because of noise restrictions. **Pearl** has more restaurants than bars and clubs, though there are a couple of nice ones here, including **Jazz, TX** ★★★ (p. 125) and the **Blue Box** bar (312 Pearl Pkwy.); more are slated to open in the future. Downtown's **Sunset Station,** 1174 E. Commerce St. (www.sunset-station.com; ✆ **210/474-7640**), a multivenue entertainment complex in the city's original railroad station, has yet to generate much buzz except for spillover from events at the nearby Alamodome, but the neighborhood east of the freeway is beginning to establish its own identity, so check local listings or the Sunset Station website.

What can you expect to pay? When judged from a big-city entertainment perspective—Houston, Dallas, New Orleans, Nashville—cover charges are very affordable. Small joints on the Strip may be free or charge $2 to $5 to get in on weekdays, $5 to $10 on weekends. A larger venue like Paper Tiger (p. 125) or a fancier one like Jazz, TX (p. 125) may charge $12 to $15 for shows that don't involve advance tickets. Even high-end dance clubs rarely charge more than $20 to $25 for non-ticketed events.

Comedy

Bexar Stage ★ Located near the Pearl, Bexar Stage is the newest home for local improv comedy, hosting live performances Thursday through Saturday and classes and workshops the rest of the week. 1203 Camden St. (off Jones Ave.). www.bexarstage.com. ✆ **210/281-4259.**

Salsa in Southtown

Latin American music and dancing is all the rage in the **Southtown Arts and Entertainment District** along South Alamo Street near the King William District. Several clubs swing to a Cuban, Argentinian, Mexican, or Brazilian beat. Whether you come to dance to *cumbia* at a Mexican ballroom or you try the merengue, there's a place for you in San Antonio most every night and weekend. First Fridays and Second Saturdays of the month are the main event in Southtown—shops, galleries, restaurants, and clubs stay open late, and special openings and art events flood the area.

Smoking in San Antonio

Smoking is not allowed in indoor areas of restaurants and bars, but there are exemptions for the River Walk and Alamo Plaza, and inside cigar bars.

Laugh Out Loud Comedy Club ★ You can usually find a comedy open mic at this North Central spot on Wednesdays, except when a touring act preempts it: Recent high-profilers have included Pauly Shore, Aries Spears, and Carlos Mencia. Lots of easy parking and a large lobby bar make this a good choice for entertaining a group. 618 NW Loop 410. www.lolsanantonio.com. ✆ **210/541-8805.**

Conjunto/Tejano

See box p. 126 for more details on this music genre.

VFW Post 76 ★ Housed in a beautiful Victorian mansion, this is the oldest Post in Texas, chartered in 1917 by several veterans of the Spanish-American War. On weekends, the large outdoor stage overlooking the River Walk usually showcases live music, frequently Tejano or conjunto. The Post is open to the public 7 days a week; guests can refresh themselves with snacks from food trucks on the grounds or beer from the indoor canteen. 10 Tenth St. (near Ave. B). www.vfwpost76ontheriverwalk.org. ✆ **210/223-4581.**

Country & Western

See p. 299 for **Gruene Hall,** the oldest (1878) dance hall in Texas.

Floores Country Store ★★★ John T. Floore, the first manager of the Majestic Theatre (p. 119) and an unsuccessful candidate for mayor of San Antonio, opened this country store in 1942. A couple years later, he added a cafe and a half-acre dance floor, the largest in south Texas. Not much has changed since then—boots, hats, and antique farm equipment hang from the ceiling, and the walls are lined with pictures of Willie Nelson, Hank Williams, Sr., Conway Twitty, Ernest Tubb, and other country greats who've played here. There's always live music on weekends, often by current country music legends. The cafe still serves homemade bread, homemade tamales, old-fashioned sausage, and cold Texas beer. 14492 Old Bandera Rd./Hwy. 16, Helotes (2 miles N. of Loop 1604). www.liveatfloores.com. ✆ **210/695-8827.**

Cowboy's Dancehall ★★ Local boot-scooters, often a college-age crowd, burn up the dance floor at this Texas-size place. The hijinx include dance lessons, a mechanical bull, and sometimes even big-name country bands. Be sure to wear Wranglers and boots when you go there, or folks might mistake you for a Yankee. 3030 N.E. Loop 410 at I-35. www.cowboysdancehall.com. ✆ **210/646-9378.**

Eclectic

La Botanica ★★ Featuring live music, DJs, and community events most nights, this LGBTQ-owned and -operated spot on North St. Mary's has a small menu of vegan snacks and specialty cocktails. You can sip them inside or out on a patio surrounded by the gardens from which the menu is sourced. 2911 N. St. Mary's St. www.vivalabotanica.com. ✆ **210/716-0702.**

Tycoon Flats ★★ This friendly outdoor venue is a fun place to kick back and listen to blues, rock, acoustic, reggae, or jazz. The burgers and such Caribbean specialties as jerk chicken are good, too. There's rarely any cover for the almost nightly live music; when there is one, it's generally no more than $5. 2926 N. St. Mary's St. at Woodlawn Ave. www.tycoonflats.net. ✆ **210/320-0819.**

Jazz & Blues

Jazz, TX ★★★ Owned by local bandleader Doc Watkins (who still plays there on weekends), this club is located in what was once the cellar of the bottling house of the historic Pearl Brewery. It combines the class of an upscale jazz club with the grit of a Texas dance hall, featuring jazz, blues, Texas swing, and salsa. (It serves up good eats, too.). Jazz great Jim Cullum, known for his American Public Radio program "Riverwalk, Live from the Landing," often plays there now that his longtime River Walk venue, The Landing, has closed. 312 Pearl Pkwy., Bldg. 6, Ste. 6001. www.jazztx.com. ✆ **210/332-9386.**

Luna ★★ If you're looking for a relaxed spot to listen to good live sounds—jazz, blues, soul, Latin dance, and more—it's worth making the trip to this swanky late-night club just south of Loop 410. Most nights you'll hear fine local talent, but bands from music-centric places like New Orleans turn up too. 6740 San Pedro St. www.lunalive.com. ✆ **210/573-6220.**

Sam's Burger Joint ★ Since 1999, this classic across the street from the Pearl has been serving up burgers, booze, and music. The booking agent has great taste in Americana sounds, bringing in acts like James McMurtry, Dave Alvin, Jimmie Dale Gilmore, and Alejandro Escovedo as well as occasional blues, metal, and jazz performers. Larger shows may require advance ticket purchase; check website for details. 330 E. Grayson St. at Ave. B. www.samsburgerjoint.com. ✆ **210/223-2830.**

Rock

Faust Tavern ★ Heavy and hardcore music of all kinds is played in the courtyard of this affordable, hip, and tiny dive bar sandwiched between one of San Antonio's best music shops and a legendary local *taquería* (Robot Monster Guitars and El Milagrito, respectively). The food truck–sized kitchen serves great bar snacks. 517 E. Woodlawn Ave. www.facebook.com/TheFaustTavern. ✆ **210/257-0628.**

Paper Tiger ★ The largest and most ambitious of the live music clubs on the North St. Mary's Strip, Paper Tiger hosts an eclectic mix of national, regional, and local bands in two performance spaces that hold from 200 to 1,000 patrons. They're doing it right, with a crystal-clear sound system and a top-shelf bar, but parking can be a problem; consider a ride-share to large-draw

conjunto: **AN AMERICAN CLASSIC**

Cruise a San Antonio radio dial or go to any major city festival, and you'll most likely hear the happy, boisterous sound of conjunto. Never heard of it? Don't worry, you're not alone. Although conjunto is one of our country's original contributions to world music, for a long time few Americans outside Texas knew much about it.

Conjunto evolved at the end of the 19th century, when South Texas was swept by a wave of German immigrants who brought with them popular polkas and waltzes. These sounds were easily incorporated into—and transformed by—Mexican folk music. The newcomer accordion, cheap and able to mimic several instruments, was happily adopted, too. With the addition at the turn of the 20th century of the *bajo sexto,* a 12-string guitarlike instrument used for rhythmic bass accompaniment, conjunto was born.

Tejano (Spanish for "Texan") is the 20th-century offspring of conjunto. The two most prominent instruments in Tejano remain the accordion and the *bajo sexto,* but the music melds more modern forms, including pop, jazz, and country-and-western, into the traditional conjunto repertoire. At clubs not exclusively devoted to Latino sounds, what you're likely to hear is Tejano.

Long ignored by the mainstream, conjunto and Tejano were brought into America's consciousness by the 1995 murder of Hispanic superstar **Selena.** Before she was killed, Selena had already been slotted for crossover success—she had done the title song and put in a cameo appearance in the film *Don Juan de Marco* with Johnny Depp—and a 1997 movie based on her life boosted awareness of her music even further. The rest of the country may have moved on, but Selena's reputation has only grown in San Antonio. There's a shrine to her in Mi Tierra (p. 61) and Selena cover bands have cropped up, include one called Bidi Bidi Bonda, after her song by the same name.

San Antonio is to conjunto music what Nashville is to country. The most famous *bajo sextos,* used nationally by everyone who is anyone in conjunto and Tejano music, were created in San Antonio by the Macías family—the late Martín and now his son, Alberto. The undisputed king of conjunto, **Flaco Jiménez**—a mild-mannered triple-Grammy winner who has recorded with the Rolling Stones, Bob Dylan, and Willie Nelson, among others—lives in the city. And San Antonio's **Tejano Conjunto Festival,** held each May (see Calendar of Events on p. 34), is the largest of its kind, drawing aficionados from around the world—there's even a band from Japan.

Most of the places to hear conjunto and Tejano are off the beaten tourist path, and they come and go fairly quickly; more common are bars that have designated "conjunto nights." A couple of possibilities for more regular play include **Far West,** 2502 Pleasanton Rd. (www.farwestsa.com; ✆ **210/290-4900**), specializing in live Tejano; and **VFW Post 76** (p. 124). Better yet, just attend one of San Antonio's many festivals—you're bound to hear these rousing sounds.

concerts. If your favorite band happens to be playing here, it's bound to be a good time. 2410 N. St. Mary's St. www.papertigersatx.com. No phone.

Sanchos ★ Featuring live rock with a Tex-Mex flair every night of the week, this cantina also has indoor and outside dining areas with excellent San

Antonio-inspired food and drinks. It's very popular with regulars from nearby neighborhoods as well as more far-flung parts of town. 628 Jackson St. www.sanchosmx.com. ✆ **210/320-1840.**

THE GAY SCENE

In addition to the Bonham (see below), Main Avenue just north of downtown has several gay and lesbian clubs in close proximity. They are not segregated by gender or even sexual preference so much as they are by scene—dance club versus pick-up club or sports bar. From south going north, you'll encounter **Pegasus,** 1402 N. Main Ave. (www.pegasussanantonio.com; ✆ **210/299-4222**), your basic cruise bar; **Sparky's Pub,** 1416 N. Main Ave. (www.sparkyspub.com; ✆ **210/320-5111**), a gay-friendly English pub, cafe, and wine bar; and, a few doors down, **Knockout,** 1420 N. Main Ave. (www.knockoutsa.com; ✆ **210/227-7678**), where the focus is sports. The hot dance club of the moment is **Heat,** 1500 N. Main Ave. (www.heatsa.com; ✆ **210/227-2600**). A few blocks away, the **Silver Dollar Saloon,** 1812 N. Main Ave. (✆ **210/227-2623**), is three venues under one roof: a gay Tejano bar, a heavy metal/thrash music space, and bar with a Goth/New Wave dance vibe.

Bonham Exchange ★★★ Tina Turner, Deborah Harry (aka Blondie), and LaToya Jackson—the real ones—have all played this high-tech dance club near the Alamo. The club no longer hosts live performances on a regular basis but a mixed crowd of gays and straights, young and old, still moves to the beat under wildly flashing lights. All the action—five bars, three dance floors, three levels—takes place in a restored German-style building dating to the 1880s. Roll over, Beethoven. 411 Bonham (at 3rd St.). www.bonhamexchange.net. ✆ **210/271-3811** or 224-9219. No cover for ages 21 and older before 10pm, then $5 Fri–Sat, $3 Sun.

THE BAR SCENE

Texas state law dictates that bars close at 2am, although some alternative spots stay open until 3 or 4am. Some of the hottest bars in town are also in restaurants: **Ácenar** (p. 60) and **Cured** (p. 68) make kickbutt cocktails, while **Zinc** (p. 60) has an top-notch wine selection.

Cadillac Bar & Restaurant ★★ Located downtown near the Bexar County Courthouse, this bar gets a lot of lawyers and businesspeople on the weekdays. Set in an old saloon, it's an enjoyable place to relax after a day of walking around town. On the weekend, it's a little noisier with live music on Fridays and recorded music on Saturdays. You might hear anything from cover bands to Tejano and conjunto music. Full dinners are served on a patio out back. 212 S. Flores St. (near Nueva St.). www.cadillacbarsanantonio.com. ✆ **210/223-5533.**

Esquire Tavern ★★★ Along with Menger (see below) this is one of San Antonio's oldest (and arguably, best) watering holes. It opened in 1933 to

brewing **MAKES A COMEBACK**

An abundance of good artesian well water, a location at the crossroads of major trade routes, and an influx of German immigrants—it's no coincidence that San Antonio has been home to breweries since as early as 1855, when William Menger and Charles Degan opened the Western Brewery in the basement of their hotel next to the Alamo. While some of the most successful breweries have been repurposed in the last few decades—the old Lone Star Brewery now houses the San Antonio Museum of Art (p. 82), and the Pearl Brewery was incorporated into Hotel Emma and other structures of the Pearl complex (p. 110)—beer production is thriving again, thanks to the rise of craft brewers, who are quenching San Antonians' thirst with a dizzying array of lagers, ales, and spirits. Many of these businesses have limited hours, so check the websites or call ahead before you visit.

BREWERIES WITH TASTING ROOMS OR BARS With an entrepreneurial founder and a brewmaster who is both a beekeeper and a graduate of the Culinary Institute of America, **Alamo Beer Company,** east of downtown on 202 Lamar St. (www.alamobeer.com; ✆ **210/872-5589**), is producing some fine lighter-styled beers, perfect for cooling off in the Texas summers. Opened as Texas' first urban distillery in 2013, **Dorcol Distilling and Brewing Company,** in Southtown at 1902 S. Flores St. (www.dorcolspirits.com; ✆ **210/229-0607**), started out with a Balkan-style apricot brandy (Kinsman Rakia) and expanded its offerings to include a line of tasty ales called High Wheel. **Freetail Brewing Company,** 2000 S. Presa St. (www.freetailbrewing.com; ✆ **210/625-6000**), makes a selection of beers year-round at their state-of-the-art brewery in Southtown, including a vast number of seasonal offerings and 22-ounce bombers for sale at local shops.

Just past Loop 410 in the northwest, another local favorite is **Busted Sandal Brewing Company,** 7114 Oaklawn Dr. (www.bustedsandalbrewing.com; ✆ **210/872-1486**); you'll also find its beers on tap at many San Antonio watering holes and available in cans at groceries around town. (Recommended: the El Robusto Porter, featuring notes of milk chocolate and roasted coffee.) North of the 410 Loop in the northeast, **Ranger Creek Brewing and Distilling,** 4834 Whirlwind Dr., Suite 102 (www.drinkrangercreek.com; ✆ **210/339-2282**), is a "brewstillery," making local beers AND whiskeys, sold locally both through retail outlets and at bars and pubs.

RESTAURANTS WITH BREWERIES Specializing in a wide variety of organic brews**, Blue Star Brewing Company,** 1414 S. Alamo St., #105 (www.bluestarbrewing.com; ✆ **210/212-55060**), has been keeping the growing community of Southtown locals lubricated and fed with comforting pub food since opening in 1996. A little farther south, German-born head brewer Vera Deckard and her husband Brent are producing some of the city's most interesting brews at **Künstler Brewing,** 302 E. Lachapelle St. (www.kuenstlerbrewing.com; ✆ **210/688-4519**), and pairing them with German- and Texas-style snacks and live music in this little gem of a brewpub. And chef Jeff Balfour brought back brewing to the redeveloped Pearl in 2015 when he opened **Southerleigh Fine Food and Brewery,** 136 E. Grayson St., Suite 120 (www.southerleigh.com; ✆ **210/455-5701**), pairing his Texas cross-cultural cuisine with more than 21 beers on tap.

celebrate the end of Prohibition and has been a beloved institution ever since, save for a short hiatus when it was closed from 2006 to 2011. The Esquire has the longest wooden bar in Texas—at over 100 feet, it has plenty of room to belly up. Oddly, though it's on the River Walk, the Esquire's not on tourists' radar—one reason why the best chefs in town often come here after they close up shop. The recently remodeled riverside lounge downstairs has an enviable spirits selection and serves small plates in a more intimate setting. 155 E. Commerce St. (at St. Mary's St.). www.esquiretavern-sa.com. © **210/222-2521.**

Francis Bogside ★★ Sitting just at the edge of King William, this little gem of an Irish pub has a devoted local following. Upscale pub food, clever cocktails, a mellow atmosphere, and a liberal happy hour (4–7pm Tues–Sat, all day Sun and Mon) all help make the Bogside popular. There's live music on Saturday nights. 803 S. St. Mary's St. (near S. Alamo St.). www.francisbogside.com. © **210/369-9192.**

Hanzo Bar ★ Cozy, hip, and friendly, Hanzo is tucked away inside a nondescript business strip in Alamo Heights. Offerings include Japanese-influenced cocktails and small plates, as well as excellent ramen and a very affordable happy hour, inside or at the adjacent courtyard area. 7701 Broadway St., #124. (at Nottingham Dr.). www.hanzobar.com. © **210/826-1488.**

Menger Bar ★★★ More than 100 years ago, Teddy Roosevelt recruited men for his Rough Riders unit at this dark, wooded bar (they were outfitted for the Spanish-American War at nearby Fort Sam Houston). Constructed in 1859 on the site of William Menger's earlier successful brewery and saloon, the bar was moved from its original location in the Victorian hotel lobby in 1956, but 90 percent of its historic furnishings remain intact. Spanish Civil War uniforms hang on the walls. It's still one of the prime spots in town to toss back a few. Menger Hotel, 204 Alamo Plaza. www.mengerhotel.com. © **210/223-4361.**

FILM

San Antonio is more of a "movies" than a "cinema" kind of town: There's not much in the way of an indie celluloid scene. You'll find the typical multiplexes showing first-run films here—Santikos and Regal are the local chains—and several branches of the Alamo Drafthouse eat-in-your-seat movie theaters. (Ironically, the popular concept was founded in Austin, not in the Alamo City.) **The Santikos Bijou Cinema Bistro,** 4522 Fredericksburg Rd. (www.santikos.com/san-antonio/bijou; © **210/734-4552**), has long been the place to go to catch indie and short-release movies. The food and wine is decent too.

The **Guadalupe Cultural Arts Center** (p. 121) and the **McNay** and **Witte museums** (p. 81 and p. 84, respectively) often have interesting film series. The **Esperanza Peace and Justice Center,** north of downtown at 922 San Pedro Ave. (www.esperanzacenter.org; © **210/228-0201**), usually hosts an annual gay and lesbian cinema festival.

And you can always go to see the IMAX movie *Alamo—The Price of Freedom* at the **AMC Rivercenter 11,** in the Shops at Rivercenter, 849 E. Commerce St. (www.amctheatres.com/alamomovie; ✆ **210/228-0351**). It's been running there continuously since 1988; nowadays it has reclining seats, and you can munch on more than popcorn while watching the defenders of the famous mission, located only a block away, go down in brave and glorious defeat.

SPECTATOR SPORTS

BASEBALL From early April through early September, the minor-league **San Antonio Missions** (a farm club for the San Diego Padres) play at the Nelson Wolff Stadium, 5757 Hwy. 90 W. Tickets range from $8 for adult general admission to $12 for seats in the lower box. For schedules and tickets, go to www.samissions.com or call ✆ **210/675-7275.**

BASKETBALL Spurs madness hits San Antonio every year from mid-October through May, when the city's only major-league franchise, the **San Antonio Spurs,** shoots hoops. Ticket prices range from $21 for nosebleed-level seats to $400 and above for seats on the corners of the court. Tickets are available at the Spurs Ticket Office in the AT&T Center, One AT&T Center Pkwy. (www.nba.com/spurs; ✆ **210/444-5140**), or via Ticketmaster San Antonio (www.ticketmaster.com; ✆ **210/224-9600**).

GOLF Each spring (March/April) **TPC San Antonio** (www.tpc.com), the private club open to members and guests of the JW Marriott San Antonio Hill Country Resort & Spa, plays host to the PGA Tour's **Valero Texas Open,** one of the tour's oldest professional golf tournaments, played on the AT&T Oaks Course. Visit www.valerotexasopen.com for details.

HORSE RACING **Retama Park,** some 20 minutes north of San Antonio in Selma (www.retamapark.com; ✆ **210/651-7000**), is the hottest place to play the ponies; take exit 174-A from I-35, or the Lookout Road exit from Loop 1604. Its multi-level Spanish-style grandstand is impressive, and the variety of food courts, restaurants, and lounges is almost as diverting as the horses. Live racing is generally from July through September on Tuesday, Wednesday, Friday, and Saturday. Call or check the website for thoroughbred and quarter horse schedules. Simulcasts from top tracks around the country are shown year-round. General admission for live racing is $7 adults, $4 seniors and active military, free for 12 and under. Admission is free for everyone on Tuesday and Wednesday.

ICE HOCKEY The American Hockey League's **San Antonio Rampage** play at the AT&T Center (One AT&T Center Pkwy.), where tickets cost $10 to $65. Go to www.sarampage.com or call ✆ **210/444-5554** for schedules and other information.

RODEO In early February, 2 weeks of Wild West events like calf roping, barrel racing, and bull riding are held at the annual **San Antonio Stock Show**

and Rodeo (www.sarodeo.com; ✆ **210/225-5851**). Major country music acts perform live each night during the rodeo, including concerts by big-name Nashville and Texas stars. Out in Bulverde, just north of San Antonio, the **Tejas Rodeo Co.** (www.tejasrodeo.com; ✆ **830/980-2226)** lays on a live rodeo every Saturday from March through November, followed by dancing to live bands. Another draw is the food at the adjoining **Tejas Steakhouse and Saloon,** created by chef Johnny Hernandez of La Gloria (p. 69) and La Fruiteria (p. 62) restaurants. Smaller rodeos are held throughout the year in nearby **Bandera** (p. 136), the self-proclaimed "Cowboy Capital of the World." Contact the Bandera County Convention and Visitors Bureau (www.banderacowboycapital.com; ✆ **800/364-3833** or 830/796-3045) for more information.

DAY TRIPS FROM SAN ANTONIO

9

San Antonio sits at the southern edge of one of Texas's prettiest regions, the rising and falling dreamscape of lakes, rivers, and limestone caverns called the Hill Country. In the 19th century, Germans and Czechs, fleeing social upheavals in Europe and lured by the promise of free land, established several small towns here; other settlements go back to the region's cattle-ranching past. Eventually, the Hill Country's mild climate and abundant springs gave rise to health spas, summer camps, and guest ranches. Modern tourism, in turn, brought restaurants, shops, lodgings, and a resurgent wine industry.

Any of these towns makes an easy day trip from San Antonio; you might even be able to do two in one trip (stopping in **Boerne,** for example, on the way to **Bandera**). **Fredericksburg** has the most accommodations and things to see and do; it also makes a good base for touring the other towns and attractions, including LBJ country. For a full listing of Hill Country events, see the Travel Texas website: **www.traveltexas.com/cities-regions/hill-country/events**.

Most of the towns covered here lie northwest of San Antonio, but if you head northeast via I-35, you can also visit New Braunfels, Gruene, San Marcos, Wimberley, and other destinations detailed as day trips from Austin in Chapter 17.

BOERNE

32 miles NW of San Antonio

From downtown San Antonio, it's a straight shot north on I-10 to Boerne (rhymes with "journey"), located on the banks of Cibolo Creek. The little (2¼ miles long) town was founded in 1849 by freedom-seeking German intellectuals, including Jewish-German political writer and satirist Ludwig Börne (1786–1837), for whom the town was named. In the 1880s, Boerne became a popular health resort. It's now the seat of Kendall County, with more than 16,000 residents. The **Boerne Visitors Center,** 108 Oak Park Dr., off Main

Day Trips from San Antonio

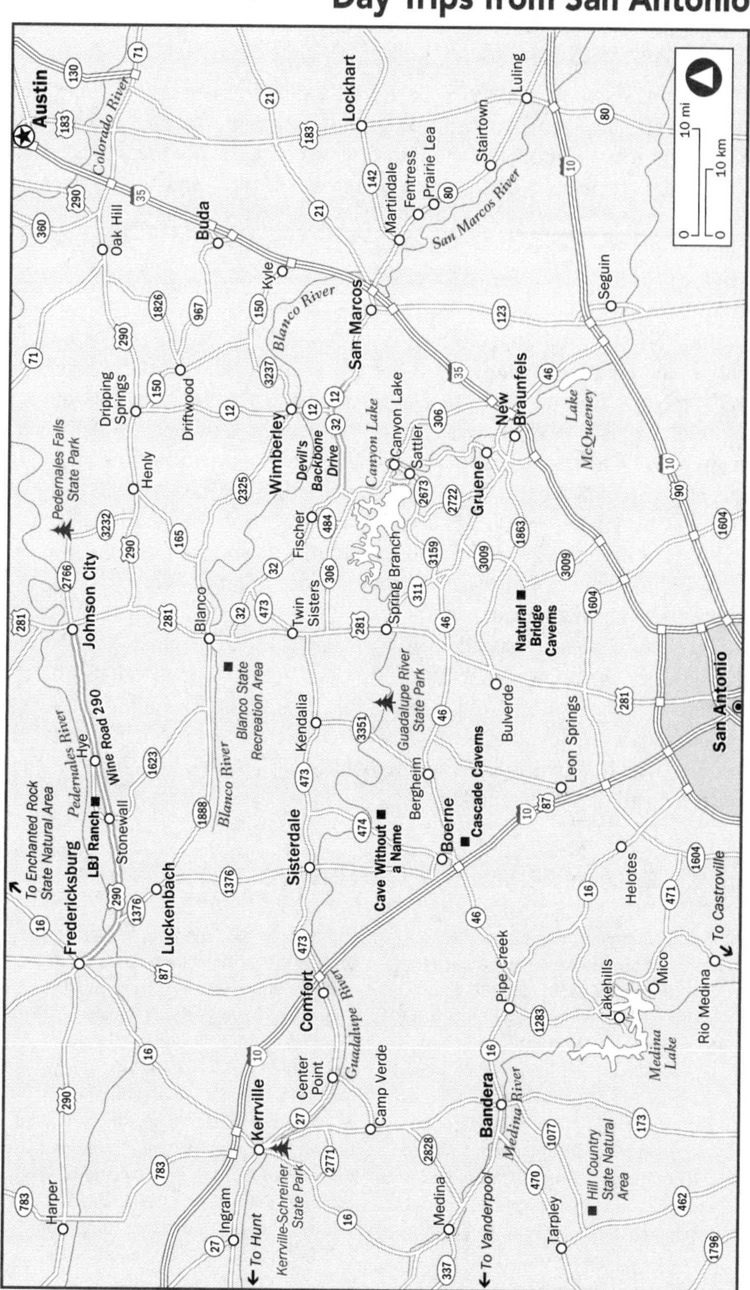

Street (www.visitboerne.org; ✆ **888/842-8080** or 830/249-7277) is open 8am to 5pm Monday through Friday, 10am to 2pm on Saturday (it's closed Sun).

Exploring Boerne

Close enough to San Antonio to be almost a suburb, Boerne is working hard to retain its small-town atmosphere—and its heritage. One of the things it's known for is the **Boerne Village Band,** which occasionally holds concerts in the gazebo on the main plaza; it first oompahed in 1860, and bills itself as the world's oldest continuously operating German band outside of Germany. A number of 19th-century limestone buildings cluster in the city's **historic district,** called the Hill Country Mile; a free self-guided tour pamphlet is available at the visitor center.

Boerne's biggest draw, however, is the antiques shops, art galleries, crafts shops, and clothing boutiques that line Main Street. The second weekend of each month, **Boerne Market Days** (www.boernemarketdays.com/boerne.html; ✆ **210/844-8193**) draws artists, crafters, and musicians to the town's main plaza. One of the best places anywhere to buy Mexican folk art is just 2½ miles north of Boerne; take exit 537 off I-10 W. to **Cosas,** 39360 I-10 W. (www.cosasonline; ✆ **830/249-1500**). The store does most of its business online, but if you're in town Friday or Saturday from 11am to 5pm, you can browse a warehouse full of south-of-the border treasures. Alternatively, call ahead to make an appointment.

Those who want to spend their time outdoors can explore four distinct ecosystems—grassland, marshland, woodland, and river bottom—at the **Cibolo Nature Center,** 140 City Park Rd., next to the Kendall County Fairgrounds (www.cibolo.org, ✆ **830/249-4616**). Behind it, on 33 Herff Rd., restored **Herff Farm** is open to the public on Saturday mornings, when it hosts a bustling farmers market.

Beneath the Hills of Hill Country

One of Boerne's most popular attractions is **Cascade Caverns** (www.cascadecaverns.com; ✆ **830/755-8080**), an active cave with huge chambers, a 100-ft. underground waterfall, and comfortable walking trails. To get there, head 3 miles south of Boerne on I-10, take exit 543, and drive 2 miles east. It's open year-round 9am to 5pm, with tours on the hour from 10am to 4pm. A 1-hr. tour costs $20 adults, $13 ages 4 to 11; reserve ahead if you want to take the 90-min. flashlight tour ($25 adults, $16 children) or the 2½-hr. adventure tour (adults only, $100). A little farther from town (11 miles northeast via Route 474 and Kreuzberg Rd.) lies the even more impressive **Cave Without a Name,** 325 Kreutzberg Rd. (www.cavewithoutaname.com; ✆ **830/537-4212**), which has more chambers, a greater amount of living rock, and a wider variety of features. Hour-long tours are offered throughout the day. From Memorial Day through Labor Day it's open daily 9am to 6pm, the rest of the year daily 10am to 5pm. Admission is $20 adults, $18 seniors and military, $10 ages 6 to 12.

A TASTE OF alsace IN TEXAS

Just 20 miles west of San Antonio (via U.S. 90 W.), **Castroville** has become something of a bedroom community for San Antonio, but the center of town retains its heritage as an old Alsatian community. It was founded in 1842, on a scenic bend of the Medina River, by Henri Castro, a Portuguese-born Jewish Frenchman who had received a 1.25-million-acre land grant from the Republic of Texas in exchange for his commitment to colonize the land. Second only to Stephen F. Austin in the number of settlers he brought over, Castro recruited 2,134 immigrants, mostly from the Rhine Valley, especially from the French province of Alsace. A few of the oldest citizens still can speak Alsatian, a dialect of German, though the language is likely to die out in the area when they do.

For insight into the town's history, visit the **Landmark Inn State Historic Site,** 402 E. Florence St. (www.thc.texas.gov/historic-sites/landmark-inn-state-historic-site; ✆ **830/931-2133**), which counts among its attractions a nature trail along the river, an old gristmill, and a stone dam. The on-site **History Store,** open daily 10am to 5pm (opens at noon on Sun), which also serves as an informal visitor center to the town, leads guided tours through the buildings ($4 adults, $3 children and seniors). The park's centerpiece **Landmark Inn** has eight simple but well-equipped rooms decorated with early Texas pieces dating up until the 1940s (rates are $120–$140 per night including breakfast). They're only available Wednesday through Saturday nights and Sundays before Monday holidays.

For a delicious taste of the Alsace, visit **Haby's Alsatian Bakery,** 207 U.S. 90 E. (www.habysbakery.com; ✆ **830/538-2118**), which sells fresh-baked apple fritters, strudels, stollens, breads, and coffeecakes. It's open Monday to Saturday, 5am to 7pm.

For additional information, contact the **Castroville Chamber of Commerce,** 1115 Angelo St. (www.castroville.com; ✆ **800/778-6775** or 830/538-3142), where you can pick up a walking-tour booklet of the town's historic buildings, as well as a map that details local boutiques and antiques shops around town. It's open 9am to 3pm Monday through Friday. ***Note:*** Downtown Castroville tends to close down on Monday and Tuesday, and some places are shuttered on Wednesday and Sunday as well. If you want to find most things open, come on Thursday, Friday, or Saturday.

Guadalupe River State Park, 13 miles east of Boerne via Hwy. 46 to 3350 P.R. 31 (www.tpwd.texas.gov/state-parks/guadalupe-river; ✆ **830/438-2656**), features 4 miles of river frontage at a particularly attractive section of the river, above Canyon Lake. You'll find a number of excellent swimming spots and some hiking trails leading through beautiful, rugged hill country. Keep an eye out and you might spot white-tailed deer, coyotes, armadillos, or even a rare golden-cheeked warbler. Camping is available; make reservations on line. Check ahead for ranger-led interpretive tours. The park is open daily 8am to 10pm; the entrance fee is $7, free for kids age 12 and under.

More and more these days, Hill Country is also wine country, and it starts 12 miles north of Boerne on FM 1376, where **Sister Creek Vineyards,** 1142 Sisterdale Hwy. (www.sistercreekvineyards.com; ✆ **830/324-6704**), is set in a converted century-old cotton gin on the main—actually the only—street in

Sisterdale. The winery creates traditional French wines using traditional French techniques, but the attitude is Texas friendly.

Where to Stay & Eat in Boerne

Peggy's on the Green, 128 W. Blanco (www.peggysonthegreen.com; ✆ **830/249-9954**), created by Mark Bohanan, chef/owner of Bohanan's steakhouse in San Antonio (p. 58), offers upscale Southern cooking—think chicken-fried quail—along with steak and seafood; entrees run from moderate to expensive. It's open for lunch and dinner Tuesday to Saturday, brunch and dinner on Sunday. Peggy's is the dining room for **Ye Kendall Inn** (www.yekendallinn.com; ✆ **830/249-2138**), a Territorial-style boutique hotel fronting the main plaza. Opened as a stagecoach lodge in 1859, it now offers a variety of rooms, suites, and cabins in the moderate to expensive price range.

The more casual and less expensive **Bear Moon Bakery,** 401 S. Main St. (www.bearmoonbakery.com; ✆ **830/816-2327**), is ideal for a hearty breakfast or light lunch. Organic ingredients and locally grown produce are used for the inventive soups, salads, sandwiches, and baked goods. You can watch ducks frolic in Cibolo Creek's old mill pond when you dine at **Dodging Duck Brewhaus,** 402 River Rd. (www.dodgingduck.com; ✆ **830/248-3825**). Sit out on the covered deck and enjoy lunch or dinner from an eclectic brewpub menu—everything from Cajun stuffed mushrooms to antelope burgers—as well as suds brewed on the premises. Prices are moderate.

BANDERA

25 miles W of Boerne; 54 miles NW of San Antonio

Bandera is a slice of life out of the Old West, a town that could easily serve as a John Ford film set. Established as a lumber camp in 1853, the self-styled (and trademarked) Cowboy Capital of the World still has the feel of the frontier. Not only are many of its historic buildings intact, rodeos are still held here on a regular basis (major rodeos are on Memorial Day weekend and Labor Day weekend, but there are also frequent smaller rodeos in between). There's a nod to contemporary attitudes—gun safety is discussed at the simulated shootouts that take place behind the visitor center, for example—but a lot of hunters live in the area, as evidenced by the taxidermist shops you'll spot. In short, Bandera is not a Western theme park, but a real town.

Genuine hospitality and friendliness to visitors are part of the local ethos. For information about local events, outfitters, and activities, stop in at the **Bandera County Convention and Visitors Bureau,** 126 Hwy. 16 S. (www.banderacowboycapital.com; ✆ **800/364-3833** or 830/796-3045), open Monday through Friday 9am to 5pm, Saturday 11am to 2pm.

Exploring Bandera

Interested in delving into the town's roots? Pick up a self-guided tour brochure of historic sites at the visitor center or head for the small **Western Trails**

Heritage Park in the main square, across from the county courthouse. Historic markers commemorate the vast Texas cattle drives that once pounded through this area, which was on the Great Western Cattle Trail, immortalized in the book and movie *Lonesome Dove*.

Immigrant families from Poland settled Bandera in the 1850s; the church they built, the beautifully restored **St. Stanislaus,** 311 E. 7th St. (www.ststanislausbandera.com; ✆ **830/460-4712**), is the country's second oldest Polish parish. The small **Frontier Times Museum,** 510 13th St. (www.frontiertimesmuseum.org; ✆ **830/796-3864**), opened its doors in 1933, an era when many museums were mainly showcases for curiosities. This one stays true to its original mandate—you'll find a taxidermied two-faced goat and a medieval birthing chair among the exhibits—but it also offers a fascinating overview of the area's history. The much newer (opened 2016) **Bandera Natural History Museum,** 267 Old San Antonio Hwy. (www.banderanhm.org; ✆ **830/328-5090**), features displays of dinosaurs and ice age animals made by the same company that created the dinos for *Jurassic Park*. The educational exhibits include real full-body mounts of animals that the museum's founder hunted, placed in replicas of their natural habitats.

BANDERA SHOPPING

If you stroll along Main Street, you'll find a variety of crafters working in the careful, deliberate style of the past. The **Leather Bank of Bandera,** 318 Main St. (✆ **830-328-5080**), is the outlet for distinctive Collins of Texas handbags (www.collinsoftexas.com), with styles ranging from vintage and bejeweled to contemporary. **Thelma and Louize,** 204 Main St. (www.themaandlouizebandera; ✆ **830/328-5060**), carries a lot of brands beloved by contemporary cowgirls, including boho-chic Ivy Jane clothing and chunky J Forks jewelry. Housed in a 1908 building, the stocked-to-the-gills **Bandera General Store,** 306 Main St. (www.banderageneralstore.com, ✆ **830/796-8176**), sells everything from boots to salsa. It has the only bookstore in town, as well as a fully functional 1950s ice-cream fountain serving malts, milk shakes, and banana splits. **Western Trail Antiques & Marketplace,** 200 Main St. (www.westerntrailantiques.com; ✆ **830/796-3838**), brings together contemporary local crafts as well as things retro, from vintage boots to farm collectibles.

Off the Main Street drag, you can buy beautiful customized belt buckles, spurs, and jewelry at **Hy O Silver,** 1107 12th St. (www.hyosilver.com; ✆ **830/796-7961**). **Suzoo's Wool Works,** 584 Hwy. 16 S. (www.suzoos.com; ✆ **949/400-4225**), is a magnet for knitters and quilters, who come for supplies and sign on for classes.

SPORTS & OUTDOOR ACTIVITIES

You don't have to go farther than **Bandera Park** (www.cityofbandera.org/2161/Park; ✆ **830/796-3765**), a 77-acre green space within city limits, to enjoy nature, whether you want to stroll along the River Bend Native Plant Trail or picnic by the Medina River. Or you can canter through the **Hill**

Country State Natural Area, 10 miles southwest of Bandera (www.tpwd.texas.gov/state-parks/hill-country; ✆ **830/796-4413**), the largest state park in Texas that allows horseback riding. Ask at the visitor center about outfitters for day rides; many guest ranches provide mounts.

About 20 miles southeast of town (take Hwy. 16 to R.R. 1283), **Bandera County Park at Medina Lake** (www.banderacounty.org/services/MedinaLakePark; no phone) is the place to hook crappie, white or black bass, and huge yellow catfish; the public boat ramp is on the north side of the lake, at the end of P.R. 37. Get a single-day license for nonresidents ($16) at the **Bandera True Value,** 1002 Main St. (✆ **830/796-3861**), and bring your own gear. If you want to kayak, canoe, or tube the Medina River, contact the **Medina River Company,** 1114 Main St. (www.themedinarivercompany.com; ✆ **830/796-3600**), which rents equipment and provides shuttle service.

Most people visit the **Lost Maples State Natural Area,** about 40 miles west of Bandera in Vanderpool (www.tpwd.texas.gove/state-park/lost-maples; ✆ **830/966-3413**), in autumn, when the leaves put on a brilliant show. But birders come in winter to look at bald eagles, hikers like the wildflower array in spring, and in summer, anglers do their best to reduce the Guadalupe bass population of the Sabinal River.

Where to Eat in Bandera

If you're looking for Tex-Mex or country cooking with lots of local atmosphere and little harm to your wallet, you've come to the right place. Typical is **O.S.T.**, 311 Main St. (www.ostbandera.com; ✆ **830/796-3836**), named for the Old Spanish Trail that used to run through Bandera; it's been open since 1921. Check out the John Wayne room, covered in photos and old movie posters of "the Duke." **Brick's River Cafe,** 1105 Main St. (www.bricksrivercafe.com; ✆ **830/460-3200**), behind the River Oak Inn at the north end of town, serves up down-home standards such as chicken-fried steak, fried catfish, and liver and onions. From a seat on the back deck (half enclosed, half open-air), you can look out over the Medina River. **Mi Pueblo,** 706 Main St. (✆ **830/796-8040**), is known for its generous portions of dishes like enchiladas verde, carnitas, and breakfast burritos. The huge **TJ's at the Old Forge,** 807 Main St. (www.tjsoldforge.com; ✆ **830/796-9990**), which calls its atmosphere "modern Western," has a nice selection of salads, fish, and lighter fare alongside its burgers and steaks. The two-tiered dining room has bars with TVs tuned to the latest games.

It's worth the 13-mile drive northwest of Bandera, via gorgeously scenic Hwy. 16, to visit the little town of Medina, which calls itself the Apple Capital of Texas. **Love Creek Orchards** (www.lovecreekorchards.com; ✆ **800/449-0882** or 830/589-2202) on the main street runs the **Apple Store Bakery & Patio Café,** which sells apple pies and other fresh-baked goods, as well as apple cider, apple syrup, apple butter, apple jam, and apple ice cream. Not feeling fruity? The restaurant out back serves some of the best burgers in the area.

STAYING AT A guest ranch

Accommodations in the Bandera area range from rustic cabins and RV hookups to upscale B&Bs, but if you're looking for lots of activities and/or a genuinely relaxing getaway, stay at one of Bandera's many guest ranches. The Bandera website (www.banderacowboycapital.com) has a full listing of them; below are some of our favorites. Rates at all the following are based on double occupancy and, unless otherwise specified, include three meals, two trail rides, and most other activities.

Note that most guest ranches have a 2-night (or more) minimum stay, but honestly, you wouldn't want to spend less time than that at a dude ranch—it'll take at least half a day to start to unwind. Expect to encounter lots of European visitors; chat with them and you'll learn about all the best beers in Texas—and Germany.

The **Dixie Dude Ranch,** 833 Dixie Dude Ranch Rd. (www.dixieduderanch.com; ✆ **800/375-YALL** [375-9255] or 830/796-7771), is still a working ranch, run by a seventh-generation Texan. You're likely to see white-tailed deer or wild turkeys as you trot on horseback through a 725-acre spread. The down-home, friendly atmosphere keeps folks coming back year after year. Rates are $150 per night for adults, $60 to $110 for children depending on age.

Tubing on the Medina River and soaking in a hot tub are among the many activities at the **Mayan Ranch** (www.mayanranch.com; ✆ **830/796-3312** or 830/460-3036), another well-established family-run operation ($170 per adult, $80–$100 per child). The ranch provides plenty of additional Western fun for its guests during high season—things like two-step lessons, cookouts, hayrides, singing cowboys, or trick-roping exhibitions.

The **Silver Spur Guest Ranch,** 9266 Bandera Creek Rd. (www.silverspur-ranch.com; ✆ **830/796-3037** or 460-3639), offers the best of both worlds: creatures and creature comforts. Horses, longhorn cattle, miniature donkeys, and pygmy goats are among the four-legged residents of the 300-acre spread, while a Healing Studio provides a serene space for treatments like aromatherapy. The ranch, which abuts the Hill Country State Natural Area (p. 138), also boasts the region's largest swimming pool and a great kids' play area. There are several different rates: You can go for all-inclusive ($130–$170 adults, $50–$95 children), non-riding ($110–135/$50–$85), or breakfast-only ($55–$105/$20–$55) plans.

Bandera Nightlife

Bandera has a lot of rustic, often loud, honky-tonks. If you're in town on an off night, you can chew the fat in peace with some of the other patrons. On Friday and Saturday, there's usually live music, so come prepared to dance.

One popular joint is **Arkey Blue's Silver Dollar Bar,** 308 Main St. (✆ **830/796-8826**), downstairs below the Bandera General Store. A well-known figure in Texas country music, Arkey has written songs for some of the biggest names in the state, including Willie Nelson. Sawdust is strewn on the floor to provide a better surface for boot scootin'. On a table in one of the corners, you can see where Hank Williams, Sr., carved his name. Just down the street, the **Chikin Coop,** 401 Main St. (✆ **830/796-4496**), is so named because it used to have chicken wire in place of windows. It has live music on Wednesdays, Fridays, and Saturdays, everything from rockabilly to Western swing. In addition to concerts, some by national recording stars, the **11th Street Cowboy Bar,** 307 11th St. (www.11thstreetcowboybar.com; ✆ **830/796-4849**), is known for its Wednesday steak nights: You bring your own meat, the bar provides the barbecue grills, utensils, and spices—and sells side dishes.

COMFORT

16 miles NW of Boerne; 48 miles NW of San Antonio

Situated about halfway between Boerne and Kerrville, the quirky town of Comfort was founded in 1854 on the banks of the Cypress Creek by German freethinkers and agnostics (the town's first church wasn't built until 1900). The town's founders were also opposed to slavery, and sided against the Confederacy in the Civil War. Look for the **Treu de Union** (Loyalty to the Union) monument in the center of town (High St., between Second and Third sts.), which honors 68 townsmen who were killed by Confederate soldiers in the 1862 Battle of Nueces.

The rough-hewn limestone buildings in the center of Comfort may contain the most complete 19th-century business district in Texas. Noted San Antonio architect Alfred Giles designed several of the structures. These days, most of the buildings, especially those on High Street, host an eclectic array of shops, such as **The Elephant Story,** 723 High St. (www.the-elephant-story.com; ✆ **830/995-3133**), a nonprofit selling merchandise—everything from sleep masks to pen holders—to benefit elephant conservation in Asia. **Christy's Boutique,** 704 High St. (✆ **830/995-2493**), carries colorful, distinctive fashions, some imports, some local, at reasonable prices. Around the corner, **The Tinsmith's Wife,** 405 7th St. (www.tinsmithswife.com; ✆ **830/995-5539**), is the go-to spot for needlecrafters, knitters, and fabric artists of all types. There are antiques shops scattered all around town, but more than 30 dealers gather on High Street at the **Comfort Antique Mall,** 734 High St. (www.visitcomfortantiquemall.com; ✆ **830/995-4678**). **Hill Country Distillers,** 723 Front St. (www.hillcountrytxdistillers.com; ✆ **830/995-2924**) creates intriguing spirits crafted with cactus and jalapeño.

In all cases, check ahead for hours, but as in other small towns around here, expect lots of places to be closed Monday through Wednesday. For more information, contact the **Comfort Chamber of Commerce,** 630 Hwy. 27 (www.comfortchamber.com; ✆ **830/995-3131**), open Tuesday through Saturday from 10am to 3pm.

WHERE TO EAT IN COMFORT

Take a shopping break on the cheery back patio of **Comfort Pizza,** 802 High St. (✆ **830/995-5959**), a converted gas station serving thin-crust pies. Toppings include everything from lime-chile spiced pineapple to fresh basil. The weekly changing menu at **814, A Texas Bistro,** 713 High St. (www.814atexasbistro.com; ✆ **830/995-4990**), might include grilled lamb chops with a balsamic glaze or sauteed salmon with spinach risotto.

WHERE TO STAY IN COMFORT

If kicking back on a rocking chair overlooking a quiet courtyard sounds appealing, consider spending the night at **Hotel Faust,** 717 High St. (www.hotelfaust.com; ✆ **830/995-3030**). A Texas Historic Landmark—it was built as an inn in the 1880s by Alfred Giles—the boutique hotel has six airy rooms ($185–$260), a log cabin ($260), and a cottage ($300).

KERRVILLE

25 miles N of Bandera; 18 miles NW of Comfort; 34 miles NW of Boerne; 65 miles NW of San Antonio

With a population of about 20,000, Kerrville is larger than the other Hill Country towns detailed here. Now a popular retirement and tourist area, it was founded in the 1840s by Joshua Brown, a shingle-maker attracted by the area's many cypress trees (and a friend of Major James Kerr, who never actually saw the town and county named after him). A rough-and-tumble camp surrounded by more civilized German towns, Kerrville soon became a ranching center for longhorn cattle and, more unusually, for Angora goats; at one time it produced the most mohair in the United States. After it was lauded in the 1920s for its healthful climate, Kerrville began to draw youth camps, sanitariums, and artists.

Exploring Kerrville

Make your first stop the **Kerrville Convention and Visitors Bureau,** 2108 Sidney Baker (www.kerrvilletexascvb.com; ✆ **800/221-7958**), where you can

A BIT OF old england IN THE OLD WEST

Several attractions, some endearingly offbeat, plus beautiful vistas along the Guadalupe River, warrant a detour west of Kerrville. Drive 5 miles from the center of town on Hwy. 27 W. to reach tiny **Ingram.** Take Hwy. 39 W. to the second traffic light downtown; after about a quarter of a mile, you'll see a sign for the Historic Old Ingram Loop, once a cowboy cattle-droving route and now home to rows of **antiques shops, crafts boutiques,** and **art galleries** and **studios.** Back on Hwy. 39, continue another few blocks to the **Hill Country Arts Foundation** (www.hcaf.com; ✆ **830/367-5121**), a complex comprising a theater, an art gallery, studios where arts-and-crafts classes are held—and a replica of Stonehenge. It's not as large as the original but, this being Texas, it's not exactly diminutive either. A couple of reproduction Easter Island heads fill out the ancient mystery sculpture group commissioned by Al Shepherd, a wealthy eccentric who died in the mid-1990s.

get a map of the area as well as of the historic downtown district. It's open weekdays 8:30am to 5pm, Saturday 9am to 3pm, and Sunday 10am to 3pm.

Then head to the restored downtown, flanked by the Guadalupe River and a pleasant park. Kerrville's historic buildings, most of them concentrated on Earl Garrett and Water streets, host a variety of restaurants and shops, many selling antiques and/or country-cute knickknacks. Among the most impressive structures is the **Schreiner Mansion Historic Site,** 226 Earl Garrett St. (www.caillouxfoundation.org/schreiner-mansion; ✆ **830/895-5222**), a mansion built of native stone by Alfred Giles for pioneer rancher and banker Capt. Charles Schreiner. The house is sometimes open for tours; call ahead. The 1935 post office now hosts the **Kerr Arts & Cultural Center,** 228 Earl Garrett St. (www.kacckerrville.com; ✆ **830/895-2911**), which exhibits work by local artists, in addition to hosting large annual exhibitions like the Southwest Gourd Fine Art Show and the Texas Furniture Makers Show.

To view work by top sculptors and painters from the mid–20th century to the present, head just outside the main part of town to the **Museum of Western Art,** 1550 Bandera Hwy. (www.museumofwesternart.com; ✆ **830/896-2553**), a high-quality collection housed in a striking Southwestern structure by O'Neill Ford. It also has an interactive children's history gallery. Outdoor enthusiasts will enjoy nearby **Kerrville-Schreiner Park,** 2385 Bandera Hwy. (www.kerrvilletx.gov/318/Kerrville-Schreiner-Park; ✆ **830/257-7300**), a 500-acre green space boasting 7 miles of hiking trails, swimming and boating on the Guadalupe River, campgrounds, and a variety of cabins for rent.

Military buffs and souvenir-seekers might want to drive 12 miles south of Kerrville on scenic Hwy. 173 to see **Camp Verde,** the former headquarters (1856–69) of the short-lived U.S. Army camel cavalry. The quixotic attempt to introduce "ships of the desert" into dry Southwest terrain never took off, due to widespread ignorance of the animals' habits; the onset of the Civil War dealt the program a final blow. There's little left of the fort itself, but the **Camp Verde General Store** (www.campverdegeneralstore.com; ✆ **830/634-7722**), with its camel statue out front, is a popular tourist stop. Established in 1857 to serve the soldiers stationed nearby, the store has been revamped several times; the most recent overhaul scrapped most of the wonderfully tacky camel-related tchotchkes in favor of more tasteful gifts, and added a cheerful casual restaurant serving hearty sandwiches and sides; it's open from 11am to 3pm.

Where to Eat in Kerrville

The setting—a beautifully restored 1915 depot with a lovely patio out back—is not the only thing outstanding about **Rails ★★**, 615 Schreiner (www.railscafe.com; ✆ **830/257-3877**), which serves some of the best food in the Hill Country. Everything, from the creative salads and Italian panini sandwiches to a small selection of hearty entrees, is made with fresh ingredients, many bought locally. The restaurant is open for lunch and dinner Monday through Saturday, and prices are moderate.

bats ALONG A BACK ROAD TO FREDERICKSBURG

It sounds like something out of a horror flick: millions of bats streaming out of an abandoned tunnel on a Texas back road. But this phenomenon, which you can view under the supervision of the Texas Parks and Wildlife Department, is fascinating—and not at all scary. From Comfort, take Hwy. 473 N. for 5 miles. When the road winds to the right toward Sisterdale, keep going straight on Old Hwy. 9. After another 8 or 9 miles, you'll spot a parking lot and a mound of large rocks on top of a hill. During the season (May–Oct), around dusk you can watch as many as three million Mexican free-tailed bats set off on a food foray. There's no charge to witness the phenomenon from the Upper Viewing Area, near the parking lot; it's open daily. If you want a closer view and an educational presentation lasting about 30 minutes to an hour, come to the Lower Viewing Area, open from Thursday through Sunday ($5 per person ages 4 and up, cash or check only). Children younger than 4 are not permitted in the Lower Viewing Area. There are 70 seats, filled on a first-come, first-served basis. Contact the **Old Tunnel Wildlife Management Area** (www.tpwd.texas.gov/state-parks/old-tunnel/bat-viewing; ✆ **866/978-2287** [recorded information]) to find out when its occupants are likely to flee the bat cave.

The name is Italian, but the menu at **Francisco's,** 201 Earl Garrett St. (www.franciscos-restaurant.com; ✆ **830/257-2995**), is eclectic, with lots of nods towards Mexico. It's housed in the 1890s Weston building. A downtown business crowd comes for soup and salad combos at lunchtime; many return on weekend evenings for such mix-it-up entrees as cilantro lime shrimp or teriyaki chipotle chicken. Francisco's is open for lunch Monday through Saturday, dinner Thursday through Saturday. Prices range from moderate to expensive.

FREDERICKSBURG

25 miles NE of Kerrville; 23 miles N of Comfort; 70 miles NW of San Antonio

A picturesque town of 10,000, about equidistant (75 miles) from San Antonio and Austin, Fredericksburg attracts visitors from both cities on weekends and holidays—with good reason. It's in a pretty rural setting, it's got lots of distinctive shops and lodgings, and it's the hub of Texas Wine Country (see box p. 148). It's also known for the peaches grown at the nearby orchards (the season runs May–Aug), and for the sweet products made from them.

Named for Prince Frederick of Prussia, Fredericksburg was founded in 1846, when Baron Ottfried Hans von Meusebach took 120 settlers in ox-drawn carts from the relative safety of New Braunfels to this site in the wild lands of the frontier. Meusebach negotiated a peace treaty with the Comanches in 1847—the only one in the United States that was never broken, it is claimed. The settlement prospered during the California Gold Rush, as this was the last place travelers could get supplies on the southern route until they reached Santa Fe, New Mexico. Fredericksburg is now the seat of Gillespie County.

Exploring Fredericksburg

IN TOWN

It's hard to find a better resource for sightseeing, dining, and lodging information than Fredericksburg's spacious and modern **Visitor Information Center,** 302 E. Austin St., (www.visitfredericksburgtx.com; ✆ **888/997-3600** or 830/997-6523), open weekdays 8:30am to 5pm, Saturday 9am to 5pm, Sunday 11am to 3pm.

On a self-guided walking tour of the historic district, points of interest include a number of little **Sunday Houses,** built by German farmers in distant rural areas as a place to stay overnight when they came to town to trade or to attend church. You'll also notice many homes built in the Hill Country version of the German *fachwerk* design, made out of limestone with diagonal wood supports.

On the town's main square, Marketplatz, the unusual octagonal **Vereins Kirche** (Society Church) was built in 1847 as a house of worship for both Lutheran and Catholic Germans. It later became a town hall, school, and storehouse. Inside the church (a 1935 replica of the original) there's a historical exhibit of the town, which can be viewed in a half-hour. (Admission by donation.) The Gillespie County Historical Society, which operates Vereins Kirche, also maintains the **Pioneer Museum,** 325 W. Main St. (www.pioneermuseum.net; ✆ **830/990-8441**). The complex is based around the 1849 Kammlah House, a family residence and general store until the 1920s, as well as its barn and smokehouse. Other historical structures, including a one-room schoolhouse and blacksmith's forge, were moved onto the site later. The museum is open Monday through Saturday from 10am to 5pm; admission is $7.50 adults, $3 ages 6 to 17.

The 1852 Steamboat Hotel, originally owned by the grandfather of World War II naval hero Chester A. Nimitz, is now part of the **National Museum of the Pacific War ★★**, 340 E. Main St. and 311 E. Austin St. (www.pacificwarmuseum.org; ✆ **830/997-8600**), the world's only museum focusing solely on the Pacific Theater of World War II. In addition to the exhibits in the steamboat-shaped museum, there are also the Japanese Garden of Peace, a gift from the people of Japan; the Memorial Courtyard, the equivalent of the Vietnam wall for Pacific war veterans; the life-size Pacific Combat Zone (2½ blocks east of the museum), which replicates a World War II battle scene; and the George H.W. Bush Gallery, where you can see a captured Japanese midget submarine and a multimedia simulation of a bombing raid on Guadalcanal. It's open daily 9am to 5pm; admission is $15 adults, $12 seniors, $10 military with ID; students and kids 6 and up $7.

Fredericksburg

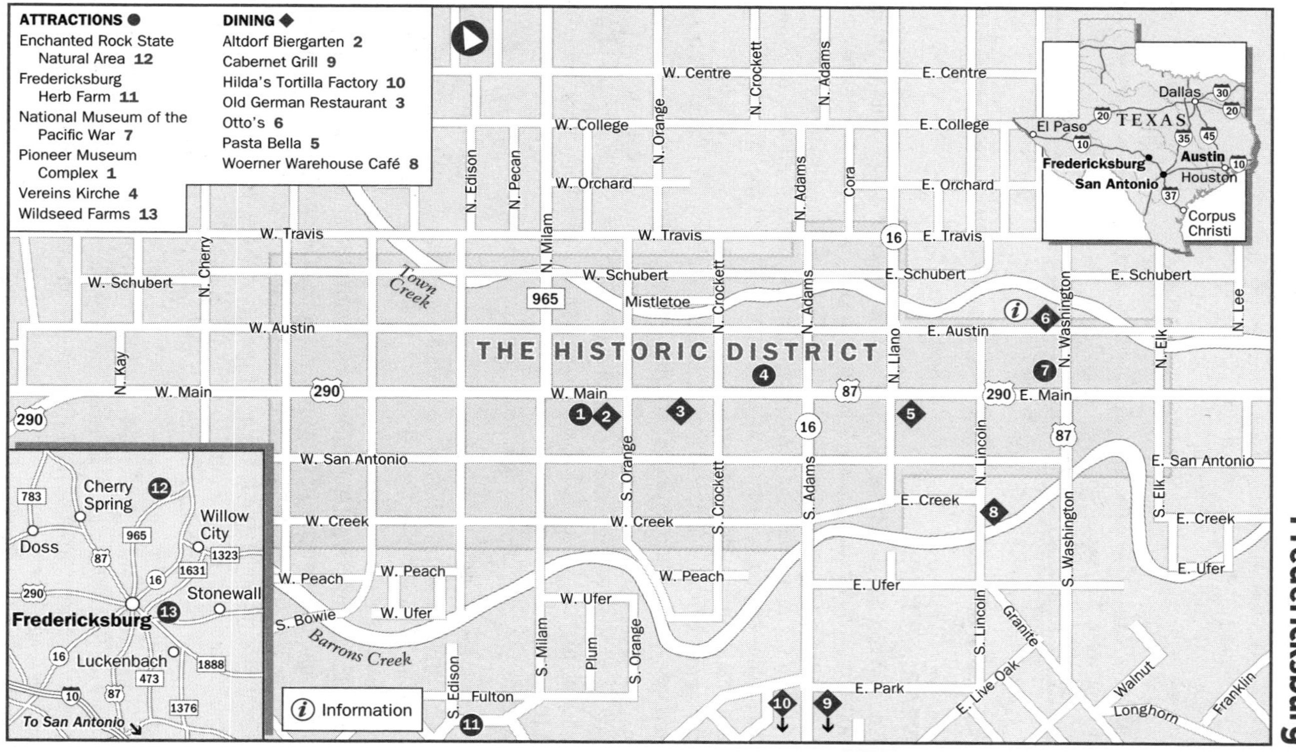

wild ABOUT TEXAS WILDFLOWERS

In mid- to late March and sometimes early April, the Hill Country is ablaze with red-topped Indian paintbrush and blue-and-white-tipped bluebonnets, the state flower of Texas. One of the most popular spots to see these and other wildflowers is the **Willow City Loop;** from Fredericksburg, head north on Hwy. 16 for approximately 13 miles to Willow City. The two-lane road passes canyons created by Coal Creek, and as you go around a bend, you spy what appears to be a pond or lake—but it's really a sea of bluebonnets. The Loop is also a popular place for cyclists, so drive slowly and watch for them. During wildflower season, the road is often clogged with traffic, giving you no choice but to crawl along.

NEAR FREDERICKSBURG

Enchanted Rock State Natural Area Take FM 965 some 18 miles north to reach **Enchanted Rock State Natural Area** (www.tpwd.texas.gov/state-parks/enchanted-rock; ✆ **830-685-3636**), a 640-acre site with a dome of solid pink granite that was pushed up to the surface by volcanic uplifting. You'll know when you get there: The smooth batholith rises almost 600 feet from the ground, in stark contrast to the surrounding hills. The creaking noises that emanate from it at night—likely caused by the cooling of the rock's outer surface—led the area's Native American tribes to believe that evil spirits inhabited the rock. The park is open daily 8am to 10pm; day-use entrance fees are $7 adults, free for children 12 and under. Tent sites in the vicinity of the parking lot cost $15 to $17; primitive backpack sites 1 to 3 miles away run $10 to $12. All campers need to pay the day-use entrance fee, too. Enchanted Rock is very popular; it's a good idea to get an early start.

LBJ Historical Parks Visiting the historical sites dedicated to Lyndon B. Johnson, the 36th president of the United States, can be a bit confusing. For one thing, they are 14 miles apart from each other. For another, they are managed by two separate government entities. In addition, within the two units, there are a variety of different sites to visit, with different opening and closing hours and an assortment of tour times to juggle. ***The good news:*** Rangers on all sites are very helpful, and you won't be paying separate entrance fees: Except for (optional) guided tours of the Texas White House, visits to both districts are free. Keep in mind too that you'll have an opportunity to swim, picnic, and even go fishing in the state park. Bring appropriate clothing and gear.

From Fredericksburg, take U.S. 290 E. for 16 miles to **The Lyndon B. Johnson State Park and Historic Site,** 199 State Park Rd. 52, Stonewall (www.tpwd.texas.gov/state-parks/lyndon-b-johnson; ✆ **830/644-2252**). At the visitor center, you'll get an overview of the Texas landscape and inhabitants that shaped LBJ's presidency; nearby, two cabins typical of life in the 1860s and 1870s add historical context. Outside, enclosures are stocked with native wildlife such as buffalo and white-tailed deer, as well as domesticated livestock: In 2014, the state park became home to part of the Official Texas State Longhorn Herd (yes, that's a thing).

From here, you can visit the **Sauer-Beckmann Farmstead,** where costumed interpreters give visitors a look at typical Texas-German farm life in 1918. Chickens, pigs, turkeys, and other farm animals roam freely or in large pens while the farmers go about their chores—churning butter, baking, feeding the animals. As interesting as Colonial Williamsburg but much less known, this is a terrific place to come with kids. Nearby are nature trails, a swimming pool (open early June to mid-Aug), and lots of picnic spots.

You can join a free (donations appreciated) hour-long guided tour of the complex, including the Sauer-Beckmann Farmstead, at the visitor center. All state park buildings, including the visitor center, are open daily 8:30am to 4pm; the Sauer-Beckmann Farmstead is open daily 10am to 4pm September through May, 9am to 3pm June to August (closed last Tues of every month). The nature trail, grounds, and picnic areas are open until dark every day.

At the state park visitor center, you can also pick up a permit and map guide for a driving tour of **Lyndon B. Johnson National Historical Park** (www.nps.gov/lyjo; ✆ **830/868-7128**), on the other side of the Pedernales River. The working ranch (here, the cattle are Herefords) was used by LBJ as a second White House, and his widow Lady Bird Johnson lived here until she died in 2007. After her death, the park service began giving half-hour-long tours of the 7,500-square-foot **Texas White House,** the only site that has a fee (adults $3, ages 17 and under free); pick up your tickets at the airplane hangar. The house feels eerily like a time warp back to the 1960s—LBJ's clothes, hats, and shoes still hang in the closet; it's as though he just walked out the door. At press time, the house was closed for repairs, but tours of the grounds were still being offered. Self-guided driving tours of the LBJ ranch are available daily from 9am to 5:30pm; driving permits are given out 9am to 4pm. Guided tours of the Texas White House are offered 10am to 4:30 pm.

It's 14 miles farther east along Hwy. 290 to **Johnson City,** a pleasant agricultural town named for founder James Polk Johnson, LBJ's first cousin once removed. Begin your visit at the **visitor center** (✆ **830/868-7128**); from U.S. 290, which turns into Main Street, take F Street to Lady Bird Lane, and you'll see the signs. Excellent interactive displays and two half-hour films (one about Johnson's presidency, the other about Lady Bird) provide background for the sites you'll see. The **Boyhood Home—**the modest white clapboard house on Elm Street where Lyndon was raised after age 5—is the centerpiece of this unit of the national historical park. From 1913 on, this house was a hub of intellectual and political activity: LBJ's father, Sam Ealy Johnson, Jr., was a state legislator, and his mother, Rebekah, was one of the few college-educated women in the country at the time. From here, head over to the **Johnson Settlement,** where LBJ's grandfather, Sam Ealy Johnson, Sr., and his great-uncle, Jessie, engaged in successful cattle speculation in the 1860s. Four buildings are still intact, including the rustic dogtrot cabin out of which the

THE FREDERICKSBURG wine connection

Texas' venerable tradition of winemaking and viticulture began with the Franciscan friars, who brought domesticated grapes up from Mexico in the late 16th century, cultivating them at the Spanish missions. Grape growing spread to the general populace and continued long after Texas and Mexico parted ways. Prohibition did real damage to Texas viticulture, however; the industry didn't begin to recover until the 1970s. A renaissance began in the 1990s, and today is in full force: At last count, there were more than 53 wineries in the Hill Country alone, some 40 of them in Gillespie County, where Fredericksburg is located. Many are on Hwy. 290, which means the road can be very congested on fair weather weekends. Pick up the **Wine Road 290** route map at the Fredericksburg visitor center, or click on www.wineroad290.com for details. Information about other Texas Hill Country Wineries is available at www.texaswinetrail.com; you can also phone ✆ **872/216-9463** for a brochure, or pick up a pamphlet at the visitor center.

If you plan to do a lot of wine tasting, the best way to visit the wineries is by van or bus tour. The **290 Wine Shuttle** (www.290wineshuttle.com; ✆ **210/724-7217**) offers lots of options: On Saturdays, a hop-on, hop-off pass ($29 for the day) lets you visit any of 14 wineries at your leisure; there are drop-offs and pick-ups at each stop every 15 minutes from 10am to 6pm. These tours depart across the street from the Fredericksburg Visitor Center. In addition, there are private group tours every day of the week.

Several excellent wineries also have tasting rooms in town. The **Narrow Path Winery,** 113 E. Main St. (www.narrowpathwinery.com; ✆ **830/624-2144**), is popular for its pretty bistro-style setting and its small batch dry wines. **Grape Creek Vineyard,** 223 E. Main St. (www.grapecreek.com; ✆ **820/644-2710**), won top awards at a major California wine competition for its Viognier and cuvee blanc. Probably the Hill Country's most famous winery, **Becker Vineyards,** 307 E. Main St. (www.beckervineyards.com; ✆ **830/644-2681**), produces classic French varietals with which it skillfully produces cabernets, pinot grigio, and chenin blancs, among others.

business was run; there's also a corral with longhorn cattle (don't bother them—they're ornery).

The visitor center is open 9am to 5pm daily. Self-guided tours of the Johnson Settlement are available daily from 9am until sunset. The Boyhood Home can be visited only by tours, offered every half hour from 9 to 11:30am, and 1 to 4:30pm. All are closed Christmas, Thanksgiving, and New Year's Day.

If you're not yet ready to call it a day, take a short detour from Hwy. 290 to **Pedernales Falls State Park,** 8 miles east of Johnson City on F.R. 2766 (www.tpwd.state.tx.us/park/pedernal; ✆ **830/868-7304**). When the flow of the Pedernales River is high, the stepped waterfalls that give the 4,860-acre park its name are awe-inspiring.

Fredericksburg Shopping

Fredericksburg has more than 150 shops, boutiques, and art galleries. You'll find candles, lace coverlets, cuckoo clocks, hand-woven rugs . . . if it's craftsy and homey, this town has got you covered. You'll find everything you need for your kitchen—and many things you don't need but want—at **Der Küchen Laden,** 258 E. Main St. (www.littlechef.com; © **830-9974937**), which is chock-a-block with high quality cutlery, gadgets, accessories, and cookbooks. Dog owners can pamper their pets at **Dogologie,** 148-B W. Main St. (www.dogologie.com; © **830/997-5855**), which carries everything the fashionable canine might need. **Texas Jack's,** 117 N. Adams St. (www.texasjacks.com; © **830/997-3213**), has outfitted actors for many Western films and TV shows, including *Lonesome Dove, Tombstone,* and *Gunsmoke.* If chocolate and spirits are two of your favorite food groups, stop in at **Chocolat,** 251 W. Main St. (www.liquidchocolates.com; © **800/842-3382** or 830/990-9382), where a rare old-world technique is employed to encase alcohol in chocolate.

In a small warehouse district on the south side, **Carol Hicks Bolton Antiques,** 301 S. Lincoln St. (www.carolhicksbolton.com; © **830/997-5551**), dedicates some 30,000 square feet to home furnishings that range from rustic (tables that look like they're straight from a farm) to romantic (wrought-iron beds with filmy white draperies). Expect to pay a premium.

Gardeners can spend a good part of the day (and in one case, night) at two spots on the outskirts of town, both well-known through their mail-order business. At **Fredericksburg Herb Farm,** 405 Whitney St. (www.fredericksburgherbfarm.com; © **800/259-HERB** [259-4372] or 830/997-8615), you can see flower beds that produce teas, fragrances, lotions, soaps, and air fresheners sold at the gift shop. The farm complex also has 14 guest cottages, modeled on the traditional Fredericksburg Sunday houses, along with a state-of-the-art spa, offering treatments that use lotions and gels made on the farm. The herb farm's **Farm House Bistro** is a lovely spot for lunches ranging from salads to flatbread pizzas and burgers (it's open for breakfast and dinner too).

A visit to **Wildseed Farms,** 7 miles east on Hwy. 290 (www.wildseedfarms.com; © **830/990-1393**), will disabuse you of any notions you may have had that wildflowers grew wild. At this working wildflower farm, you can stroll through fields of blossoms that are harvested for seeds sold throughout the world. Along with seeds, plants, and gardening accessories, the gift shop sells clothing and a wide assortment of gifts. Jams, jellies, and salsas are sold at the **Brewbonnet Biergarten,** where beer and a menu of light snacks is also available. Prefer wine? Visit **Wedding Oak Winery's** tasting room, also on the premises.

Where to Stay in Fredericksburg

Fredericksburg is known for its abundant bed-and-breakfasts and *gastehauses* (guest cottages)—more than 1,000 of them. *Gastehauses* are often romantic havens complete with robes, fireplaces, and even hot tubs; they run anywhere from $120 to $300 plus. Most visitors reserve lodgings through one of these booking services: **First Class Bed & Breakfast Reservation Service,** 909 E.

Main St. (www.fredericksburg-lodging.com; ✆ **855-422-4928** or 830/997-0443); **Gästehaus Schmidt,** 231 W. Main St. (www.fbglodging.com; ✆ **866/427-8374** or 830/997-5612); **Absolute Charm,** 711 W. Main St. (www.absolutecharm.com; ✆ **866/244-7897** or 830/997-2749); **Main Street B&B Reservation Service,** 337 E. Main St. (www.travelmainstreet.com; ✆ **888/559-8555** or 830/997-0153); **Fredericksburg Guest House Reservations** (www.cccottage.com; ✆ **830/997-5839**); or **Vacasa,** 417 E. Main St. (www.vacasa.com/usa/Texas/Fredericksburg; ✆ **830/515-4787**).

There are also several hotels and motels in town, including the **Hangar Hotel,** 155 Airport Rd. (www.hangarhotel.com; ✆ **830/997-9990**), which banks on nostalgia for the World War II flyboy era. Located at the town's tiny private airport, this hotel hearkens back to the 1940s with its clean-lined Art Moderne–style rooms, as well as an officer's club (democratically open to all) and retro diner. The re-creation isn't taken too far: Rooms have all the mod-cons. Rates run from $149 Sunday through Thursday to $189 on Friday and Saturday.

Where to Eat in Fredericksburg

See also the **Farm House Bistro** at the Fredericksburg Herb Farm (above) and **Hondo's on Main** (below).

Fredericksburg's dining scene is diverse, catering to the traditional and trendy alike. Some places are closed for Sunday dinner (though Sun brunch is big in town) and all day Monday, and not all restaurants take reservations; make them in advance for weekend dinners if possible.

The line sometimes extends out the door for breakfast tacos like "El Especial" (poblanos, eggs, beans, bacon, and tomatoes) at **Hilda's Tortillas,** 149 Tivydale Rd. (www.hildastortillas.com; ✆ **830/997-6105**); don't worry, the line moves quickly. A bit off the beaten tourist path, **Woerner Warehouse Café + Catering,** 305 S. Lincoln St. (woernerwarehouse.com; ✆ **830/997-2246**), is a good bet for a lunch of from-scratch pizza, panini, or a farm-fresh salad in an antiques-filled warehouse.

Want to relate to the town's history? Then start your day with German pancakes or apple strudel at the **Old German Restaurant & Bakery,** 225 W. Main St. (www.oldgermanbakeryandrestaurant.com; ✆ **830/997-9084**). For lunch, the patio of **Altdorf Biergarten,** 301 W. Main St. (www.altdorfs.com; ✆ **830/997-7865**), makes a great perch to munch on a Reuben sandwich or a pair of brats washed down a cold Pilsner. **Otto's,** 316 E. Austin St. (www.ottosfbg.com; ✆ **830/307-3336**), does a contemporary spin on traditional German cooking, with a weekly changing menu that relies on local and organic products—you might find duck schnitzel with apple-mustard lyonnaise sauce for a main course, Cambozola cheesecake for dessert. The killer cocktails alone justify a visit.

Another foodie magnet at dinnertime, the **Cabernet Grill,** 2805 Hwy. 16 S. (www.cabernetgrill.com; ✆ **830/990-5734**), looks to local ranches and farms

GOING BACK (IN TIME) TO luckenbach

Originally founded as a trading post by German immigrant Jacob Luckenbach in 1849, **Luckenbach** (www.luckenbachtexas.com; ✆ **888/311-8990** or 830/997-3224), about 10 miles southeast of Fredericksburg, almost faded away until the late John Russell "Hondo" Crouch entered the picture. A political commentator, swimmer, writer, goat farmer, and humorist, Crouch bought the entire town in 1971, primarily so he would have a place to drink beer. Declaring himself mayor, Crouch set to work establishing as many wacky traditions as possible, including women-only chili cook-offs and no-talent contests. The outdoor stage emerged as a favorite venue of Willie Nelson, Jerry Jeff Walker, Waylon Jennings, and other legends, and the catchphrase, "Everybody's somebody in Luckenbach," caught on, appearing on bumper stickers and T-shirts. Jerry Jeff's famed *Viva Terlingua* album was recorded here live, but it was Willie & Waylon's hit song "Luckenbach, Texas," that put this quirky ghost town on the map. Centered around the old general store to this day, Luckenbach remains one of the best places to catch live music in all of Texas (shows 7 days a week; tickets are often free, but can run up to about $30). Souvenirs, food, and ice-cold beer are available. Each day, people sit around the stovepipe heater inside the bar and play guitar and sing. Outside, they're singing too. Hondo passed away soon after pushing for the "Non-Buy Centennial" as his personal protest against the commercialization of the bicentennial of the Declaration of Independence in 1976. His memorial is on-site. ***Tip:*** Luckenbach sometimes tends to shut down early at night on weeknights and even some weekends. Best to get there in the afternoon.

Whenever you visit, lots of beer is likely to be involved, so consider staying at the **Full Moon Inn,** 3234 Luckenbach Rd. (www.luckenbachtx.com; ✆ **800/997-1124** or 830/997-2205), just half a mile from the action on a rise overlooking the countryside. The best of the accommodations, most of which range in price from $125 to $200, is the 1800s log cabin ($290), large enough to sleep four.

for such entrees as bacon-wrapped grilled quail and oak-smoked pork tenderloin, and to Texas vineyards for its wines. For a more casual repast, try the intimate and colorful **Pasta Bella,** 103 S. Llano St. (www.pastabellarestaurant.com; ✆ **830/990-9778**), where you get a choice of portion size, sauces, and toppings for your spaghetti or other pasta. Carb-free and gluten-free options are available too.

Fredericksburg Nightlife

Yes, Fredericksburg's got nightlife, or at least what passes for it in the Hill Country. Some of the live music action takes place a bit outside the center of town. On Fridays and Saturdays, you'll usually find Johnny Nicholas (formerly of Austin's Asleep at the Wheel) jamming with friends at the **Hill Top Café,** 10661 N. Hwy. 87 (www.hilltopcafe.com; ✆ **830/997-8922**), an old country gas station that Nichols and his late wife, Brenda, converted into a restaurant. Luckenbach (see box above) also hosts lots of good bands.

Lately, Fredericksburg's main (and side) streets have also come alive with the sound of music—everything from rockabilly and jazz to oompah—from Thursday through Saturday nights. An offshoot of the Luckenbach Dancehall created by the late Hondo Crouch, **Hondo's on Main,** 312 W. Main St. (www.hondosonmain.com; ✆ **830/997-1633**), tends to feature Texas roots bands. The burgers, ribs, and stacked enchiladas are reason enough to come.

SUGGESTED AUSTIN ITINERARIES

10

There's an in-joke that Austinites tell about how to entertain visiting family and friends. At some point in discussing sightseeing plans, someone is bound to ask, "So when are you taking them to San Antonio?"

It's not that Austin doesn't have places of interest to travelers. There are plenty of great historic sights and abundant outdoor activities, though some of the latter can only be enjoyed seasonally. It's just that a taste of genuine Austin is less about standard sightseeing, more about absorbing the city's vibe. Thus this 3-day itinerary is geared toward those who want to experience the best of what Austin has to offer, including lifestyle activities in addition to typical tourist attractions. Many of the stops are low-cost or free, though several offer the opportunity to drop a lot of money. That's true too of the separate itinerary designed for those traveling with kids.

And, hey, if you're up for more sightseeing, the first half of this book is devoted to San Antonio, which is less than an hour and a half away.

Note: Austin's attractions are fairly spread out. Because you're going to be packing a lot into your 3 days, driving is generally your best option, though it's not always ideal. See chapter 18 for more details about parking and getting around Austin.

THE BEST OF AUSTIN IN 1 DAY

This first day of highlights doesn't take you very far from the downtown core, but you'll mostly be on its periphery. The first few stops are within walking distance of each other, but for the others you'll need wheels—and parking can be a hassle in several of these popular spots. If you're only in town for 1 day, consider ride-shares, which are not very expensive within these relatively short distances, or take advantage of the B-Cycle bike-sharing program, a great option for those willing to two-wheel it around town for at least part of this itinerary.

The Best of Austin in 1, 2 & 3 Days

The Best of Austin in 1 Day

1. Paperboy
2. Texas State Capitol
3. Blanton Museum of Art
4. West 6th Street and North Lamar Blvd.
5. Zilker Metropolitan Park
6. Bat Flight
7. South Congress Avenue
8a. Broken Spoke
8b. Continental Club
8c. Saxon Pub

The Best of Austin in 2 Days

1. Fareground
2. Hike-and-Bike Trail
3. LBJ Library and Museum
4. Hyde Park
5. Mount Bonnell
6. Cactus Cafe

The Best of Austin in 3 Days

1. Lady Bird Johnson Wildflower Center
2. Zilker Metropolitan Park/ South Congress Ave.
3. East Austin
4. Bar Hopping

0 1 mi
0 1 km

ALLANDALE
Emma Long Metropolitan Park
Northland Dr.
Shoal Creek
W. Koenig Ln.
Airport Blvd.
35
Mount Bonnell Rd.
Westlake Dr.
Toro Canyon Rd.
1
Colorado River
ROSEDALE
E. 51st St.
W. 35th St.
N. Lamar Blvd.
E. 45th St.
HYDE PARK
Wild Basin Wilderness Park
WESTLAKE HILLS
W. 38th St.
Airport Blvd.
Exposition Blvd.
Shoal Creek Greenbelt
Enfield Rd.
Windsor Rd.
UNIVERSITY OF TEXAS
290
Manor Rd.
Lake Austin Blvd.
Pease Park
Westlake Dr.
E. Martin
WEST AUSTIN
E. 19th St.
Capital of Texas Hwy.
ROLLINGWOOD
E. 12th St.
Bee Caves Rd.
35
DOWNTOWN
Zilker Park
W. Cesar Chavez St.
EAST AUSTIN
E. 5th St.
360
Mopac Expy.
Lady Bird Lake
E. Cesar Chavez St.
Barton Creek
SOUTH AUSTIN
Pleasant Valley Rd.
S. Lamar Blvd.
W. Oltorf St.
Barton Creek Greenbelt
S. Congress Ave.
S. 1st St.
E. Riverside Dr.
Montopolis Dr.
290
E. Oltorf St.
Brodie Ln.
Manchaca Rd.
71
35
Burleson Rd.
290
SOUTH AUSTIN
W. Stassney Ln.
S. Congress Ave.
E. St Elmo Rd.
To Austin-Bergstrom International Airport
McKinney Falls State Park
Burleson Rd.

Bike Trail

1 Paperboy

You can't say you've been to Austin if you haven't eaten in a food trailer, and **Paperboy** (p. 213), just east of I-35 from downtown, specializes in breakfast, from cinnamon toast to a hash of sweet potatoes, pork belly, poached egg, and pecan mole.

Your next stop is only a few blocks to the west, but if you opt to walk, cars will be whizzing overhead on the freeway. If you're driving, you get 2 hours of free parking in the Texas State Capitol garage (1201 San Jacinto St.), a short walk from the main building.

2 Texas State Capitol ★★★

You might expect the Texas State Capitol (p. 224) to be BIG and you won't be disappointed by this grand pink-granite structure on 22 acres of immaculately tended grounds; its spire rises 14 feet higher than the U.S. Capitol building in Washington, D.C. To learn all the fascinating details of its history and construction, catch one of the frequent free half-hour tours, or pick up a self-guided tour pamphlet. Keep an eye out for such details as the decorative door hinges, so gorgeous that they kept getting stolen; now you can buy replicas in the excellent **Texas Capitol Gift Shop.**

3 Blanton Museum of Art ★★★

Less than a 15-minute walk north of the Capitol, the University of Texas's **Blanton Museum of Art** (p. 226) is a must-visit for many reasons—its stunning modern architecture, its wide-ranging and in-depth holdings (everything from Dutch Renaissance masters to contemporary Latin American abstractionists), and Ellsworth Kelly's "Austin," the first and only building by the late abstract artist. ***A bonus:*** It's a relatively small museum, so you should be able to get a good taste in an hour or so.

4 West 6th Street and North Lamar Boulevard

About a 10-minute drive south from the UT campus, this intersection on the west side of downtown spotlights three Austin-sprung retailers who embody the city's spirit: **BookPeople** (p. 260), one of the top indie bookstores in the country; **Waterloo Records** (p. 265), a magnet for every type of music lover; and the 80,000-square-foot **Whole Foods** (p. 258), on the site of the original upscale organic grocer (and next door to its world headquarters), which has everything you might want to consume, fresh or packaged, flesh or fowl, cooked or raw.

5 Zilker Metropolitan Park

Continue south on Lamar Boulevard across Lady Bird Lake to the liveliest green space in town, spread over 347 acres. A few top options at Zilker Park: Join the throngs splashing around the spring-fed **Barton Springs Pool** ★★★ (p. 237); stroll through the gracious **Zilker Botanical Garden** (p. 245); or visit the **Umlauf Sculpture Garden & Museum**

(p. 238), the home, studios, and garden of artist Charles Umlauf. If you're up for some exercise, **rent a kayak or canoe** (p. 250) to take on Lady Bird Lake; the vistas from the water can't be beat.

6 Bat Flight

Less than 10 minutes east from the park, you'll reach the *Austin-American Statesman* Bat Observation Center, on the southeast side of the Congress Avenue Bridge. From late March through early November, the largest urban bat colony in North America—that's some 1.5 million Mexican free-tailed bats—swarm out from under Congress Avenue Bridge at around dusk to go on an insect hunt. See p. 237.

7 South Congress Avenue

Half a mile south of the Congress Avenue Bridge, the shops, restaurants, and nightspots of trendy SoCo offer lots of shopping options (see chapter 15) and the city's best concentration of good restaurants (see chapter 13).

8 Live Music

South Austin—not only South Congress Avenue but also South Lamar and South First avenues, nearby—has several great live music venues; check out who's playing at the **Broken Spoke** (p. 277), the **Continental Club** (p. 274), or the **Saxon Pub** (p. 274).

THE BEST OF AUSTIN: DAY 2

This day starts at the southern end of downtown, near the Congress Avenue Bridge; this time, you're heading northwest. You won't go much beyond the central part of town, but put on comfortable shoes. You'll be doing a bit of walking around.

---

1 Fareground

You'll be spoiled for choice at **Fareground** (p. 203), Austin's first food hall, located in the lobby of a high-rise office building just north of the Congress Avenue Bridge. Go for a coffee and pastry at **Easy Tiger,** perhaps, or a sausage-and-egg burrito at **Henbit.**

2 Hike-and-Bike Trail

Fareground is a block from the north shore of the 10-mile lakeside loop around Lady Bird Lake, known as the **Hike-and-Bike Trail** (p. 232). Austinites of all ages and professions congregate here, from parents with baby carriages to speed walkers and casual amblers.

3 LBJ Library and Museum ★★★

Head back north to the University of Texas campus, where the fascinating **Lyndon Baines Johnson Library and Museum** (p. 229) affords your best view of the UT campus. Inside the library, behind glass windows, you'll see the presidential papers boxed in red Moroccan leather, but it's the museum you'll really want to visit, including an animatronic version of LBJ and displays of editorial comics, some of them rather brutal.

4 Hyde Park ★★

Just north of the UT campus, stroll the leafy streets of Austin's first suburb, a planned community where you'll find a mix of home styles, including Queen Anne, Tudor Revivals, and Craftsman. Perhaps the most impressive—and also the oddest—structure is your ultimate destination: The **Elisabet Ney Museum** ★★★ (p. 228), a startlingly large limestone residence and studio built in 1893 by the feminist sculptor and philosopher. Formosa, as Ney dubbed the place, showcases over 100 of her works. Grab something light to eat at the Hyde Park branch of **Kerbey Lane** (p. 210).

5 Mount Bonnell ★★

Less than 15 minutes northwest of Hyde Park, the limestone outcropping known as Mount Bonnell (p. 242)—the highest point in Austin—provides unbeatable vistas of Lake Austin as well as downtown. It's the perfect place to enjoy the sunset. Then return to the UT area to have dinner at **Olamaie** ★★★ (p. 218), which raises southern dining to an art form.

6 Live Music

If you want to experience great singer/songwriter talent—whether up-and-coming or tried-and-true—go to the **Cactus Cafe** (p. 278), on the UT campus.

THE BEST OF AUSTIN: DAY 3

On the third day, you can wind down a bit. You'll be heading about half an hour outside town in the morning, then returning to the center of the city. Have breakfast near your hotel before heading out to:

---

1 Lady Bird Johnson Wildflower Center ★★★

A small native plant research center in East Austin, co-founded by the former first lady and actress Helen Hayes, the **Lady Bird Johnson Wildflower Center** (p. 231) was moved to the southwest part of town and eventually became part of the University of Texas. There's so much to ogle on this 284-acre spread that you can end up spending more time here than you planned, especially in spring when the wildflowers are in bloom.

2 Zilker Metropolitan Park / South Congress Avenue

You'll be near Zilker Park (see Day 1, stop #5) as you head back toward the city center, so consider visiting one of the attractions you missed on the first day. Then head east on Barton Springs Road to get a barbecue fix at **Terry Black's** (p. 215) and enjoy it on the restaurant's laid-back patio.

3 East Austin

Cross the river and head northeast to explore one of Austin's trendiest areas, the historically black and Hispanic neighborhood just east of downtown across I-35. To learn about the neighborhood's history, visit the **George Washington Carver Museum, Cultural and Genealogy Center** ★★ (p. 241), which explores Texas' African-American roots. You won't find as many shops and galleries in East Austin as you will in SoCo (for now), but the ones there are arguably more cutting edge, though not necessarily less expensive. For dinner, you've got a lot of options, from Japanese Texan (**Kemuri Tatsu-ya** ★★; p. 216) to classic French (**Justine's Brasserie** ★★; p. 215).

4 Bar Hopping

You'll find several bars scattered around the **East Austin Entertainment District** (p. 277). Just strolling around this hip neighborhood, with its street art and food trucks, is a great way to feel the pulse of Austin's nightlife.

AUSTIN WITH KIDS

The family who loves to play outdoors together will find heaven in Austin, but those who are less fresh-air inclined will also find plenty to do.

DAY 1

Let's start in the historic downtown.

1 Bullock Texas State History Museum ★★★

Your kids might come away from the **Bullock Texas State History Museum** (p. 228) thinking that Texas is the center of the universe—that's pretty much the goal of this big, bold, appealing institution. Interactive exhibitions include historical artifacts from *La Belle*, a shipwrecked French boat dating back to 1684, and the original Goddess of Liberty that stood on top of the Texas State Capitol. The two multi-sensory films shown in the Spirit Theater are loads of fun and an on-site IMAX theater plays the latest box office hits.

Austin with Kids

Day 1

1. Bullock Texas State History Museum
2. West 6th Street and North Lamar Boulevard
3. Zilker Metropolitan Park
4. Bat Viewing
5. Güero's

Day 2

1. Austin Zoo
2. Lady Bird Johnson Wildflower Center
3. Austin Central Library

Day 3

(1) Schlitterbahn Waterpark

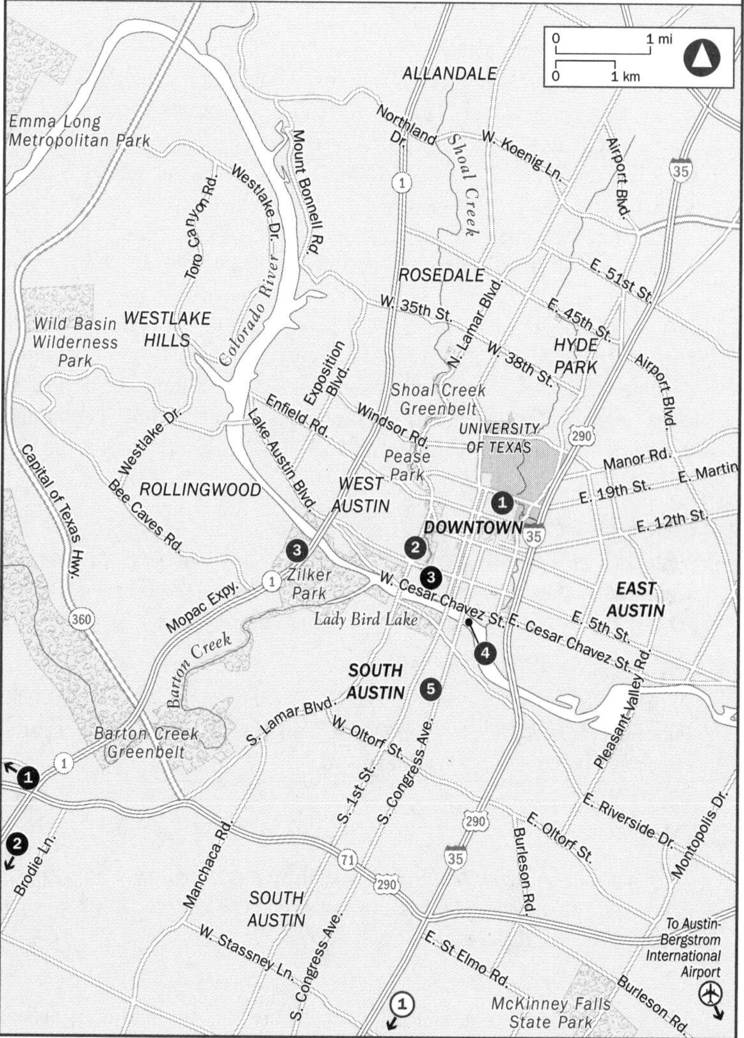

2 West 6th Street and North Lamar Boulevard

Southwest of downtown, all ages will find something to like at the three stores that share this intersection. There's a large section for kids at **BookPeople** (p. 260); teenagers will especially love **Waterloo Records** (p. 265) if you hold back on the nostalgic tales about the music you grew up on. The vast **Whole Foods** (p. 258) is a perfect spot for lunch or take-away; even picky eaters are bound to find something to suit their taste. (***Little known fact:*** For the last several years, there's been an ice skating rink atop this Whole Foods from late November to late January. The price ($10) includes skate rentals.)

3 Zilker Metropolitan Park

Head south a couple of blocks on Lamar Boulevard to reach Zilker Park, which is a great place to spend the entire afternoon. If the weather's warm enough, you can splash in the **Barton Springs Pool** ★★★ (p. 237); its former bathroom is now a kid-friendly attraction, **Splash! Into the Edwards Aquifer** ★★ (p. 246), which simulates entering a sinkhole in the ecosystem that created the natural swimming pool. At the 80-acre **Austin Nature and Science Center** ★★ (p. 246), exhibits range from dinosaur tracks to a wildlife rehabilitation facility, with rescued birds of prey, mammals, and more. Not far from Barton Springs Pool, the narrow-gauge **Zilker Zephyr Miniature Train** ★ (p. 247) departs on a 25-minute journey through the park every hour on the hour during the week, every half hour on the weekend, weather permitting. If you time things right, your family can be on Lady Bird Lake at dusk for the next activity.

4 Bat Viewing

Watching the 1.5 million Mexican free-tailed bats emerge from under the Congress Avenue Bridge from a vantage point on the lake—a **Capital Cruise** (p. 248) is a good option—is great fun.

5 Güero's ★★★

A perfect place for a post-bat watching meal for the family, Tex-Mex favorite **Güero's** (p. 209), on South Congress Avenue, has a separate children's menu and a fun atmosphere.

DAY 2

Two top sights for kids are in the southwest part of town, so it makes sense for you to start your day in this area. The rest of Day 2 has you heading back to the center of town.

1 Austin Zoo ★

The concept of keeping animals in enclosures of any kind is controversial, so it's no surprise that this ethically oriented city's nonprofit **Austin**

Zoo (p. 246) exists as a sanctuary for creatures that can't survive in the wild. More than 800 different species from all over the world are gathered here, from domestic goats, sheep, and deer to exotics like tigers and giant Galapagos tortoises.

2 Lady Bird Johnson Wildflower Center ★★★

The Luci and Ian Family Garden at the **Lady Bird Johnson Wildflower Center** (p. 231) has several natural playscapes for kids, including a shallow creek to wade through, tree stumps to sit on, and caves to crawl through.

3 Austin Central Library ★★★

Return to downtown to check out the spacious new (2017) **Austin Central Library** (p. 234), which has something for all ages, including teens who want to spend time online—visitors are given free access to computers with an ID card from an adult—or small kids who want to play or yell or touch things. If you spend the afternoon here, you can have dinner at the library's **Cookbook Café** ★★★ (p. 203), which offers menu items from kids' cookbooks, and cocktails for adults who might need "A Midsummer Night's Dram" at the end of a long day.

DAY 3

If you're visiting from late April to mid-September, consider heading out of town to visit the large **Schlitterbahn Waterpark** (p. 301) in New Braunfels, about 50 miles from Austin. Like any theme park, this one has lots of thrill rides, but it's also in a natural setting on the Comal River so you don't feel like you're in an entirely artificial environment. Tubing, surfing, and every other way you can think of to get wet are the order of the day.

CITY LAYOUT

In 1839, Austin was laid out in a grid on the northern shore of the Colorado River, bounded by Shoal Creek to the west and Waller Creek to the east. The section of the river abutting the original settlement is now known as Lady Bird Lake, and the city has spread far beyond its original borders in all directions. The land to the east is flat Texas prairie; the rolling Hill Country begins on the west side of town.

MAIN ARTERIES & STREETS **I-35,** forming the border between central and east Austin, is the main north-south thoroughfare; **Loop 1,** usually called MoPac Boulevard (it follows the course of the Missouri-Pacific railroad), is the major north-south road on the west side of town. On the far west side of town, the scenic **Loop 360** is a good north-south alterative road when MoPac is jammed. East-west **Hwy. 290** enters the city on the north side of town, merges with I-35 to run through downtown, then reestablishes its separate identity on the south side of town to proceed west, merging with east-west **Hwy. 71** (also called **Ben White Boulevard** for a stretch just west of the airport). Hwy. 290 and Hwy. 71 split up again in Oak Hill, on the west side of town. The **Pickle Parkway** (Texas State Hwy. 130), Austin's infamous 80–85 mph toll road, runs north-south on the east side of town. (Looking at a map should make all this clear as mud.)

Important north-south city streets include **Lamar Boulevard, Guadalupe Street,** and **Burnet Road.** If you want to get across town north of the river, use **Cesar Chavez Street** (once known as First St.), **15th Street** (which turns into Enfield Rd. west of Lamar Blvd.), **Martin Luther King, Jr., Boulevard** (the equivalent of 19th St., and often just called MLK), **38th Street,** or **45th Street.**

FINDING AN ADDRESS Congress Avenue was the earliest dividing line between east and west, while the Colorado River divided the north and south sections of the city. Addresses were designed to move in increments of 100 per block, so that 1500 N. Guadalupe, say, would be 15 blocks north of the river. This system still works reasonably well in the older sections of town, but breaks down where the neat street grid does (look at a street map to see where the right angles end). All the east-west streets were originally named after trees native to the city (for example, Sixth Street was once Pecan Street); most that run north and south, such as San Jacinto, Lavaca, and Guadalupe, retain their original Texas river monikers.

Austin Neighborhoods in Brief

Although Austin, designed to be the capital of the independent Republic of Texas, has a grand planned city center similar to that of Washington, D.C., the city has spread out far beyond those original boundaries in all directions. Rather than easily delineated small areas, locals often speak in terms of landmarks (near the University of Texas), intersections (close to 183 and MoPac), or large geographical sections (East Austin). And with the exceptions of such established historic neighborhoods as Hyde Park, newer neighborhoods are often in flux; those that are trendy one year may be forgotten the next. So with those caveats, these are some useful designations. For now.

DOWNTOWN

The original city, laid out by Edwin Waller in 1839, runs roughly north-south from Lady Bird Lake/Cesar Chavez Street to Martin Luther King, Jr., Boulevard (around 20th St.) and east-west between I-35 and Lamar Boulevard. The main north-south drag, **Congress Avenue,** runs from Lady Bird Lake to the State Capitol. With its many historic buildings and blocks, this is the prime sightseeing hub, as well as an entertainment district. It's also home to the Convention Center and many major businesses and financial institutions. As might be expected, it has the highest concentration of hotels in town.

Once known as Austin's live music hub, **Sixth Street** has a dual personality these days. Locals refer to East Sixth Street between Congress Avenue and I-35 as Dirty Sixth; it's lined with small live music venues, endless bars offering dollar shots, and pool halls. West Sixth, from Congress Avenue to Lamar Avenue, appeals more to the young professional crowd. Serious music lovers head for the **Warehouse District,** centered on Third and Fourth streets just west of Congress, and the **Red River District,** on (where else?) Red River Street, between 6th and 10th streets.

SOUTH AUSTIN

For a long time, south of Lady Bird Lake was largely a working class residential area. In the 1990s, **South Congress,** the once-derelict stretch of Congress that extends (roughly) to Oltorf Street, began getting gentrified by shop and restaurant owners who liked the proximity to downtown without the high rents. Now dubbed SoCo, it's one of Austin's trendiest places to shop, eat, and—increasingly, as boutique hotels crop up—sleep in town. **South Lamar** has also become established as a hot area, with trendy bars and restaurants opening along South Lamar Boulevard. A few blocks east, **South First Street** offers everything from food trucks to upscale dining rooms. Austin's first settlements south of the river, **East Riverside** and **Travis Heights** (adjacent neighborhoods between Congress and I-35), are popular with young professionals who can afford the high prices. Farther south and west, toward the Lady Bird Johnson Wildflower Center, South Austin begins to reassert its rural roots, with less construction and more businesses that cater mostly to locals.

EAST SIDE

The residential area east of I-35 between Cesar Chavez Street and Manor Road was long home to many of Austin's Hispanic and African-American residents. But the parts closest to downtown and the university are increasingly popular, forcing many poorer residents to move farther east. **Cesar Chavez, East Sixth Street, East Seventh Street,** and **Manor Road** are now packed with bars, restaurants, and coffee shops, and experimental theaters are popping up. Hip lodgings are beginning to appear in the area closest to downtown.

CENTRAL

North of Lady Bird Lake/Cesar Chavez Street up to 45th Street, between I-35 and MoPac, Central Austin includes downtown (see above) as well as several neighborhoods on its fringes. Just north of the Capitol and the state government office complex, the original 40-acre site allotted for the **University of Texas** has expanded to 357, and **Guadalupe Street,** along the west side of the campus, is now a popular shopping street known as the Drag. Many visitors come to what's often called the Cultural Campus to see the Blanton Museum of Art, the Bullock Texas State History Museum, the Harry Ransom Center, the LBJ Library and Museum, and the Texas Memorial Museum. North of the university, from 35th to 51st streets, **Hyde Park** was laid out in 1891 as one of Austin's first planned suburbs; renovation of its Victorian and early Craftsman houses began in the 1970s, and now it has a real neighborhood feel.

Beyond Hyde Park, numbered streets disappear. The older neighborhoods in this area are also experiencing a renaissance. Just north of Hyde Park, the shabby-chic **North Loop** is fast becoming Austin's bohemian epicenter, with hip indie shops and restaurants taking over North Loop Avenue. It's bounded on the west by North Lamar Boulevard, on the east by Airport Boulevard (some say I-35), and on the north by Koenig Lane. For a lot of Austinites, **Research Boulevard** is where central Austin ends and north Austin begins.

WEST / LAKES

Just west of downtown and the shopping enclave at Lamar and West Sixth is **Clarksville,** a black community founded in the 1870s by freed slaves. It's now a neighborhood of small, old houses that command high prices. To the west of Clarksville, on the other side of the MoPac Freeway, tony **Tarrytown** extends as far as Lake Austin (another dammed section of the Colorado River). Both neighborhoods are close enough to the heart of town that they're sometimes folded into the "Central" designation.

For many, "West" refers to the townships on the opposite side of Lake Austin from West Austin. This affluent suburban area includes the communities of **Rollingwood** and **Westlake Hills.** If you head upstream to the next dam, you come to Lake Travis, a large lake with lots of marinas and lakeside communities, such as **Lakeway.** Those who live in Central Austin come here to splash around and kick back on nice weekends.

NORTHWEST

This high-growth area, Austin's version of the suburbs, is where most of the high-tech industry is located. It includes the **Arboretum** mall, a prime area of restaurant and retail growth in the late 1980s and 1990s; and the newer, still expanding, **Domain** and **Domain NORTHSIDE** mall complex. This manufactured mixed-use community, with apartments, retail, and restaurants and hotels, is an anchor for the otherwise sprawling North Austin neighborhoods. It's not quite the "second downtown" that its promoters make it out to be, but it has lots of lively nightspots. Farther north are the bedroom communities of **Round Rock** and **Cedar Park.**

AUSTIN IN CONTEXT

11

A rapidly growing city that's struggling to define itself, Austin contains multitudes. It's relaxed and friendly, yet high-tech and competitive; it has some of the most beautiful green spaces of any metropolitan area, and some of the worst traffic. And if locals aren't arguing about an issue, it's probably not worth trying to accomplish. This chapter provides some insight into the many factors that give Austin its unique character.

Planning a trip to Austin can be complex. As the Calendar of Events (p. 174) shows, there's almost always something going on in town. But if an event is interesting enough to draw crowds of out-of-towners, as many are, there's likely to be a run on hotel rooms. Similarly, while it can be uncomfortably warm in summer, that's also when many outdoor activities are at their peak. Try to figure out your priorities, and see if they match your budget: Although Austin's supply of hotel rooms is growing, it's still far from keeping up with tourist needs. Naturally, rates are at a premium when the demand is high.

AUSTIN TODAY

Read anything about Austin and the most common characterization you'll find of the city is "laid-back." First-time visitors may therefore be shocked to encounter bearish traffic, pushy drivers, and a downtown that's beginning to look a lot like Houston or Dallas. "Keep Austin Weird"—the ubiquitous slogan on T-shirts, bumper stickers, and mugs—has become less of a declaration of pride in the city's iconoclasm than a plaintive plea for a return to kinder, quirkier times. While Austin is still known as the country's live music capital, the success of the tech industry has earned it another nickname: "Silicon Hills."

So the struggle for Austin's soul is ongoing. Who's winning? It depends on where you look and who you talk to.

A love of the outdoors is key to Austin's identity, and that remains unchanged. The parks, nature preserves, rivers, and lakes that thread through and around town are revered with an almost religious fervor. Austinites of all walks of life run or amble on the hike-and-bike trail edging downtown's Lady Bird Lake; even Lady

Bird herself, late in life, enjoyed being pushed around it in her wheelchair. Access to, and preservation of, Austin's green spaces are taken very seriously, reflecting the city's strong environmental consciousness and devotion to the Americans with Disabilities Act. Austin prides itself on being one of the most accessible cities in the United States, and leads the nation in green energy production. It has the most aggressive recycling and energy conservation programs in the state.

The city's legendary passion for live music hasn't abated either. On any given night, you can find great bands playing around town, and at very reasonable (for the audience) prices.

There's the rub. Austin's musicians, along with other creatives, are being priced out of many of the city's neighborhoods—especially the ones that host the clubs and bars where they play. To cite just one example: There's now a gated community in South Austin right across the street from the Continental Club, a magnet for striving bands since 1955.

It's not just musicians who are being displaced, of course. Longtime lower- and even middle-income residents can no longer afford to live in central city neighborhoods that have become trendy. The premier example of this in recent years is East Austin, historically a Hispanic and African-American area. From 2000 to 2016, the median family income in the neighborhood rose from $28,929 to $69,570. The result? Austin was the only one of the fastest growing U.S. cities to see a decline in its black population between 2000 and 2010.

Austin's overall population (currently at 947,000) is exploding; it's estimated that some 150 new people move to the city every day. Many are in search of jobs with tech giants like Dell, IBM, National Instruments, and Oracle—and, increasingly, Apple. The company's north Austin campus is the second largest one outside of Cupertino, California, and in late 2018, Apple announced that it will be building another 133-acre campus about a mile from the original site, adding at least 5,000 jobs to the 6,200 already there (and potentially 15,000 more in the future). That will make it the largest private employer in Austin.

All this has resulted in a real estate boom, but little in the way of affordable housing. Visitors only need to look at downtown for evidence. What began with a move to convert former warehouses and commercial lofts into residential housing has turned high-rise. At 56 stories, the Austonian is the tallest building in Austin and the tallest residential tower west of the Mississippi; when completed in 2019, the 58-story Independent will overtake it in both respects—and unit prices will range from $600,000 to $3.5 million. Downtown hotels are literally skyrocketing, too, with the openings of the JW Marriott (32 stories; 2015), Aloft/Element (31 stories; 2017), and Fairmont (37 stories; 2018).

As housing for the affluent continues to metastasize in the urban core, middle-class families are fleeing to the suburbs of the north and northwest—which has helped create out-of-control traffic, with frequent jams and delays on the freeways, especially I-35.

Though it's likely too little too late, Austin has been working on solutions for reducing traffic and urban sprawl. Capital Metro Rail, a commuter line running from the northern satellite community of Cedar Park to downtown, started service in 2010, and to the east of town, Hwy. 130 was completed in 2012 (a toll road, it's officially Pickle Parkway, after Jake Pickle, who represented the Austin area in Congress from 1963–1995). Both have the goal of getting cars off the central roads. Also in 2012, the city created Imagine Austin, a 30-year plan to make the city more livable; a key element, CodeNEXT, aims to revise the city's old zoning code to increase density and affordability.

Transportation bonds to finance an electric streetcar system have been voted down twice, but many believe that a 2020 plan, which would connect downtown to the university, Zilker Park, the airport, and some central neighborhoods, is likely to succeed. Demographics may help—millennials are more likely to use public transportation, ride-shares, bicycles, and electric scooters than previous generations.

Time will tell. Austin may never be truly weird again—if it ever was—but it may become more weird-friendly.

LOOKING BACK: AUSTIN'S HISTORY

A vast territory that rejected foreign rule to become an independent nation, Texas has always played a starring role in the romance of the American West. So it's only fitting that Texas' capital should spring, full-blown, from the imagination of a man on a buffalo hunt.

A Capital Dilemma

The man was Mirabeau Buonaparte Lamar, who earned a reputation for bravery in Texas' struggle for independence from Mexico. In 1838, Lamar was vice president of the 2-year-old Republic of Texas, under president Sam

AUSTIN: DATELINE

- 1730 Franciscans build a mission at Barton Springs, but abandon it within a year.
- 1836 Texas wins independence from Mexico; Republic of Texas established.
- 1838 Jacob Harrell sets up camp on the Colorado River, calling the settlement Waterloo.
- 1839 Congressional commission recommends Waterloo as site for new capital of Texas republic. The town is renamed Austin.
- 1842 President Sam Houston re-establishes Houston as Texas' capital, and orders archives moved there. Austinites resist.
- 1844 Anson Jones succeeds Houston as president and returns capital to Austin.
- 1845 Constitutional convention in Austin approves annexation of Texas by the United States.
- 1850s Austin undergoes a building boom.

continues

Why Waterloo?

Most Austinites are aware that their city was originally called Waterloo—Waterloo Records, Waterloo Park, and other local sites all attest to that fact—but nobody really knows why. When a reader posed the question to the *Austin-American Statesman*, the newspaper asked several local historians, and came up empty. The only point of consensus was why Lamar was eager to change the city's original appellation: After all, his middle name was Buonaparte.

Houston, the even more renowned hero of the Battle of San Jacinto. Both were strong-willed, but they had very different ideas about the future of the republic. Houston tended to look eastward, toward union with the United States, while Lamar saw independence as the first step to establishing a Texas empire that would stretch to the Pacific.

That year, an adventurer named Jacob Harrell set up a camp called Waterloo at the western edge of the frontier, on the northern banks of Texas' Colorado River (not to be confused with the larger waterway up north). Some 100 years earlier, the Franciscans had established a temporary mission here, nestled against the same gentle hills; Stephen F. Austin, Texas's earliest and greatest land developer, had had the area surveyed in the 1820s, for the smaller of two colonies he was to establish on Mexican territory. But otherwise the place had seen few Anglos before Harrell arrived. Natural springs in the area had attracted various Native American tribes, including the Comanche, Lipan Apaches, and Tonkawas, but none settled there. In the autumn of 1838, when Harrell invited his friend Mirabeau Lamar on a buffalo hunting expedition, Lamar gazed at the pristine rolling woodlands surrounding Waterloo and thought it was an ideal place to settle.

1861	Texas votes to secede from the Union (Austin's Travis County votes against secession).
1865	General Custer and troops come to restore order in Austin during Reconstruction.
1871	First rail line to Austin completed.
1883	University of Texas opens.
1923	Santa Rita No. 1, an oil well on University of Texas land, strikes a gusher.
1937	Lyndon Johnson elected U.S. representative from 10th Congressional District, which includes Austin.
Late 1930s–early 1950s	Six dams built on the Colorado River, forming the Highland Lakes chain.
1960s	High-tech firms, including IBM, move to Austin.
1972	Willie Nelson moves back to Texas from Nashville; helps spur live-music scene on Sixth Street.
1976	PBS's *Austin City Limits* airs for the first time.
1980	Whole Foods Market is founded.
1987	South by Southwest (S×SW) Music Festival debuts.
1999	Opening of Austin-Bergstrom International Airport.

In December of the same year, Lamar succeeded Houston as president of the Texas Republic. He promptly ordered the congressional commission charged with selecting a site for a permanent capital to check out Waterloo. This news was not well received by Houston residents, who hoped their city would remain the republic's capital. They argued that Waterloo was a dangerous and inconvenient outpost, unsuitable as a capital. The commission, however, was made up of those who favored Texas' westward expansion, and they believed moving the capital to the west would help this endeavor. Lamar's pet site won their recommendation.

In early 1839, Lamar's friend Edwin Waller was dispatched to lay out a new Texas capital, to be named in honor of Stephen F. Austin (besides Washington, D.C, Austin is the only U.S. city originally designed as an independent nation's capital). The first public lots went on sale on August 1, 1839, and by November of that year, Austin was ready to host its first session of Congress.

Austin's position as capital was far from entrenched, however. Attacks on the republic by Mexico in 1842 gave Sam Houston, now president again, sufficient excuse to order the national archives relocated out of remote Austin. When 26 armed men came to repossess the historic papers, resistant Austinites greeted them with a cannon. After a struggle, the men returned empty-handed, and Houston abandoned his plan, thus ceding to Austin the victory in what came to be called the Archive War.

Although Austin won this skirmish, it was losing a larger battle. President Houston refused to convene the Congress in Austin, and by 1843, Austin's population had dropped down to 200, and its buildings lay in disrepair. Help came in the person of Anson Jones, who succeeded to the presidency in 1844. The constitutional convention he called in 1845 not only approved Texas's annexation to the United States, but also named Austin the capital until 1850, when voters of what was now the state of Texas could choose their

2002 The tech recession hits, but Austin's still partying like it's 2000, as the Austin City Limits Music Festival debuts.

2004 Debut of Austin's tallest building, the Frost Bank Tower, on Congress Avenue.

2007 Town Lake renamed Lady Bird Johnson Lake.

2010 Capital Metro Rail, a commuter line running from the northern satellite community of Cedar Park to downtown, begins operation.

The 56-story Austonian, the tallest all-residential building west of the Mississippi, is completed.

2012 Austin Food & Wine Alliance established, signaling the coming-of-age of Austin's culinary scene.

The Circuit of the Americas Grand Prix racetrack opens, bringing Formula One racing to Austin.

2018 Austin City Council votes to build a stadium in north Austin to house a major league soccer team.

Apple announces expansion of its Austin presence, adding a $1-billion campus in north Austin.

governmental seat for the next 20 years. In 1850, Austin campaigned hard for the position and won by a landslide.

A Capital Solution

Austin thrived under the protection of the U.S. Army. During the 1850s construction boom that followed statehood, the city's first permanent buildings included an impressive limestone capitol. It no longer exists, but two of the buildings in its complex, the **General Land Office** (p. 234) and the **Governor's Mansion** (p. 236), still stand today.

The boom was short-lived, however. In 1861, although Austin's Travis County voted against secession, Texas decided to join the Confederacy. By 1865, Union army units—including one led by General George Armstrong Custer—were sent to restore order in a defeated and looted Austin.

But once again Austin rebounded. With the arrival of the railroad in 1871, the city's recovery was secured. The following year Austin re-won election as state capital.

More battles for status followed. Back in 1839, the Republic of Texas had declared its intention to build a "university of the first class," and in 1876, a new state constitution mandated its establishment. It took another bout of heavy electioneering for Austin to win the right to have the flagship of Texas's higher educational system on its soil. In 1883, classrooms not yet completed, the first 221 students met the eight instructors of the **University of Texas** (p. 230), which nowadays boasts a student body of more than 50,000.

The university wasn't the only Austin institution without permanent quarters that year. The old limestone capitol had burned in 1881, and a new, much larger home for the legislature was being built. In 1888, after a series of mishaps, the current **capitol** (p, 224) was completed. The grand red-granite edifice towering above the city symbolized Austin's arrival.

Dams, Oil & Microchips

The new capitol notwithstanding, the city was once again in a slump. Although some believed that quality of life would be sacrificed to growth—a view still widely held today—most townspeople embraced the idea of harnessing the fast-flowing waters of the Colorado River as the solution to Austin's economic woes. A dam, they thought, would provide a cheap source of electricity for residents, and also supply power for irrigation and new factories. Dedicated in 1893, the Austin Dam did indeed fulfill these goals—but only temporarily. The energy source proved to be limited, and when torrential rains pelted the city in April 1900, Austin's dreams came crashing down with its dam.

Another dam, attempted in 1915, was never finished. It wasn't until the late 1930s that a permanent solution to the water power problem was found. A young Lyndon Johnson, the newly elected representative from Austin's 10th Congressional District, made a successful plea to President Roosevelt for federal funds to construct six dams along the lower Colorado River. These dams not only afforded Austin and central Texas all the hydroelectric power and drinking water they needed, they also created the seven **Highland Lakes** (p. 242)—aesthetically appealing and a great source of recreational revenue.

Still, Austin might have remained a backwater capital abutting a beautiful lake had it not been for the discovery of oil on University of Texas (UT) land in 1923. Huge amounts of money subsequently flowed into the Permanent University Fund—worth some $20 billion today—enabling Austin's campus to become truly first class. During the Depression, while most of the country was cutting back, UT went on a building binge and began hiring a faculty as impressive as the new halls in which they were to hold forth.

Impressions

Like the ancient city of Rome, Austin is built upon seven hills, and it is impossible to conceive of a more beautiful and lovely situation.

—George W. Bonnell, Commissioner of Indian Affairs of the Republic of Texas, 1840

The indirect effects of the oil bonus reached far beyond College Hill. In 1955, UT scientists and engineers founded Tracor, the first of Austin's more than 250 high-tech companies. Lured by the city's natural attractions and its access to a growing bank of young brainpower, many outside companies soon arrived: IBM (1967), Texas Instruments (1968), and Motorola's Semiconductor Products Section (1974). In the 1980s, two huge computer consortiums, MCC and SEMATECH, opted to make Austin their home. Wunderkind Michael Dell, who started out selling computers from his dorm room at UT in 1984, became the CEO of the hugely successful Austin-based Dell Technologies, and spawned a generation of local "Dellionaires" by rewarding his employees with company stock. Not until 2018, when Apple announced that it was expanding its presence in Austin, did the possibility exist of Dell being surpassed as the city's #1 tech employer.

During the 1990s, Austin's population increased by 41 percent (from 465,600 to 656,600). Many of the new residents moved to the suburban west and northwest, but the economic expansion also fueled a resurgence in the older central city. Projects in the last decade of the 20th century and the first of the 21st included the restoration of the Capitol and its grounds; the refurbishing of the **State Theatre;** and the renovation of the **Driskill Hotel** (p. 178) and the reopening of the **Stephen F. Austin Hotel** (p. 183), two grand historic properties. The convention center doubled in size. The University of Texas created what's called the "cultural campus," adding to its visitor attractions the **Bob Bullock Texas History Center** (p. 228) and the **Blanton Museum of Art** (p. 226).

Willie Nelson's return to Austin from Nashville in 1972 didn't have quite as profound an effect on the economy as the tech boom, but it certainly had one on the city's live-music scene. For the first time, hippies and country music fans found common ground at the many clubs that began to sprout up along downtown's Sixth Street, which had largely been abandoned. These music venues, combined with the construction that followed in the wake of the city's high-tech success, helped spur downtown's resurgence—and, eventually, helped price out living quarters for many of the artists who helped created that revitalization.

AUSTIN IN LITERATURE & POP CULTURE

Austin's central role in Texas politics has long been a topic for writers. William Sydney Porter, better known as O. Henry, published a satirical newspaper in Austin in the late 19th century. Among the many short tales he wrote about the area—collected in *O. Henry's Texas Stories*—are four inspired by his stint as a draftsman in the General Land Office.

Serious history buffs might want to dip into Robert Caro's excellent multivolume biography of Lyndon B. Johnson, the consummate Texas politician, who had a profound effect on the Austin area, or *Let the People In: The Life and Times of Ann Richards* by Jan Reid, which explores the career of one of Texas' most colorful governors.

Set largely in Austin, Billy Lee Brammer's *The Gay Place* is a fictional portrait of a political figure based loosely on LBJ. The city's most famous resident scribe, James Michener, placed his historical epic *Texas* in the frame of a governor's task force operating out of Austin.

Lawrence Wright's *God Save Texas* combines memoir with an up-to-date (2018) look at how Texas fits into the national conversation; the chapter about Austin includes notes from covering two legislative sessions.

Molly Ivins (& Ann Richards) Can't Say That, Can They?

Longtime friends and fixtures on the Austin scene, writer Molly Ivins and Texas governor Ann Richards proved that well-behaved women seldom make history. They were witty, iconoclastic, bold . . . anything but ladylike.

Until she died in 2007, Molly Ivins was Austin's resident scourge. She pilloried the foibles of the Texas "lege"—along with those of Congress and the rest of Washington—in her syndicated newspaper columns, published in several collections, including *Molly Ivins Can't Say That, Can She?* and *Who Let the Dogs In?*

Richards, who was governor of Texas from 1991 to 1995, first came to national attention when she delivered the keynote address at the 1988 Democratic National Convention; it included the oft-quoted line "Poor George [H.W. Bush], he was born with a silver foot in his mouth." Another claim to fame: Richards' *Texas Monthly* magazine cover, showing her straddling a large motorcycle and wearing white leathers—which matched her white hair.

Both of these larger-than-life Austinites had one-woman plays devoted to them. In 2012, Kathleen Turner took on the role of Ivins in *Red Hot Patriot* by Margaret and Allison Engel, while Holland Taylor wrote and played the title role in *Ann: The Ann Richards Play,* which debuted in 2013. Both plays have been reprised with different lead actors in subsequent years.

For background into the city's unique music scene, try Jan Reid's *The Improbable Rise of Redneck Rock,* or Barry Shank's more scholarly *Dissonant Identities: The Rock 'n' Roll Scene in Austin, Texas.* Danny Garret's *Weird, Yet Strange: Notes from an Austin Music Artist,* is a visual chronicle of the scene. The author of *Armadillo World Headquarters: A Memoir* is formally Edward O. Wilson, but everyone knows the founder of the venue where the city's live music scene began as Eddie Wilson.

Chainsaws, Slackers, and Spy Kids: 30 Years of Film Making in Austin, Texas, by Alison Macor, traces the development of the city's storied indie cinema (p. 281).

Sarah Bird has won acclaim for such humorous Austin-based novels as *The Mommy Club, Virgin of the Rodeo, The Boyfriend School*, and *How Perfect is That;* she turned to nonfiction in 2016 to write her (also very funny) *Love Letter to Texas Women.*

WHEN TO GO

In planning a visit, keep in mind the calendars of the state legislature and the University of Texas. Lawmakers and lobbyists converge on the capital from January through May of odd-numbered years, so you can expect tighter bookings. The start of fall term, graduation week, and football weekends—UT's football stadium now seats 100,000—will also fill lots of hotel rooms. Formula 1 Grand Prix events may also result in room scarcities.

The busiest season, however, is the month of March, when the ever-growing South by Southwest conference (p. 279) fills entire hotels. Another part of the year when the hotels are busy is in early October for the Austin City Limits Music Festival (p. 269). Not only are rooms hard to come by during S×SW and ACL but rates tend to skyrocket. All in all, the best time to find a hotel room is during the hottest late-summer days—when most out-of-towners have enough good sense to stay home in cooler climes.

Climate

May showers follow April flowers in the Austin/Texas Hill Country area; by the time the late spring rains set in, the bluebonnets and most of the other wildflowers have already peaked. It's a lovely anomaly: The weather for enjoying the glorious flower arrangements in early spring is mild and dry, making it an ideal and deservedly popular time to visit. Summers can be steamy—more and more years are seeing triple digit temps for long stretches—but Austin offers plenty of places to cool off, among them the Highland Lakes (p. 242) and Barton Springs (p. 237). Fall foliage in this leafy area is another treat, and it's hard to beat a Texas evening by a cozy fireplace—admittedly more for show than warmth in Austin, which generally enjoys mild winters.

For a temperature chart and list of national holidays, see p. 34.

Austin Calendar of Events

Many of Austin's festivals capitalize on the city's large community of local musicians and/or on the great outdoors. The major annual events are listed here. See also chapter 16 for information on various free concerts and other cultural events held throughout the year. Additional local events may also be found by logging on to www.austintexas.org/events, www.austin360.com, and www.austinchronicle.com.

JANUARY

Red Eye Regatta, Austin Yacht Club, Lake Travis. The bracing lake air at this keelboat race should help cure the aftereffects of too much New Year's Eve. www.austinyachtclub.net/annual-red-eye-regatta; ✆ **512/266-1336.** New Year's Day.

MLK March, Festival, and Food Drive, multiple venues. Marchers go from the MLK statue on the UT campus to the historically African-American Huston-Tillotson University, where vendors and musicians celebrate Martin Luther King's birthday. www.mlkcelebration.com; ✆ **512/657-3064.** Third Monday in January.

FronteraFest, Hyde Park Theater, other venues. Five weeks of fringe theater and performance art keep things lively in what is now the largest festival of its type in the Southwest. www.hydeparktheatre.org; ✆ **512/479-7530.** Mid-January to mid-Februrary.

FEBRUARY

Carnival Brasileiro, Emo's. Conga lines, elaborate costumes, samba bands, and confetti are all part of this sizzling Carnaval-style event, started in 1975 by homesick Brazilian UT students. www.sambaparty.com. First or second Saturday in February.

OUTsider Festival, various venues. Academics, artists, musicians, filmmakers, and other creatives in the LGBTQI community come together for 5 days of performances and discussions. www.outsiderfest.org. Third week in February.

MARCH

South by Southwest (S×SW) Conference & Festivals, various venues. The Austin Music Awards kick off this 2-week-long conference, with hundreds of concerts at more than 50 city venues, in addition to various lectures and symposia. Aspiring music-industry and tech professionals sign up months ahead. www.sxsw.com; ✆ **512/467-7979.** Usually around 2nd week in March.

Rodeo Austin, Leudecke Arena. This 2-week Wild West extravaganza features rodeos, cattle auctions, a youth fair, BBQ cookoffs, and lots of live country music. www.rodeoaustin.com; ✆ **512/919-3000.** Mid- to late March.

Jerry Jeff Walker's Texas Bash, various locations. Each year, singer/songwriter Walker performs at such venues as Gruene Hall and the Paramount Theatre; proceeds benefit music education for young people. www.jerryjeff.com; ✆ **512/477-0036.** Late March, early April.

ABC Kite Festival, Zilker Park. Colorful handmade kites fill the sky during this popular annual contest, one of the country's oldest of its kind. www.abckitefest.org; ✆ **512/837-9500.** Last Sunday in March.

APRIL

Statesman/Cap10k, downtown. Texas' largest 10K race winds from the state capitol through West Austin, ending up at Lady Bird Lake. www.cap10k.com; ✆ **512/445-3598.** Early April.

Art City Austin Fine Arts Festival, Palmer Center. This 3-day fair features a large juried art show, fine art performances, and lots of kids' activities. www.artallianceaustin.org; ✆ **512/609-8587.** Mid-April.

Austin Food + Wine Festival, Auditorium Shores. Cooking demonstrations; beer, wine, and food tastings; book signings; and celebrity chef dinners fill this 3-day foodfest; book in advance. www.austinfoodandwinefestival. Third or fourth weekend in April.

Old Settlers Music Festival, Tilmon. More than two dozen bluegrass bands descend on

Tilmon, about 10 miles southeast of Austin, for this Americana roots music fest, which also includes workshops, craft booths, and kid's entertainment. www.oldsettlersmusicfest.org. Mid-April.

MAY

Old Pecan Street Spring Arts and Crafts Festival, Sixth Street. Eat and shop for crafts along downtown's entertainment drag while bands play nearby. www.pecanstreetfestival.org. First weekend in May.

O. Henry Museum Pun-Off, backyard of the O. Henry Museum. This annual battle of the wits is for a wordy cause—the upkeep of the three Brush Fair Museums, including O. Henry's former house. www.punpunpun.com. Mid-May.

Hot Luck, multiple venues. One of Austin's newer (and hipper) festivals is devoted to two local favorites: chef-driven food and local music. Proceeds benefit a domestic violence prevention group. www.hotluckfest.com. Memorial Day weekend.

JUNE

ATX Television Festival, multiple downtown venues. This 4-day tubefest is geared toward both fans and those looking to work in the industry. www.atxfestival.com; ✆ **512/551-1330.** First weekend in June.

Republic of Texas Biker Rally, Travis County Expo Center. The city fills with the sound of rolling thunder during this downtown bike parade that ends at the State Capitol. Custom bike makers display their newest creations at the Expo Center. www.rotrally.com; ✆ **512/906-9954.** Usually second weekend in June.

Juneteenth, various venues, mostly in East Austin. This celebration of African-American emancipation (designated a Texas state holiday in 1980) generally includes a parade, gospel singing, and many children's events. For info, contact the George Washington Carver Museum and Cultural Center. www.austintexas.gov/carvermuseum; ✆ **512/974-4926.** June 19.

JULY

H-E-B Austin Symphony Concert & Fireworks, Vic Mathias Shores. Cannons, fireworks, and a rousing rendition of the "1812 Overture" are highlights of this noisy freedom celebration. www.austinsymphony.org/events; ✆ **888/4-MAESTRO** (888/4-6237876) or 512/476-6064. July 4.

AUGUST

Bat Fest, Congress Ave. Bridge/Austin American Statesman parking lot. A bat costume contest, arts and crafts, food, and music are key to this 1-day event, starring 1.5 million free-tailed bats that emerge from under the bridge at dusk. www.roadwayevents.com/event/bat-fest. Mid-August.

***Austin Chronicle* Hot Sauce Festival,** Waterloo Park. The largest hot-sauce contest in the world features more than 350 salsa entries, judged by celebrity chefs and food editors. www.austinchronicle.com/hot-sauce; ✆ **512/454-5766.** Last Sunday in August.

SEPTEMBER

Diez y Seis, Fiesta Gardens Park, Plaza Saltillo, and other sites. Mariachis and folk dancers, conjunto and Tejano music, plus fajitas, piñatas, and clowns help celebrate Mexico's independence from Spain. The highlight is the crowning of the Fiestas Patrias Queen. www.diezyseis.org; ✆ **512/974-6797.** Weekend around September 16.

OCTOBER

Austin City Limits Music Festival, Zilker Park. Yet more evidence of Austin's devotion to live music, this music extravaganza mounts a superb lineup of musical talent. www.aclfestival.com; ✆ **888/512/7649.** First 2 weekends in October.

Austin Film Festival, Paramount Theatre and other venues. Screening 100 films in a little over a week—everything from restored classics to new indie releases—this filmfest attracts movie fans, aspiring screenwriters, and filmmakers galore. www.austinfilmfestival.com; ✆ **800/310-FEST** (3378) or 512/478-4795. Mid-October.

Texas Book Festival, State Capitol. One of the largest literary events in the Southwest, this 2-day fundraiser for Texas public libraries draws literati from all over the U.S. www.texasbookfestival.org; ✆ **512/477-4055.** Late October.

Viva La Vida, Fourth St./Congress Ave. Co-sponsored by the City of Austin and the Mexic-arte Museum, the city's longest Day of the Dead festival features a grand procession, food booths, live music, crafts, and a low-rider exhibition. www.mexic-arte museum.org; ✆ **520/480-9373.** Last Saturday in October or first in November.

NOVEMBER

Austin Powwow, Travis County Expo Center. Native American dancers, singers, musicians, artists, and crafters come together at this American Indian Heritage festival, the largest of its kind in Texas. http://austinpowwow.net; ✆ **520/371-0628.** Early November.

Celtic Fest, Jourdan Bachman Pioneer Farms. Dancing, a dog parade, men in kilts, demonstrations of Viking fights . . . you don't have to be a Celt to enjoy this lively, family-friendly 2-day event. www.austinceltícfestival.com. First weekend in November.

Austin Area Jazz Festival, Emma S. Barrientos Mexican American Cultural Center. A good cure for the holiday frazzles, this day of smooth jazz includes national acts as well as up-and-comers. www.austinareajazzfestival.com; ✆ **512/541-6297.** Late November.

Chuy's Christmas Parade, Congress Ave. With giant balloons, marching bands, floats, and gifts for needy kids, this is a great way to ring in the season. www.chuysparade.com. Saturday after Thanksgiving.

DECEMBER

Zilker Park Tree Lighting. The lighting of a magnificent 165-foot tree is followed by the Trail of Lights, a mile-long display of life-size holiday scenes. A 5K run is also involved. https://austintrailoflights.org. First Sunday of month (tree lighting); second Sunday through December 23 (Trail of Lights).

Armadillo Christmas Bazaar, Palmer Events Center. Revel in Tex-Mex food, live music, and a full bar at this high-quality art, craft, and gift show, lasting 11 days. www.armadillo bazaar.com; ✆ **512/447-1605.** Begins approximately 2 weeks before Christmas.

WHERE TO STAY IN AUSTIN

12

Austin is one of the most popular cities in Texas, attracting techies, Hollywood types, academics, politicos, and vacationers drawn to the town's music scene and outdoor activities. Add the influx of new residents who need temporary places to stay while apartment hunting or waiting for houses to close, and you've got a hotel room shortage. New properties are cropping up like mushrooms to meet the demand—so much so that complaints about a room glut are beginning to appear in the press—but in the meantime hotels don't have to try too hard to court visitors (see "When to Go," p. 173, for the busiest times).

Still, people manage to go to Austin throughout the year without breaking the bank. Most hotels catering to business travelers offer weekend discounts and, of course, corporate discounts. You'll find lots of Austin room deals online—see p. 38 for our advice on snagging those deals and for information about alternative lodgings such as VRBO and Airbnb.

Most hotel rooms are **downtown,** in the blocks just east and west of Congress Avenue between the Capitol and Lady Bird Lake, where nightlife, dining, and historic sights are concentrated. Many of the newest hotels are rising on the southernmost part of this stretch, convenient for not only Lady Bird Lake but also the very big and very busy Austin Convention Center. Skip the car if you're staying downtown: Traffic is horrendous and parking is hard to find (or extremely expensive).

Hotel construction continues apace just across Lady Bird Lake in **South Austin,** especially on and around South Congress Avenue. Zoning restrictions here keep out the brand-name high-rises; most hotels are boutique-size and strive to outdo each other in quirkiness and hipness. If you bed down here you'll have access to great dining, unique shopping, and the many recreational activities on the south shore of Lady Bird Lake.

East Austin, especially the area just across the I-35 from downtown, is the up-and-coming place to stay; so far, there are only a few privately owned boutique hotels here, but watch this space for

Arrive East Austin, part of a small hotel group. There are also a few small hotels and B&Bs **near the University of Texas,** with newer and (somewhat) larger properties in the works.

In the **Northwest,** more and more brand-name hotels are opening along the U.S. 183/Parmer Lane tech corridor—a trend unlikely to change with the arrival of Apple's new campus. Many hotels are clustered around the upscale Arboretum and Domain/Domain NORTHSIDE malls. A couple of the more distinctive lodgings are covered here. It's not a bad area to stay in if you want access to the western green spaces and lakes, as well as upscale shopping. You're not far from the University of Texas, either.

Several spa/resorts on the outskirts of town, especially on the **far west,** provide relaxing getaways in proximity to Austin's attractions while being sufficient unto themselves. (For the glamorous camping known as glamping, see box, p. 295.)

Tip: If you're on a tight budget, Austin has two major clusters of economical lodgings, including extended-stay chains. One surrounds the intersection of I-35 and Ben White Boulevard (Hwy. 71), south of downtown and near the airport; the other is north of downtown, where I-35 intersects Hwy. 290 E. The latter is generally preferable—it's closer to downtown, has better dining options, and offers alternative routes to I-35 for getting around.

Note that rates listed below do not include the city's **9% hotel tax.**

Wherever you bunk in Austin—even B&B rooms—it is safe to expect high-speed Wi-Fi; even when fees are noted, below, they're often waived if you sign up for the hotel's corporate clubs. Almost all hotels in Austin are entirely smoke-free and you can expect to see recycling bins and other serious eco-friendly programs—not just the standard "we won't change your towels or sheets for the environment"—everywhere. Finally, Austin is exceedingly pet friendly; several hotels charge no fees for bringing your dog and have no size or number restrictions. You just have to sign a good behavior waiver (for the dog; unfortunately, guests are not required to commit to similar restrictions).

DOWNTOWN

Expensive

The Driskill ★★★ The wealthy cattle baron for whom it is named built this grand Romanesque hotel in 1886, and it remains an Austin icon. The lobby has hand-inlaid marble floors and tall columns, the bar upstairs is topped with a magnificent stained-glass dome, and the hallways of the guest floors are lined with original art. This hotel is Texan to the core, epitomizing old-school luxury but not dated and stuffy. It was here that Lyndon Johnson awaited his election results, and the Texas Rangers gathered to plan their ambush of Bonnie and Clyde. The hotel has two parts; the Historic section (the original 1886 building) and the Traditional section (a 1929 addition).

Central Austin Hotels

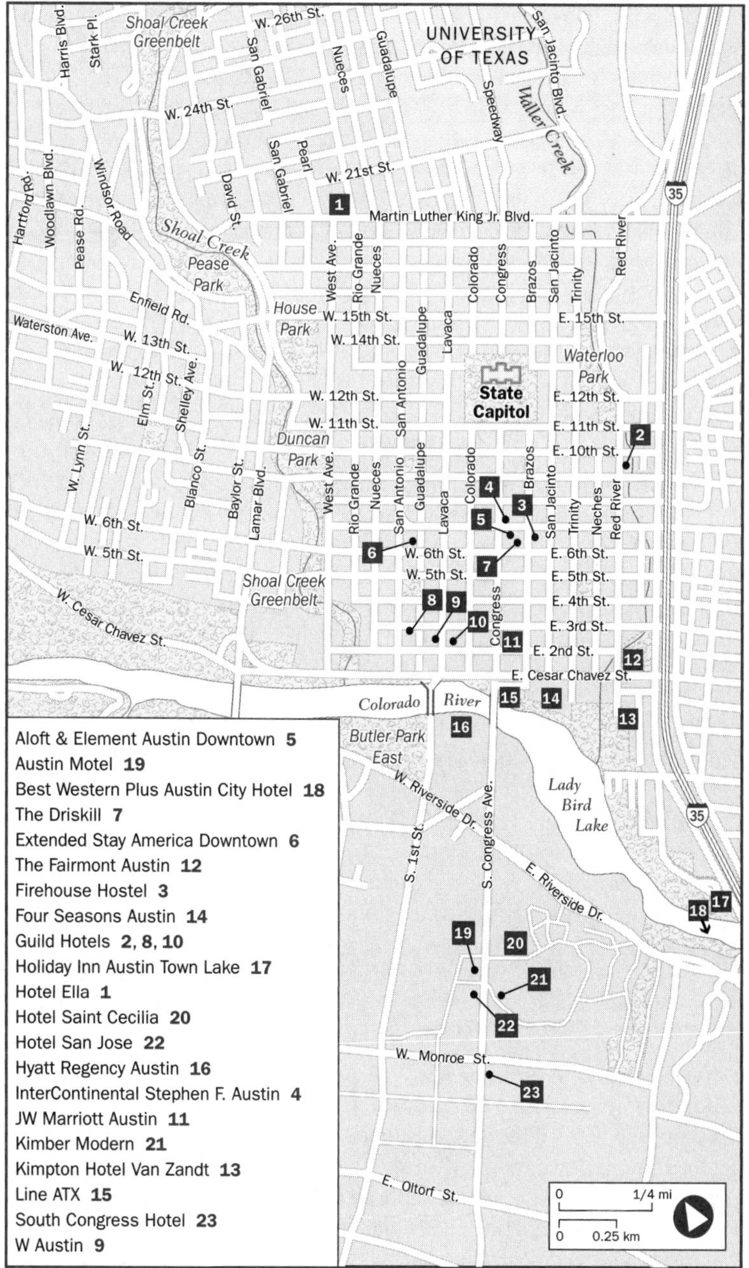

Meticulous renovations and maintenance have kept the hotel from getting stale. Rooms are furnished with understated elegance—heavy draperies in muted shades, fine linens—and subtle Texas touches like wrought iron headboards designed around the Driskill cattle brands. The smallish bathrooms are clad in black Brazilian marble or Art Deco tile. Room picks: The Historic section's corner rooms, with big windows, and the high-ceilinged rooms on the 12th floor. The **Driskill Bar** (p. 280) has live music nightly, and is popular on Sunday for its Blues Brunch. Many locals reserve a spot at the **Driskill Grill** for any occasion that calls for crystal wineglasses and flickering candles. Enjoy a hearty Southern breakfast or a light lunch at the **1886 Café & Bakery.**

604 Brazos St. (at E. 6th St.). www.driskillhotel.com. ✆ **800/233-1234** or 512/439-1234. 189 units. $229–$349 double; $419 and up suite. Valet parking $45. Pets accepted, $100 fee. **Amenities:** 2 restaurants; bar; concierge; 24-hr. exercise room; room service; Wi-Fi (free).

The Fairmont Austin ★★ This bustling 37-story glass tower, opened in 2018, is the definition of a convention hotel: It's attached to the Austin Convention Center through a sky bridge, has enough meeting space to fill a football stadium, and can hold 1,800 conventioneers on its outdoor deck. It can hold even more in its rooms, too—this is the largest hotel in Austin, with 1,048 units, including those in **Gold,** a separate luxury hotel-within-a-hotel on the top floors. Bright and attractive standard accommodations have all the perks business travelers would want, including nice-size desks and lots of outlets with USB ports; views of Lady Bird Lake and/or the city skyline are a bonus. The five on-site restaurants include the upscale **Garrison** steakhouse and the internationally flavored **Review,** as well as a coffee shop, lobby bar, and cocktail lounge. A full-service spa and exercise facility rank among the top in downtown. The location, near the Red River entertainment district and Lady Bird Lake, can't be beat. In short, the hotel has everything you might need or want—except local character. ***Tip:*** Right across the street, the shack-like **Iron Works BBQ** (p. 214) is both a great place to eat and a reminder of the old Austin that's literally losing ground.

101 Red River St. www.fairmont.com/austin. ✆ **512/600-2000.** 1,048 units. $200–$350 double; $280 and up suite; $450 and up Gold suite. Valet parking $45. Pets 25 lb. or under accepted, $150 fee. **Amenities:** 5 restaurants; coffee shop; 2 bars; concierge; health club; business center; room service; Wi-Fi ($14)

Four Seasons Austin ★★★ Having completed the third phase of a $10-million renovation in 2018, this link in the luxe Four Seasons chain can now compete with all the new kids in the neighborhood—and then some. It's got the formula down for a perfect stay, whether for work or play: understated elegance, superb service, plus a whole lot of fun. Take the rooms, for example. They have windows that open, a white noise machine, pillow-top mattresses that can be changed depending on how firm or soft you want your bed—and a button on your phone specially dedicated to summoning a margarita cart (from 3–6pm). And, this being Austin, there's a guitar concierge on staff who will provide you with a Taylor guitar to play while you're on the property (it's available for purchase of course, but the Four Seasons logo pick is free). The hotel also makes the most of its location, with the hike-and-bike trail and Lady Bird Lake abutting its lush backyard; it's the perfect spot for guests to play lawn games, gather around a BBQ grill and listen to live music, or stroll down to the nearby dock to rent a kayak. Adding to the kick-back experience: An outdoor saltwater pool (environmentally friendly, since it relies on few chemicals); a state-of-the-art spa with a Himalayan sea-salt wall; and the **Ciclo** restaurant, serving Texas fare with Latin influences in all indoor and outdoor dining areas and bars.

98 San Jacinto Blvd. (at Cesar Chavez St.). www.fourseasons.com/austin. ✆ **512/478-4500.** 291 units. $450–$800 double; $699 and up suite. Valet parking $45. Pets 60 lb. or under accepted, $100 fee. **Amenities:** Restaurant; bar; babysitting; bikes; concierge; exercise room; outdoor pool; 24-hr. room service; spa; Wi-Fi (free).

JW Marriott Austin ★★★ At 1,002 rooms, this is North America's largest member of Marriot's luxury JW brand. What with all the people hustling off to meetings or schmoozing on the lower-level floors, it's not exactly serene. Nevertheless, the hotel doesn't feel sterile—partly because the staff prides itself on catering to individual needs (even with so many individuals to cater to), and partly because of its organic design aesthetic. Subtle allusions to Texas' natural history are sprinkled throughout, and the earth-toned decor is enlivened with plants and other touches of color in the downstairs public areas. In the rooms, headboards resemble tufted leather and bathrooms have distinctive shell light fixtures. The hotel doesn't just pay lip service to nature: This is one of the most eco-friendly properties in town. There's an excellent full-service spa and well-equipped exercise room, but this JW really outdid itself with the Edge rooftop pool, which has the shape of Texas outlined on the bottom; it's flanked by curtained cabanas, cushioned banquettes surrounding fire pits, and, of course, a fully-stocked bar. Of the many top-notch food concessions, standouts are the indoor/outdoor **Corner** restaurant, drawing locals to its farm-to-table Texas fare and people-watching patio overlooking Congress Avenue; and the **Burger Bar,** which adds shakes, breakfast tacos, fries, and other comfort food to its array of gourmet patties.

110 E. 2nd St. www.marriott.com/austin. ✆ **888/236-2427** or 512/474-4777. 1002 units. $199–$450 double; $600 and up suite. Self-parking $32; valet parking $45. **Amenities:** 4 restaurants; 2 bars; coffee shop; outdoor pool; fitness room; spa; concierge; business center; 24-hr. room service; Wi-Fi ($15).

Kimpton Hotel Van Zandt ★★★ If you're a fan of Kimpton hotels, known for highlighting the distinctive character of their host cities, you won't be disappointed in this locally owned link, which pays tribute to Austin's live music scene. It's named for late singer/songwriter Townes Van Zandt, who lived in Austin (mostly; the Van Zandt family is generally influential in Texas). Artwork in the lobby includes a chandelier made from trombones and a collage of birds fashioned from vinyl 45s. There's even a director of music, who curates playlists for each public space (there's an underwater one for the rooftop pool), and books the live bands featured daily at **Geraldine's,** home to "elevated Austin grub." The 16-story hotel stands a stone's throw from the Rainey Street music district (for better and worse—ask for a room on the highest floor farthest from Rainey Street, or you may be kept up on Fri–Sat nights). Spacious modern guest rooms feature plush bedding, soft carpeting, and draperies tangled up in blue. Some suites offer deep oversize bathtubs with big-window views of nearby Lady Bird Lake.

605 Davis St. (near Rainey St.). www.hotelvanzandt.com. ✆ **800/546-7866** or 512/542-5300. 319 units. $199–$439 double; $399 and up suite. Valet parking $40 per night. Pets stay free. **Amenities:** Restaurant; bar; cafe; fitness center; outdoor rooftop pool; 24-hr. room service; concierge; Wi-Fi ($13).

LINE ATX ★★ It's amazing what a few coats of white paint—and a $75-million revamp—can do. Returning Austin visitors might recognize the arched windows and boxy shape of the 1960s Radisson Hotel, but it's now the chic LINE, with siblings in Los Angeles and D.C. The lobby has become light and airy, with a Zen-meets-the-Hill-Country vibe. Furnishings are sleek and minimalist, while floor-to-ceiling windows drink in views of the foliage-fringed shores of Lady Bird Lake. All concessions have been carefully chosen for the world stage: The main restaurant, **Arlo Grey,** is the first dining venture of Kristen Kish, who won season 10 of *Top Chef*, while **Alfred's Coffee,** with its gourmet sips, baked goods, and grab-and-go selections (Scotch eggs, anyone?), has branches only in Tokyo and LA. If all this sounds a bit too cool for school, evoking a side of Austin that's overly status conscious, it's balanced by genuinely friendly Texas hospitality. Also, a no-fee-or-size-restriction pet policy ensures there are usually lots of dogs around to keep folks from taking themselves too seriously. Only one tower of rooms was open for business at the end of 2018 and the rooftop fine-dining restaurant wasn't yet finished, but it's clear that this is destined to be a downtown gathering spot for locals as well as guests; they already attend al fresco yoga and kickboxing classes here.

111 E. Cesar Chavez St. www.thelinehotel.com. ✆ **512/478-9611.** 428 units. $179–$335 double; $269 and up suite. Valet parking $39. Pets stay free. **Amenities:** 3 restaurants; 2 bars; coffee shop; outdoor infinity pool; 24-hr. concierge; business center; free bike rentals; Wi-Fi (free).

W Austin ★★ One the first (2010) of a flurry of downtown hotels catering to the young, hip, and affluent, the W has something the others don't: A perch right next to the Moody Theater (p. 269) and near Second Street's glitzy nightspots and boutiques. But you don't have to leave the premises to chill out at night: The lobby-level **Living Room** splits into three clubby elements: the Tequila Bar; the intimate Secret Bar, featuring an amplifier system from the

LET THE guild PUT YOU UP

This Austin-born and -tested hospitality concept is perfect for a city under construction: Units in not-yet-completed luxury apartment buildings are furnished and rented out to visitors, who receive a personalized key code to enter. The Guild Hotels' attractively furnished guest quarters have all the amenities of hotels, such as hair dryers and ironing boards, plus several that most don't have, including fully equipped kitchens and in-room washer/dryers. All the buildings offer covered parking, fitness rooms, pools, and free Wi-Fi. In addition, to compensate for the lack of front desk and room service, guests can take advantage of a 24-hour phone concierge. Just call any time of the day or night and you'll get advice about where to eat, what to see and do—not to mention help with troubleshooting any problems that may occur in your room. The organization has a total of 250 units to let, at prices from $145 to $339. There are three properties in downtown Austin, at 421 3rd St., 201 Lavaca St., and 901 Red River St. Another three are in East Austin (1000 E. 5th St.; 1621 E. 6th St.; and 1620 E. 6th St.), and one is in South Austin (1100 S. Lamar Blvd.). Most of the units are studios or one-bedrooms, but several properties also have two-bedroom options. To see what's available, contact the company at www.theguild.co/properties-austin or call ✆ **512/623-7480.**

1970s; and the Records Room, with more than 8,000 vinyl disks. On weekends, brunch in the indoor/door **Trace** restaurant might feature a Puppy Bowl contest or Britney Spears drag show. Wherever you go in the hotel, you'll see red: It's the accent color in all public spaces (except the Secret Bat, where red runs wild) and in the guest rooms, otherwise done in muted blues and whites. Detox (or socialize) at the spa, workout room, or pool. This is a fun place to bunk, with excellent service and amenities—just be aware you're paying extra for the brand name.

200 Lavaca St. (at Second St.). www.whotelaustin.com. ✆ **866/946-8357** or 512/542-3600. 251 units. $239–$469 double; $550 and up suite. Valet or self-parking $45; $50 for oversized vehicles. Pets accepted, $100 per stay plus $25 per day. **Amenities:** Restaurant; 3 bars; concierge; health club; outdoor pool; 24-hr. room service; spa; Wi-Fi ($15).

Moderate/Expensive

InterContinental Stephen F. Austin ★★ Built in 1924 to compete with the nearby Driskill (p. 178), the Stephen F. Austin was another favorite spot for state legislators, as well as celebrities like Babe Ruth and Frank Sinatra. Unlike the Driskill, it stood abandoned for a while before being gutted and reopened as an InterContinental property. The public areas aren't as grand as those of the Driskill—the lobby is rather dark—but the guest rooms are elegant, with touches of red giving them a regal air (stars on the rugs symbolize Texas). They also have nice tech touches, including USB ports on the bedside phones and a bedside unit that lets you remotely turn off lights in other parts of the room. Two other assets: **Stephen F's Bar and Terrace,** with sweeping views of Congress Avenue and the capitol, and the **Roaring Fork** restaurant, known for its "bigass burgers" and Southwest flair.

701 Congress Ave. (at E. 7th St.). www.austin.intercontinental.com. ✆ **800/424-6835** or 512/457-8800. 189 units. $159–$329 double; $339 and up suite. Valet parking $42 ($46 SUVs and larger vehicles). **Amenities:** 2 restaurants; bar; club-level rooms; concierge; exercise room; Jacuzzi; indoor pool; room service; sauna. Wi-Fi ($10).

Moderate

Aloft & Element Austin Downtown ★★/★★★ The trend for co-branded lodgings is manifest in this dual personality hotel where the happening Aloft, often described as a budget W offshoot, shares a high-rise with the more serene Element, an extended-stay Westin line (both now come under the Marriott aegis). When you walk in the front door—which is also the entryway to the bustling coffee bar/casual-chic restaurant **Caroline/Coffeehouse at Caroline**—a sign directs you to separate lobbies for the hotels on different floors. If all this sounds a bit confusing, that's because it is.

It doesn't get much clearer when you reach the **Aloft ★★** check-in on the second floor, because this is also home to **Upstairs at Caroline,** where you can play lawn games, drink tiki cocktails, and eat food that can be held in your hand (because you're pitching cornhole with the other hand, naturally). There's an array of Allens cowboy boots to the other side of the reception desk, which you can borrow should the urge to bootscoot hit you. When you finally get to your room, you'll find it to be small and fairly basic—bed, shallow desk, table, ergonomic chair—the premise being that you probably won't spend much time in it.

In contrast, stepping into the reception area of **Element ★★★** is like entering a yoga studio. There are no games, and the only drinks are organic kombucha and the like in a cold case; here, you can borrow bicycles rather than boots. The guest rooms, intended to be homes-away-from home, are large, with Heavenly Beds (there's that Westin brand), comfy couches, and lots of light wood. All have kitchenettes with full-size refrigerators, microwaves, and stovetops, the better to prepare the gourmet meals available through the Blue Apron "chef yourself" program. An upscale continental breakfast—think granola and a Chobani yogurt bar—is included in the room rate.

Most, though not all, of the Aloft and Element rooms are on separate floors, but hard partiers and early-to-bedders may mingle in the elevators, the 24-hour fitness room, and the various Carolines.

109 E. 7th St. (off Congress Ave.). www.aloftandelementhotels.com. ✆ **866/912-1073** or 512/476-2222 (Aloft), 512/473-0000 (Element). 278 units (Aloft); 144 units (Element). $149–$239 double (Aloft); $149–$269 double, $259 and up suite (Element). Valet parking $43. Pets free, no size restriction (Aloft); pets free, 40 lb. and under (Element). Amenities: 2 restaurants; coffee shop; bar; fitness room; concierge; room service; Wi-Fi (free).

Holiday Inn Austin Town Lake ★★ Location, location, location. This budget hotel spread across two towers is a convenient, value-friendly find. It's close to the bars, restaurants, and live-music venues of Rainey Street, just a 1⅓-mile walk to the convention center, and a sneaker's throw from the hike-and-bike trail, with a boat ramp nearby. The staff is welcoming and knowledgeable—many of them have worked on the property for years—and rooms are larger and nicer than you might expect for this price range. All have microwaves and small refrigerators, and some feature pullout sofa sleepers; many have views of either the Austin skyline or Lady Bird Lake. A full renovation completed in 2017 has given everything a fresh look. Other assets include the family-friendly **Pecan Tree Restaurant,** an outdoor rooftop pool, and an inviting sports bar/lounge just off the lobby. Free parking—a downtown rarity—adds value.

20 N. I-35 (exit 233, Riverside Dr./Lady Bird Lake). www.hiaustintownlake.com. ✆ **800/593-5676** or 512/472-8211. 322 units. $109–$249 double. Free self-parking. **Amenities:** Restaurant, lounge; business center; fitness center; outdoor rooftop pool; bike rentals; Wi-Fi (free).

Hyatt Regency Austin ★★★ Although this is largely a convention hotel, the Hyatt Regency's location makes it appealing to leisure travelers too. It sits on Lady Bird Lake's south shore (strictly speaking, this is South Austin, but its size and feel are more characteristic of downtown than hip SoCo). This gives the north-facing rooms lake vistas with the downtown skyline as a backdrop. The dock for boat tours on Lady Bird Lake, including those to view the bats emerging from under the Congress Avenue Bridge, sits right below the hotel (p. 248). You can rent paddle boats and canoes from this dock too (p. 250), or take advantage of the hike-and-bike trail with one of the hotel's cycles. Restaurant options include the atrium's **SWB,** serving casual fine dining with Southwest appeal (and a great breakfast buffet); and **Marker 10,** featuring sushi, craft cocktails, local microbrews, and a super kicked-back patio. This is an older property, but a $27-million room refurbishing in 2016 brought all the rooms up to date; they have excellent business-oriented amenities and nice touches such as padded window seats, the better to gaze at the vistas below. Accommodations come in a lot of different configurations, from viewless standard kings to river-view suites with patios. If you're willing to forgo a peek at the water until you get downstairs, you can get some good bargains.

208 Barton Springs Rd. (at S. Congress Ave.). www.austin.hyatt.com. ✆ **800/233-1234** or 512/477-1234. 448 units. $129–$365 double; $275–$600 suite. Valet parking $32. Pets 75 lb. or under accepted, $100 fee. **Amenities:** Restaurant; bar; coffee shop; bike rental; concierge; fitness center; outdoor pool; room service; Wi-Fi (free).

Inexpensive

See also the "Hip Hosteling" box, p. 190, for the **Firehouse Hostel.**

Extended Stay America Downtown ★ You get just what you'd expect—a generic, but largish, studio with a tiny kitchen, geared for travelers in town for longer stays. But the rooms are clean (the hotel is 100% non-smoking), well-equipped, and convenient, and the prices are some of the lowest in the downtown area (per day rates get lower the more days you book). You won't get much in the way of amenities, other than a grab-and-go breakfast bar and a laundry room, and daily maid service costs extra. But then again, you're not paying for amenities you don't use, so it may be a worthwhile trade-off.

600 Guadalupe St. (at 6th St.). www.extendedstayamerica.com. ✆ **800/398-7829** or 512/457-9994. $105–$219 double. Pets accepted, $25 per day per pet. Rates include continental breakfast. **Amenities:** Coin-op laundry; Wi-Fi (free).

SOUTH AUSTIN

See also the **Hyatt Regency** (above).

Expensive

Hotel Saint Cecilia ★★ A shrine to the patron saint of music and poetry, this converted historic home makes for a quiet getaway near the heart of hip SoCo. It has a fun, exclusive vibe: Beat writers and 1960s rock musicians are the prevailing spirits. A neon sign near the pool, which is surrounded by lush greenery, reads "Soul"; the rooms—five suites, three studios, and six swanky poolside bungalows—nod to the rock gods with Rega retro-style turntables and Geneva sound systems, the better to listen to vinyl albums from the hotel's music library. The hotel concierge can arrange for you to rent a Gibson guitar or have your hair done in-room before you hit the hot clubs. Suites have nice features—#4 has a yard and outdoor fireplace, #5 an upright piano, #2 an outdoor bamboo shower—but the poolside bungalows are cozier. Mattresses from Sweden and organic spa products add to the cachet. Celebrities visiting Austin often stay at the Four Seasons, but some hide out in the bungalows here—which require a celebrity bankroll on weekends (rates on weekdays are

THE BOUTIQUE HOTEL queen

Everyone in the Austin hospitality business—and many outside of it—has heard of Liz Lambert, who seems to have the descriptor "hip hotelier" permanently attached to her name. The creator of the Bunkhouse Group of boutique hotels, represented in San Antonio, Marfa, TX, San Francisco, and Todos Santos, Mexico, Lambert got her start on South Congress Avenue in 1999, when she converted the rundown San Jose motor court into a trendy place to stay. This was one of the keys to SoCo's resurgence. Now Lambert has a mini-empire in the area: In addition to the **San José ★★★** (p. 188), there are the **Hotel St. Cecilia ★★** (see above) and the **Austin Motel ★★** (p. 188). A fourth hotel, the **Magdalena,** is being built from scratch in a quiet patch just down the block from the Cecilia; slated to open at the end of 2019, it will be larger than the others and offer a dedicated events space. The style of each lodging is different but, to varying degrees, they're all boho chic—reclaimed antiques, mismatched furnishings, colorful original art, and tongue-in-cheek touches such as old-style radios and retro candy in the mini-bars.

lower). If you're beyond millennial age and looking for a splurge, you might be better off buying a book of Allen Ginsburg's poems, loading some Stones onto your iPhone, and going for the Four Seasons.

112 Academy Dr. (1 block E. of S. Congress Ave.). www.hotelsaintcecilia.com. ✆ **512/852-2400.** 14 units. $385–$500 double; $385–$875 suite; $510–$630 bungalow. Rates include breakfast. Free parking. Pets under 25 lb. accepted, $25 fee per day. **Amenities:** Bar; bikes; concierge; outdoor pool; room service; Wi-Fi (free).

Kimber Modern ★★★ Stunning architecture by namesake Kimber Cavendish, a serene setting just a block from the SoCo action, and minimal human contact (including no small children) . . . for many, this adds up to the perfect getaway. The owners call it "elevated self-sufficiency": You get a keyless entry code to access the property and your room, though there's always someone around or on quick call to assist you. Accommodations are sleek and sophisticated Euro-minimalist-style with lots of light, splashes of primary colors, and cushy seating areas; luxe bath products and original art add to the appeal. Kimber built the property around a 300-year-old live oak, and a courtyard deck anchoring the hotel's seven units offers conversation-area seating beside a 25-foot-long water feature. You can read outside your room on a hammock made out of recycled seat belts or in an indoor common area with floor-to-ceiling windows—and a stocked refrigerator. This place also offers surprising value: A self-serve organic breakfast and limitless supply of beer and wine, gourmet coffee, tea, and soft drinks are included in the room rate. Only children 15 and older are permitted.

110 The Circle (1 block E. of S. Congress Ave.). www.kimbermodern.com. ✆ **512/912-1046.** 7 units. $199–$299 double; $299–$399 suite. Max. 3 adults per room, $75 fee per night for 3rd adult. Entire property can be rented. Rates include breakfast & beer and wine. No children 14 and under. Free parking. **Amenities:** Concierge; access to nearby health club; business center; Wi-Fi (free).

South Congress Hotel ★★★ SoCo's namesake hotel is not only in the heart of the district's hottest shopping and restaurant row, it contributes to that hipness, drawing locals to its trendy dining and retail spaces. Built from the ground up—this is one of the few hotels in the neighborhood that hasn't been converted from something else—and designed to fit the site unobtrusively, from the street it resembles a 1960s doctor's office block. Inside, however, it's rustic chic, with leather ottomans, potted plants, and large ceramics. The restaurants include **Otoko,** celebrity chef Paul Qui's tiny sushi bar, tucked away upstairs speakeasy-style; **Central Standard,** serving oysters, small plates, craft cocktails, and local brews in a steakhouse-style setting; and the indoor/outdoor **Café No Sé,** perfect for healthy salads and lighter fare. There's also a juice bar/bakery/coffee shop. Retail outlets include a nail salon, a women's clothing boutique with personal shopping service, and a vintage motorcycle shop. Guests gather at the 24-hour fitness center and plant-fringed outdoor pool. Rooms are spacious and serene, with wood floors, painted brick walls, and simple blue-and-white color schemes; among many different configurations, some have large patios. TVs not only get the usual premium channels, but also play indie movies from the Drafthouse cinema, gratis.

1603 S. Congress Ave. www.southcongresshotel.com. ✆ **512/920-6405.** 83 units. $219–$549 double; $359–$1,349 suite. Valet parking $32. Pets up to 50 lb. accepted, $125 fee per stay up to 7 days. **Amenities:** 3 restaurants; 2 bars; coffee shop; bike & motorcycle rental; shops; 24-hr. fitness center; 24-hr. concierge; outdoor pool; car service (up to 3 miles from hotel); Wi-Fi (free).

Moderate/Expensive

See also "Let the Guild Put You Up," p. 183.

Hotel San José ★★★ The hotel that launched the Bunkhouse group empire in SoCo (see box p. 186), this revamped 1936 motor court gets a lot of press for its Texas-meets-Tokyo design. There are nods to Austin—red Spanish tile roofs, native-pattern throw rugs, and Texas pine beds—but the dominant feel is Zen, with rooms so stripped down (white walls, cement floors) that they border on stark; seafoam green is the dominant color accent. Many rooms have pretty outdoor sitting areas, with Japanese-style landscaping. The swimming pool would be an oasis of tranquility too, if it weren't for its popularity with guests. Locals like to gather in the afternoon at the courtyard lounge, with its vine-covered trellises and frosé (frozen rosé) cocktails; coffee and breakfast tacos draw the morning crowd to **Jo's.** Right across Congress Avenue, the famous Continental Club has the best musical happy hour in town (p. 274). Book a room in the back to avoid the Congress Avenue traffic noise and passing partiers.

1316 S. Congress Ave. (south of Nellie St.). www.sanjosehotel.com. ✆ **800/574-8897** or 512/444-7322. 40 units. $125–$200 double w/ shared bathroom; $200–$400 double w/ private bathroom; $400–$650 suite. Free parking. Dogs accepted, $20 per dog per day, 2 dog limit. **Amenities:** Bar/lounge; coffee shop; bikes, Polaroid cameras, and typewriters available; outdoor pool; breakfast-only room service; Wi-Fi (free).

Inexpensive

See also "Hip Hosteling" box, p. 190, for **Hostelling International–Austin.**

Austin Motel ★★ You get a lot of fun for your buck at this revamped 1938 motor court in SoCo's action hub. The Austin Motel sign is a local landmark; instead of posting vacancy information, the neon billboard announces "Let Love In" or makes topical comments like "I Believe Her." The retro-chic decor is playful, with lipstick-red or lemon-yellow vinyl headboards, 1950s-inspired seating, push-button phones, and vintage silkscreened music posters. The spiffed-up pool (classic kidney-shaped, natch) and lounge area is outfitted with vinyl lounge chairs and vintage tables beneath red-and-white-striped umbrellas. Poolside activities include punk-rock water ballet, water aerobics, and live music. The small reception area shares space with a general store that sells tropical kitsch items as well as beverages and snacks you can take back to your room (in a beach cooler—what else?). **Joann's** restaurant and bar, opened in 2018, continues the retro theme with cushy blue vinyl booths and counter stools; its Tex-Mex comfort food and comfort drinks and a palm-fringed patio on Congress Avenue became instant hits.

1220 S. Congress Ave. www.austinmotel.com. ✆ **512/441-1157.** 41 units. $115–$250 double; $200 and up suite. Free parking. Pets accepted, $20 fee. **Amenities:** Restaurant; outdoor pool and bar; gift shop; Wi-Fi (free).

Best Western Plus Austin City Hotel ★★★ You won't be in the heart of SoCo if you stay at this Best Western, but you'll be 5 minutes from all the action—and you'll save considerable amounts of money. Good insulation in the spacious, attractive rooms keep you from hearing the nearby freeway—the hotel is on the I-35 frontage road—which is convenient for trips to central Austin and out of town. Lots of grassy areas, a tiled garden patio with a pool and hot tub, and a good on-site bar and grill make a stay here pleasant, while in-room refrigerators and microwaves and the inclusion of a full breakfast, parking, and Wi-Fi in the room rate add to the pocketbook appeal.

2200 S. I-35 Frontage Rd. www.austincityhotel.com. ✆ **800/780-7234** or 512/444-0561. 145 units. $96–$155 double; $155–$205 suite. Rates include full breakfast. Free self-parking. Pets 80 lb. or under accepted, $20 per night ($100 per week max). **Amenities:** Restaurant; bar; convenience store; laundromat; exercise room; outdoor pool; hot tub; business center; Wi-Fi (free).

EAST AUSTIN

Expensive

Heywood Hotel ★★★ This 7-room boutique hotel, opened in late 2012, anticipated the need for lodging in gentrifying East Austin and set a high bar for it. It's an architectural delight, a 1925 Craftsman bungalow beautifully furnished with mid-century modern pieces, local art (many pieces are for sale), comfy throw pillows, and colorful textiles. Several guest rooms have high ceilings and skylights; some have patios. All offer handcrafted walnut platform beds dressed in high-quality linens, reclaimed longleaf pine floors, white noise machines, and refrigerators stocked with Texas beer. But one of the best things about staying here is the personalized service; you'll get a great introduction to the latest food trucks and restaurants in the area, as well as to downtown sights, just a 10-minute walk away. The staff is only on property from 7am to 7pm, so you're on your own at night, which adds to the homey atmosphere.

1609 E. Cesar Chavez St. www.heywoodhotel.com. ✆ **512/271-5522.** 7 units. $189–$389. Min. 2-night stay weekends. Free on-site parking. No children age 9 and under. Full property available for rental. **Amenities:** Coffee bar; bike rentals; Wi-Fi (free).

Moderate/Expensive

Hotel Eleven ★★★ First, to get the celebrity news out of the way: Louis Vuitton, the uncharacteristically friendly (semi-)resident feline at this appealing

HIP hosteling IN AUSTIN

Perennially popular with the young and the budget-conscious, hostels have also become entertainment hubs in Austin. Two recent arrivals on the communal lodging scene offer guests the dubious advantage of being able to go straight from bar to bed—though not necessarily a private one. All three hostels covered here provide free Wi-Fi, free continental breakfast, and shared guest kitchen facilities. Rates are per person per night, and are averages for the year.

You can listen to soft jazz or blues while sipping a craft cocktail in Austin's oldest (1885) fire station, now downtown's **Firehouse Lounge and Hostel,** 605 Brazos St. (www.firehousehostel.com; ✆ **512/201-2522**). Rooms are dorms with shared bathroom ($29–$32); private but shared bathroom ($99); or suites with private bathrooms ($139–$149).

The eco-friendly **Hostelling International–Austin** in South Austin, 2200 S. Lakeshore Blvd. (www.hiusa.org/hostels/texas/austin/austin; ✆ **512/444-2294**), occupies a spot on the hike-and-bike trail with views of Lady Bird Lake that many pay through the nose to get. You can rent bikes and kayaks here. Room options include: dorms ($23) or private rooms ($79), all with shared hallway bathrooms.

A converted lock-and-safe warehouse, **Native Experiential Hostels,** 807 E. 4th St. (www.nativehostels.com; ✆ **512/551-9947**), is an East Austin destination for casual dining and sipping at both lunch and dinnertime; daytime use of the conference room is not uncommon, and evening often brings live bands. The most upscale of the three, with fewer beds per dorm room and some comfy private accommodations, this is a prototype for what may be an expanded brand. Rooms range from dorms with shared bathroom ($39–$40) to a king room with private bathroom ($150) or a loft room with private bathroom ($275).

eastside property, was featured in the book *Hotels with Cats*. Among the other reasons to stay at this boutique hotel: It was built from scratch by architect/co-owner Mark Vornberg and decorated by his wife Shelly Leibham, who is also the general manager; they both drew on their favorite travel experiences to create stylish but warm guest rooms with all the mod cons, as well as inviting public spaces; these include a rooftop deck with expansive city views, and a friendly downstairs bar and lounge, which feels like a mini-"Cheers." Everyone may not know your name there right away but at least one person will: You'll get a handwritten welcome note awaiting you in your room, as well as a personal greeting from Shelly, who can help acclimate you to the neighborhood. You'll be within easy walking distance of downtown sights like the Capitol, and even closer to such East Austin attractions as the Texas State Cemetery (p. 241), not to mention to several food trucks and restaurants. It's right near Franklin Barbeque (p. 214); if you don't want to wait in line for several hours, find someone to hold your place and text you back in your room when the 'cue's ready.

1123 E. 11th St. www.hotelelevenaustin.com. ✆ **512/675-0011.** 14 units. $159–$279 double; $259 and up suite. Limited free parking. **Amenities:** Bar/lounge; concierge; Wi-Fi (free).

Inexpensive

See box above for the **Native Experiential Hostels.**

CENTRAL AUSTIN

Moderate/Expensive

Hotel Ella ★★★ Proud UT parents and Longhorn alums, businesspeople, and couples are all regulars to this impeccable West Campus boutique hotel. Along with its prime location in an area with a dearth of lodgings, Hotel Ella is known for its casual-chic restaurant, attentive service, and gorgeous Greek Revival architecture; the house was built in 1900 for Goodall Wooten and his new wife, the former Ella Newsome. All the rooms in the mansion—as the main building is called—as well as those in the 1983 North Wing addition are old-style elegant, but with modern amenities such as 47-inch LED TVs. In the mansion, the second-story signature rooms are the most fun; most of them open onto a sweeping wraparound porch and have high ceilings and large bathrooms. The third-floor rooms are a little smaller, while those in the North Wing have patios and surround a tree-shaded courtyard centered by a pool. **Goodall's Kitchen** offers fresh seasonal fare in a casual, minimalist atmosphere. The original Ella's role as a patron of the arts is reflected in the lobby's art photographs and prints and the hotel's monthly salon series.

1900 Rio Grande St. www.hotelella.com. ✆ **512/495-1800.** 47 units. $169–$459 double; $249–$509 suite. Valet parking $25 per night. Pets accepted. **Amenities:** Restaurant with bar/lounge; 24-hr. fitness center; outdoor pool; Wi-Fi (free).

Inexpensive

Habitat Suites ★★ This all-suites property is probably the greenest budget hotel in town—and has been since 1991, when its owners made that their goal. From the beginning, they've recycled, conserved water, grown organic food, generated their own solar electricity, used only natural materials and cleaning products, and even allowed guests to cook for themselves—making this a lodging like none other in Austin. Each large, hypoallergenic suite has a full kitchen and a small outdoor seating area, most overlooking the nicely shaded pool; several have fireplaces. The furniture is basic and occasionally worn-looking; older pieces are sometimes reupholstered to avoid adding to the waste stream. The location is just 2 miles north of the UT Austin campus, but this is not a hotel for college students and partiers. It even has a "quiet time" between 9pm and 9am. Too bad it's not a bit closer to downtown—and to the owners' **Casa de Luz** macrobiotic restaurant in South Austin (p. 209). That said, this hotel is on the Capital Metro Rail Red Line and Capital Metro bus routes, both of which go downtown.

500 E. Highland Mall Blvd. www.habitatsuites.com. ✆ **800/916-4339** or 512/467-6000. 96 units. $109–$159 1-bedroom suite; $159–$259 2-bedroom suite. Packages available. Rates include breakfast and afternoon wine & snacks (except Sun). Free parking. **Amenities:** Jacuzzi; outdoor saltwater pool; Wi-Fi (free).

NORTHWEST

The transformation of the 220-acre Travaasa Austin into the **Miraval Austin Resort & Spa,** 13500 FM2769 (www.miravalaustin.com; ✆ **855/234-1672**), hadn't yet been completed when we went to press, but the setting, in a northwest Austin nature preserve, combined with the brand's track record for award-winning wellness and pampering programs, guarantee a top-rate (if not inexpensive) experience.

Expensive

The Archer ★★★ The Domain NORTHSIDE (p. 257) likes to bill itself as an alternate entertainment hub to downtown Austin. That's seriously stretching it, but the stylish Archer proves that you don't have to feel like a dweeb for staying at a mall. The high-ceilinged lobby is a fun mash-up of styles—a giant chandelier dripping sparkly crystal strings, a mural of wild horses, and leather chairs flanking a blazing fireplace (the cranked up air-conditioning makes sitting near it plausible). The lobby also hosts the **Second Bar + Kitchen,** a farm-to-table restaurant helmed by CIA-trained chef David Bull. It's adjacent to an outdoor patio lounge, centered around a small pool with a Texas star on the bottom. Rooms are similarly tongue-in-cheek chic, with local art and touches of whimsy like his-and-her fuzzy slippers (if you don't do pink lips, go for the black mustache ones). Lots of outlets and USB ports, plus a well-stocked mini-bar/caffeine center, make holing up and working here convenient for the many guests who have business on the nearby tech corridor (the Apple store is also a handy two doors down). Turn-down treats from local businesses like Bakery Lorraine are another nice touch.

3121 Palm Way, Domain NORTHSIDE. www.archerhotel.com/austin. ✆ **855/437-9100** or 512/836-5700. 171 units. $179–$299 double; $239 and up suite. Free self-parking; valet parking $25. Pets under 50 lb. accepted, $150 fee. **Amenities:** Restaurant; bar; business center; concierge; outdoor pool; fitness room; day spa (next door); Wi-Fi (free).

Moderate/Expensive

Renaissance Austin Hotel ★★ Anchoring the upscale Arboretum mall, the Renaissance has been catering to travelers doing business in northwest Austin since the mid-1980s, making it a pioneer in the tech corridor. Regular upgrades and new development in the area—including the Domain and Domain NORTHSIDE malls, just a 10-minute drive away—have kept the hotel thriving. On Friday and Saturday, rates are often discounted, drawing shoppers. The huge atrium lobby is dramatic (though rooms facing it can be noisy), while exterior rooms have attractive views of the thickly wooded rolling hills surrounding the mall. Chic, larger-than-normal guest rooms feature pillow-top bedding, local art, and plushly upholstered furniture in soothing earth tones. All have mini-fridges and state-of-the-art business

Greater Austin Hotels

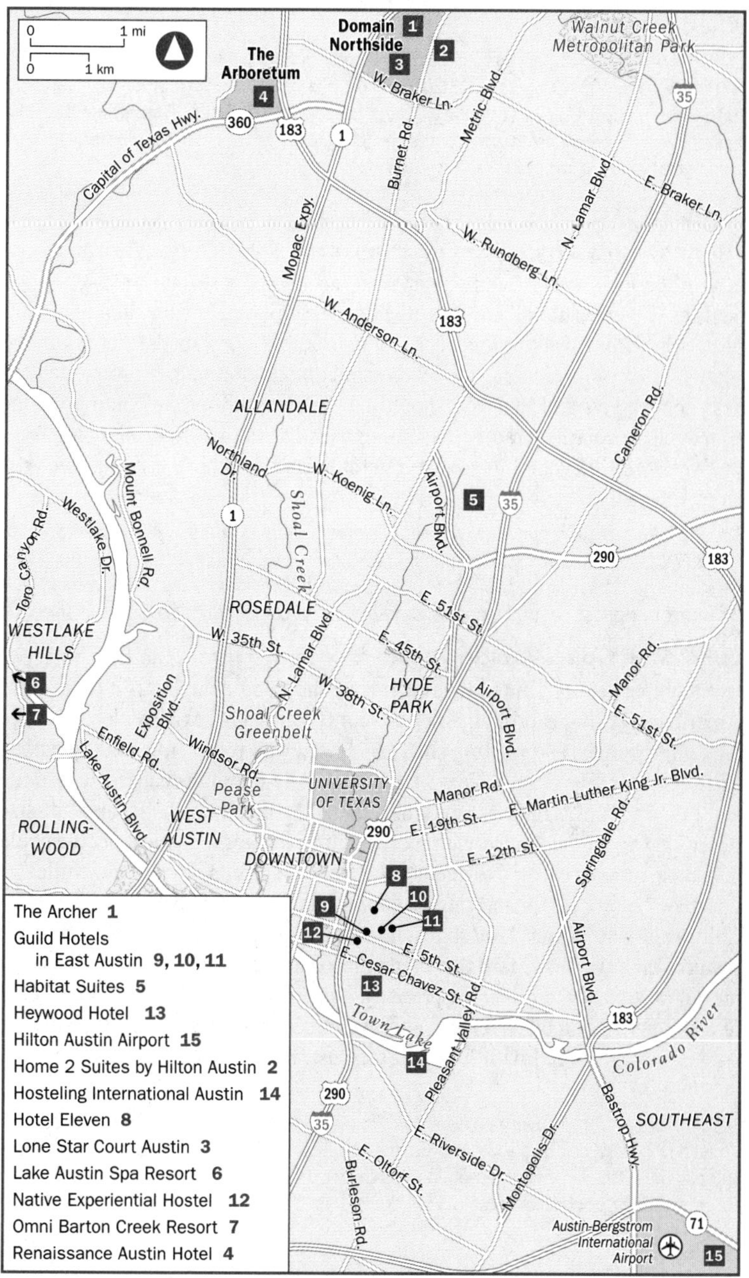

perks. The **Knotty Deck & Bar** has an appealing outdoor patio and creative cocktails, while you can get made-to-order pizza and local brews at **@austinbytes.**

9721 Arboretum Blvd. (off Loop 360, near Research Blvd.). www.marriott.com. ✆ **800/HOTELS-1** (468-3571) or 512/343-2626. 478 units. $229–$299 double; $260 and up suite. Self-parking $10; valet parking $25. Pets accepted, $75 fee. **Amenities:** 2 restaurants; bar; convenience store; concierge; club-level rooms; fitness center; Jacuzzi; indoor pool; outdoor pool; sauna; room service; car rental; Wi-Fi ($15).

Moderate

Home 2 Suites by Hilton Austin North ★ This extended-stay property in the tech corridor is popular with businesspeople, but it's also a good deal for leisure visitors, who like its proximity to the Domain shopping complex (it's within walking distance, though across busy roads), its pool, and such nice (if guilt-inducing) touches as a combination laundry room and fitness center; you feel like you should hit the treadmill while waiting for the spin cycle to complete rather than going back to your room, drinking the beer you've stored in your full-size refrigerator, and watching a movie on your large-screen TV.

2800 Esperanza Crossing. www.home2suites3.hilton.com. ✆ **888/225-9664** or 512/339-2400. $105–$169 studio suites; $145–$205 1-bedroom suites. Free self-parking. Pets under 50 lb. accepted, $100 fee. Rates include breakfast buffet. **Amenities:** Outdoor pool; exercise room; business center; laundry; convenience store; Wi-Fi (free).

Lone Star Court Austin at the Domain ★★★ The last thing you would expect to find in the toney Domain shopping complex is a bit of retro Americana. A re-creation of a motor court from 1950s Texas, replete with fire pits, grassy areas, and rocking chairs on breezeway patios, this boutique hotel might come off as corny if it were less skillfully done; instead, it's charming and fun. The rooms have braided rugs, cowhide director's chairs, and full-size SMEG refrigerators loaded with more adult beverages than most people could consume in a week, not to mention—shhh—such fancy-pants amenities as gourmet coffee, Egyptian cotton bedding, and boutique bath products from California. The **Water Trough** restaurant and bar—in a faux barn, naturally—features creative Texas fare like brisket tacos and cocktails served in a Mason jar. There's plenty to do on the property—lawn games, Ping-Pong, swimming in an outdoor pool, bikes rentals, and live music from Wednesday to Saturday. And if you get bored with living in the past, there's always the mall outside the door.

10901 Domain Dr., in Domain Mall. www.lonestarcourt.com. ✆ **512/814-2625.** 123 units. $139–$219 double; $409 and up suite. Rates include continental breakfast. Free self-parking. Max. 2 pets under 50 lb., $50 per pet. Amenities: Restaurant; bar; exercise room; outdoor pool; bike rental; Wi-Fi (free).

WEST/LAKES

Expensive

Lake Austin Spa Resort ★★★ This all-inclusive wellness retreat in a picture-perfect setting is quintessential Austin: It's set along a serene body of water, offers lots of outdoor activities, and serves fresh, healthful foods. Just west of town near the Highland Lakes area and the Balcones Canyonlands Nature Preserve, the resort is the kind of place where you can sit in a breezy cabana by a pool, take to the water in kayaks, hydro-bikes, and stand-up paddleboards, venture out on hiking excursions . . . or just relax and get pampered in a gorgeous setting. Natural herbs and flowers growing in the resort's garden are used for soothing spa treatments such the signature "Lake House Lavender" sugar scrub, or sourced by the chef for dishes served in the resort restaurants.

You can't go wrong with any of the different room configurations: The "standard" signature rooms, luxury garden rooms, luxury lakeview rooms, or the hot tub cottages—all are beautifully outfitted, so it just depends on which views you want, how many beds you need, and how much money you can afford to spend. The resort's luxury watercraft delivers guests to the Lake Austin shores of its 25,000-square-foot **LakeHouse Spa** from downtown Austin or the 360 Bridge.

1705 S. Quinlan Park Rd. (at Steiner Ranch, 5 miles S. of Hwy. 620). www.lakeaustin.com. ✆ **800/847-5637** or 512/372-7300. 40 units. $625 and up (per person) double without spa treatments, $775 with treatments; packages available. Rates include all meals, classes, and activities. Alcoholic beverages, spa treatments/personal trainers extra. Free parking. Dogs accepted in Garden Cottage rooms, $300 fee. No children 13 and under. **Amenities:** 2 restaurants; boutiques; 24-hr. fitness center; 1 indoor and 2 outdoor pools; salon; spa; watersports equipment; room service; Wi-Fi (free).

Omni Barton Creek Resort ★★★ Austin's only real full-service resort—one that caters to business travelers, couples, singles, and families alike—Barton Creek sits on 4,000 gently rolling, wooded acres near Lake Travis. The resort feels rural, but it's close enough to central Austin (about 20 min. away) that you can easily sightsee or party there.

To mark its 30th anniversary, the resort is undergoing a $150-million expansion and renovation, expected to be completed in May 2019; the resort is temporarily closed until then. It's adding a tower of rooms, several restaurants, and the Mokara Spa, while refreshing its already top-notch accommodations and recreational facilities: four 18-hole championship golf courses and the Chuck Cook Golf Academy, tennis courts and a tennis clinic, and a state-of-the-art fitness center with an indoor track. Restaurants include **Bob's Steak & Chop House,** an appropriately clubby fine dining room; **Nopales,** a hip Latin-flavored spot to sip and sup, named for the prickly pear cactus; and **Blind Salamander**—an allusion to a local endangered species—which serves light,

family-friendly HOTELS

Element Austin (p. 184) Large rooms with full-size kitchens that can be stocked with healthy Blue Apron meals make this hotel in the heart of downtown convenient for those traveling with kids. Other family-friendly features include free bike rentals and the casual Caroline's Upstairs restaurant, where youngsters can play lawn games and eat finger foods with the big kids—and maybe even get a mocktail with a little umbrella as a treat.

Four Seasons Austin (p. 180) Tell reservations that you're traveling with kids and you'll be automatically enrolled in the free amenities program, which gets you everything from child-size bathrobes and baby toiletries to age-appropriate toys and books. You don't have to schlep your baby gear along either; the hotel can provide car seats, strollers, playpens, disposable diapers and pacifiers, and more. There's a kid-friendly menu, lots of fun things to do on the property—and bonded babysitting services should you need some grown-up alone time.

Habitat Suites (p. 191) These low-key guest lodgings offer spacious, commonsense living quarters, plus the convenience (and economy) of kitchen facilities; free parking and a central location are assets too. This super eco-friendly place will especially appeal to kids who are concerned more about the environment than they are with glitz.

Lone Star Court (p. 194) Reasons for families to stay here include lawn games, Ping-Pong tables, an outdoor pool, fire pits for marshmallow roasting, and a big barn dining room with a menu that's not too frou-frou for picky kids. In addition, you're smack in the middle of a major shopping mall, thus lowering the potential for boredom even more.

healthful fare in a room with a panoramic view. Guest rooms in all three buildings—the European chateau-style reception building and two modern towers—are generously sized, with those in the new tower starting at a whopping 425 square feet. Mixing heavy wood furnishings with lighter, more casual fittings, the look is elegant without being stuffy—in short, typical upscale Texas.

8212 Barton Club Dr. (1 mile W. of intersection Loop 360 and R.R. 2244). www.bartoncreek.com. ✆ **800/336-6158** or 512/329-4000. 493 units. $308–$479 double; $389–$769 suite. **Amenities:** 6 restaurants; coffee shop; bar; children's center and programs; 4 golf courses; mini-golf; health club; indoor pool; outdoor pool; spa; 10 tennis courts; room service; Wi-Fi (free).

AIRPORT/SOUTHEAST

See also Chapter 17, p. 290, for the **Hyatt Regency Lost Pines Resort & Spa.**

Moderate

Hilton Austin Airport ★★ So close to the airport you can almost see your gate, this hotel—known as "the Donut" for its round shape—has a central atrium, a restaurant and bar, and a coffee shop. It also has quite a history:

It's the former headquarters of Bergstrom Air Force Base and also one of three Cold War bunkers where the president of the United States could be taken for safety in the event of a nuclear attack. (Ask for the hotel fact sheet on the fascinating history of this building.) So it was built to be solid—which means, for the hotel guest, it's also virtually soundproof. The Donut is nicer in other ways than most airport hotels. Large, comfortable rooms are equipped with all the amenities, and the hotel has an outdoor saltwater pool, Jacuzzi, and 24-hour fitness center. If you get stuck in a storm at the airport or have a quick overnight layover, this is a good choice. It's also convenient for those heading to the Circuit of the Americas (p. 283).

9515 New Airport Dr. (½ mile from airport, 2 miles E. of intersection hwys. 183 and 71). www3.hilton.com. ✆ **800/445-8667** or 512/385-6767. 273 units. $109–$199 double; $189 and up suite. Valet parking $20; self-parking $14. Pets accepted, $50 fee. **Amenities:** Restaurant; lounge; free airport transfers; concierge; executive-level rooms; exercise room; outdoor pool; room service; Wi-Fi (free).

13

WHERE TO EAT IN AUSTIN

Austin has plenty of down-home barbecue joints, Tex-Mex holes-in-the-wall, and hippie diners, but the city has also become known for its serious culinary scene. This is a town where people will wait more than 4 hours for the pit-smoked brisket of Aaron Franklin, who won the Best Southwest Chef award from the James Beard Foundation, and where you can expect to hear terms like "locally sourced," "snout-to-tail," and "scratch kitchen" casually dropped into dining conversations.

The city lacks ethnic enclaves like Chinatown and Little Italy, or a major Mexican section, but compensates with its food trucks or trailers; there were more than 2,000 of them at last count. You'll see them everywhere—downtown, along South Congress and South Lamar, and in a lot of unexpected places. Many chefs use their mobile kitchens as incubators for new recipes and concepts they'd like to try. Some of the most popular ones turn into brick-and-mortar restaurants; others stay where they are and acquire large followings—and long lines. I cover a handful of them in "Meals on Wheels in Austin" (p. 213) and "Austin's Offbeat Sweet Treats" (p. 206).

Downtown has the highest concentration of restaurants, but the most exciting dining is found in two adjacent areas: south of Lady Bird Lake, especially along South Congress, First, and South Lamar avenues; and east of I-35, where Cesar Chavez, East Sixth, and Manor are major culinary corridors. In other parts of the city, restaurants tend to cluster along major commercial corridors and in malls, but you'll find a few tucked away on the quiet streets of some old neighborhoods.

Wherever you eat, think casual. There isn't a restaurant in Austin that requires men to put on a tie and jacket, and many upscale dining rooms are far more elegantly attired than their tech-industry customers.

Dining out can be a competitive sport in Austin. Make reservations if at all possible, or dine at off hours. If you turn up at some of the most popular spots around 7:30pm, you might wait an hour or more. Austin restaurants tend to be noisy; if you're looking for conversation rather than (literal) buzz, that's another reason to dine at off hours. (Of course, you have no choice with brunch, one of Austin's most popular meals, which only takes place at, well, brunch hours.)

Assume parking will be a problem downtown and on South Congress Avenue. Taking a ride-share is your best bet—also freeing you to indulge in some of the well-crafted cocktails you'll find in most top dining rooms.

One of the best things about dining in Austin is that restaurants take food allergies and sensitivities seriously. It's the rare server in an upscale restaurant who doesn't ask patrons if there are ingredients they need to avoid, the rare chef who won't take the time to suggest appropriate substitutes. And (no surprise) ethical preferences are honored in Austin too: You'll find vegetarian and vegan options on nearly every menu, and several restaurants are entirely meat-free. Smoking is not allowed in public places in Austin, including the outside areas of restaurants or bars, so expect a fume-free experience too.

Which leads to the last point: Many restaurants around town offer patio dining, which not only gives them a setting for live music, but also makes them kid- and pet-friendly. Austinites may get pretentious about dining, but they also know how to have fun at mealtimes.

DOWNTOWN

Expensive

There's also a downtown branch of **Eddie V's,** p. 220.

Emmer and Rye ★★★ NEW AMERICAN The name of this deservedly-acclaimed restaurant is derived from the fact that owner/executive chef Kevin Fink mills his own heirloom grains for pastas, breads, and dessert—perhaps durum wheat spaghetti noodles for the signature *cacio e pepe*, made with Swiss challerhocker cheese; or the buckwheat chocolate cake with crème fraîche. Carefully constructed carbs are by no means all you'll find here, however. Fresh produce, meat, and seafood get equal attention on the daily changing menu. It's hard to describe the preparation processes without sounding a bit clinical (there's a lot of fermentation, reduction, and dehydration involved). Perhaps alchemical, in the sense of magical, might be a better way to put what happens when these disparate flavors and textures combine. You might never have heard of *hoja santa* (Mexican pepperleaf), say, but when it comes on an apple baked with dehydrated pork loin, you know it tastes amazing. You have two dining options: Order small plates, pastas, entrees, and desserts from a fixed menu, or wait for the servers to describe your choices from around a dozen dim sum-style plates. If all this sounds a bit intimidating, don't worry: You're on an equal footing with the foodiest of the food geeks, that is, likely to be ignorant about much of what you'll be introduced to. The staff is very knowledgeable without being condescending. With all the servers

Downtown & SoCo Restaurants

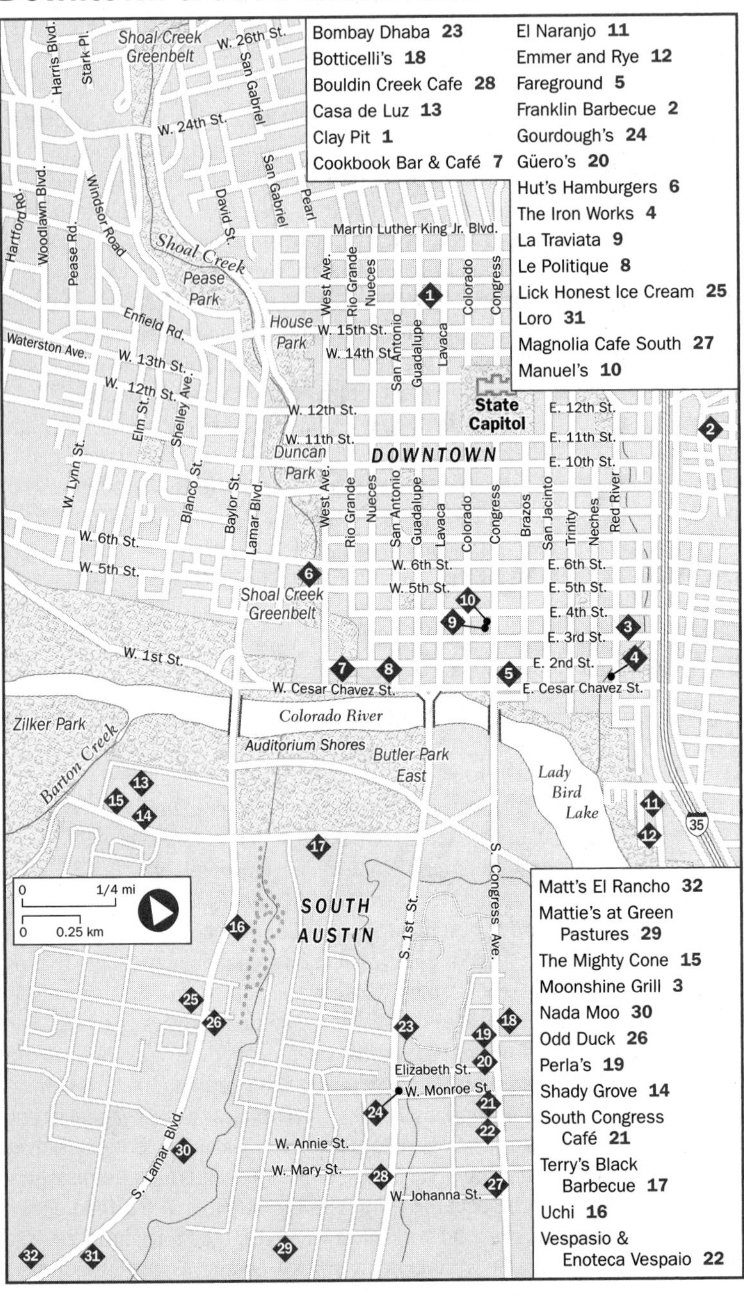

bustling around, the rooms—modern and bright—can be noisy. Opt for the patio if weather permits.

51 Rainey St., Ste. 110. www.emmerandrye.com. ✆ **512/366-5530.** Dinner main courses $11–$22; brunch $11–$16. Reservations accepted. Tues–Thurs 5:30–10pm; Fri–Sat 5:30–11pm; Sun 11am–2pm and 5:30–10pm.

El Naranjo ★★ MEXICAN In a simple yellow bungalow on Rainey Street, you can get some of the city's best *tacos dorados,* here filled with goat cheese, potatoes, or chicken, swathed in a creamy green avocado salsa. Other standouts include the duck with mole *negro,* shrimp with mole Colorado . . . really, any of the mole dishes, since owners Iliana de la Vega and Ernesto Torrealba hail from Oaxaca, a city renowned for these intricate sauces. Chef Iliana worked as an instructor at the Culinary Institute of America before the couple moved to Austin and opened a food truck on Rainey Street. Now, in this brick-and-mortar shop, she can bake fresh bread, Mexican pastries, and tortillas each day and create spicy fresh salsas, as well as the aforementioned moles. The space is intimate and cheerful, with two small dining rooms, a lively bar with killer cocktails, and a happening patio.

85 Rainey St. www.elnaranjorestaurant.com. ✆ **512/474-2776.** Plates $14–$44. Tues–Sat 5:30–10pm; brunch Sat–Sun 11am–2pm.

La Traviata ★★ ITALIAN If you're tired of Italian restaurant clichés, you'll love this Euro-chic trattoria, with textured limestone walls complementing the hardwood floors, sleek bar, and soaring ceilings. The food is just as unfussy and fresh. Chef/owner Marion Gilchrist allows the quality ingredients to take center stage, and creates sauces that are delicious without being overwhelming. That's why such classics as chicken parmesan or spaghetti Bolognese remain so popular here. The same is true of the crispy polenta with Gorgonzola cheese or the duck confit. One of the nice features of this place is that you can make size adjustments for some dishes: Order a second leg for the duck confit, for example, for $8 extra. The narrow room bustles with energy, especially on weekend pre-theater evenings, but the staff never seems overwhelmed. Don't miss the tiramisu, wonderfully light with toasted hazelnuts and a dusting of espresso.

314 Congress Ave. www.latraviatatx.com. ✆ **512/479-8131.** Pasta $12–$16; main courses $16–$26. Reservations highly recommended. Mon–Thurs 11:30am–2pm and 5:30–9:30pm; Fri 11:30am–2pm and 5:30–10:30pm; Sat 5:30–10:30pm.

Le Politique ★★ FRENCH In a city where Mexican, Asian, Italian, and fusion restaurants rule, many will be comforted to find classic French food in a classic French setting, replete with black-and-white tiled floors, caned chairs, and a blue awning-covered patio. Comfort is the operative word: You're not going to find excitement in such skillfully prepared dishes as escargots, French onion soup, trout almandine, or beef bourguignon. Rich and buttery (and in the case of the escargots, garlicky) is what you're signing on for and what you're getting. Some quibbles: A salad niçoise needs to have anchovies in it to be a salad niçoise. And having to pay for bread—even excellent bread—is irritating. Some compensations: The pastry chef, who worked at Napa's French Laundry, turns out Paris-worthy *bombe au chocolat* and macarons, and the wine list is well rounded, with some interesting by-the-glass selections.

110 San Antonio St. www.lepolitiqueaustin.com. ✆ **512/580-7651.** Lunch main courses $12–$20; dinner main courses $15–$43; brunch $12–$18. Reservations accepted. Mon–Wed 11am–10pm; Thurs–Fri 11am–11pm; Sat 10:30am–3pm and 5–11pm; Sun 10:30am–3pm and 5–10pm.

Moderate

Clay Pit ★★ INDIAN An elegant setting—a historic building with wood floors and exposed limestone walls, softly lit with lamps and votive candles—and creative recipes raise this restaurant to gourmet status. The Clay Pit is known for Indian cooking with a bit of a twist. Try the perfectly cooked coriander calamari served with a piquant cilantro aioli as an appetizer. For an entree, consider *khuroos-e-tursh,* baked chicken breast stuffed with nuts, mushrooms, and onions, and smothered in a cashew-almond cream sauce; or one of the many dazzling vegetarian dishes. At night, the dining room is romantic; during the day, it's a place to grab a quick, economical lunch from the buffet, something to keep in mind when you're touring either the nearby capitol or the university campus.

1601 Guadalupe St. www.claypit.com. ✆ **512/322-5131.** Lunch buffet $7.50–$10; main courses $10–$20. Reservations recommended. Mon–Fri 11am–2:30pm and 5–10pm (till 11pm Fri); Sat noon–3pm and 5–11pm; Sun noon–3pm and 5–10pm.

Manuel's ★★ MEXICAN With large windows facing Congress Avenue and a bright, glittery vibe, Manuel's has Mexico-style flair—and a Mexico City–style menu. It was one of the first (1984) restaurants in town to introduce regional cuisine to a town weaned on Tex-Mex. Using high-quality local and seasonal ingredients, Manuel's menu includes such entrees as *enchiladas suizas* topped with a savory chile verde sauce, and *chile relleno en nogada*, a roasted poblano chile stuffed with shredded pork, almonds, and raisins. Wild-caught fish from certified sustainable waters is hand cut daily; salad dressings and fried foods are made with canola and virgin olive oils; and gluten-free, dairy-free, and vegetarian options abound. The restaurant is popular with the after-work happy-hour crowd, and there's often a wait here at night, so reservations are a good idea. Don't miss the popular Sunday Jazz brunch at both the downtown and Great Hills (10201 Jollyville Rd., ✆ **512/345-1042**) locations.

310 Congress Ave. www.manuels.com. ✆ **512/472-7555.** Lunch main courses $12–$18; dinner main courses $14–$34. Reservations recommended. Sun–Thurs 11am–9pm; Fri–Sat 11am–10pm; Sunday 11am–3pm. Happy hour daily 4–6pm.

A GOURMET food court

One of downtown's most anticipated recent (2018) additions, the **Fareground** food court, 111 Congress Plaza (www.faregroundaustin.com), is ideal for traveling companions with different culinary tastes and checkbook sizes. You can sample the wares of some of Austin's top chefs in the lobby and plaza of a high-rise just north of the Congress Avenue Bridge. You might start your day with a breakfast bowl of poached eggs, short ribs, and sweet potatoes at **Henbit,** brought to you by the Emmer and Rye team (p. 199); savor Sonoran wheat tacos filled with wild boar carnitas from **Dai Due Taqueria;** or enjoy a hamachi roll with avocado and cucumber from **Ni-Kome.** Bread or savory pastries from the excellent **Easy Tiger** bakery might be perfect with cheese and wine from other outlets. Prices are reasonable for most of the places, and menu lengths are limited; check the website for details on all the vendors and for the live music schedule. Office workers in the building have complained of weight gains but agree that their productivity has increased as reasons to leave the premises have decreased.

Moonshine Grill ★ SOUTHERN This friendly kitchen has a loyal following of politicos and other downtown workers who like the historic setting, the generous portions of well-prepared comfort food, and the chance to kick back a few shots of moonshine (it's available by the flight). The chicken and waffles and Hatch chile mac and cheese are deservedly popular; so is the signature skillet apple pie with salted caramel (do not attempt to eat this on your own unless you intend to walk back to your hotel room and it's at least a mile away). If you don't make a reservation and have to wait, nibble the complimentary popcorn and read about the history of the building: it's the last Sunday house in the region (see Fredericksburg, p. 144 for details) and sits on the site of the city's original Waterloo settlement. There's a second location in Avery Ranch, 10525 W. Parmer Ln. (✆ **520/551-8669**), about half an hour north of downtown near Cedar Park.

303 Red River St. www.moonshinegrill.com. ✆ **512/236-9599.** Plates $9–$34. No reservations. Mon–Thurs 11am–10pm; Fri–Sat 11am–11pm; Sun 9am–2pm and 5–10pm.

Inexpensive

Cookbook Bar & Café ★★★ NEW AMERICAN If you're both a food lover and a book lover, you'll find this cafe in Austin's new Central Library (p. 234) irresistible. A 5,000-volume collection of cookbooks donated by late local food critic Virginia Wood is the source of the recipes; you order at a counter, cafeteria-style, and your food is brought to you in one of the light-filled indoor dining rooms or on the patio. While paying tribute to seasonal local ingredients, the menu highlights classic items from well-known chefs: perhaps a greens, pear, walnut, and Parmesan salad from Jamie Oliver's *The Naked Chef*; fried chickpeas courtesy of *The Martha Stewart Cookbook*; or a chicken pot pie that draws on the expertise of Thomas Keller's *Ad Hoc at*

Home. The cafe has a full liquor license, leading to such concoctions as the Last of the Mojitos and The Adventures of Huckleberry Gin. Prices are reasonable, and executions are as clever as the concept.

710 W. Cesar Chavez St. inside Central Library. www.cookbookatx.com. No phone. Plates $5–$15. Mon–Thurs 9am–9pm; Fri–Sat 9am–7pm; Sun 11am–7pm.

Hut's Hamburgers ★★ AMERICAN Sometimes you're just in the mood for a burger, fries, and a shake, and you don't want to spend big bucks. This classic burger shack has been an Austin favorite since it opened in 1939 as Sammie's Drive-In. Now it offers more than 20 varieties of its specialty, from classic patties made with fresh (never frozen) Texas beef to buffalo, chicken, and vegan burgers. Regular blue-plate specials include chicken-fried steak, meatloaf, and fried catfish, as well as Texas-size onion rings. Get some takeout for a picnic on the grounds of Zilker Hillside Theatre during the summer musicals.

807 W. 6th St. www.facebook.com/hutshamburgersatx. ✆ **512/472-0693.** Sandwiches and burgers $6–$10; plates $8–$11. Sun–Tues 11am–9:30pm; Wed–Sat 11am–10pm.

SOUTH AUSTIN

Expensive

Botticelli's ★★ ITALIAN Tucked beneath a black awning on a popular part of the South Congress strip, this is the place to come for Italian comfort food. It's got big storefront windows, high ceilings, exposed brick, and a large outdoor patio for alfresco dining; seats out front are perfect for people watching. The lasagna is superb, as are house-made raviolis (try the sage butternut squash), and the veal/pork/beef meatballs, with a well-seasoned marinara sauce made with freshly diced tomatoes; you can't miss with the fresh fish offerings or wood-fired pizzas, either. Wine and beer lists are well curated, and a concise cocktail menu offers drinks such as a Hemingway daiquiri and a peach sangria made in-house. Botticelli's is newer and buzzier than Italian standby Vespaio (p. 206), just across the road; both have their devoted fans and any Austinite will be happy to argue preferences with you.

1321 S. Congress Ave. www.botticellissouthcongress.com. ✆ **512/916-1315.** Main courses $16–$32. Reservations accepted. Sun–Wed 5–10:30pm; Thurs–Sat 5–11pm.

Mattie's at Green Pastures ★★ NEW AMERICAN/SOUTHERN In 1946, a stately 1894 mansion in remote south Austin was converted into a restaurant called Green Pastures. Fast forward to 2019: The area's buzzing and, following a thorough renovation, the restaurant has re-emerged as Mattie's, the nickname of one of the original owners. The menu fits today's trend for lighter versions of Southern comfort food, but in a far less casual setting than you'd expect in this category: If you've ever wanted to eat fried chicken with fancy cutlery, this is the place. Cornmeal dumplings, grilled pork ribs, and superb buttermilk biscuits also lay on the Southern charm. The grounds are gorgeous, lush with live oaks and peacocks strutting their stuff. This is the ultimate special occasion/brunch restaurant, a place Austinites favor for taking out visiting family members. Too bad it's not open for lunch Monday through Friday; it would be the perfect spot for leisure travelers to sip a mint julep and play lord or lady of the manor.

811 W. Live Oak St. www.mattiesaustin.com. ✆ **512/444-1888.** Main courses $18–$32; brunch $15–$22. Reservations accepted. Tues–Thurs 5–10pm; Fri 5– 11pm; Sat 11am–2pm and 5–11pm; Sun 11am–2pm.

Perla's ★★★ FISH/SEAFOOD You hit the trifecta at Perla's: a perfect patio for people-watching, killer bloody marys, and some of the best seafood in town. The restaurant is known for its raw oyster bar, with whatever's fresh from the coasts served up on a half shell, but cooked fish dishes with a Southern spin—crab Louie with cornbread-crusted fried green tomatoes, say, or bouillabaisse with saffron *rouille*—are justly popular too. The restaurant also has a way with lobster, with a creamy bisque and a sandwich (roll) that do credit to the pricey crustacean. Oak-grilled Niman Ranch steaks make good turf complements to the surf, and desserts such as the salted butterscotch pot de crème are surprisingly delicate. About that patio: It's a tree-shaded wooden deck with blue umbrellas for additional coverage and strings of tiny lights for additional romance. None of this comes cheap; this is the type of place you take someone you want to impress but who hates ostentation.

1400 S. Congress Ave. www.perlasaustin.com. ✆ **512/291-7300.** Main courses $31–$60. Reservations accepted. Mon–Thurs 11:30am–10pm; Fri 11:30am–11pm; Sat 10:30am–11pm; Sun 10:30am–10pm.

Uchi ★★★ ASIAN/JAPANESE This foodie favorite is popular for its playful and inventive take on Asian dishes as well as for having the freshest and finest sushi in town. James Beard award–winning chef and co-owner Tyson Cole trained at restaurants in Tokyo and New York. His menus change daily but may include such delights as Uchiviche, a whitefish and salmon ceviche with cilantro, chiles, and tomatoes; the Muru Kai mussels in a dreamy light sauce; or short-ribs cooked low and slow for 72 hours and served with wasabi. But sushi is always the main draw. For a near-perfect (though pricey) meal, go with the chef's tasting menu, ideally paired with selections from Uchi's long list of cold sakes. Uchi, Japanese for "house," is set in a converted 1930s bungalow decorated in dark rouge wallpaper with touches of black. Space is limited, and since Uchi has a cult following in Austin, you'll need to make reservations far in advance, or wait (hours) for a table at the bar. ***One downside:*** It's hard to have a conversation here. Sister restaurant **Uchiko** is in a larger, brighter space at 4200 N. Lamar Blvd. (www.uchikoaustin.com; ✆ **512/916-4808**), and there are also Uchi restaurants in Dallas, Denver, and Houston.

801 S. Lamar Blvd. www.uchiaustin.com. ✆ **512/916-4808.** Main courses $18–$30. Chef's tasting menu $100 per person. Reservations recommended. Sun–Thurs 5–10pm; Fri–Sat 5–11pm.

Vespaio ★★ ITALIAN Vespaio's swanked-up old storefront with lots of exposed brick and glass is elegant, and the food is worth waiting for, but you can drop quite a bit of dough on expensive wines while you're doing so; one of the oddities is that reservations are limited to off-peak hours and days. Your best bet is to get an order of the crispy calamari (they're huge) while you're waiting for a table. The spaghetti alla carbonara is super, as is veal scaloppine with mushrooms. Many come for the pizza—try the *boscaiola,* topped with wild boar sausage and Cambozola cheese. Among the chalkboard specials offered nightly, mixed meat and seafood grills are usually top-notch. Next door, the more informal **Enoteca Vespaio** (✆ **512/441-7672**) is a bit less expensive and offers lighter fare, including lunch and brunch. The attractive dining room is slightly more cramped but it's perfect for an afternoon coffee, panini, or glass of wine; there's a small outdoor patio, too. One of the starters served here is a plate of *arancini,* crispy fried risotto balls filled with fontina.

AUSTIN'S offbeat SWEET TREATS

Although Austin has lots of standard bakeries and sweets shops, several of the top places to get a sugar fix think outside the (candy) box.

Austin's homegrown brand of ice cream, introduced in 1984 and now available nationally, **Amy's** (www.amysicecream.com) is wonderfully rich and creamy. Watching the colorfully clad servers juggling the scoops is half the fun, however; check them out at any of Amy's 12 Austin locations, including one in west downtown, 1012 W. Sixth St., at Lamar Blvd. (✆ **512/480-0673**); one in SoCo, 1301 S. Congress Ave. (✆ **512/440-7488**); and one just north of the UT campus, 3500 Guadalupe (✆ **512/458-6895**). If you don't get a chance to try it in the city, you can catch this tasty treat at the airport.

If the road to excess leads to the palace of wisdom, you'll be a genius after visiting **Gourdoughs,** in an airstream trailer at 1503 S. First St. (www.gourdoughs.com). Bacon and chicken strips are among the ingredients you might find in these oversized fried-dough concoctions; peanut butter and fried bananas are others (they feature in The Elvis, of course). There's also a brick-and-mortar store where you can enjoy these meals-in-the-round with a cold beer: **Gourdough's Public House,** 2700 S. Lamar Blvd. (✆ **512/912-9070**).

Known for unusual flavors based on the availability of seasonal ingredients—roasted beets and fresh mint, say, or dewberry corn cobbler—**Lick Honest Ice Cream** (www.ilikelick.com/austin) sells its all-local, natural, sustainable sweets at three locations, including one in South Austin at 1100 S. Lamar Blvd. (✆ **512/363-5622**).

Vegans don't have to forgo creamy summer coolers in Austin. You can get a nondairy fix at **NadaMoo,** 1701 S. Lamar Blvd. (www.nadamoo.com/scoop-shop; ✆ **512/566-4964**), with flavors of coconut milk-based confections that include caramel cold brew and cookies (so Austin!) and birthday cake cookie dough. If you find yourself addicted, you'll likely find the nationally distributed product at a Whole Foods, Sprouts, or any other natural grocer near you. Lick (see above) also offers several non-dairy flavors.

There's a small cold case filled with Italian delicacies—perfect for taking something back to your hotel room.

1610 S. Congress Ave. www.austinvespaio.com. ✆ **512/441-6100.** Pizzas $18–$23; pastas and main courses $15–$23. Reservations accepted for Sun–Thurs 5:30–6:30pm only. Tues–Fri 5:30–10:30pm; Sat 5–10:30pm; Sun–Mon 5:30–10pm.

Moderate/Expensive

Odd Duck ★★★ ECLECTIC The menu at this food truck-turned-gourmet cafe is known for offbeat combinations: a fried quail sandwich with smoked egg salad and hot caramel, perhaps, or head-on shrimp sided by kimchi and pork belly. But James Beard–nominated chef Bryce Gilmore doesn't do novelty for novelty's sake: His devotion to local farmers and whole animal ethos means coming up with creative combinations to sync with the season and avoid waste. The cocktails are as creatively constructed as the dishes—you can choose such top-shelf spirits as Suerte Anejo Tequila or Balcones Texas Rye for an Old Fashioned— and this is the place to come if you want to sample the best craft beers in the region. The dining room has a foresty feel, with lots of natural light and knotty-pine tables complemented by deep green linens. You might end up dropping a lot of money here (a burger runs $19, for example, without sides, and bread and butter cost extra), but most likely you'll feel the meal was worth it. Its slightly more upscale sister restaurant **Barley Swine,** 6555 Burnet Rd., Ste. 400 (www.barleyswine.com; ✆ **512/394-8150**), has the same food philosophy but is open only for dinner and happy hour ("swine time"); it offers a tasting menu ($95) and chef pairing ($55) options. The more casual **Sour Duck Market,** 1814 E. Martin Luther King Jr. Blvd. (www.sourduckmarket.com; ✆ **512/394-5776**), specializing in sandwiches, salads, and pastries, is the latest addition to the duck pond.

1201 S. Lamar Blvd. www.oddduckaustin.com. ✆ **512/433-6521.** Main courses $9–$36; brunch $10–$14. Reservations accepted. Mon–Fri 11:30am–2:30pm and 5–10pm (until 11pm Fri); Sat 5–11pm; Sun 10:30am–2:30pm and 5–10pm.

South Congress Cafe ★★ SOUTHWEST/NEW AMERICAN This is the go-to spot for locals and visitors who love brunch but don't want to wait for the weekend to enjoy it. Among the standouts are the *migas* (Austin's favorite breakfast—eggs scrambled with strips of tortillas, tomatoes, onions, and chiles) and eggs Benedict with chipotle hollandaise and a side of crab cakes. Recommended on both the brunch and dinner menus is the hearty gumbo with duck and oysters. The dinner menu changes seasonally but, as with most Southwestern cooking, you'll usually find a variety of grilled meats and updated versions of comfort food standbys. The stylish modern dining room is a bit cramped, but high ceilings and tall windows facing South Congress give it a light and airy feel; you can always retreat to the spacious back deck when it's not too warm or cool. Brunch during the week is as popular as the Friday and Saturday versions; since midday reservations are not accepted, you may have to wait in line for a while.

1600 S. Congress Ave. www.southcongresscafe.com. ✆ **512/447-3905.** Main courses $11–$30. Reservations accepted for dinner. Mon–Fri 10am–10pm; Sat–Sun 9am–10pm.

Moderate

Loro ★★ ASIAN/FUSION When two of the city's top chefs, barbecue master Aaron Franklin (see Franklin Barbecue, p. 214) and sushi king Tyson Coleman (see Uchi, p. 205), opened this fast casual concept in 2018, you can bet Austin diners paid attention. Few left the restaurant disappointed, except those who were expecting to get straight-up versions of the dishes for which both restaurateurs are known, only without the wait (Franklin) or high prices (Coleman). Yes, the famed meat is present, but it's prepared with Asian spices—brisket with chili gastrique and Thai herbs, for example, or pork belly with house hoisin sauce. But that's not a complaint. It's worth coming here for the Thai green curry sausage sandwich alone. This is a bustling place, with a two-tiered outdoor deck and a light-filled dining room with wooden booths and a bar overhung by TVs tuned to sports channels. Ordering is a bit complicated: Elbow your way to one of the bartenders, pay, take a number, and wait until your order is brought to you. But the food is excellent, the beer is cold, and this is a great slice of Austin life, with families and foodie hipsters rubbing shoulders (and elbows).

2115 S. Lamar Blvd. www.loroaustin.com. ✆ **512/916-4858.** Main courses $11–$18. No reservations. Sun–Thurs 11am–10pm; Fri–Sat 11am–11pm.

Matt's El Rancho ★ TEX-MEX The year was 1952. Lyndon Johnson hadn't been serving in the U.S. Senate very long when Matt Martinez, a former prizefighter, opened his namesake restaurant downtown. Although Matt outlived LBJ, plenty of his original patrons followed when he moved his restaurant to south Austin some 3 decades later. Now in the hands of his grandkids, Matt's is still a must-stop for generations of Austinites, who make the pilgrimage for more reasons than nostalgia. They come for dependable Tex-Mex staples such as enchiladas, chiles relleno, fajitas, and the perennial favorite queso, named for former land commissioner Bob Armstrong. Matt's gets crowded on Friday and Saturday nights, especially if there's a university event, and you might have to wait up to an hour; show up by 6pm to avoid the queue. Then again, as luck would have it, there's a bar area and terrace where you can sip a fresh-lime margarita until your table is ready.

2613 S. Lamar Blvd. www.mattselrancho.com. ✆ **512/462-9333.** Main courses $11–$25. Reservations not accepted after 6pm Sat–Sun, except for large groups. Sun–Mon and Wed–Thurs 11am–10pm; Fri–Sat 11am–11pm.

Inexpensive

Bouldin Creek Café ★★★ VEGETARIAN/AMERICAN An Austin classic for a new generation, this colorful vegetarian cafe is more hippie than hipster in attitude. While it's a popular gathering spot for aspiring artists, filmmakers, and other young tattooed creatives, all ages and professions are made to feel welcome here. Patrons find common ground in such well prepared and reasonably priced fare as the South Austin stir fry (rice noodles, broccoli, mushrooms, and carrots in a teriyaki ginger miso sauce) and hearty breakfast dishes like zucchini and cheese *migas,* or sweet-potato-and-pecan tamales with eggs or tofu. The drinks—coffee and tea, wine, beer, and cocktails—match the food in quality. Many of the dishes are vegan or can be prepared that way; all allergies and food sensitivities are accommodated; and organic and locally sourced ingredients are emphasized. Events notices, tongue-in-cheek signs, and changing artwork—for sale—decorate the walls of the small bar and large dining room, and there's an enclosed dog-friendly patio.

1900 S. First St. www.bouldingcreekcafe.com. ✆ **512/416-1601.** Main courses $9–$13. No reservations. Mon–Fri 7am–midnight; Sat–Sun 8am–midnight; happy hour 3–7pm.

Casa de Luz ★ VEGETARIAN/AMERICAN A longtime favorite with Austin's large vegetarian community, this is part of a complex that includes a Montessori school, a book/gift shop, massage rooms, and a yoga studio. A shaded walkway leads to the large, attractive dining room, its many windows shaded with bamboo. Lunch and dinner consist of a set menu of soup, salad, and entree for a fixed price; check the website or phone to find out what's cooking. All the food is organic, vegan, macrobiotic, and gluten-free. Those with a sweet tooth can grab a piece of pie or cake at the dessert bar. There is no waitstaff—you pick up the food from a counter—and no tipping, as you're expected to bus your own dishes.

1701 Toomey Rd. www.casadeluz.org. ✆ **512/476-2535.** Breakfast $10; lunch or dinner $13. No reservations. Daily 7–8:30pm.

Güero's Taco Bar ★★★ TEX-MEX Opened in an old feed store in 1993, Güero's has become the unofficial center of the SoCo scene. It's quintessential Austin. The room is homey rustic—airy, clean, and bright, but with well-worn wood floors, exposed brick walls, and a rattling tin roof—and the food is fresh, authentic, and delicious, including tortillas made on the premises. Zesty fish tacos, creamy spinach enchiladas, and big bowls of guacamole are among the favorites, along with generous Tex-Mex combo platters. Live music, cold Mexican beer, and a margarita list as long as the Austin summer add to the restaurant's appeal. It's the perfect spot to cool off after shopping the SoCo strip, and a great place to enjoy breakfast tacos on Saturday and Sunday—though half the town wakes up with the same idea.

1412 S. Congress Ave. www.gueros.com. ✆ **512/447-7688.** Main courses $7–$20. No reservations. Mon–Wed 11am–10pm; Thurs–Fri 11am–11pm; Sat 8am–11pm; Sun 8am–10pm.

Shady Grove ★★ AMERICAN If your idea of comfort food involves chiles, don't pass up Shady Grove, named for the pecan trees that overlooked

red-eye SPECIALS

It's 3am and you've got a hankering for a huge stack of pancakes to soak up the excess alcohol you shouldn't have downed at a local club. No worries—Austin's got you covered with its all-night cafes. In addition to the usual diner-type offerings, you can get local favorites, including Tex-Mex items such as *migas*, queso, and breakfast tacos; vegetarian versions of traditional Texas fare; and large creative salads.

Started in 1980 in an old house on the street for which it is named, **Kerbey Lane** (www.kerbeylanecafe.com) now has eight locations around town, most of them open 24/7; it's also gone a bit upscale, adding a cocktail menu, gluten-free options, and (heaven help us!) a nutritional breakdown of its menu. The original north central location, 3704 Kerbey Lane (✆ **512/451-1436**), is probably the most popular, with the one near the university, 2606 Guadalupe St. (✆ **512/477-5717**), a close runner-up.

Musicians finishing up late-night gigs at the Continental Club often head over to the **Magnolia Cafe South,** 1920 S. Congress Ave. (www.magnoliacafeaustin.com; ✆ **512/445-0000**), but west siders have an abiding affection for the original **Magnolia Cafe West,** near the Deep Eddy Pool, 2304 Lake Austin Blvd. (✆ **512/478-8645**). Both have excellent neon signs, loads of local color, and breakfast dishes—say, eggs Zapatiano, scrambled and smothered in queso and served with home fries—that'll rev your engines any time of day.

what was an RV park in the 1950s. The inside dining room, with its Texas kitsch roadhouse decor and cushy booths, is plenty comfortable but most people head for the large shaded patio when weather permits. When your appetite is whetted by a day of fresh air at nearby Zilker Park, a hearty bowl of Freddie's Airstream chili or tortilla-fried queso catfish might hit the spot. All the burgers are made with high-grade ground sirloin (the green chile cheeseburger is a standout) and if you've never had a Frito pie (Fritos topped with chili, jalapeños, and cheese), this is the place to try it. The hippie sandwich (grilled eggplant, veggies, and cheese with pesto mayonnaise) is another good bet. On spring and summer Thursdays since 1993, the free **Shady Grove Unplugged** concert series, now done in coordination with Austin City Limits radio, takes place here from 8 to 10pm; check www.acl-radio.com for the schedule.

1624 Barton Springs Rd. www.theshadygrove.com. ✆ **512/474-9991.** Main courses $9–$18. No reservations. Sun–Thurs 11am–10pm; Fri–Sat 11am–11pm.

EAST SIDE

Expensive

Pitchfork Pretty ★★ NEW AMERICAN This Zen chic eatery didn't invent garden-to-table fare, the creative mix of culinary cultures, or family-style sharing of different-size plates, but it often takes these trends to a higher

Greater Austin Restaurants

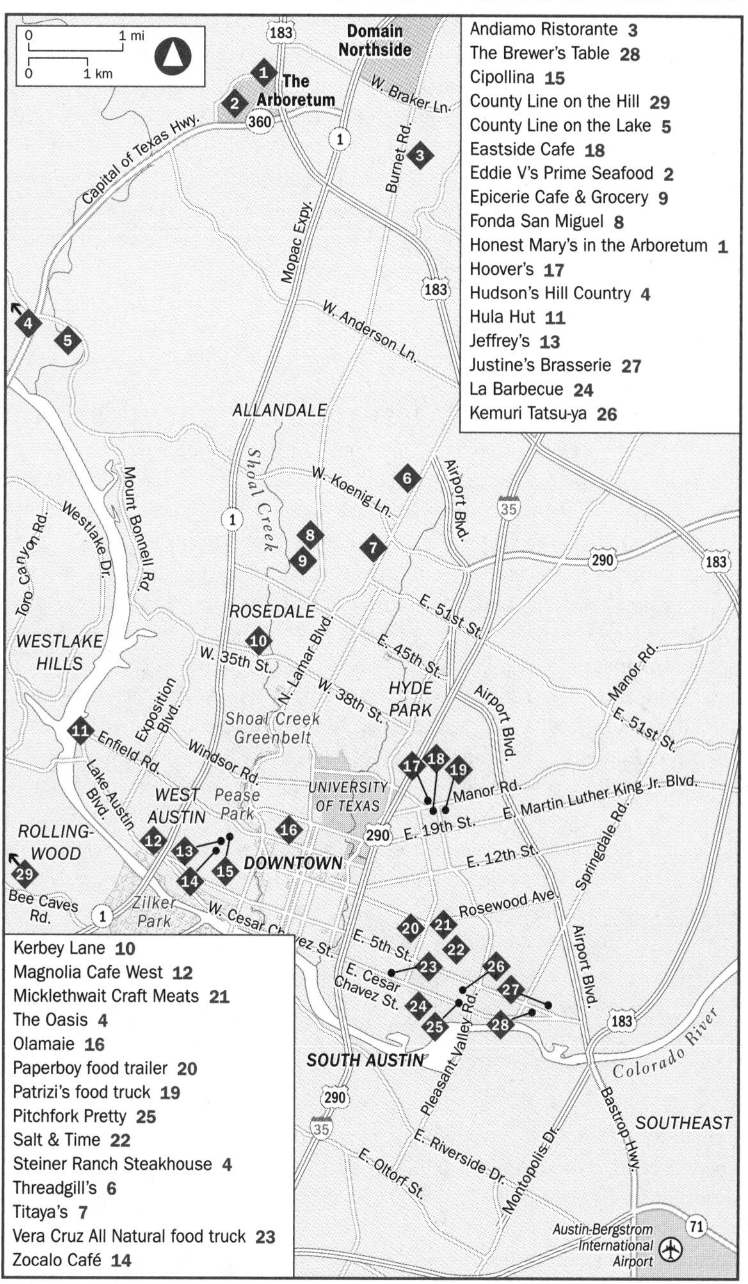

level. The restaurant's small farm gets esoteric with its herbs and edible flowers, for example, cultivating a variety of basils and mints to match the seasonal meats and fishes. And everything from the baked goods down to the cheese curds is made on the premises. Chicken fried in chickpea batter with habanero vinaigrette is a big hit with those avoiding gluten, while the fluffy light biscuits are celebrated by those who are not. Some dishes cater to the adventurous (goat loin with spiced ghee, say), others to those who walk on the mild side (potato gnocchi with arugula, broccoli, and sunflower seeds). The Monday night prix-fixe ($29) Korean barbecue is a nice way to kickstart the week, and you can sample some dishes, well-crafted cocktails, and local beers and wines at a discounted price during happy hour.

2708 E. Cesar Chavez. www.pitchforkpretty.com. ✆ **512/494-4593.** Main courses $21–$37. Tues–Thurs 5–10pm; Fri–Sat 5–11pm; Sun 10am–2pm.

Expensive/Moderate

The Brewer's Table ★★★ BREW PUB/NEW AMERICAN It's a brewpub, because beer is produced on the premises by skilled brewer Drew Durish; it's a gastropub, because the food quality is assured by stellar executive chef Zach Hunter. At the same time, Brewer's Table is an entirely new concept: The restaurant and brewery have a symbiotic relationship, with beer or ingredients from the beer-making process incorporated into the dishes, and vice versa. Sometimes it's subtle; you won't notice that the *chicharrones* snacks are cooked down with lager, for example, or that food scraps are used in the beer fermentation process. The bonding message comes through loud and clear, however, in a scooplet of toasted barley ice cream with hop honey served in a tiny beer-grain waffle cone. Several different dining experiences are offered: Indoors, you can order from a large a la carte menu, with chicken paprikash and smoked rabbit carnitas among the entrees, or opt for a "shareable feast" for two, a prix-fixe meat, seafood, or vegetarian dinner. Outside, the casual lager garden has a small menu of sandwiches and sides. Weekend brunch and daily happy hour add to the configurations. This place is located way east, in an industrial area—you may wonder if you've gone astray, but look for the distinctive Quonset hut and strings of lights illuminating the beer garden.

4715 E. 5th St. www.thebrewerstable.com. ✆ **512/520-8199.** Brunch $9–$16; main courses $8–$18; feasts $80 (meat), $70 (fish), or $40 (vegetarian). Mon–Thurs 4–10pm; Fri 4–11pm; Sat 11am–11 pm; Sun 11am–10pm.

Salt & Time ★★ BUTCHER SHOP/STEAKHOUSE Strange but true: Not everyone in Austin wants their meat smoked in a pit. Carnivores who crave a good grilled steak or burger will find their bliss in this small dining room in the back of a butcher shop and grocery, which also creates its own charcuterie. You know that the meat, from select Texas ranches, is fresh because you can see it in the cold cases out front, where you can also sample the latest salumi and other dried cured meats. There are a few entrees for those

MEALS ON wheels IN AUSTIN

Airstreams and RVs and trailers, oh my. Austin's compact, not-so-mobile kitchens—especially those in South and East Austin—turn out some of the most interesting food in town at very reasonable prices. Here are some top spots to try if you don't mind eating outdoors. All offer seating, and some even string lights on nearby trees to provide atmosphere.

Bombay Dhaba: Satisfying vegetarians and carnivores alike, this truck specializes in Indian classics: crispy *pakoras*, creamy *kormas*, and spicy masalas and curries (lamb and goat meat are options). The lunch special combos are a delicious bargain. 1207 S. 1st St. www.bombaydhabaaustin.com. ✆ **737/247-4323.**

The Mighty Cone: Known for hot and crunchy fried wraps—aka "cones"—made with chicken, shrimp, or avocado and served with mango aioli and slaw, The Mighty Cone got its start at the acclaimed Hudson's on the Bend (p. 222), and then moved on to make perfect carry-around food for the Austin City Limits festivals. Now you can find these treats year-round near Zilker Park. 1720 Barton Springs Rd. www.mightycone.com. ✆ **737/300-1054.**

Paperboy: This East Austin food trailer is perfect for creative breakfast grub, including Texas hash (roasted sweet potatoes, poached egg, pork shoulder, and grilled onions) and *chilaquiles* (goat chorizo, cotija cheese, and a sunny-side-up egg on tortilla chips). There's a second Paperboy on Manchaca Road in central Austin. 1203 E. 11th St. www.paperboyaustin.com.

Patrizi's: With family recipes for house-made (truck-made?) pastas, meatballs, the simple Roman dish *cacio e pepe,* and a hearty signature red sauce, Patrizi's is a favorite casual go-to. It's located on Manor Road just east of I-35 in the Vortex Theater courtyard. www.patrizis.com. ✆ **512/522-4834.**

Vera Cruz All Natural: It's hard to find consensus about any food item in Austin, but everyone agrees that Veracruz-born sisters Reyna and Maritza Vazquez turn out some of the town's best *migas* breakfast tacos. In addition to the original trailer in East Austin, there are two other trailers, and two brick-and-mortar stores. 1704 E. Cesar Chavez St. www.veracruzallnatural.com.

who don't eat red meat—perhaps a chicken pot pie, lentil salad with shrimp, or pan-roasted octopus—but most people come for the perfectly cooked beef patties, ribeye, and other steaks and chops with beef fat fries. Cheese or charcuterie boards make good starters to share, and the wine and beer lists highlight good local producers. Service can be spotty, however.

1912 E. 7th St. www.saltandtime.com. ✆ **512/524-1383.** Burgers and other main courses $14–$23; steaks and chops market price (up to around $50). Lunch reservations accepted for parties of 6 or more. Tues–Fri 11am–3pm and 5–10pm; Sat–Sun 10am–3pm and 5–10pm.

Moderate

Eastside Cafe ★★ AMERICAN Opened in 1988, long before East Austin became trendy, this cafe tapped into the local zeitgeist—and has kept up with the competition. This is still a top pick for locals seeking a well-prepared,

AUSTIN'S WORLD-FAMOUS barbecue

As the urban hub of the rural region famed for its smoked meat, Austin is only about half an hour from small towns such as Lockhart, dubbed the "BBQ capital of Texas," and Driftwood, where the **Salt Lick** draws Austinites bearing ice chests full of beer to its smoked meat and music every week. For details about the best places to chow down in the area, see "Exploring Texas Barbecue" in chapter 17, p. 285.

If you need a barbecue fix closer to town, however, here are a few top options (see also **Stubb's** in Chapter 16, p. 276). Prices are generally inexpensive to moderate, unless you can eat an entire giant beef rib on your own. The order is alphabetical, but Franklin and La Barbecue rank highest on the recommended list, with Micklethwait close behind.

The original location of what has become a small Texas chain, **County Line on the Hill,** 6500 W. Bee Cave Rd. (www.countyline.com; ✆ **512/327-1742**), opened in 1975 on a spot once occupied by a 1920s speakeasy. Today it draws crowds who love big ribs and great Hill Country views. If you don't mind a heavy midday meal, come for lunch—it's often so crowded at suppertime you may wait as long as an hour. Unless you request it "moist," the brisket here is generally lean, something many BBQ purists disdain. **County Line on the Lake,** 5204 FM 2222 (✆ **512/346-3664**), offers the same menu and a lovely setting at Bull Creek just off Lake Austin.

There are those who say that the tender smoked brisket at **Franklin Barbecue,** 900 E. 11th St. (www.franklinbbq.com; ✆ **512/653-1187**), cooked over a low-heat oak fire for 18 hours, justifies waiting in line for up to 4 hours. Others contend that nothing's worth that much of a time investment. I fall into the latter category, so I can only pass along the praise garnered for pitmaster Aaron Franklin, including a 2015 Best Chef Southwest James Beard award, his own PBS show, and frequent appearances on *Jimmy Kimmel Live*! In addition to more traditional BBQ offerings, Franklin serves pulled pork and an espresso-flavored barbecue sauce. You can skip the queue if you pre-order your meat online for takeout, with a 5-pound minimum order. Open Tuesday through Sunday, from 11am until the 'cue is sold out.

The historic setting is part of the draw of **The Iron Works,** 100 Red River St. (www.ironworksbbq.com; ✆ **512/478-4855**), a slice of old Austin amidst downtown's new high-rises. Until 1977, this ramshackle tin building housed the ironworks of the Weigl family, who came

healthful meal with a local orientation: Each morning, the gardener and the chef discuss what herbs and vegetables are available from the huge organic garden in the back and farm just outside town. You can dine on a tree-shaded patio overlooking the gardens or in one of a series of small, homey rooms in the turn-of-the-century bungalow. The menu ranges from panko-and-pecan breaded chicken breasts and artichoke manicotti (one of several good vegetarian options) to sesame-crusted catfish, baked brie, and salads topped with warm goat cheese and pine nuts—all served with the cafe's signature warm jalapeño cornbread. Look for daily chef specials and seasonal soups. Also on the property and named for the owner is the smaller **Elaine's** over from Germany in 1913 (you can see their ornamental craft all around town, including at the state capitol). Cattle brands created for Jack Benny ("Lasting 39"), Lucille Ball, and Bob Hope are displayed in front of the restaurant. Beef ribs are the most popular order, with brisket running a close second. Lean turkey breast and juicy chicken will please those who want the smoke but not the red meat. Closed Sundays.

LeAnn Mueller, founder of **La Barbecue,** 2027 E. Cesar Chavez St. (www.labarbecue.com; ✆ **512/605-9696**), hails from smoked meat royalty: Her father, Bobby Mueller, and grandfather, Louie Mueller, are behind one of the top BBQ spots in Taylor (p. 290). That expertise shows in the spicy house-made sausage, the peppery crust on the brisket, and the traditional butcher paper presentation, though LeAnn puts her own spin on the tried-and-true, using leaner grass-fed brisket, for example. You've gotta love a place that revels in being woman-owned, saying "in the sausage fest of the BBQ industry, we're proud the future is female." Closed Mondays and Tuesdays.

Selling a variety of signature house-made sausages along with sliced pork shoulder, beef ribs that weigh a pound and a half, and sides like jalapeño cheese grits, **Micklethwait Craft Meats,** 1309 Rosewood Ave. (www.craftmeatsaustin.com; ✆ **512/791-5961**), operating out of a tree-shaded East Austin trailer, has racked up kudos from the local and national food press—a write-up in *Bon Appetit,* a coveted top 50 BBQ spot in *Texas Monthly*, and a 2017 nod for best barbecue in town by *Austin Monthly*. Owner Tom Micklethwait started out his culinary career as a baker, and his buttermilk pie and fruit cobblers are well worth saving room for. Closed Mondays, closes at 3pm on Sundays.

There's a complicated family story behind **Terry Black's Barbecue,** 1003 Barton Springs Rd. (www.terryblacksbbq.com; ✆ **512/394-5899**), not to be confused with the Black's on Guadalupe Road, though both are related to the venerable Black's in Lockhart (p. 287). Suffice it to say that a lot of history and experience go into this smoked meat venture, and it shows. A huge open dining room with a nice deck is the setting for the cafeteria-style experience. Don't worry that the plastic knives won't cut through the sausage, ribs, or brisket—the meat's so tender, it yields at the slightest touch. Neighbors have complained about the smoke from the traditional wood-fired boxes out back, but patrons are more than pleased with the results.

(✆ **512/494-1464**), serving a pared-down menu that's a boon for the indecisive: pulled-pork sandwiches, house-made pies, and assorted hard and soft beverages.

2113 Manor Rd. www.eastsidecafeaustin.com. ✆ **512/476-5858.** Main courses $11–$24. Reservations recommended. Mon–Fri 11:15am–9pm; Sat–Sun 3–9pm.

Justine's Brasserie ★★ FRENCH This Paris-style bistro in an old house on the east side feels like a special-occasion spot without special-occasion prices. It's laid-back, unfussy Austin, with creaky wooden floors, wobbly cafe tables, and vintage Neil Young warbling in the background.

Young bohemian types huddle at the bar, and old friends sit around the patio firepit. The food is solidly pleasing classic French fare: steamed mussels, *pommes frites,* French onion soup, and a Belgian endive-pear-and-Roquefort salad with roasted beets and walnuts. Look for chalkboard wine specials daily. It's a good idea to arrive very early or very late (the kitchen keeps European hours); the place gets noisy and crowded, and if the dining room is full you might be consigned to Siberia—the quirky and less cozy tent out front. If you walked into Justine's in the morning, you might think it was a dive, but at night with the music playing, votive candles flickering, and bordello-red walls casting a warm rosy glow, you just might think it's the best place in town.

4710 E. 5th St. www.facebook.com/Justinesbrasserie. ✆ **512/385-2900.** Main courses $12–$35. Reservations recommended. Wed–Mon 6pm–2am; closed Tues.

Kemuri Tatsu-ya ★★ JAPANESE/TEXAN What do you get when you cross an *izakaya* (Japanese pub) with an old barbecue joint? The latest darling of the Austin food scene. The owners already had an excellent track record with their three **Ramen-Tatsuya** (www.ramen-tatsuya.com) restaurants, so locals felt confident in going along with them on a wild cross-cultural ride. The Guaca-poke, for example, mixes tuna, wasabi, and red onion with avocado; another dish tops octopus fritters with Texas chili and smoked jalapeños; sticky rice tamales are made with beef tongue and chorizo . . . you get the picture. The list of sakes, beer, whiskey, and cocktails—including the Puff Puff Pass, sweet-potato soshu and rum delivered in a huge ceramic vessel shaped like a deadly blowfish—is twice as long as the food menu, which probably gets patrons feeling more adventurous. This is the type of place you can enjoy just as much with a large raucous group or sitting solo at one of the bars (on your own, you can order whatever oddity suits your palate—and you don't have to share!).

2713 E. 2nd St. www.kemuri-tatsuya.com. ✆ **512/893-5561.** Main courses $3.50–$15; ramen $12–$13. Reservations accepted for groups up to 7. Sun–Thurs 5–11pm; Fri–Sat 5pm–midnight.

Inexpensive

Hoover's ★ AMERICAN/SOUTHERN When native Austinite Alexander Hoover, long a presence on the local restaurant scene, opened up his own place near where he grew up, he looked to his mother's recipes and added a bit of Cajun and Tex-Mex for inspiration. Fried catfish, meatloaf, and gravy-smothered pork chops, with sides of mac and cheese or jalapeño-creamed spinach, come to the table in generous portions. If you're in the mood for a sandwich, try the muffuletta. And if you haven't yet tried that Texas standard, the chicken-fried steak, this is a great place to do so. Check the chalkboard for daily specials, seasonal side dishes, and available desserts. If coconut cream pie is on the list, that clinches your decision. The crowd is a mix of the East Side African-American community, UT students, and country food lovers from all around town. Truth be told, this place is hit and miss; service can be spotty. But you can't beat the prices and Hoover's is one of the last holdouts of genuine old East Austin. It'd be a pity to see it shutter its doors.

2002 Manor Rd. www.hooverscooking.com. ✆ **512/479-5006.** Sandwiches $10–$12; main courses $10–$15. No reservations. Daily 11am–10pm.

CENTRAL/WEST AUSTIN

Expensive

Fonda San Miguel ★★ MEXICAN Chefs all over Texas mourned the 2017 passing of Miguel Ravago, credited as being the first to introduce Mexican fine dining to Texas in 1975; even now, there are few restaurants in the state quite like Fonda San Miguel. In recent years, Ravago was a consulting (rather than hands-on) chef, so his menu legacy is largely unaffected. And in 2018 owner Tom Gillibrand helped refresh the look of the gorgeous hacienda-style complex. Massive hand-carved wooden doors open into a lush interior courtyard; from there, you enter into a series of high-ceilinged, low-lit dining rooms with wildly colorful original Mexican art, including fantastical animal sculptures. It's a wonderful atmosphere in which to savor such dishes as *cochinita pibil,* pork roasted Yucatan-style in a banana leaf; or an ancho chile relleno stuffed with chicken, olives, and almonds and topped with a delicate cilantro cream sauce. The margaritas are equally creative, some incorporating smoky mezcals rather than tequilas, others celebrating fresh fruit like watermelon. The popular brunch buffet offers an array of choices such as fruit gazpacho and *chilaquiles* that you'll rarely find elsewhere. Now that the North Loop area is trendy again, maybe a new generation will discover this Austin treasure.

2330 W. North Loop Blvd. www.fondasanmiguel.com. ✆ **512/459-4121.** Main courses $18–$42; brunch $39. Reservations recommended. Mon–Thurs 5:30–9:30pm; Fri–Sat 5:30–10:30pm; Sun 11am–2pm.

Jeffrey's ★★★ NEW AMERICAN This intimate bistro in the Clarksville neighborhood has been a top destination for Austin food lovers since 1975. It's gotten swankier in recent years, having taken on a roving cocktail cart, caviar service, leather-bound menus, and servers who are dressed better than the average Austin executive, but with that comes a consistency in quality and service. Lighting is soft, tables are draped in white linen, and you know you'll be cosseted from start to finish, yet not condescended to. Most of the appetizers rotate with the seasons, but the sesame-fried oysters are perennial favorites. Those who want to eat lighter can't go wrong with seafood entrees such as a Gulf snapper with subtle Thai spices, but the top sellers are the grilled meat, especially cuts of tender Waygu beef from Beeman Ranch. A reinvented baked Alaska, with pistachio semifreddo, lemon sorbet, and lemon-poppy olive oil cake, is just one of many dessert delights. ***Tip:*** For the same flavor and cachet with a more casual vibe, go next door to sister restaurant **Josephine House** (www.josephineofaustin.com; ✆ **512/477-5584**), serving breakfast, lunch, brunch, and dinner in a sweet cottage. The Monday night prix-fixe dinner is a local favorite way to start the week.

1204 W. Lynn St. www.jeffreysofaustin.com. ✆ **512/477-5584.** Main courses $38–$130. Reservations recommended. Mon–Thurs 5:30–10pm; Fri–Sat 5:30–11pm; Sun 5:30–9:30pm.

Olamaie ★★★ SOUTHERN/NEW AMERICAN Austin's mash-ups of dining traditions can be fun, but if you're looking for food that digs deep into a region's roots while being tailored to contemporary tastes, Olamaie is your place. The recipient of many major food awards, this restaurant brings you Southern cooking at its subtlest and its most sublime. The menu draws on careful historical cookbook research and recipes passed along to chef Michael Fojtasek, whose mother—and grandmother and matriarchs spanning five generations—was named Olamaie; ingredients come from purveyors within an 80-mile radius. You can make a meal out of smaller dishes like the flavorful and rich boiled peanuts with winter squash, buttermilk, and molasses, perhaps complemented by the zing of shrimp, red rice, and shishito peppers, or go for heartier fare like a sorghum-brined pork chop. The cocktails are as creative as the food, with obscure liqueurs like Melletti Amoro and Suse mixed with rye and orange bitters to create the dark magic of the Knight of Cups, for example. Occupying a small art-decked house dating to the 1920s, Olamaie is in the fine dining desert near the University of Texas. Locals in the know keep the restaurant hopping, however; be sure to make a reservation. And while you're at it, order some biscuits to take away; flaky with a perfectly crusty bottom, they're the Platonic ideal of what a biscuit should be.

1610 San Antonio St. www.olamaieaustin.com. ✆ **512/474-2796.** Main courses $30–$45 (Waygu steak $120). Reservations recommended. Daily 5–10pm.

Moderate

Cipollina ★★ ITALIAN/NEW AMERICAN This West Lynn eatery has long been a neighborhood favorite for delicious wood-fired pizza and Italian sandwiches. But Cipollina was created by the team behind Jeffrey's (p. 217), so it transcends typical pizzeria fare. The bread on the sandwiches comes from the local Easy Tiger bakery, for example; the signature pizza is topped with mushrooms, sweet-and-sour agrodolce, chevre, and balsamic; and a fresh seasonal menu offers everything from pan-seared redfish or roast chicken to hanger steaks. Pastas like tagliatelle (served a la Bolognese) or linguini (in the shrimp scampi) are house-made. The roomy dining room has a casual, unfussy Austin aesthetic, and there's a good wine list with reasonable prices. Want to retreat to your hotel room and eat in your sweats? Cipollina does takeaway for that, too.

1213 W. Lynn St. www.cipollina-austin.com. ✆ **512/477-5211.** Sandwiches and pizzas $9–$17; main courses $14–$32. Daily 11am–10pm. Happy hour 3–6pm daily.

Epicerie Cafe & Grocery ★ FRENCH/AMERICAN This vine-covered restaurant and gourmet deli in Allandale has the feel of a European neighborhood bistro by way of New Orleans. A display case of assorted fine cheeses, shelves filled with gourmet foods, and a selection of affordable wines greeting you as you enter the light-filled room will whet your appetite for the house-made soups, fresh salads, hot sandwiches, and powdery beignets. The menu changes seasonally, but a classic French onion soup, cheeseburger with aioli and frîtes, and mussels with sauce étouffé and chorizo are reliable picks. The food can be hit-or-miss but when it's good, it's very, very good.

2307 Hancock Dr. www.epicerieaustin.com. ✆ **512/371-6840.** Sandwiches $12–$16; main courses $15–$22. Mon–Thurs 8am–9:30pm; Fri–Sat 8am–10:30pm; Sun 10:30am–3pm.

Threadgill's ★ AMERICAN/SOUTHERN When the South Riverside location of this Austin icon closed in late 2018, a little bit of local history was lost. This North Lamar location (aka Old No. 1) was the original gas-station-turned music venue, yet the one to the south sat next door to—and paid tribute to—Austin's famous and beloved Armadillo World Headquarters (see the Threadgill's website for details of this tangled history). But that was then. The question remains: Will the original dining spot thrive now that it has owner Eddie Wilson's undivided attention? It's worth coming here to try the chicken-fried steak, burgers, cheese-stuffed jalapeños, fried okra, garlic-cheese grits, black-eyed peas, and other down-home dishes. The Sunday brunch buffet with live music (11am–1pm) is definitely worth checking out.

6416 N. Lamar Blvd. www.threadgills.com. ✆ **512/451-5440.** Sandwich and burgers $8–$13; main courses $12–$22; brunch buffet $13 (children $6). No reservations. Mon–Tues 11am–9:30pm; Wed–Sat 11am–10pm; Sun 10am–9:30pm.

Titaya's ★ THAI In a strip mall on North Lamar, you'll find some of the best Thai food in Austin—though more so on quieter weekdays than weekends. Look for a nondescript building on the east side of the street, by a large Half-Price Books. The Thai standards, such as pad Thai (not too sweet and with the right amount of tamarind) and *pad kee mao* are well prepared as is the typical Vietnamese noodle bowl (called "vermicelli lover" on the menu). The highly aromatic green curry is perhaps the best of the curries. For something more off-the-beaten-menu-path, try spicy fried catfish in garlic sauce.

5501 N. Lamar Blvd. (just south of Koenig). www.titayasthaicuisine.com. ✆ **512/458-1792.** Main courses $9–$16. No reservations. Tues–Fri 11am–2:30pm and 5–10pm; Sat–Sun noon–3pm and 5–10pm.

Inexpensive

Hula Hut ★ TEX-MEX/AMERICAN A favorite, if slightly cheesy, place to bring out-of-town guests since the 1990s, the Hula Hut has found its calling now that fusion cuisine is in. Along with Tex-Mex standards, you'll find dishes like Mexonesian shrimp flautas: fried wontons stuffed with shrimp, bacon, jalapeños, and cheese. The Hawaiian-inspired fajita plates (think grilled pineapple and plum sauce) are especially good; for a group, try the pu pu platter (ribs, nachos, flautas, tacos, chopped salad, and queso). The main

family-friendly **RESTAURANTS**

Terming eateries "family friendly" in Austin is often just a question of degree. It's safe to assume that most moderately-priced restaurants with patios will welcome pint-sized diners. The following, however, are standouts in welcoming kids to the table.

Güero's (p. 209), **Shady Grove** (p. 209), and **Kerbey Lane** (p. 210) all have special menus for ages 12 and under, not to mention casual, kid-friendly atmospheres and food inexpensive enough to feed everyone without taking out a second mortgage.

The **Cookbook Bar & Café** (p. 203) at Austin's Central Library has a children's menu that might include a chicken, carrot, and potato kebab recipe out of Alain Ducasse's *Cooking for Kids*—and absolutely no shushing librarians.

At **County Line on the Hill** and **County Line on the Lake** (p. 214), kids' plates for ages 12 and under offer everything from corn dogs to sausage and brisket, along with fries, pickles, a fountain drink, and a scoop of ice cream (with parent permission).

Sports pennants, Elvis trinkets, and 1950s memorabilia, combined with a menu of familiar American favorites, make **Hut's** (p. 204) a great place for kids, especially teens.

dining room is brash and colorful, but the best thing about this place is the outdoor dining on a pier extending out into Lake Austin, with a view of the hills across the way. Parking is sometimes a problem, so go early or late if possible.

3825 Lake Austin Blvd. www.hulahut.com. ✆ **512/476-4852.** Main courses $9–$15. No reservations. Mon–Thurs 11am–10pm; Fri 11am–11pm; Sat 10:30am–11pm; Sun 10:30am–10pm.

Zocalo Café ★ MEXICAN This fast-casual Mexican cafe in the Clarksville neighborhood offers light, healthful fare for reasonable prices. Ingredients are fresh, and the tortillas handmade. Soft tacos, which come three to the order, accompanied by rice and beans, make for just the right amount to satisfy any reasonable appetite; unlike Tex-Mex tacos, they don't come smothered with cheese. Specialties include the Zocalo plate, a version of *chilaquiles con pollo* made of tortilla pieces cooked with chicken in a green sauce and topped with crumbled fresh cheese and sour cream. Look for the daily weekday specials. The dining area is flooded by natural light from tall windows, and the patio is a nice place to sip sangria when the weather is agreeable.

1110 W. Lynn St. www.zocalocafe.com. ✆ **512/472-8226.** Main courses $9–$12.50. Mon–Fri 11am–10pm; Sat–Sun 10am–10pm (brunch served 10am–2pm).

NORTHWEST

Expensive

Eddie V's Prime Seafood ★★ SEAFOOD/STEAK Yes, Eddie V's was bought out by a corporation that owns a lot of restaurant chains, but it was founded in Austin and lots of its patrons are loyal from way back. With good reason. The supper club atmosphere—white tablecloths, lots of black accents—and top-notch seafood are a winning combination. The crispy calamari appetizer and lump crab cake make great starters, but take care not to indulge too much; this place doesn't stint on portion sizes. Top seafood choices include Parmesan-crusted lemon sole or Norwegian salmon with mustard vinaigrette, but don't overlook the steaks—prime black Angus, well-aged, and perfectly grilled. Whatever you choose, try to leave room for the bananas Foster butter cake, served tableside and flambéed. The downtown Eddie V's, 301 E. Fifth St. (✆ **512/472-1860**), has the same menu, decor, and see-and-be-seen cachet, but it doesn't have the Arboretum's Hill Country sunset views. Both offer good happy hours (4:30–7pm), with half-price appetizers and $1 off wines and cocktails.

9400-B Arboretum Blvd. www.eddiev.com/locations/tx/austin/austin-arboretum/8502. ✆ **512/342-2642.** Main courses $33–$54. Reservations recommended. Mon–Sat 4–10pm; Sun 4–9pm.

Moderate

Andiamo Ristorante ★★★ ITALIAN Though only a 5-minute drive from the Domain and DomainNORTHSIDE shopping complexes, Andiamo feels like it's a world away—specifically, in the boot of Europe. Owner Daniela Marcone was born in Naples, and she ensures that all the recipes she oversees remain true to the details and principles of Italian cooking. This includes using the best and freshest ingredients available; buying wines from select Italian distributors; and making the preparations simple, the presentations artful. The ravioli de zucca, filled with pumpkin and ricotta cheese and sautéed in brown butter and sage, makes a good first course. The kitchen has a way with fish, so for a second consider the baked salmon with kalamata olive sauce. Desserts like warm profiteroles are rich but delicate. Service is attentive without being overbearing, and the large open dining room is elegant but not stuffy. It's a cliché to call something a hidden gem, but this restaurant isn't on the foodie radar and you won't happen on this modest strip shopping center unless you know to look for it. It's worth the effort.

2521 Rutland Dr. www.andiamoitaliano.com. ✆ **512/719-3377.** Main courses $14.50–$17.50. Reservations suggested. Mon–Fri 11am–1:45pm and 5–9pm; Sat 5–10pm.

Inexpensive

Honest Mary's in the Arboretum ★ HEALTH FOOD/AMERICAN Seeking something inexpensive and healthy? These meals in a bowl fit the bill. There are two ways to go: Opt for one of the signature bowls and be presented with an chef-designed array of veggies and dressings atop such grains as quinoa or basmati rice; here the only decision is whether to add a suggested extra protein (for example, grilled naturally raised chicken) to the otherwise vegetarian mix. (The exception is the poke bowl, which includes ahi tuna.) Alternatively, micromanage your meal by selecting a base protein, then layering on whatever grains, veggies, and toppings you choose—perhaps avocado, pickled onions, organic apples, or toasted pecans. All the meat is antibiotic- and hormone- free, refined sugars are eschewed, oils are non-GMO, and local seasonal ingredients are favored. The presentations are aesthetically pleasing and so is the room—lots of light wood, greenery, and books. You'll be dining in a mall next door to a TJ Maxx, so this makes a nice oasis.

9828 Great Hills Trail, Ste. 300. www.honestmarys.com. ✆ **512/953-8427.** Bowls $8–$13. No reservations. Daily 11am–9pm.

WESTLAKE/LAKE TRAVIS

Expensive

Hudson's Hill Country ★★ NEW AMERICAN The former Hudson's on the Bend has a slightly different name and slightly different menu under new ownership. Much will be familiar to those who've dined here in the past, however. Set in an old house some 1½ miles southwest of the Mansfield Dam, near Lake Travis, Hudson's has several softly lit, romantic dining rooms. Exotic meats, including a hot and crunchy alligator appetizer, are still in evidence and, as before, the emphasis is on game dishes like smoked venison topped with king crab, wild boar skewers, and chicken-fried venison. More traditional options include smoked duck, beef tenderloin, and roast chicken; there's also a (very slight) nod to vegetarians. Hudson's indoor dining rooms can be noisy on Friday and Saturday. Opt for the terrace if the weather permits.

3509 Ranch Road 620 N. www.hudsonshillcountry.com. ✆ **512/266-5644.** Main courses $25–$50. Weekend reservations essential. Tues–Wed 4:30–9pm; Thurs–Sat 4:30–10pm; Sun 10:30am–2pm and 4:30–9pm.

Steiner Ranch Steakhouse ★★ STEAK/SEAFOOD For a special evening, take a scenic drive along a curvy canyon-edged road to this stylish steakhouse in the northwest lake country. The 35-minute journey is justified by both the food and the sunset views of Lake Travis from every room. Dine outside to live music on the patio, or slide into a big roomy booth in the clubby main dining room, with its casual but upscale vibe. This quintessential Texas steakhouse stands on land that was once part of a 5,200-acre ranch, home base to the founders and livestock of the Steiner rodeo company. It's the perfect place to enjoy hand-selected premium cuts of beef. Lighter fare includes blackened Atlantic salmon topped with grilled jumbo shrimp, sautéed spinach, and sun-dried tomato butter. For a romantic winter dinner, grab a spot near the fireplace in the Great Room, or cozy up in a booth and sip a cocktail or a selection from an award winning wine list.

5424 Steiner Ranch Blvd. www.steinersteakhouse.com. ✆ **512/381-0800.** Main courses $25–$50. Reservations recommended. Mon–Thurs 4–10pm; Fri–Sat 4–11pm; Sun 10am–10pm.

Moderate

The Oasis ★ AMERICAN/TEX-MEX When friends visit from out-of-town, it's required that Austinites take them to the Oasis to see the sunset. It's a ritual. At this enormous place with multilevel decks burrowed into the hill-side hundreds of feet above Lake Travis, guests applaud and whoop it up when the sun finally descends behind the hills. This (and the margaritas) is why they came, and few leave unimpressed. The food can be iffy, however—this is not the place to try your first enchilada or order a big steak. Stick to the basics, like burgers, nachos, and chicken-tender–topped salads, and you'll be fine. Then add an icy margarita for the sunset wait. Before the night is over, you'll be planning your next trip back to Austin. It's more than a little touristy (exit through the gift shop), but it's worth it for the views, not only of the lake, but of the scenery along the way out along Ranch Road 2222 from MoPac.

6550 Comanche Trail, overlooking Lake Travis off RM 620. www.oasis-austin.com. ✆ **512/266-2442.** Main courses $12–$20. No reservations. Mon–Thurs 11:30am–9pm; Fri 11:30–10pm; Sat–Sun 11am–10pm (closing times may vary with weather).

EXPLORING AUSTIN

14

Stroll up Congress Avenue and you'll see much the same sight visitors to Austin did more than 100 years ago: a broad thoroughfare, gently rising to the grandest of all state capitols. Long obsessed with its place in history, the city continues to pay tribute to its past with ongoing restorations of old buildings, many of them tourist draws. Most of the city's top historical and cultural sights reside near the Capitol, clustered in the downtown area to the south, and on the campus of the University of Texas to the north.

But it is Austin's myriad natural attractions that put the city on many "most livable" lists. From bats and birds to Barton Springs, from the Highland Lakes to the hike-and-bike trails, Austin lays out the green carpet for its visitors. You'd be hard-pressed to find a city that has more to offer fresh-air enthusiasts.

Be sure to take full advantage of the city's immensely helpful **Visitor Information Center** at 602 E. 4th St. (www.austintexas.org/plan-a-trip/visitor-center; ✆ **866/GO-AUSTIN** [462-8784] or 512/478-0098). Designed as a one-stop welcome and orientation hub, it's the place to book tours and hammer out an itinerary, shop for Austin-centric gifts, recharge your phone, check your email, use the bathroom (the most frequent visitor request, according to a staff member), and even check your luggage for the day.

THE TOP ATTRACTIONS

With a few exceptions, this section focuses on indoor cultural attractions, but don't skip the sights detailed in "Parks & Natural Attractions," p. 241—even if you're not the athletic type.

Downtown

State Capitol ★★★ The history of Texas's legislative center is as turbulent and dramatic as that of the state itself. The current capitol, erected in 1888, replaced a limestone statehouse that burned down in 1881. Construction was financed by a land-rich but otherwise impecunious Texas government by trading 3 million acres of public lands. Gleaming pink granite was donated to the

Downtown Austin Attractions

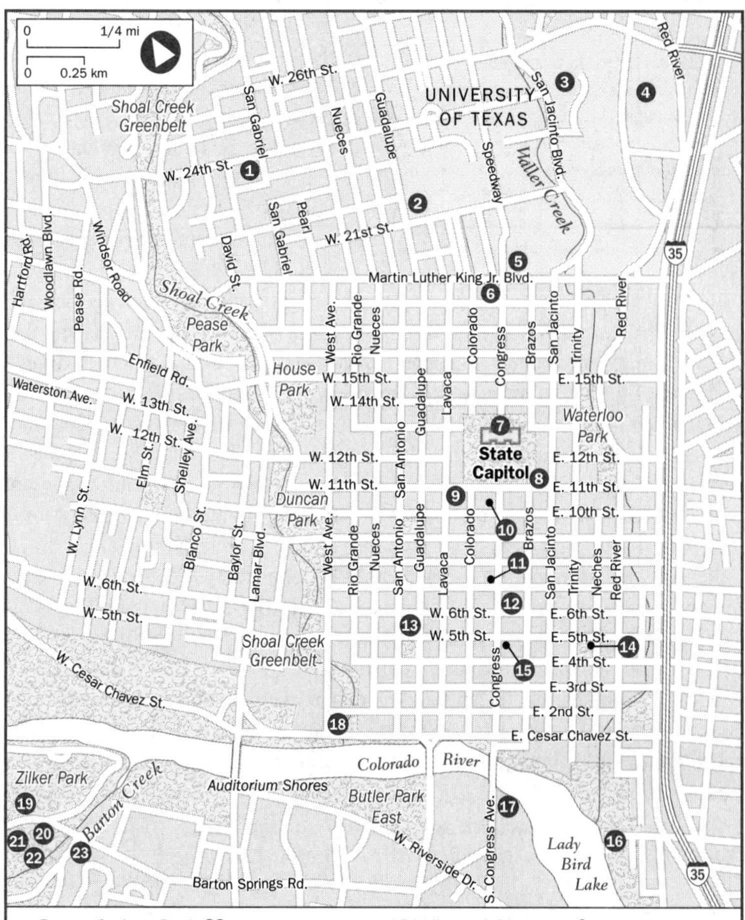

Barton Springs Pool **22**
Bats **17**
Blanton Museum of Art **5**
Brush Square Museums **14**
Bullock Texas State History Museum **6**
Bremond Block **13**
Capitol Complex Visitors Center **8**
Central Library **18**
Contemporary Austin Jones Center **11**
Driskill Hotel **12**
Emma S. Barrientos Mexican American Cultural Center **16**
Harry Ransom Center **2**
LBJ Library & Museum **4**
MEXIC-ARTE Museum **15**
Neill-Cochran Museum House **1**
Old Bakery & Emporium **10**
Splash **21**
State Capitol **7**
Texas Governor's Mansion **9**
Texas Memorial Museum **3**
Umlauf Sculpture Garden & Museum **23**
University of Texas at Austin **3**
Zilker Botanical Garden **19**
Zilker Metropolitan Park **20**
Zilker Zephyr Miniature Train **20**

Lone Star Lawmaking

To see how politics are conducted Texas-style, go up to the state capitol's third-floor visitors' gallery during legislative sessions, which occur almost every weekday from January through May of odd-numbered years. The galleries look down upon the House and Senate chambers, which are located at opposite ends of the second level.

cause, but a railroad had to be built to transport the material some 75 miles from Granite Mountain, near the present-day town of Marble Falls. Texas convicts labored on the project alongside 62 stonecutters brought in from Scotland. The result is the largest state capitol building in the country, covering 3 acres; it's second in size only to the U.S. Capitol (but still, in typical Texas style, measuring 14 feet taller). The cornerstone alone weighs 12,000 pounds, and inside, approximately 7 miles of wooden wainscoting run along the walls. A splendid rotunda and dome lie at the intersection of the main corridors. Marble statues of Sam Houston and Stephen F. Austin by Texas sculptor Elisabet Ney (p. 228) stand near the south entrance. In the 1990s, a massive renovation and expansion restored the grandeur of the capitol building, which had become dingy and overcrowded. The expansion project was fascinating in its own right: Almost 700,000 tons of rock were chiseled out to create an underground annex (often called the "inside-out, upside-down capitol"), constructed with similar materials and connected via tunnel to the capitol and four other state buildings. To prevent the annex from seeming too much like a cave, skylights were installed and the main corridors designed as atriums.

Free 30-minute guided Capitol tours depart every 30 or 45 minutes from the South Foyer, or you can explore the buildings on your own. Be sure to stop at the **Capitol Complex Visitors Center** (p. 234) beforehand to give context to your visit.

1100 Congress Ave. www.tspb.texas.gov/prop/tc/tc/capitol.html. © **512/463-4630.** Free admission. Mon–Fri 7am–10pm; Sat–Sun 9am–8pm; hours extended during legislative sessions. Closed major holidays. Free guided tours Mon–Fri 8:30am–4:30pm; Sat 9:30am–3:30pm; Sun noon–3:30.

Central

Blanton Museum of Art ★★★ The University of Texas' art collection, showcased here, is ranked among the U.S.'s top university collections. But the Blanton's superb presentation, world-class visiting exhibitions, and striking architecture make it stand out beyond academia. Another bonus: The museum is comparatively small and thus possible to take in on a single visit—though you're likely to want to return.

There's something for every aesthetic interest here, from Greek sculpture and paintings by Renaissance masters to Latin American conceptual works. The most outstanding piece is outside and a few yards away: **Ellsworth Kelly's "Austin" ★★★**, a soaring stone building with light filtered through

Greater Austin Attractions

Austin Nature & Science Center **12**	George Washington Carver Museum, Cultural & Genealogy Center **9**
Austin Zoo **13**	Hyde Park **6**
Barton Creek Greenbelt **15**	Lady Bird Johnson Wildflower Center **14**
The Contemporary Austin - Laguna Gloria **5**	McKinney Falls State Park **16**
Covert Park at Mt. Bonnell **4**	Texas State Cemetery **10**
Elisabet Ney Museum **7**	The Thinkery **8**
Emma Long Metropolitan Park **1**	Westcave Preserve **3**
French Legation State Historic Site **11**	Wild Basin Wilderness Preserve **2**

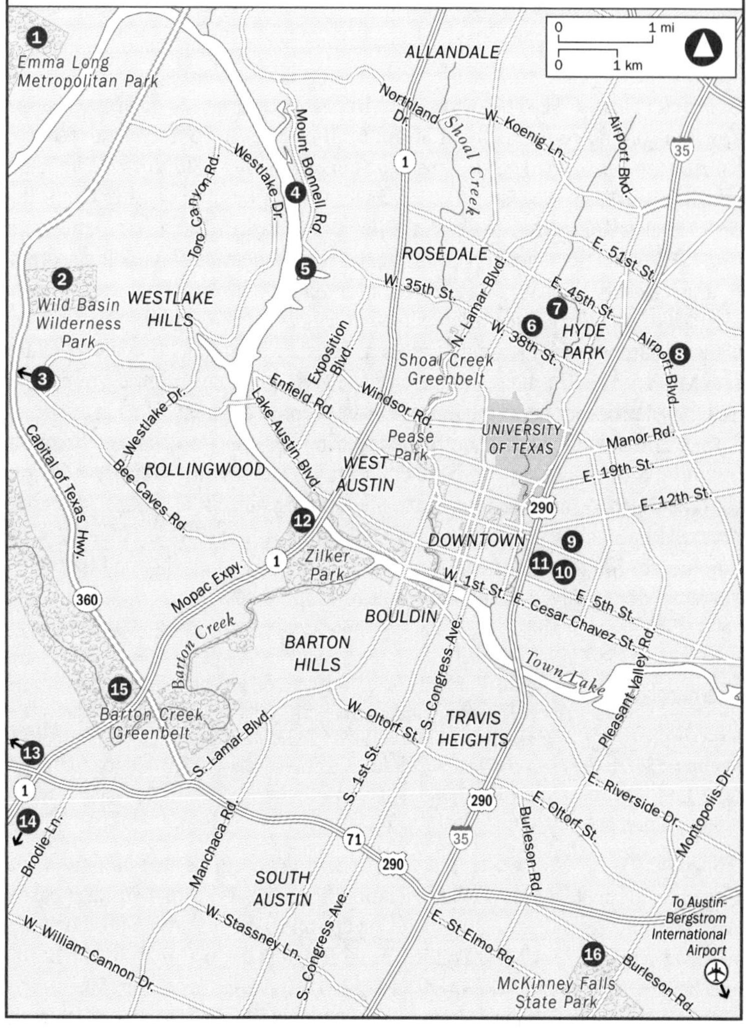

colored glass panes—a modern temple of art, which Kelly deeded to the museum in 2015. Inside, you ascend from the atrium to the second floor via another impressive art installation: Teresa Fernandez's "Stacked Waters," a staircase that gives the illusion you're emerging from a deep pool of water. Across a small plaza from the Blanton's main door, its Museum Shop carries an entertaining selection of arty gifts (see www.pinterest.com/blantonmuseum shop for a sampling), while the adjacent cafe is an attractive place to recharge with a coffee or light bite.

University of Texas, 200 E. Martin Luther King Jr. Blvd. www.blantonmuseum.org. ✆ **512/471-5482.** $12 adults; $10 seniors (65+); $5 ages 13–21; free for ages 12 and under, teachers, and active military/retired veterans. Free admission Thurs. Tues–Fri 10am–5pm; Sat 11am–5pm; Sun 1–5pm. Open until 9pm 3rd Thurs of month. Closed Mon and major holidays. Bus: UT Shuttle.

Bullock Texas State History Museum ★★★ A gleaming copper dome, a soaring rotunda, and a 35-foot-tall bronze star out front set the tone for this museum, devoted to Texas boosterism; it's as bold as the state itself, and loads of fun. The story of Texas is told through special exhibits that explore everything from rodeo to roller derby, with related live demonstrations. The eclectic collection of artifacts on permanent display includes ornate Spanish colonial stirrups, a skull cast of a giant prehistoric crocodile, and the Goddess of Liberty, who once stood atop the State Capitol. The museum offers a number of kid-friendly interactive exhibits, and it's home to the largest IMAX screen in the state; the films shown on it have nothing to do with Texas, but proceeds go to the museum's upkeep. In contrast, films at the **Texas Spirit Theater** are often state related; during the day, you can see the multisensory "Star of Destiny," where the story of Texas comes replete with surround-sound storms, rumbling seats, and misting rain. At night, the film series includes one called B Movies and Bad History. The **Story of Texas Cafe** emphasizes Southwestern comfort food—chili con queso, chopped BBQ brisket sandwiches, say—with locally sourced ingredients.

1800 N. Congress Ave. www.thestoryoftexas.com. ✆ **512/936-8746.** Exhibit areas: $13 adults; $11 seniors (65+), military, college students; $9 children 4–17; free for children 3 and under. IMAX Theater (documentaries): $9 adults; $8 seniors, military, college students; $7 children. IMAX Theater (feature films): $14 adults; $12 seniors, military, college students; $11 children. Texas Spirit Theater: $6 adults; $5 seniors, military, college students; $5 children. Combination tickets available. Mon–Sat 9am–5pm; Sun noon–5pm. Phone or check website for additional IMAX evening hours. Closed Jan 1, Easter, Thanksgiving, and Dec 24–25. Bus: UT Shuttle.

Elisabet Ney Museum ★★★ Tucked away in the trees along Waller Creek in the historic Hyde Park neighborhood (p. 239), this striking castle-like structure served as a studio and reception room for artist and iconoclast Elisabet Ney (1833-1907). Trained in the art schools of Munich and Berlin, she became confidante to King Ludwig II of Bavaria, for whom she created classically styled Romantic sculptures. After emigrating to the U.S. in the

1860s, she took a similarly exalted role in the art society of Austin, where she was commissioned to create the monumental statues of Stephen F. Austin and Sam Houston that now stand at the Texas State Capitol. William Jennings Bryan, Enrico Caruso, and four Texas governors were among the many visitors to Ney's studio, which she called Formosa.

Among the works showcased here today are a variety of working studies, including an enormous plaster cast of Lady Macbeth (the final marble is on display at the Smithsonian), and several marble busts. The museum also holds Ney's collection of studio portraits of European dignitaries, including Schopenhauer, Garibaldi, and Bismarck, which she retrieved from Germany in 1902. ***Tip:*** Climb the little tower above the museum for a view above the treetops. Half of the grounds of the 2½-acre site re-create the prairie landscape that existed when Ney first arrived on the property.

304 E. 44th St. www.austintexas.gov/ElisabetNey. ✆ **512/974-1625.** Free admission. Wed–Sun noon–5pm; closed Mon–Tues. Bus: 1, 5, 7 and 338.

Harry Ransom Center ★★★ This place is not only the pride of the University of Texas, it's the pride of the entire state. A museum, research library, and archive, with a focus on cultural and literary artifacts, the Ransom Center is the caretaker and keeper of European and American treasures: about a million rare books, including one of only six complete Gutenberg Bibles in the U.S.; 42 million literary manuscripts; 5 million photographs, including the world's first permanent photograph from nature; and more than 100,000 works of art, including pieces by Picasso and Kahlo. This material is most often accessed by scholars (though anyone can request to see it), but parts of the collection are regularly exhibited in the ground-floor gallery. Some examples: handwritten manuscripts of short stories by Hemingway; poetry scribbled on a lunch bag by e. e. cummings; Woodward and Bernstein's Watergate papers; a handwritten journal kept by Jack Kerouac; and Houdini's private papers. There's also an impressive collection of rare vintage comic books. Check the website for the various lectures, plays, and poetry readings held here day and night.

University of Texas, Harry Ransom Center, 21st and Guadalupe sts. www.hrc.utexas.edu. ✆ **512/471-8944.** Free admission. Galleries Mon–Fri 10am–5pm (until 7pm Thurs); Sat–Sun noon–5pm. Library Reading/Viewing Rooms Mon–Sat 9am–5pm; closed Sun. Tours daily at noon, Thurs at 6pm, Sat–Sun 2pm. Closed university holidays. Bus: UT shuttle. Metro-Rail: Red Line to MLK, Jr. Station with transfer to 464 MLK, Jr./Capitol Connector or local route 18.

LBJ Library and Museum ★★★ A presidential library is only as interesting as the president it honors: The 36th president of the United States was a bigger-than-life boot-wearing, cigar-smoking character, and his presidential library and museum on the UT campus is equally fascinating. Lyndon Baines Johnson's popularity in Texas and his many successes in Washington are sometimes overlooked in light of his handling of the Vietnam War, but that's not the case here. Through photographs, papers, campaign souvenirs, and personal mementos, the Library tells the tale of Johnson's long political career—beginning with his early years as a congressman all the way up to the Kennedy assassination, civil-rights battles, and groundbreaking Great Society legislation. LBJ recorded hundreds of hours of telephone conversations, and visitors can pick up one of many phones to listen to him laconically conducting presidential business. Some highlights: The remarkable (though not quite to scale) replica of LBJ's White House Oval Office, where an animatronic LBJ, speaking in his thick Texas drawl, is simultaneously fascinating and creepy; and LBJ's shiny black, custom-built 1968 Lincoln Continental stretch limo, equipped with then state-of-the-art cassette player, TV, telephone, and reserve gas tank. The library was dedicated in 1971, and until his death in 1973, LBJ kept an office here, no doubt drinking in the impressive views of the UT campus. The first presidential library to be built on a university campus, the huge travertine marble structure oversees a beautifully landscaped 14-acre complex.

University of Texas, 2313 Red River St. www.lbjlibrary.org. ✆ **512/721-0200.** $10 adults, $7 seniors (62+) & retired military, $3 ages 13–18 and college students, free for ages 12 and under & active duty military. Daily 9am–5pm. Closed Thanksgiving, Dec 25, and Jan 1. Bus: 15; UT shuttle.

University of Texas at Austin ★★★ No ivory tower, the University of Texas is fully integrated into Austin's economic and cultural life. To explore the vast main campus is to glimpse the city's future as well as its past. Here, state-of-the-art structures sit next to fine examples of 19th-century architecture. In 1839, the Congress of the Republic of Texas ordered a 40-acre site set aside to establish a "university of the first class" in Austin. Some 4 decades later, the flagship of the new University of Texas system opened, with its first two buildings on that original plot, dubbed College Hill. Although there were attempts to establish master-design plans for the university from the turn of the 20th century onward, they were only carried out in bits and pieces until 1930, when money from an earlier oil strike on UT land allowed the school to begin building in earnest. Between 1930 and 1945, consulting architect Paul Cret put his mark on 19 university buildings, most showing the influence of his education at Paris's Ecole des Beaux-Arts. The entire 357-acre campus may never achieve stylistic unity, but its earliest section has grace and cohesion, making it a delight to stroll through. Self-guided walking-tour maps of the campus are available at the **Visitor Center,** on the second floor of Walter Webb Hall, 405 W. 25th St. (www.admissions.utexas.edu/visit/general-visitors; ✆ **512/471-1000**). It's open Monday through Friday, 8am to 5pm. You can also download the maps from the Visitor Center website.

Texas Union Information Center, 2308 Whittis Ave. on West Mall. www.universityunions.utexas.edu/texas-union. ✆ **512/475-6636.** Mon–Fri 7am–1am; Sat 10am–1am; Sun noon–1am.

South Austin

Lady Bird Johnson Wildflower Center ★★★ Most first ladies devote themselves to public causes that become their signature projects. For the wife of Lyndon Baines Johnson, that cause was the preservation of wildflowers and native plants. Lady Bird was a pioneer in promoting the idea that natural habitats and native species were beautiful in their own right, and that they could even be economically beneficial. She prevailed upon the state highway agency to seed the roadsides with wildflowers, which now flourish throughout the state—especially in central Texas, where bluebonnets, Indian paintbrush, evening primrose, and other wildflowers paint the landscape in rich colors. And, with actress Helen Hayes, she founded the National Research Wildflower Center to help preserve—and showcase—the region's natural glory.

The center was later renamed for her and, in 2006, became part of the University of Texas; it's an off-campus complement to UT's LBJ Library and Museum (p. 229), demonstrating the power couple's impact on the state. The facility's research library is the nation's largest for the study of native plants, and the university uses the center's habitats to study fire prevention, water conservation—its elaborate rainwater collection system could serve as a national model—and other topics key to environmental health. In 2017, the center was dubbed the State Botanic Garden and Arboretum of Texas, further recognizing its importance.

But what grabs visitors is the dramatic proof of what's in peril. This place is especially spectacular in springtime, when wildflowers (especially bluebonnets) paint the 284-acre spread in a palate of primary colors. You'll see some 900 species of native plants in their distinctive habitats; a series of gardens, including one where kids can wade in a stream and sit on tree stumps; several hothouses; an arboretum with a gathering of historic oak trees; 2 miles of trails; and an observation tower built out of native limestone. There is also a large and colorful gift shop, a children's playroom, and a cafe serving light fare. Free lectures and guided walks are usually offered on the weekends; check the website for current programs. Even if you're not a gardening geek, you can find yourself spending the better part of a day here.

4801 La Crosse Ave. www.wildflower.org. ✆ **512/232-0100.** $12 adults, $10 students & seniors (65+), $6 ages 5–17, free ages 4 and under. Daily 9am–5pm. Take Loop 1 (MoPac) south to La Crosse Ave. and turn left. Open most major holidays.

Zilker Metropolitan Park ★★★ Everybody's favorite weekend place, this park serves as Austin's living room, swimming pool, outdoor theater, music arena—the Austin City Limits Festival is held here—and park. There's always something fun happening here. Spread out over 347 green acres of rolling hills, Zilker Park is like a big friendly public playground with a wonderful swimming hole, the **Barton Springs Pool** (p. 237). Families picnic,

ON TWO FEET OR TWO wheels

Flanking downtown's Lady Bird Lake in a 10-mile loop, the **Anne and Roy Butler Hike and Bike Trail** (www.austintexas.gov/department/ann-and-roy-butler-hike-and-bike-trail) is arguably the country's best example of an urban fresh air route, catering to bicyclists, runners, and casual amblers alike. It's unquestionably Austin's most beloved pathway, one that exemplifies the city's unique combination of natural and man-made attractions. Look across the lake from the south shore and you'll see a glittering skyline, with ever-higher structures competing for attention. Take a gander from the north shore, and it's all lush greenery.

A few fun trail facts:

- While it's named for a former Austin mayor and his wife (few people outside Austin have heard of them), no one in town calls it anything but the hike-and-bike trail.
- Its two sides are connected at a major point by the Ann W. Richards Congress Avenue Bridge, renamed in 2006 for a well-known Texas governor, but no one in town calls it anything but the Congress Avenue Bridge.
- It surrounds a lake that's really a portion of the dammed Colorado River.
- Everyone agrees that Lady Bird Johnson deserved to have the misidentified body of water named for her, but people who have lived in Austin before 2007 still have a hard time calling it by anything but its former name, Town Lake.
- The railings of the paved Boardwalk portion of the trail, completed in 2014, are lined with an artwork called "Belting it Out." Created by Ken Little, it consists of 36 bronze Western-style belts embossed with lyrics by Texas singers and songwriters. Several are fairly obscure. For example, "I'd be working in the Kremlin with a two-headed dog" was penned by Roky Erickson (of the 1960s band the 13th Floor Elevators), from his song "Two-Headed Dog."

kids ride the **Zilker Zephyr Miniature Train** (p. 247), and nature lovers rent canoes (p. 250) to take on Lady Bird Lake. Visitors also flock to the nearby **Zilker Botanical Garden** (p. 245), **Austin Nature & Science Center** (p. 246), and **Umlauf Sculpture Garden & Museum** (p. 238), a short bike ride from the main part of the park. In addition to athletic fields (nine for soccer, one for rugby, and two multi-use), the park has a 9-hole disk (Frisbee) golf course and a sand volleyball court. There are also greenbelt areas and trails that you can access from the park. The **Zilker Hillside Theater**'s summer musical productions (p. 272) are free, and during the winter holidays, Zilker's historic **Moonlight Tower** (p. 240) becomes the town's biggest holiday tree during the annual Trail of Lights (see Calendar of Events, p. 174).

2201 Barton Springs Rd. www.zilkerpark.org. ✆ **512/476-9044.** Free admission. Daily 5am–10pm. Bus: 30

OTHER ATTRACTIONS

Downtown

See also the **State Capitol,** p. 224.

Bremond Block ★ "The family that builds together, bonds together" might have been the slogan of Eugene Bremond, an early Austin banker who established a mini-real-estate monopoly for his own kin in the downtown area. In the mid-1860s, he started investing in land on what was Block 80 of the original city plan. In 1874, he moved into a Greek revival home made by master builder Abner Cook. By the time Bremond was through, he had created a family compound, purchasing and enlarging homes for himself, two sisters, a daughter, a son, and a brother-in-law. Some of these private buildings were destroyed, but those that remain on what is now known as the Bremond Block are exquisite examples of elaborate late-19th-century homes. ***Note:*** None of the houses are open to the public and they're on a one-way street with difficult parking. Architecture buffs who find themselves in this area, however, will enjoy seeing how the other half lived in the gilded era.

Btw. Seventh and Eighth, San Antonio and Guadalupe sts.

Brush Square Museums ★★ Brush Square, one of the oldest parks in Texas (plotted in 1839), is a mini-museum row with three mini-museums. The best is the **O. Henry House Museum,** the 1883–1895 home of author William Sydney Porter, who wrote indelible short stories (like "The Gift of the Magi") and novellas under the pen name O. Henry. He worked for several years as a draftsman in the Texas Land Grant office (now the Capitol Complex Visitors Center, below). In Austin, Porter published a popular satirical newspaper called *Rolling Stone* and was a teller at the First National Bank of Austin (it's rumored he embezzled from the bank, too). The little Victorian cottage where Porter lived with his wife and daughter houses artifacts and memorabilia from his Austin years, including original furniture and personal belongings. If you're visiting in May, check the calendar for the annual O. Henry Pun-Off. Next door, the **Susanna Dickinson Museum** was the home of one of only 22 Anglo adult survivors of the Battle of the Alamo. She became known as the "Messenger of the Alamo" because she carried the news of the battle to Sam Houston, who exhorted his troops to "Remember the Alamo!" when he fought the (successful) Battle of San Jacinto. The small "rubble-rock" house was built in 1869 by Joseph Hannig for his new bride; he built much of the furniture too. Next door, the little **Austin Fire Museum** occupies space in the still functioning Fire Station #1, built in 1939. It houses photographs and artifacts from Austin's early fire-fighting days.

409 E. 5th St. www.brushsquaremuseums.org. ✆ **512/477-1566.** Free admission. Wed–Sun noon–5pm.

Austin's Power Hotel

Only 5 blocks from the State Capitol, the historic **Driskill Hotel ★★** (604 Brazos St.; www.driskillhotel.com; ✆ **512/439-1243**) exudes class, Texas-style, with inlaid marble floors, massive columns, hand-painted friezes, and a lounge with leather and cowhide and bronze sculptures of cowboys and cattle. Texas legislators and lobbyists gather here on oversize Chesterfield sofas, glasses of bourbon in hand. Built in 1886 by cattle baron and oilman Col. Jesse Driskill, who modestly named it after himself, the hotel was so handsome and grand that the state legislature met here while the 1888 capitol was being built. Look for the busts of Driskill and his two sons, mounted over the hotel entrances. For a full hotel review, see p. 178; for a review of the bar, see p. 280.

Capitol Complex Visitors Center ★★ Texas's oldest surviving state office building still in use, the 1857 General Land Office stands on the capitol grounds in the southeast corner, making it a convenient spot to house the Capitol Complex Visitors Center. With its Norman/Germanic-medieval style, mock-crenellated towers, parapets, and faux stone walls made of scored stucco, the building looks oddly out of place in the heart of downtown—but that also makes it easy for visitors to find. An exhibit on the building's first floor honors short-story writer O. Henry (see above), who worked as a draftsman here from 1887–1891 (and based two stories on his experiences). Also on the first floor are a gift shop selling Texas books and souvenirs, and a Texas Travel Center information desk. The second floor is home to engaging exhibits on other aspects of Texas history, including photographs tracing the evolution of the land office building. A stop here before touring the Capitol is highly recommended.

112 E. 11th St. (SE corner of capitol grounds). www.tspb.state.tx.us/prop/tcvc/cvc/cvc.html. ✆ **512/305-8400.** Free admission. Mon–Sat 9am–5pm; Sun noon–5pm.

Central Library ★★ Voted one of *Time* magazine's Top 100 Great Places on Earth in 2018, Austin's new main library is the Platonic ideal of a 21st-century center of learning. It's community oriented, with lots of public and private spaces, and equipped with the latest technology, which is shared for free as much as possible. The huge (200,000-square-foot) open structure was Platinum LEED certified for its sustainability; among other things, it is 80% day-lit and powered by downtown's largest solar array. Art throughout the building adds to the visual appeal; most striking is "CAW" by Christian Moeller, a 37-foot-tall, bright red sculpture inspired by Austin's grackle population. Visitors can't use such features as free laptop checkout, video-conferencing, and 3D printing, but the high-speed Wi-Fi and public computers are available to all, as is the "technology petting zoo," which lets everyone play with the latest tech devices. There are always free events and lectures open to the general public; check the website. A prime reason to come is the

Cookbook Bar & Café, with dishes gleaned from the library's huge cookbook collection; see p. 203 for details.

710 W. Cesar Chávez St. www.library.austintexas.gov/central-library. ✆ **512/974-7400.** Mon–Thurs 10am–8pm; Fri–Sat 10am–6pm; Sun noon–6pm.

The Contemporary Austin-Jones Center ★ This downtown gallery, affiliated with the art school and sculpture garden/museum at the Contemporary-Laguna Gloria (p. 238), has gone through more reincarnations than the Dalai Lama; the website explores the history of both institutions in great detail. The Jones Center's current incarnation is a mixed bag. Some of the exhibitions, all devoted to contemporary work, are excellent; others not so much. But it's inexpensive, air-conditioned (hey, it can get hot strolling around the concrete canyon of Congress Avenue), and you might hit it on a great day. One of the best works of art is on the edge of the museum's roof, viewable for blocks around at night: Huge neon letters spell out "With Liberty and Justice For All"—which artist Jim Hodges jokingly calls "a work in progress," even though it's a permanent fixture. Behind the letters, the **Moody Rooftop** serves as an open-air lounge for galas and gatherings.

700 Congress Ave. www.thecontemporaryaustin.org. ✆ **512/453-5312.** $5 adults, $3 seniors & students, free for 17 and under & military. Tues–Sat 11am–7pm; Sun noon–5pm.

The Emma S. Barrientos Mexican American Cultural Center ★ Celebrating Mexican- and Latin-American heritage, this popular cultural arts center—nicknamed MACC—has rotating exhibits in its two galleries on Lady Bird Lake. It's fronted by a 22,000-square foot outdoor plaza with a sculpture garden and a pleasant *zocalo* (central plaza) on an inviting expanse of lawn; performances are often held here. Interest in MACC has grown since its 2007 opening; plans are in the works to expand the original space—an open circular structure by Mexican architect Teodoro Gonzalez de Leon—to include a theater, among other things.

600 Red River St. www.austintexas.gov/esbmacc. ✆ **512/974-3772.** Free admission. Mon–Thurs 10am–6pm; Fri 10am–5:30pm; Sat 10am–4pm.

Mexic-Arte Museum ★★ One of very few Mexican-American art museums in the country, this is home to a small collection of 20th-century Mexican art, photos from the Mexican revolution, masks from the Mexican state of Guerrero, and prints by Mexican political printmaker and engraver José Guadalupe Posada. But the museum is perhaps best known for its annual "Young Latino Artists" show held each summer (check website for exact dates). The museum also hosts the *Viva la Vida* (Live the Life) festival and parade, the city's largest and longest-running annual Day of the Dead celebration (last weekend in October). The elaborate Day of the Dead shrines showcased during this period are not to be missed.

419 Congress Ave. at 5th St. www.mexic-artemuseum.org. ✆ **512/480-9373.** $7 adults, $4 seniors & students, $1 children 12 and under. Mon–Thurs 10am–6pm; Fri–Sat 10am–5pm; Sun noon–5pm.

THE RISE & FALL (& RISE AGAIN) OF sixth street

Formerly known as Pecan Street (all downtown Austin's east-west streets were originally named for Texas trees, with north-south streets named for Texas rivers), **Sixth Street** was the main connecting road to the older settlements east of Austin. During the Reconstruction boom of the 1870s, the street's wooden wagon yards and saloons began to be replaced by the more solid masonry structures you see today. After the new state capitol was built in 1888, however, the center of commercial activity began shifting toward Congress Avenue; by the middle of the 20th century, Sixth Street had become a skid row. Then 9 blocks were designated as a Historic District by the National Register of Historic Places, and restoration began in the late 1960s. In the 1970s, the street started gaining a reputation as a live-music hub—an identity that held into the beginning of the 21st century. But as serious music venues migrated elsewhere, the stretch of Sixth Street from Congress Avenue east to I-35 got a new name: Dirty Sixth. It's perfectly fine during the day, but after dark the drag takes on an air of decadence that reminds many of Bourbon Street; it's a place where a lot of college kids go to get wasted on cheap shots. No doubt the next makeover is just around the bend.

Old Bakery and Emporium ★ On the National Register of Historic Places, the Old Bakery was built in 1876 by Charles Lundberg, a Swedish master baker, and continuously operated until 1936. You can still see the giant oven and wooden baker's spade inside. Rescued from demolition by the Austin Heritage Society and now owned and operated by Austin's Parks and Recreation Department, the brick-and-limestone building is one of the few unaltered structures on Congress Avenue. A gallery inside showcases the arts and crafts of locals aged 50 or older, sold here on consignment, and a hospitality desk dispenses visitor brochures.

1006 Congress Ave. www.austintexas.gov/obemporium. ✆ **512/974-1300.** Free admission. Tues–Fri 9am–4pm. Closed most holidays.

Texas Governor's Mansion ★★ Built by Abner Cook in 1856, this Greek Revival–style manor boasted a sunny veranda, floor-to-ceiling windows, and broad hallways—but no indoor toilets (there are now seven). It is said to be the oldest continuously inhabited house in Texas. Sam Houston lived here with his large family; the nation's second female governor, Miriam "Ma" Ferguson, hosted Will Rogers here; and Governor John Connally recuperated here after being shot in Dallas when President John F. Kennedy was assassinated. Arsonists set fire to the mansion in 2008, causing severe damage; restoration was completed in 2013 and the house reopened for tours. Among the many historical artifacts are a desk belonging to Stephen F. Austin and portraits of Davy Crockett and Sam Houston.

1010 Colorado St. www.txfgm.org. ✆ **512/305-8524.** Free admission. 30-min. tours Wed–Fri 2–4pm by appointment only (email Mansion.Tours@tspb.texas.gov). All visitors must pass background security screening and provide name, date of birth, and government ID info at least 1 week prior to tour. Closed some holidays and at governor's discretion. Parking in Capitol Visitors Parking Garage, 1201 San Jacinto St., btw. Trinity and San Jacinto sts.

South Austin

See also the **Lady Bird Johnson Wildflower Center,** p. 231, and **Zilker Metropolitan Park,** p. 231.

Barton Springs Pool ★★ If the University of Texas is the seat of Austin's intellect, and the state capitol is its political pulse, Barton Springs is the city's soul. The Native Americans who settled near here believed these waters had spiritual powers, and today's residents still attest to the springs' refreshing and restorative gifts. The pool was privately owned until 1918, when Andrew Jackson Zilker deeded the land to the city. In the 1920s, the city enlarged the pool by damming the springs and building sidewalks. Although the original

GOING batty

Austin has the largest urban bat population in North America—much to the delight of Austinites. Some visitors are dubious at first, but it's impossible not to be impressed by the sight of 1.5 million Mexican free-tailed bats emerging en masse from under the Ann W. Richards Congress Avenue Bridge. They leave their roosts shortly before dusk and fly over Lady Bird Lake, moving eerily through the air like a column of smoke above the river.

Each spring (usually around March), free-tailed bats migrate from central Mexico to various roost sites in the Southwest U.S.. In 1980, when a deck reconstruction of Austin's bridge created an ideal environment for bringing up babies (called pups), some 750,000 pregnant bats began settling in. At dusk every evening, they'd take off from the bridge to hunt for bugs. Their numbers grew over time, and today the bat population may consume anywhere from 10,000 to 30,000 pounds of insects in a single night—just another reason why locals go so batty over their bats. Austin is so crazy about its bats that folks celebrate with an annual **Bat Fest** (www.roadwayevents.com/event/bat-fest; ✆ **512/441-9015**) on the bridge each August (p. 175). By fall (usually November), the pups are old enough to fly back south on the winds of an early cold front.

When the bats are in town, a kiosk designed to educate visitors and dispel some scary bat myths is set up on the south bank of the river, east of the bridge. You'll learn, for example, that bats are not rodents, they're not blind, and they're not in the least bit interested in getting in your hair. Austin-based **Bat Conservation International** (www.batcon.org; ✆ **512/327-9721** or 800/538-2287 for catalog) offers interesting bat facts, as well as bat-related retail items. If you want to know what time the bats are expected to emerge from the bridge, phone the *Austin American-Statesman* **Bat Hot Line** (✆ **512/327-9721**, ext. 2). ***Tip:*** If you think you've arrived at the bridge too late and fear you may have missed the bats, sit tight: Sometimes the bats don't leave all at once. If you can still hear chattering sounds from beneath the bridge, it's a sign that more bats may yet emerge.

limestone bottom remains, concrete was added to the banks to give uniform sides to what is now a swimming pool of about 1,000×125 feet.

Each day, approximately 32 million gallons of water from the underground Edwards Aquifer bubble to the surface here. Maintaining a constant 68°F (20°C) temperature, the amazingly clear water actually feels colder in the summer than it does in winter, when a few brave souls unwilling to do without their daily swim have the huge pool all to themselves. Lifeguards are on duty most of the day, and a large bathhouse offers changing facilities and a gift shop. This is a favorite gathering spot for Austinites, but if you're not up for swimming, you're not likely to visit. For details about the Splash! environmental information center, see p. 246.

Zilker Park, 2201 Barton Springs Rd. www.austintexas.gov/department/barton-springs-pool. ✆ **512/974-6300.** $5 adults ($9 non-resident), $3 ages 12–17 ($5 non-resident), $2 seniors ($5 non-resident); $2 ages 11 and under ($4 non-resident). Admission charged only after 8am mid-Mar–Oct; free before 8am. Daily 5am–10pm except during pool maintenance (Thurs 9am–7pm). Bus: 30 (Barton Creek Square).

Umlauf Sculpture Garden & Museum ★★ More a park than a museum, this is one of the most peaceful places in Austin. "Art framed by nature" is the concept behind this pleasant wooded garden and small studio museum at the edge of Zilker Park, near Barton Springs. In 1985, famed sculptor and former UT professor Charles Umlauf and his wife, Angeline, donated their home, studio, and 168 pieces of sculpture to the city of Austin. Today Umlauf's whimsical and often oversized art, which ranges in style from realism to abstract expressionism to lyrical abstraction, can be seen in both permanent and changing exhibitions. Locals recall how late in his life, Umlauf often walked these grounds and warmly greeted visitors. Though he used several models, the one you're likely to recognize is Farrah Fawcett, Umlauf's most famous UT student.

605 Azie Morton Rd. www.umlaufsculpture.org. ✆ **512/445-5582.** $5 adults , $3 seniors (60+), $1 students (with ID), free for ages 12 and under & active military & their families. Tues–Fri 10am–4 pm; Sat–Sun noon–4pm. Bus: 30.

Central

A number of top-notch museums, research libraries, and special archives are within walking distance of one another on the campus of the **University of Texas at Austin** (p. 230). Collectively known as **Austin's Cultural Campus,** they also include the **Blanton Museum of Art** (p. 226), the **Bullock Texas State History Museum** (p. 228), the **Elisabet Ney Museum** (p. 228), the **Harry Ransom Center** (p. 229), and the **LBJ Library and Museum** (p. 229), reviewed above.

The Contemporary Austin-Laguna Gloria ★★ A Mediterranean-style villa built in 1916 for Clara Driscoll—best known for her successful crusade to save the Alamo from commercial development—is the architectural centerpiece of this site. While it no longer houses the main art collection—that has been moved to the Contemporary Austin-Jones Center (p. 235)—the mansion now hosts a small arts school for young people, along with exhibits highlighting historic aspects of the mansion and grounds. The main artistic focus these days is the **Betty and Edward Marcus Sculpture Park,** with works of cutting edge artists and (some) traditionalists integrated into the lush landscape of the 14-acre grounds. ***Tip:*** If the weather's nice, bring a picnic lunch to enjoy by the lake. It's one of the prettiest spots in the city and, during the week, one of the most peaceful.

3809 W. 35th St. (exit W. 35th St. heading north on MoPac/Loop 1). www.thecontemporaryaustin.org. ✆ **512/458-8191. $5** adults, $3 seniors (55+) and students, free for military & ages 18 and under; $1 admission on Tues. Driscoll Villa open Tues–Sun 10am–4pm, closed Sun; grounds open Mon–Sat 9am–5pm, Sun 10am–5pm.

Hyde Park ★★ Unlike Eugene Bremond (p. 233), developer Monroe Martin Shipe built homes for the middle, not upper, classes. In the 1890s, he created, and tirelessly promoted, this complex-cum-resort in what was at that time the northern edge of Austin, and even built an electric streetcar system to connect Hyde Park with the rest of the city. After the streetcar stopped operating in the 1940s, with the rising availability of cars, the neighborhood entered a slow decline. By the 1960s, Austin's first planned suburb had become somewhat shabby. Subsequent decades of gentrification have turned the tide, however; now visitors can amble along pecan-shaded streets and look at beautifully restored residences, many in pleasing combinations of late Queen Anne and early Craftsman styles. Shipe's own architecturally eclectic home can be seen at 3816 Ave. G.

Btw. E. 38th and E. 45th, Duval and Guadalupe sts. Bus: 1 or 7.

Neill-Cochran Museum House ★ Abner Cook, the architect-contractor responsible for the governor's mansion (p. 236) and many of the city's other Greek Revival mansions, built this home in 1855. It bears his trademark portico with six Doric columns and a balustrade designed with crossed sheaves of wheat. Almost all its doors, windows, shutters, and hinges are original, which is rather astonishing when you consider the structure's history: The house was used as the city's first Blind Institute in 1856 and then as a hospital for Union prisoners near the end of the Civil War. Its well-maintained furnishings, dating from the 18th and 19th centuries, are eye-catching, but many people come just to see the painting of bluebonnets that helped convince legislators to designate these native blooms as the state flower.

2310 San Gabriel St. www.nchmuseum.org. ✆ **512/478-2335.** $5 adults, $4 seniors (65+) & students; free for ages 12 and under. Wed–Sat 1–4pm; call to book a guided tour.

Texas Memorial Museum ★ Housed in a blocky Art Moderne building designed by Paul Cret—for a while, the supervising architect of the UT campus—this 1939 museum is devoted to natural history and geology. The most impressive display is the one you can't miss when you come in: a skeleton of the Texas Pterosaur, the largest flying creature on record, suspended from the ceiling. With its 40-foot wingspan, it looks very threatening—the better to thrill dino-loving kids. Other dinosaur skeletons, fossils, and rocks will impress geo-geeks of all ages. And in a state where many textbooks present creationism as one side of a complex issue, displays on evolution and the HIV virus are standouts. The staff is very knowledgeable too. Several exhibits, including taxidermied animals, look outdated and worn, however. For many years, there was no admission price, making this worth a quick visit. Now that there's a fee, albeit a reasonable one, consider beforehand whether the subject matter really matches your interests.

University of Texas, 2400 Trinity St. www.tmm.utexas.edu. ✆ **512/471-1604.** $7 adults & teens, $5 ages 2–12, $2 college students. Tues–Sat 9am–5pm.

East Side

French Legation State Historic Site ★ Occupying 2½ acres on a hilltop above downtown, this small house museum is a holdover from Texas's brief stint as an independent nation—and from its days as a slave-holding state. The oldest surviving house in Austin still standing in its original location, it was built by Count Alphonse Dubois de Saligny, France's representative to the short-lived Republic of Texas (1836–1845). Dubois sold the house to Dr. Joseph W. Robertson in 1848; he, his wife, their 11 children, and nine enslaved workers all lived on the site, and it remained in their family's possession for close to 100 years. The house is furnished with antiques dating from

Old-Fashioned Moonlight

If you saw the cult-classic 1993 Richard Linklater film *Dazed and Confused*, set in Austin, you may remember the line, "Party at the moon tower!" and the scene set under one of Austin's Moonlight Towers. So what's a "moon tower"? Standing 165 feet above their 15-foot base, these old-fashioned towers shed bright lights over Austin, creating a moonlight-like glow. Popular in the late 1800s across the U.S. and Europe, the original moonlight towers were established in Austin between 1884 and 1885. Each one originally contained six carbon arc lamps, illuminating a 1,500-foot-radius circle, which is said to have burned "brightly enough to read a watch from as far away as 1,500 feet." Originally, the towers were connected to generators on the Colorado River. In the 1920s, the carbon arc lamps were changed to incandescent lamps, and in the 1930s, mercury vapor lamps were lit by a switch at each tower's base. During World War II, a central switch controlled the lights, allowing citywide blackouts in case of air raids. In 1970 the towers were officially recognized as state antiquities and were collectively listed in the National Register of Historic Places in 1976. As a part of a $1.3-million project in 1993, the City of Austin dismantled and meticulously restored each piece of the 15 remaining towers (there were originally 31). The only ones still in existence in the world, the towers are scattered all over town, with the greatest concentration near the State Capitol. Don't try to look for the one in Linklater's film, however—it was built as a film set and bore little resemblance to the real thing.

the 1840s to the 1870s, some belonging to Count Dubois or the Robinsons. At the rear of the house is a reconstructed kitchen of the era (the original burned down). In late 2017, the house came under the aegis of the Texas Historical Commission; the state allotted $1.56 million to address its many structural problems. The site is currently closed for restoration; check the website for status reports.

802 San Marcos. www.thc.texas.gov/historic-sites/french-legation-state-historic-site.

George Washington Carver Museum, Cultural and Genealogy Center ★★ The first museum in Texas devoted to African-American history, this spacious facility serves as a resource center for the Austin black community, hosting art galleries, a dance studio, a theater, and genealogical archives. The permanent exhibition on Juneteenth explains the genesis and evolution of the Texas-born holiday, now spread to other parts of the country: It commemorates June 19, 1865, when Union general Gordon Granger read the Emancipation Proclamation to the public in Galveston.

1165 Angelina St. www.austintexas.gov/page/carver-history. ✆ **512/974-4926.** Free admission. Mon–Fri 10am–6pm (Thurs until 9pm); Sat 10am–4pm.

Texas State Cemetery ★★ The city's namesake, Stephen F. Austin, is the best-known resident of this East Side cemetery, established by the state in 1851. Judge Edwin Waller, who laid out the grid plan for Austin's streets and later served as mayor, also rests here, as do eight former Texas governors, various fighters in Texas's battles for independence, author James Michener, and Barbara Jordan, the first black woman from the South elected to the U.S. Congress (in 1996, she became the first African American to gain admittance to these grounds). Perhaps the most striking monument is one sculpted by Elisabet Ney (p. 228), for the tomb of Confederate general Albert Sidney Johnston, who died at the Battle of Shiloh. Interestingly, in the 1990s, restoring the graveyard's grounds was a pet project of Lt. Gov. Bob Bullock, a politician who was nothing if not resourceful. Unable to get funding from the state legislature, Bullock had the narrow drive that runs through the cemetery officially designated as a state highway so he could allocate funds from the Texas Department of Transportation. (Note the highway signs at the entrances.) Bullock himself resides here now, in quite a fancy tomb.

Free self-guided walking and audio tours are available at the visitor center/museum, which is designed to resemble the long barracks at the Alamo; you can also download walking tours onto your phone.

909 Navasota St. www.cemetery.tspb.texas.gov. ✆ **512/463-0605.** Free admission. Grounds daily 8am–5pm; visitor center Mon–Fri 8am–5pm. Bus: 4 and 18 stop nearby.

PARKS & NATURAL ATTRACTIONS

If you look up as you pass along Balcones Drive on the city's west side, you can glimpse a portion of the Balcones Escarpment, a fault zone that marks the boundary between the rich Blacklands Prairie to the east and the hilly Edwards Plateau to the west. The limestone comprising the plateau, uplifted millions of years ago from the bottom of the shallow sea that covered most of Texas, renders the underground water that rises at such pools as Barton Springs (p. 237) remarkably clear. It also acts as a filter for the waters of the Highland Lakes, a sparkling 150-mile-long chain created by a series of dams, which spreads northwest from the city in an ever-widening pattern. This all makes the Austin a remarkable place to play outdoors.

Lakes

Highland Lakes ★★ From the late 1930s to the early 1950s, six dams were built by the Lower Colorado River Authority to control the flooding that had plagued the areas surrounding Texas's Colorado River (not to be confused with the river of the same name that flows through the Grand Canyon); they transformed the waterway into a sparkling chain of lakes, stretching some 150 miles northwest of Austin. The narrowest of them, **Lady Bird Lake,** runs through downtown, traversed by the Congress Avenue Bridge; it's the heart of urban recreation in Austin, its banks lined by trails and a shoreline park. Just upstream, **Lake Austin** divides West Austin from Westlake Hills; on its banks you'll find **Emma Long Park** (p. 244). Next in the series is **Lake Travis,** the longest lake in the chain, which offers the most options for boating and general recreation. Together with the other Highland Lakes—**Marble Falls, LBJ, Inks,** and **Buchanan**—these comprise the largest concentration of freshwater lakes in Texas. See "Sports & Outdoor Activities," p. 250, for recreation details.

Mountains

Covert Park at Mount Bonnell ★★ For the best views of the city, Lake Austin, and some of the Hill Country stretching out westward, take a drive up to this hilltop park. At 785 feet, it's the highest point in Austin—and also the oldest tourist attraction in town. It was used by Native Americans as an outlook, and it was a popular tourist attraction in the 1850s and 1860s, when General Sam Houston and George Armstrong Custer were among the visitors (though not together). It has long been a favorite spot for romantic trysts; rumor has it that any couple who climbed the 106 stone steps to the top together would fall in love (an emotion often confused with exhaustion). The peak was named in 1836 for George W. Mount, Sam Houston's Commissioner of Indian Affairs, while the far-from-secret park at the summit gets its moniker from Frank M. Covert, Jr., who donated the land to the city in 1939.

3800 Mt. Bonnell Rd. www.austintexas.gov/department/mount-bonnell. ✆ **512/974-6700.** Free admission. Daily 5am–10pm. Take Mt. Bonnell Rd. 1 mile past west end of W. 35th St.

Nature Preserves

City of Austin Nature Preserves ★ In 2,200 acres of city-run nature preserves, Austin boasts a remarkably diverse group of natural habitats.

AUSTIN'S MIGHTY (HISTORIC) oaks

Austin is not the only city to have trees designated as historic sites, but in this leafy metropolis, it makes perfect sense. These two landmarks are live oaks, a species commonly seen from Florida to Texas, which can grow to be very tall, often 50 feet high. Their spreading branches may be draped with moss—an image often used by filmmakers to telegraph that a scene is set in the South.

Treaty Oak Legend has it that Stephen F. Austin signed the first boundary treaty with the Comanche under the spreading branches of this 500-year-old live oak, the sole remaining tree in what was once a grove of 14 known as Council Oaks. When the Treaty Oak was deliberately poisoned in 1989 by a mentally unstable man (he almost managed to kill it), the attack shocked the community. A large international team of forestry experts managed to save the tree through extraordinary efforts, largely funded by one-time presidential candidate Ross Perot. For a long time, it was the subject of prayer circles and energy healers, and surrounded by everything from get-well cards and letters to bottles of Maalox and Tums. Located downtown on Baylor Street between West Fifth and Sixth streets, the Treaty Oak is a bit lopsided and about one-third of its original size but is no longer in any danger.

Battle Oaks The three oldest members of this small grove of live oaks on the University of Texas campus are said to be about 250 to 300 years old. They survived the destruction of most of the grove to build a Civil War fortress, and a later attempt to displace them with a new Biology Building. It was this last, near-fatal skirmish that earned them their name. Legend has it that Dr. W. J. Battle, a professor of classics and an early university president, holed up in the largest oak with a shotgun to protect the three ancient trees. The Battle Oaks are located at the southwest corner of Whitis Avenue and 24th Street, near the Barbara Jordan statue.

Blunn Creek, 1200 St. Edward's Dr. (www.austinparks.org/blunn-creek-preserve; ✆ **512/974-6700**), is 40 acres of upland woods and meadows traversed by a spring-fed creek; one of its two lookout areas is made of compacted volcanic ash. Spelunkers will like **Goat Cave,** 3900 Deer Lane (www.austinparks.org/goat-cave-karst-preserve), which is honeycombed with limestone caverns and sinkholes. To arrange for cave tours, contact the **Austin Nature Center** (www.austintexas.gov/page/about-austin-nature-science-center; ✆ **512/974-3888**). Directly abutting the Barrow Brook Cove of Lake Austin, lovely **Mayfield Park,** 3505 W. 35th St. (www.austintexas.org/listings/mayfield-park-and-preserve/6859; ✆ **512/974-6797**), features peacocks and peahens roaming freely around lily ponds, and trails crossing over bridges in oak and juniper woods. Visitors to the rock-walled ramada at the **Zilker Nature Preserve,** 301 Nature Center Dr., with its meadows, streams, and cliff, can look out over downtown Austin (see the Austin Nature and Science Center, p. 246, for more details). All the preserves are maintained in a primitive state with natural surface trails and no restrooms. Admission is free and they're open daily from dawn to dusk. For additional information, including directions, log on to www.austintexas.gov/naturepreserves or phone ✆ **512/974-9461.**

Westcave Preserve ★ If you don't like the weather in one part of Westcave Preserve, you might like it better in another: Up to a 25° difference in temperature has been recorded between the highest area of this beautiful natural habitat, an arid Hill Country scrub, and the lowest, a lush woodland spread across a canyon floor. Because the ecosystem here is so delicate, this 30-acre preserve on the Pedernales River may be entered only by guided tour. Reservations are taken for weekday visits; on weekends, only the first 30 people who show up at the allotted times are allowed in. To get here, take Hwy. 71 to RR 3238, and follow the signs 15 miles to Hamilton Pool, across the Pedernales River Bridge from the preserve.

Star Rte. 1, Dripping Springs. www.westcave.org. ✆ **830/825-3442.** Guided tours Tues–Fri 10am–2pm, Sat–Sun 9:30am–4:30pm, weather permitting. Canyon tours $15 adults, $7 children 4–17; Upland trails tours $7 adults, $4 children 4–17.

Wild Basin Wilderness Preserve ★ In the Westlake section of Austin, this 227-acre peninsula is part of the larger Balcones Canyonland Preserve, which protects several protected species, including the golden warbler. It's a lovely place to hike, with 2.5 miles of trails; it also serves as an ecological education center for St. Edwards University. Some of the programs offered to students are also open to the public.

805 N. Capital of Texas Hwy. www.parks.traviscountytx.gov/parks/wild-basin. ✆ **512/854-7275.** Preserve open Mon–Fri sunrise–sunset; office daily 9am–4pm.

Parks & Gardens

See also **Zilker Metropolitan Park,** p. 231.

Barton Creek Greenbelt ★ When locals refer to "The Greenbelt," they almost always mean this verdant creekside stretch in south-central Austin, known for hiking, mountain biking, swimming, bird-watching, and rock climbing. There are many access points, but the one best known to hikers is at 2212 William Barton Dr.: It's the trailhead for not only the Barton Springs Greenbelt but also for the **Violet Crown Trail,** which will be 30 miles long when completed. For information on all access points, see www.austinparks.org/barton-creek-greenbelt, or phone the Austin Parks Foundation (✆ **520/477-1566**).

Emma Long Metropolitan Park ★ More than 1,100 acres of woodland and a mile of shore along Lake Austin make Emma Long Park—named after the first woman to sit on Austin's city council—a most appealing space. You'll find boat ramps, a fishing dock, and a protected swimming area, guarded by lifeguards on summer weekends. This is the only city park to offer camping, with permits ($10 for primitive camping, $20–$25 utility camping, in addition to entry fee) available on a first-come, first-served basis. If you hike through the stands of oak, ash, and juniper to an elevation of 1,000 feet, you'll get a view of the city spread out before you. Note that the park closes whenever its maximum capacity is reached. To get here, exit I-35 at 290 W., then go west to City Park Rd. (near Loop 360); turn south (left) and drive 6¼ miles to park entrance.

1600 City Park Rd. www.austintexas.gov/department/emma-long-metropolitan-park. ✆ **512/974-1831.** Admission $5 per vehicle Mon–Thurs; $10 Fri–Sun and holidays. Daily 7am–10pm.

McKinney Falls State Park ★ In the southeast part of Austin, not far from the airport (consider this when you have a long layover), this wooded preserve lies at the confluence of two streams, with waterfalls flowing over limestone ledges. It offers a 2.8-mile hike-and-bike trail, as well as fishing, swimming, and camping; there's even a small historic site. This is a popular spot on fine-weather weekends and sometimes gets closed when it reaches capacity—call ahead or check the park's Twitter feed or Facebook posts (links are on the website).

5808 McKinney Falls Pkwy. www.tpwd.texas.gov/state-parks/mckinney-falls. ✆ **512/243-1643.** $6 adults, free for children 6 and under. Daily 8am–10pm; park office daily 8:30am–4:30pm (Fri until 6:30pm).

Zilker Botanical Garden ★ Austinites love the natural beauty of their city, and perhaps nowhere is that beauty so gracefully displayed as at the Zilker Botanical Garden, set on the south banks of Lady Bird Lake, not far from downtown. These 26 acres of fenced gardens are especially lovely in the spring, or almost anytime from March to October. Highlights include the **Oriental Garden,** created by Japanese landscape architect Isamu Taniguchi when he was 70 years old. You'll also encounter a rose garden, a succulents garden, and children's gardens. In April and October the **Douglas Blachly Butterfly Trail** is aflutter with migrating butterflies. The dinosaur tracks in the 1½-acre **Hartman Prehistoric Garden** were discovered in the early 1900s and date back 100 million years. And if you come in spring, don't miss the annual creation of the award-winning **Woodland Faerie Trail,** when Austin-area gardeners, architects, artists, families, and school groups create tiny woodland fairy houses and host tea parties, crafts workshops, and moonlight walks.

2220 Barton Springs Rd. www.zilkergarden.org. ✆ **512/477-8672.** $3 adults ($2 residents), $1 seniors & children. No credit cards. Garden center 9am–5pm daily. Bus: 30.

ESPECIALLY FOR KIDS

The **Bullock Texas State History Museum** (p. 228) and the **Texas Memorial Museum** (p. 239) are kid-friendly, but outdoor attractions are still Austin's biggest draw for children. There's lots of room for children to splash around at **Barton Springs Pool** (p. 237) and even youngsters who thought bats were creepy are likely to be converted on further acquaintance with the critters. In addition, the following attractions are especially geared toward children.

Austin Nature and Science Center ★★ Bats, bees, and crystal caverns are among the subjects of the Discovery Lab at this museum in the 80-acre Nature Center, which features lots of interactive exhibits. Tortoises, lizards, and vultures in the Animal Exhibits—including orphaned or injured creatures brought here from the wild—also hold kids' attention. An Eco-Detective trail highlights pond-life awareness. The Dino Pit, with its replicas of Texas fossils and dinosaur tracks, lures budding paleontologists. A variety of specialty camps, focusing on everything from caving to astronomy, are offered from late May through August.

Zilker Park, 301 Nature Center Dr. www.austintexas.gov/page/about-austin-nature-science-center. ✆ **512/974-3888.** Free admission; added charge for some special exhibits. Mon–Sat 9am–5pm; Sun noon–5pm. Closed July 4, Thanksgiving, and Dec 25. Bus: 30.

Austin Zoo ★ This small zoo, some 14 miles southwest of downtown, may not feature the state-of-the-jungle habitats of larger facilities, but it's easy to get up close and personal with the critters here. It began as a rescue facility, and most of the residents, who range from turkeys and potbellied pigs to marmosets and tigers, were mistreated, abandoned, or illegally imported before they found a home here. There are no food concessions here for humans (you can buy feed for the animals at the gift shop), but there are plenty of picnic tables. To get there, take Hwy. 290 W. to Circle Drive, turn right, go 1½ miles to Rawhide Trail, and turn right.

10808 Rawhide Trail. www.austinzoo.org. ✆ **512/288-1490.** $12 adults, $11 seniors & students, $9 children 2–12, free for children 1 and under. Daily 10am–6pm. Closed Thanksgiving and Dec 25.

Splash! Into the Edwards Aquifer ★★ The Edwards Aquifer, Austin's main source of water, is fed by a variety of underground creeks filtered through a large layer of limestone. You'll feel as though you're entering one of this vast ecosystem's sinkholes when you walk into this dimly lit enclosure—formerly the bathhouse at Barton Springs Pool—where a variety of interactive displays grab kids' attention. Young visitors can make it rain on the city, identify water bugs, or peer through a periscope at swimmers. Splash! is part of the Beverly S. Sheffield Education Center, which has rotating exhibitions—perhaps one on the endangered Barton Springs salamander—and partners with the Austin Nature and Science Center (p. 246) on special educational programs.

Zilker Park, 2201 William Barton Dr. www.austintexas.gov/splash. ✆ **512/974-6350.** Free admission. Tues–Sat 10am–5pm; Sun noon–5pm. Bus: 30 (Barton Creek Sq.).

Thinkery ★★ Longtime residents may remember this as downtown's Children's Museum, but it's much bigger (40,000 square feet) and better in its new iteration as the Thinkery in the Mueller area of east central Austin. The focus is on STEAM (Science, Technology, Engineering, Arts, Math) learning

african-american **HISTORY TRAIL**

In a city where the African-American population is decreasing in spite of the general growth trend, it's especially important to recognize the many contributions of this community. The most comprehensive place to explore that history is the **George Washington Carver Museum, Cultural and Genealogy Center** (p. 241). But other sites on the East Side are worth visiting too. Less than two blocks from the Carver, on the corner of Hackberry and San Bernard streets, the **Wesley United Methodist Church,** established at the end of the Civil War, became one of the leading black churches in Texas; it's still an active parish. Diagonally across the street, the **Zeta Phi Beta Sorority,** Austin's first black Greek letter house, occupies the 1877 Thompson house, which is also the archival center for the sorority's Texas chapter. Nearby, at the **State Cemetery** (p. 241), you can visit the gravesite of congresswoman and civil rights leader Barbara Jordan, the first African-American to be buried there.

About half a mile away, the sparsely furnished **Henry G. Madison Cabin** was built around 1863 by a black homesteader; during Reconstruction, Madison became Austin's first African-American city council member. In 1973, the cabin—enclosed in a larger frame house that Madison also built—was donated to the city, which moved it to its present site in Rosewood Park at 2300 Rosewood Ave. (✆ **512/472-6838**).

A contemporary of Madison, Charles Clark founded **Clarksville,** a small utopian community of freed blacks in 1871; it's just to the west of the city center around what is now West 10th Street. Clarksville was designated a historic district in 1976 but is now a mostly white neighborhood.

On the University of Texas campus, sites on the self-guided Diversity Tour (www.admissions.utexas.edu/visit/general-visitors) include statues of **Martin Luther King, Jr.** (in the center of the East Mall), **Barbara Jordan** (beneath the Battle Oaks, to the northwest of the UT Tower), and 1977 Heisman Trophy winner **Earl "Tyler Rose" Campbell** (southwest side of the Darrell K. Royal-Texas Memorial Stadium).

See also p. 249 for Preservation Austin's self-guided tour app covering African-American historical sites.

through a variety of creative hands-on and interactive displays. The outdoor Backyard offers fresh air and some gentle activities. Age categories for exhibits (0-4 and 4-12) are not hard and fast, but the entire facility is turned over to toddlers and their handlers in special Baby Bloomers hours (for ages 0-3). There's always something going on here—even an adult night. Check the website for listings.

1830 Simond Ave. www.thinkeryaustin.org. ✆ **512/469-6200.** Admission $12, free for children 23 months and under. Mon 9am–noon (Baby Bloomers only); Tues, Thurs, Fri 10am–5pm; Sat 10am–6pm (Baby Bloomers 9–10am); Sun 10am–6pm.

Zilker Zephyr Miniature Train ★ Take a scenic 25-minute ride through Zilker Park on a narrow-gauge, light-rail miniature train, trundling at a leisurely pace along Barton Creek and Lady Bird Lake. The train departs approximately every hour on the hour during the week, every half-hour on the weekend, weather permitting.

Zilker Park, 2100 Barton Springs Rd. (just across from Barton Springs Pool). www.zilkerpark.org/zilker-park-amenities/zilker-park-train. ✆ **512/478-8286.** $3 adults, $2 seniors & ages 11 and under, free for infants (age 1 and under) on guardian's lap. Daily 10am–5pm. Bus: 30

ORGANIZED TOURS

See also **Westcave Preserve,** p. 244.

Boat Tours

Capital Cruises ★★ From March through October, Capital Cruises ply Lady Bird Lake with electric-powered boats heading out on a number of popular tours. The bat cruises are especially big in summer, when warm nights are perfect for enjoyable, educational hour-long excursions. The high point is seeing thousands of bats stream out from under their Congress Avenue Bridge roost. Afternoon sightseeing tours are a nice way to while away an hour on the weekend. Dinner and lunch cruises are offered, with catering from the Hyatt Regency kitchen. Rates depend on the size of your group (min. 2 people) and the meals you choose.

Hyatt Regency Lady Bird Lake boat dock, 208 Barton Springs Rd. www.capitalcruises.com. ✆ **512/480-9264.** Bat and sightseeing cruises $10 adults, $8 seniors, $5 children ages 3–12. Bat cruise daily 30 min. before sunset (call ahead for exact time), weather permitting; sightseeing cruise Sat–Sun at 1pm; hours and days of tours change seasonally. Reservations required for lunch and dinner cruises; for bat and sightseeing cruises, arrive at dock at least 30 min. in advance.

Lone Star Riverboat ★★ You'll set out against a backdrop of Austin's skyline and the state capitol, then move upstream past Barton Creek and Zilker Park, along the way glimpsing 100-foot-high cliffs and million-dollar estates. These scenic tours, accompanied by knowledgeable narrators, last about 90 minutes; slightly shorter bat-watching tours leave around half an hour before sunset. For a romantic experience, hop aboard the BYOB Moonlight Cruise and enjoy the lights of the city under the stars.

South shore of Lady Bird Lake, btw. Congress Ave. and S. First St. bridges, next to Hyatt Regency. www.lonestarriverboat.com. ✆ **512/327-1388.** Sightseeing and bat tours $12 adults, $10 seniors, $7 children ages 4–12. Bat tours nightly Mar–Oct only; call for exact times. Moonlight tours $12. Reservations recommended; times and frequency change with the season.

Segway Tours

Gliding Revolution ★ Guided scooter tours of downtown, the Capitol, East Austin, and South Austin run from 1 to 3 hours. You can also rent Segways to zip around on your own for $35 an hour (2-hr. min.) or $175 for a 9-hour day. Electric bikes are also available for rent.

1403 Lavaca St. www.glidingrevolution.com. ✆ **512/495-9250.** Tours $49–$59 adults. Daily tours; call to check schedule.

Tower Tour

University of Texas Tower Observation Deck Tour ★ Off-limits to the public for nearly a quarter of a century, the infamous observation deck of the UT Tower—where gunman Charles Whitman went on a deadly shooting spree in 1966—now has a webbed safety dome. Billed as self-guided tours, these excursions to the top of the tower are really supervised visits, although a guide gives a short, informative spiel and stays on hand to answer questions. It would probably be better if these visits—about 45 minutes—were half as long and half as expensive. ***Note:*** You are permitted to bring a camera, binoculars, or phone to take advantage of the observation deck's spectacular 360-degree view of the city and environs, but you must leave behind everything else, including purses, camera bags, tripods, and strollers. (Lockers are available at the Texas Union for $1.)

UT Campus, Texas Union Bldg. www.universityunions.utexas.edu/food-fun/tower-tours. ✆ **512/475-6636.** Tours $6. Schedules vary according to academic schedule; late May–late Aug, tours offered Sat–Sun evenings only.

Van Tours

Austin Detours ★★ This local company uses local talent (including some between-gigs actors and musicians) for their knowledgeable insider tours. The Real Austin highlights tour ($35 for 2 hr.) is a great introduction or reorientation to the ever-changing city; the price includes a food truck snack. Other themes on regular rotation include the nighttime Live Music Crawl ($50, 2 hr.) and a fun interactive Murder Mystery Tour ($40, 2 hr.). You can also choose from a long menu of private tours, or have one tailored to you.

602 E. 4th St. www.austindetours.com. ✆ **512/962-8636.**

Walking Tours

You won't find better guided walks than the informative and entertaining downtown walking tours offered by **Visit Austin** (www.austintexas.org/plan-a-trip/downtown-walking-tours; ✆ **866/GO-AUSTIN** [462-8784]). Tours are about 90 minutes long and cost $10 per person; there's no charge for children under age 12 with paying parents. Three types of tours are offered year-round, weather permitting: one of Upper Congress Avenue, which starts at the Capitol; another covering Lower Congress Avenue, Willie Nelson Boulevard, East Sixth Street, and Lady Bird Lake; and the third exploring Historic Downtown West–Bremond Block and Guadalupe Street. See details online.

Alternatively, download a free app to take one of the self-guided historic tours created by **Preservation Austin** (www.preservationaustin.org/programs/historic-austin-tour-app; ✆ **512/474-5198**). In addition to general tours covering Congress Avenue and East Sixth Street, you'll also find ones catering to special interests, such as iconic music venues and African-American sites.

SPORTS & OUTDOOR ACTIVITIES

BIKING Austin has been designated a Gold Level Bicycle Friendly Community by the League of American Bicyclists. For an overview of bicycling in the city, including route maps and laws and regulations, see www.austintexas.gov/bicycle.

If you want to ride on park trails, you have your choice of the mellow hike-and-bike trail around Lady Bird Lake (10 miles), or the more challenging Barton Creek Greenbelt (7.8 miles). Contact **Austin Parks and Recreation,** 200 S. Lamar Blvd. (www.austintexas.gov/department/parks-and-recreation; ✆ **512/974-6700**), for more information on these and other bike trails. There is also a paved **Veloway,** a 3.1-mile paved loop devoted exclusively to bicyclists and in-line skaters, in Slaughter Creek Metropolitan Park in far South Austin (www.austintexas.gov/department/veloway). For rougher mountain-bike routes, try the **Austin Ridge Riders** (www.austinridgeriders.com).

Austin's public bike share program, **Austin B-Cycle,** has B-station stands throughout the city. Get the details, plus B-station locations and bike routes, at **www.austin.bcycle.com** or download the B-Cycle app. A number of downtown hotels also rent or provide free bikes to their guests. You can also rent mountain and city bikes from **Mellow Johnny's Bike Shop,** in the Warehouse District at 400 Nueces between 4th and 5th streets (www.austin.mellowjohnnys.com; ✆ **512/473-0222**); it even has kids' bikes for rent. MJ's, as it's known locally, is owned by Austin Tour de France biker Lance Armstrong, though you won't get that information from the website.

For information on weekly road rides, contact **Bike Austin,** 1000 Brazos St., Suite 100 (www.bikeaustin.org; ✆ **512/282-7413**).

BIRD-WATCHING Endangered golden-cheeked warblers and black-capped vireos are among the many species you might spot around Austin. The **Travis Audubon Society** (www.travisaudubon.org; ✆ **512/300-2473**) organizes regular birding trips and even has a rare-bird hotline. Texas Parks and Wildlife's *Guide to Austin-Area Birding Sites* points you to the best urban perches; it's available online at www.tpwd.texas.gov/publications/pwdpubs/pwd_br_w7000_0328. Avid birders might also enjoy ***Adventures with a Texas Naturalist,*** by Roy Bedichek, reprinted many times since it was first published in 1947.

CANOEING & KAYAKING You can rent canoes and kayaks at **Zilker Park,** 2101 Andrew Zilker Rd. (www.zilkerboats.com; ✆ **512/478-3852**), for \$18 an hour or \$54 per day. **Capital Cruises,** at the Hyatt Regency boat dock (www.capitalcruises.com; ✆ **512/480-9264**), offers rentals on Lady Bird Lake for \$15 per hour.

FISHING **Git Bit** (www.gitbitfishing.com; ✆ **512/773-7401**) provides guide service for half- or full-day bass-fishing trips on Lake Travis.

GOLF For information about Austin's six municipal golf courses, log on to www.austintexas.gov/department/golf. The 9-hole **Hancock** course, built in 1899, is the oldest course in Texas; the **Lions** course is where Tom Kite and Ben Crenshaw played college golf for the University of Texas. All but the Hancock course offer pro shops and equipment rental, and greens fees tend to be reasonable.

HIKING Austin's parks and preserves abound in nature trails. Contact the **Sierra Club** (www.texas.sierraclub.org/austin; ✆ **512/477-1729**) if you're interested in organized hikes. **Wild Basin Wilderness Preserve** (p. 244) is another source for guided treks, offering periodic "Haunted Trails" tours along with its more typical hikes.

ROCK CLIMBING Those with the urge to hang out on cliffs can call **Texas Climbing Adventures** (www.texasclimbingadventures.com; (✆ **512/590-2988**), which holds weekend rock-climbing courses at Enchanted Rock, a stunning granite outcropping in the Hill Country (p. 146). **Austin Rock Gym** (www.austinrockgym.com; ✆ **512/416-9299**) offers two family-friendly indoor climbing facilities, as well as a variety of classes and guided outdoor trips. **Austin Bouldering Project** (www. austinboulderingproject.com; ✆ **512/645-4633**) holds beginning and intermediate climbing classes at its indoor gym.

PADDLEBOARDING Since no motorized boat traffic is permitted on Lady Bird Lake, paddleboarding (along with kayaking and canoeing) is very popular there. It'll run you $15 to $20 an hour ($35–$45 max.), depending on the day of the week, to rent a board from **Rowing Dock ATX** (www.rowing dock.com; ✆ **512/459-0999**) or the **Texas Rowing Center** (www.texasrowing center.com; ✆ **512/467-7799**).

SAILING Lake Travis is the perfect place to let the wind drive your sails; among the operators offering sailboat rentals in the Austin area are **Commander's Point Yacht Basin** (www.commanderspointmarnia.com; ✆ **512/266-2333**) and **Texas Sailing Academy** (www.texassailing.com; ✆ **512/261-6193**). Both offer instruction.

SCUBA DIVING The clarity of the water in Lake Travis varies a good bit; on days when the lake is full and the wind is mild, conditions are good for diving there. Boat wrecks and metal sculptures have been planted on the lake bottom of the private (paying) portion of **Windy Point Park,** 6506 Bob Wentz Park Rd. (www.windypointpark.com; ✆ **512/266-3337**), while nature has provided the park's advanced divers with an unusual underwater grove of pecan trees. Equipment rentals and lessons are available nearby from **Dive World** (www.diveworldaustin.com; ✆ **512/219-1220**).

SPELUNKING The limestone country in the Austin area is rife with dark places in which to poke around. In the city, two wild caves you can crawl into with the proper training are **Airman's Cave,** on the Barton Creek Greenbelt (p. 244), and **Goat Cave Preserve,** in southwest Austin (p. 243). Check the website of the Texas Speleological Association (www.cavetexas.org), and that of the University Speleological Society (www.utgrotto.org) for links to underground attractions statewide. See chapter 9 for other nearby caves in the Hill Country.

SWIMMING The best known of Austin's natural swimming holes is **Barton Springs Pool** (p. 237), but it's by no means the only one. Another scenic outdoor spot to take the plunge is **Deep Eddy Pool,** 401 Deep Eddy Ave. at Lake Austin Blvd. (www.austintexas.gov/department/deep-eddy-pool; ✆ **512/472-8546**). For lakeshore swimming, consider **Emma Long Metropolitan Park** on Lake Austin (p. 244), or **Hippie Hollow** on Lake Travis, 2½ miles off FM 620 (https://parks.traviscountytx.gov/find-a-park/hippie-hollow), where you can let it all hang out in a series of clothing-optional coves.

SHOPPING IN AUSTIN

The Austin retail scene isn't as glitzy as those in larger Texas metropolises like Houston or Dallas—at least not yet. Most locals pride themselves on the fact that the city excels in the unique and the home grown, from clothing to crafts and, especially, groceries; this is, after all, where Whole Foods originated. But Austin itself has come to be seen as a brand—one that, much like Brooklyn, telegraphs young, hip, and wired. As rents have risen in several popular shopping districts, many independents have gotten pricey. And of course Whole Foods is now a corporation.

Still, there are enclaves with less expensive wares in parts of town where the rents have not yet skyrocketed. Pop-up shops—online retailers who gather to sell their wares in vacant lots or on the properties of established businesses as one-time or recurring events—have also kept things interesting and competitively priced. The retail equivalent of food trucks that test the waters for chefs, these temporary shops sometimes decide to go the brick-and-mortar route. To find out what's popping up while you're visiting, check www.eventbrite.com/d/tx--austin/pop-up.

THE SHOPPING SCENE

Once the hub of Austin's independent retail scene, **Downtown** still has some treasures, especially along Congress Avenue and West Sixth Street. However, the only area that might be identified as a real shopping district these days is **West Second Street,** known for its trendy, high-end boutiques.

Across Lady Bird Lake from downtown, **South Congress Avenue** is chock-a-block with art galleries, vintage clothing emporia, and folk art shops, along with upscale retailers, mostly concentrated from the 1200 block to the 2500 block. The popularity of this area, however, has meant higher rents, which results in higher prices passed along to consumers. Just a few blocks west, **South First** and, to a lesser degree, **South Lamar Boulevard** are what South Congress used to be: drags where you can still find fun local wares at prices that aren't prohibitive. **East Austin,** across I-35 from

FIRST thursdays

As if there weren't already enough street theater in Austin, the merchants on South Congress Avenue decided a few years back to host a monthly street festival. They began keeping their doors open late and providing food, drinks, and entertainment on the first Thursday of every month. Soon impromptu open-air markets sprang up, and jugglers, drum circles, and of course live bands performed indoors, outdoors, and in between.

First Thursdays are popular for their mix of shopping, entertainment, people-watching, and the surprise factor—you never know what you're going to meet up with. It's also a way for locals to celebrate the approach of the weekend. The street festival occupies about 8 blocks along both sides of South Congress. Traffic along the avenue is not cordoned off, but everyone drives slowly because of the crowds crisscrossing the avenue, from around Academy Drive to Crockett Street. It kicks off around 5pm and runs until 10pm.

downtown, draws up-and-coming artists and indie retailers, especially along East Cesar Chavez Street; it's the place to browse the latest in understated home design and personal adornment, Austin style.

In the older **West End,** near where downtown's Fifth and Sixth streets cross Lamar Boulevard, you'll find mega-shops of well-known brands like Anthropologie, REI, and Austin-grown Whole Foods, Waterloo Records, and Book-People, along with smaller boutiques dotted on side streets and north along Lamar to 12th street. In the vicinity of **Central Market,** between West 35th and 40th streets and Lamar and MoPac, such small shopping centers as **26 Doors** and **Jefferson Square** have charming selections.

Many stores on **The Drag**—the stretch of Guadalupe Street bordering the University of Texas campus—are student-oriented, but a wide range of upscale options complement the expected tie-dye. **North Loop,** the newest shopping destination for the boho-chic, lies just north of UT, specializing in vintage shops, used bookstores, and one-off quirky boutiques.

Specialty shops in Austin tend to open around 10am, Monday through Saturday, and close at about 5:30 or 6pm; many have Sunday hours from noon to 6pm. Malls tend to keep the same Sunday schedule, but Monday through Saturday they stay open until 9pm. Sales tax in Austin is 8.25%.

Malls/Shopping Centers

Much of Austin's shopping has moved out to the malls. **Barton Creek Square** drew wealthy shoppers from all parts of town when it opened in the southwest in 1980, but since then far more malls have opened up in the northwest, especially as it became a hot tech corridor. Bargain hunters go farther afield to the huge collection of **factory outlet stores** just south of San Marcos (p. 294).

Downtown Austin Shopping

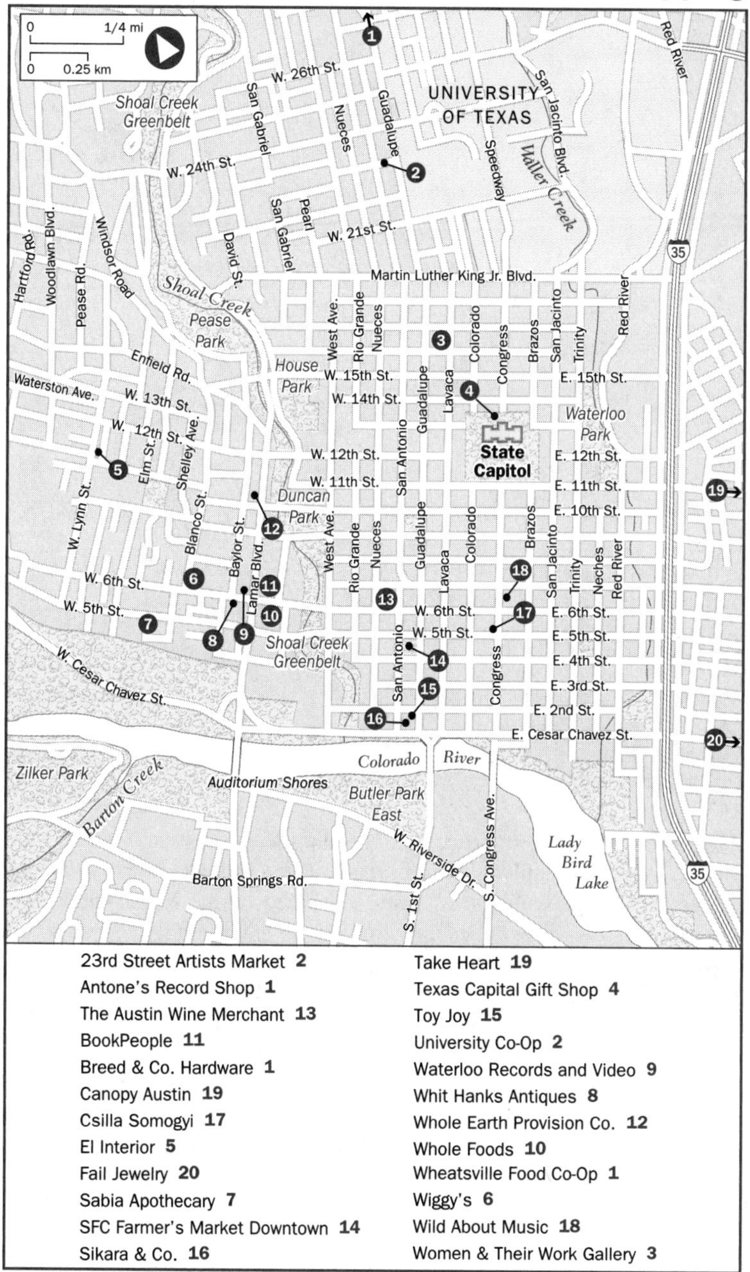

23rd Street Artists Market **2**
Antone's Record Shop **1**
The Austin Wine Merchant **13**
BookPeople **11**
Breed & Co. Hardware **1**
Canopy Austin **19**
Csilla Somogyi **17**
El Interior **5**
Fail Jewelry **20**
Sabia Apothecary **7**
SFC Farmer's Market Downtown **14**
Sikara & Co. **16**
Take Heart **19**
Texas Capital Gift Shop **4**
Toy Joy **15**
University Co-Op **2**
Waterloo Records and Video **9**
Whit Hanks Antiques **8**
Whole Earth Provision Co. **12**
Whole Foods **10**
Wheatsville Food Co-Op **1**
Wiggy's **6**
Wild About Music **18**
Women & Their Work Gallery **3**

SoCo Shopping

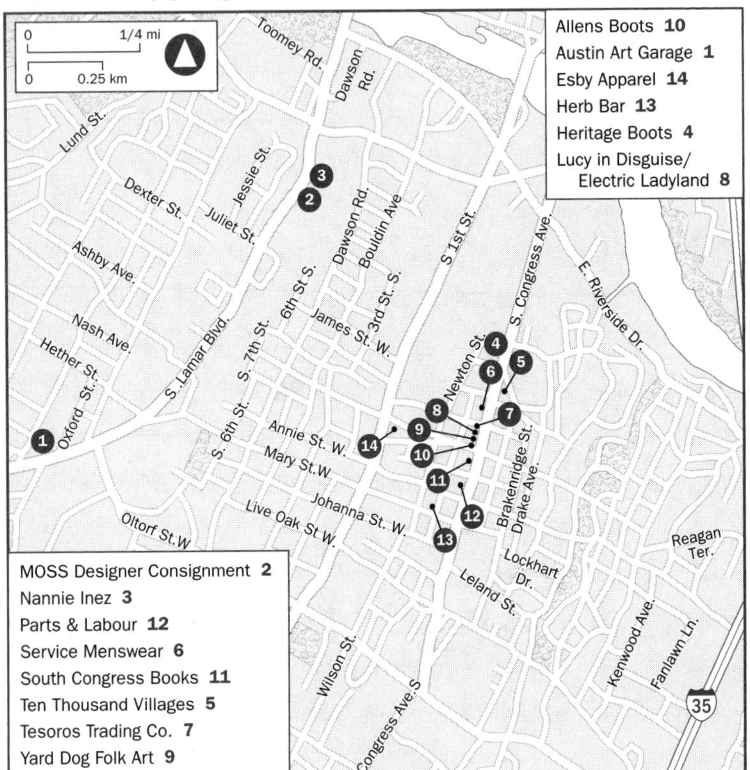

The Arboretum ★★ The first of the northwest's upscale shopping complexes, the Arboretum lives up to its name with a leafy, park-like setting and a tongue-in-cheek sculpture of cows. Anchored by the Renaissance Hotel (p. 192), this two-level collection of outdoor boutiques doesn't include any department stores, but it does have a Barnes & Noble Superstore and a huge Pottery Barn. You'll find your basic selection of mid-range shops—Chico's, Gap, Lenscrafters, Z Galerie—along with local businesses. Dining options include some chains and some local tastes, among them Estancia, a Brazilian steakhouse, and an outlet for the home grown Amy's ice cream (p. 206). Compared to some outdoor mega-malls, this is a fairly small and pleasant place to spend an afternoon. The nearby **Arboretum Market** extends the retail experience with Trader Joe's and Williams-Sonoma, among other shops. 10000 Research Blvd. (Hwy. 183 and Loop 360). www.thearboretum.com. ✆ **512/338-4755.**

Barton Creek Square ★ Set on a bluff with a view of downtown, Barton Creek has a wide-ranging collection of more than 180 shops, anchored by Nordstrom, Dillard's, Macy's, Sears, and JCPenney. One of the earliest of

Austin's high-end malls, it's kept up with the times, but it had more distinctive character before it was taken over by mall overlord Simon Property Group. It's probably the kid-friendliest mall in town, with its 14-plex movie theater, Disney Jr. Play Zone, and lots of casual dining options. One of the city's few enclosed malls, it's a comfortable place to shop when it's hot outdoors. 2901 S. Capital of Texas Hwy. www.simon.com/mall/barton-creek-square. ✆ **512/327-7040.**

The Domain ★★ Anchored by Macy's and Neiman Marcus, this mall hosts such high-end brands as Tiffany and Louis Vuitton, along with chain stores like Dick's Sporting Goods. Restaurants range from the pricey Flemings steakhouse to fast casual chains like Shake Shack, along with some local places. Add yoga and Pilates studios, an IPic movie complex, and a shuttle to move you around, and you've got a lifestyle center more than a shopping complex. Don't want to leave? There are also two hotels here, a large Westin and the boutique Lone Star Court (p. 194). 11410 Century Oaks Terrace (off MoPac, between Braker Lane and Burnet Rd.). www.simon.com/mall/the-domain. ✆ **512/795-4320.**

The Domain NORTHSIDE ★★★ Welcome to the Mall Wars. Though they share a first name and are adjacent to each other, this newer shopping complex is locally owned and under different management than its Simon Property Group counterpart The Domain—thus the capitalized NORTHSIDE and the separate mall map that reads "Our SIDE has it all." This vast retail complex does have a lot of fun local shops in addition to name brand boutiques like Apple and Ray Ban and anchors Nordstrom and Neiman Marcus. Dining here is a mix of local and national fast casual chains; there's also a Whole Foods. The place to bunk is the hip Archer (p. 192). The Warehouse District and SoCo have nothing to worry about, but lots of techies are likely to party at the bars and clubs of this complex's **Rock Rose** entertainment district rather than driving downtown. Add the assets of the other mall that shall not be named, and you've got a pretty nifty mini-city—which is, of course, the goal of both. 11700 Domain Blvd, off MoPac. www.domainnorthside.com. ✆ **512/758-7937.**

Gateway Shopping Centers ★ Comprising three not-so-distinct shopping areas, the Gateway Courtyard, the Gateway Market, and Gateway Square, this large, open complex includes mainly national chains such as Crate & Barrel, REI, Old Navy, and Nordstrom Rack; there's also a branch of Whole Foods. A 16-plex cinema provides entertainment, but there are only a couple of dining options. This is a good bet for shoppers who are not looking to break the bank; other malls in the area—including the Arboretum, just across Hwy 183—are glitzier. 9607 Research Blvd. at Hwy. 183 and Capital of Texas Hwy. www.gatewayshoppingcenters.com. ✆ **512/338-4755.**

Markets

FLEA

Austin Country Flea Market ★ Every Saturday and Sunday year-round, more than 300 covered spaces are filled with merchants selling all the usual flea market goods and then some—new and used clothing, fresh herbs and produce, electronics, antiques. This is the largest flea market in central Texas, covering more than 130 paved acres. There's live music every weekend—generally a spirited Latino band—to step up the shopping pace. 9500 Hwy. 290 E. (4 miles E. of I-35). www.austincountry.citymax.com. ✆ **512/928-2795** or 928-4711.

23rd St. Artists' Market/Renaissance Market ★ Flash back or be introduced to tie-dye and other hippie wares at this crafts market near the UT campus, where vendors are licensed by the City of Austin (read: no commercial schlock). Started in the early 1970s and billed as the only continuously operated open-air crafts market in the United States, it's theoretically open daily 8am to 10pm, but most merchants turn up only on Saturday and Sunday. You'll find everything from silver jewelry and hand-carved flutes to batik T-shirts. Many of the artisans come in from small towns in the nearby Hill Country. W. 23rd St. and Guadalupe St. (the Drag). www.23rdstreetartistsmarket.com. ✆ **512/974-4000.**

AUSTIN'S UPSCALE grocers

If you're visiting Austin for the first time at the end of the 2010s, it's easy to forget that the national grocery-as-theater trend got its start in Austin with the opening of **Whole Foods** in 1980. **Central Market,** founded in 1994, two years after Whole Foods went public, upped its competitor's game by featuring chef programs and cooking classes. The trends they pioneered are now common around the country: to have organics and other health foods readily available at stores that don't smell like patchouli; to offer vast sections of prepared foods; to feature cafes and other sit-down sections; and to host a variety of culinary events.

Austinites love to dispute whether they prefer **Whole Foods,** headquartered in Austin, or **Central Market,** now the elite brand of H-E-B, headquartered in San Antonio. Both have hometown cred and comparable offerings. Some argue Central Market has better prices (true); others say Whole Foods has a better organics selection (also true, especially at its flagship store). Mostly, though, it's a question of personal taste.

Central Market has two branches in the city, the original just north of UT, 4001 N. Lamar Blvd. (www.centralmarket.com. ✆ **512/206-1000**), and a newer one at Westgate Shopping Center in South Austin, 4477 S. Lamar Blvd. (✆ **512/899-4300**). Both are equally impressive. A monthly newsletter announces what's fresh in the produce department, which jazz musicians are entertaining on the weekend, and which gourmet chef is holding forth at the market's cooking school.

Austin hosts six Whole Foods stores, including branches at Gateway Market (see above) and the Domain NORTHSIDE (see above), but the really wow-worthy one is the 80,000-square-foot flagship near the original downtown location (and corporate headquarters), at 525 N. Lamar Blvd. (www.wholefoods.com; ✆ **512/476-1206**). With its 600-seat amphitheater, wine bar, taco bar, makeup center, rooftop skating rink (winter only), gardens, on-site massages, and more, it's among the city's most popular tourist attractions.

FOOD

In addition to Whole Foods and Central Market (see box above), Austin has several co-ops and farmers markets. A standout is counter-cultural **Wheatsville Food Co-op,** 3101 Guadalupe St. (✆ **512/478-2667**), which has excellent service and makes maximum use of its limited floor space, including a good selection of beer and wine and a deli.

Perhaps the most notable farmers market is the **SFC (Sustainable Food Center) Farmers' Market Downtown,** held at Republic Square Park, 422 Guadalupe St. (www.sustainablefoodcenter.org/programs/sfc-farmers-market; ✆ **512/236-0074**), every Saturday from 9am to 1pm March through November. It not only features fresh produce and prepared food, but also offers live music, cooking demonstrations, kids' activities, and workshops on everything from organic gardening to aromatherapy. A similar array of activities, plus a lakeside setting, graces the local favorite **Texas Farmers' Market at Mueller,** 4209 Airport Blvd. (www.texasfarmersmarket.org/mueller; ✆ **512/953-7959**), held every Sunday from 10am to 2pm and Wednesday from 5 to 8pm.

SHOPPING A TO Z

Antiques/Vintage Furnishings

In addition to the antiques markets listed below, a number of smaller shops line Burnet Road north of 45th Street.

Austin Antique Mall ★ You can spend anywhere from five bucks to thousands of dollars in this huge collection of antiques stores. More than 100 dealers occupy a 30,000-square-foot indoor space, offering Roseville pottery, Fiesta dishes, Victorian furniture, costume jewelry, and much, much more. 8822 McCann Dr. www.austinantiquemall.com. ✆ **512/459-5900.**

Room Service ★★ This is one of those fun stores where you're never quite sure what you'll find. The focus is on home furnishings from the 1950s, '60s, and '70s, but you'll also find clothing, funky jewelry, and assorted other artifacts. It's always worth a few chuckles; a couple of neighboring stores in this North Loop strip have similar wares. 107 E. North Loop Blvd. www.roomservicevintage.com. ✆ **512/451-1057.**

Uncommon Objects ★★ Carrying some of the quirkiest and weirdly wonderful items in townfrom clothed taxidermied animals to serious early Americana—this store brings together 24 dealers with the same strange sensibility. 1602 Fortview Rd. www.uncommonobjects.com. ✆ **520/442-4000.**

Whit Hanks Antiques ★ Seven high-end dealers gather at tony Whit Hanks, just across the street from the historic Treaty Oak. This is Austin's premier outlet for fine antiques. Even if you can't afford to buy anything, it's fun to ogle items from fine crystal and vases to Chinese cabinets and neoclassical columns. 1009 W. Sixth St. www.whithanksantiques.com.

Art Galleries

Austin Art Garage ★ Showcasing emerging and established Austin artists working in a variety of styles, this non-intimidating gallery is a great place for newbies and established collectors alike. 2200 S. Lamar Blvd., Ste. J. www.austinartgarage.com. ✆ **512/351-5934.**

Canopy Austin ★★ A converted East Austin warehouse hosts three galleries, a cafe, and 45 working artists' studios. This is a good snapshot of creative endeavors in this hipster neighborhood. 916 Springdale Rd. www.canopyaustin.com ✆ **512/939-6665.**

Women & Their Work Gallery ★★ Founded in 1978, this nonprofit gallery is devoted to more than visual art; it also promotes and showcases women in dance, music, theater, film, and literature. Regularly changing exhibits have little in common except innovation. The gift shop has a great selection of unusual crafts and jewelry by female artists. 1710 Lavaca St. www.womenandtheirwork.org. ✆ **512/477-1064.**

Yard Dog Folk Art ★★ Pop art, folk art, fine art, art by Austin musicians—what started out as a gallery to highlight Southern "Outsider" art slowly expanded its holdings so that now the work is wonderfully eclectic. If there's a dominating tendency, it's that the artists tend to use a lot of color and don't take themselves overly seriously. 1510 S. Congress Ave. www.yarddog.com. ✆ **512/912-1613.**

Bookstores

As might be expected, there are several bookstores in the University of Texas area. The **University Co-Op,** 2246 Guadalupe St. (www.universitycoop.com; ✆ **512/476-7211**), opened in 1896, has many volumes of general interest, along with the requisite burnt-orange-and-white Longhorn T-shirts, mugs, and other UT souvenirs.

For a good selection of used and remaindered books, check out **Half-Price Books** at 5555 N. Lamar Blvd. (www.hpb.com/005; ✆ **512/451-4463;** five other locations). You'll also find a large selection of vinyl as well as DVDs in this link of the family-run chain founded in Dallas.

BookPeople ★★★ One of the largest and best independent bookstores you're likely to find these days, BookPeople expanded in the mid-1990s from its New Age roots, but remains stubbornly quirky and independent, stocking more than 250,000 titles ranging over a wide variety of subjects. It also sells technical videos, audiobooks, and gift items, including lots of KEEP AUSTIN WEIRD merch. Intimate sitting areas and an espresso bar prevent this huge store—the largest in Texas—from feeling overwhelming. More than 200 author signings and special events are held here every year. 603 N. Lamar Blvd. www.bookpeople.com. ✆ **512/472-5050.**

BookWoman ★★ Offering the largest selection of books by and about women in Texas, this store is also one of the best feminist resource centers, the place to find out about women's organizations and events statewide. Readings and discussion groups are regularly held here, and BookWoman carries a great selection of T-shirts, cards, posters, and music. 5501 N. Lamar Blvd. www.ebookwoman.com. ✆ **512/472-2785.**

South Congress Books ★★ When Sheri Tornatore, creator of a thriving online book business, opened a brick-and-mortar store in South Austin, it was a fast success. The well-stocked shop, focusing on rare and used volumes, caters to serious bibliophiles as well as those just looking for a good book to curl up with at night. 1608 S. Congress Ave. www.southcongressbooks.com. ✆ **512/916-8882.**

Fashion

For children's clothing, see **Terra Toys,** p. 266.

MEN'S

See also **Esby Apparel,** p. 262.

Capra & Cavelli ★★ Image-conscious men come to this West End store for hip and classic fashions—both high-end rack labels and, increasingly, custom-made threads. The sales staff is extremely knowledgeable and helpful. There's another store downtown at East Fifth Street and Red River, in the Hilton Hotel; it doesn't do bespoke tailoring but carries women's clothing as well as men's. 3500 Jefferson St., Ste. 110. www.capracavelli.com. ✆ **512/450-1919.**

Service Menswear ★★ Originated in Brooklyn by founder Kirk Haines and distributed to men's fashion retailers around the country, Service clothing is sold with other chic brands in a SoCo store devoted to customer service. Casual styles and materials are hallmarks, including lots of denim pre-washed to ensure a proper fit. 1400 S. Congress Ave., Ste. A160. www.servicemenswear.com. ✆ **512-447-7600.**

VINTAGE

Maybe it's the bent toward recycling, but vintage wear shops have cropped up all over Austin, especially in the North Loop area. A group of businesses devoted to reclaiming—and reselling—the past have compiled **Vintage Guide Around Town** (www.vintagearoundtownguide.com), which includes details of participating stores as well as a map pinpointing their locations.

Lucy in Disguise/Electric Ladyland ★★ Feather boas, tutus, flapper dresses, angel wings, and the occasional gorilla suit overflow the narrow aisles of Austin's best-known costume and vintage clothing outlet. You'll find floral-print dresses and bold-striped shirts, lots of costume jewelry, outrageous Western belt buckles, and the most bodacious selection of sunglasses you've ever seen. 1506 S. Congress Ave. www.lucyindisguise.com. ✆ **512/444-2002.**

WOMEN'S

See also **Capra & Cavelli,** p. 261.

Esby Apparel ★ Careful attention to fabrics (washed and unwashed) and to style and cut make the casual clothing designed and crafted at Esby popular in chic boutiques around the country. Although women are the main audience, the store also caters to men with "a menswear mentality." 1601 S. First St. www.esbyapparel.com. ✆ **512/243-8901.**

MOSS Designer Consignment ★★ Wealthy Austinites looking to make some extra dosh by clearing out their closets find common ground with their cash-strapped counterparts at this south Austin shop, which carries designer labels like Gucci, Stella McCartney, Chanel—even such shoe gods as Jimmy Choo and Christian Louboutin. Sister store **Garment ★**, three doors down at 701 S. Lamar Blvd. (www.shopgarment.com; ✆ **512/462-4667),** buys and sells vintage clothing of a wider range, as well as new designs. 705 S. Lamar Blvd. www.mossaustin.com. ✆ **512/916-9961.**

Csilla Somogyi ★★ Women who dare to wear bright, boldly patterned clothes gravitate to this cheerful downtown shop, where owner/designer Csilla Somogyi and her staff create all the dresses and tops, and alter them to each customer's shape. Accessories by local artists are sold here too. 504 Congress Ave. www.csillawear.com. ✆ **512/499-0039.**

Folk Art & Crafts

El Interior ★ Nestled in a small cluster of restaurants in Clarksville, this intimate and fun import shop gathers merchandise from Mexico and Guatemala, as well as from the Navajo and Pueblo Indians of the American Southwest. Several kinds of crafts are for sale, but the emphasis is on textiles and clothing. 1009 W. Lynn St. www.elinterior.com. ✆ **512/474-8680.**

Hill Country Weavers ★★★ The de facto center of the local fabric arts community, this store has the largest selection of yarns in Texas, many of them made by independent artisans. The store also sells basket-making and felting supplies, dyes, spinning wheels, and more. It offers a variety of classes, as well as a kids' summer camp that takes a new generation far beyond lanyards and potholders. 4102 Manchaca Rd. www.hillcountryweavers.com. ✆ **512/707-7396** or 512/707-7397.

Ten Thousand Villages ★ The local retail outlet for a national nonprofit dedicated to fair trade for folk artists, crafters, and small farmers from developing nations, this store sells all kinds of merchandise: jewelry, toys, decorative objects, coffee, chocolate, and more. 1317 S. Congress Ave. www.tenthousandvillages.com/austin. ✆ **512/440-0440.**

Tesoros Trading Co. ★★★ A dazzling variety of objects both large and small from around the world are offered here: bronze figurines from

Indonesia, *milagro* charms from Mexico, wood cuts from Brazil, talismans from Turkey, and more. It's easy to walk in, intending to spend 15 minutes, and get sucked in for a couple of hours. 1500 S. Congress Ave. www.tesoros.com. ✆ **512/447-7500.**

Food

See Markets, p. 257.

Gifts/Souvenirs

Texas Capitol Gift Shop ★★★ Souvenirs ranging from silly (mugs with batwing handles) to serious, such as reproductions of historic maps, have one thing in common: They celebrate all things Texas. Some items are related to the Capitol itself, such as reproductions of the Texas seal, doorknobs, and bookends. There are also a variety of educational toys and an excellent selection of books. In addition to the one in the Capitol Visitors Center, there's a shop in the Capitol Extension at 1400 N. Congress Ave. (✆ **512/475-2167**). 112 E. 11th St. (SE corner of capitol grounds). www.texascapitolgiftshop.com. ✆ **512/385-8408.**

Parts & Labour ★★ This is the place to come for quirky Austin-centric souvenirs: a tea towel that says "queso" on it, say, or a print of Willie Nelson as a popsicle (I said quirky, didn't I?). Greeting cards, crafts, and clothing sold here tend towards the tongue-in-cheek too. 1704 S. Congress Ave. www.partsandlabourstore.com. ✆ **512/326-1648.**

Wild About Music ★★★ Austin's obsession with music is indulged at this popular souvenir shop, where all the merchandise is music-themed. Much of it is kitschy (a KISS beach towel, for example, or glow-in-the-dark drumsticks), but not many items are expensive, and you may get a good laugh out of how your favorite musicians are represented. 615 Congress Ave. www.wildaboutmusic.com. ✆ **512/708-1700.**

Health and Beauty

See also **Nannie Inez,** p. 264.

Herb Bar ★ Opened on a quiet street off South Congress Avenue before the area became trendy, this shop devoted to natural health and healing offers teas, tinctures, flower essences, and more, along with herbs. It's the place to find a gift for your favorite hippie friend—perhaps a ceramic teapot or singing bowl. 200 W. Mary St. www.theherbbar.com. ✆ **512/444-6251.**

Sabia Apothecary ★★ All those soothing oils and lotions in their pretty bottles on the shelves seem to whisper, "Buy me, I'll make you feel better." Anti-aging products promise that you'll look better too, and you can get help from the on-site salon, which offers facials, waxing, makeup, and hair services. 1213 W. Fifth St., Ste. B1. www.sabia.com. ✆ **512/469-0447.**

Home Decor

Breed & Co. Hardware ★★ You don't have to be a power-drill freak to love Breed & Co. This darling of Austin DIYers has everything from nails to tropical plants, organic fertilizer, gardening books and cookbooks, pâté molds, and cherry pitters. Breed & Co. became part of Ace Hardware in 2015, but is still a family-owned franchise. Three more branches in the Austin area include one in the prosperous Westlake Hills area, 3663 Bee Cave Rd. (✆ **512/328-3960**). 718 W. 29th St. www.breedandco.com. ✆ **512/474-6679.**

Eco-Wise ★★ It's hard to typecast a shop that sells everything from greeting cards, natural insect repellent, and hand-woven purses to building materials and home decorating supplies. The common denominator? Everything here is created with an eye toward the environment—recycled, made from natural fabrics, and/or chemical free. Staff is knowledgeable and helpful, and customers are passionately loyal. 209 E. Ben White Blvd., Ste. 103. www.ecowise.com. ✆ **512/326-4474.**

Nannie Inez ★ The latest furniture designs from around the world are represented at this South Austin boutique, which also carries votive candles and book ends. Jewelry and beauty and skincare products are sold here too. Hey, if your home is going to look good, you'll want to look good in it. 701 S. Lamar Blvd. www.nannieinez.com. ✆ **512/428-6639.**

Take Heart ★★ This is the place to come for items that you won't see in other people's homes—everything from delicate wind chimes to handcrafted dolls to incense holders (and a wide selection of incense to burn in them). Many of the designers represented here come from Japan, which tells you a lot about the aesthetic of this lovely east side shop. 1211 E. 11th St., Ste. 100. www.takeheartshop.com. ✆ **512/366-5667.**

Jewelry

See also **Tesoros,** p. 262.

Fail Jewelry ★★ In her East Austin studio, Christine Fail creates jewelry classics for men and women. Some pieces are intended for everyday wear, others for special occasions, including weddings. Deceptively simple and clean lined, the pieces tend to look more expensive than they're likely to be. 2612 E. Cesar Chavez St., Ste. 100. www.failjewelry.com. ✆ **512/666-5446.**

Sikara & Co. ★★ The jewelry by shop owner Mousimi Shaw is inspired by different international locations—including India, the country of her heritage—but it's not "ethnic" in the usual sense of the word. While the pieces often incorporate colorful stones and intricate designs, they're elegant rather than chunky. 417 W. Second St. www.sikara.com. ✆ **512/476-1298.**

Russell Korman ★ You'd never know it from his current posh digs, but Russell Korman got his start in Austin's jewelry trade by selling trader beads on the Drag. Although he's moved on to 14-karat gold, platinum, and diamond pieces, along with fine watches—there's an experienced watchmaker on premises—prices are competitive, even for the most formal baubles, and service is excellent. 5011 Burnet Rd., Ste. 100. www.russellkormanjewelry.com. ✆ **512/451-9292.**

Music

See also **Wild About Music,** p. 263.

Antone's Record Shop ★★ As might be expected from a record shop affiliated with Austin's famous blues club (p. 278), this shop's strength is blues and Texas artists. But you'll find plenty of other sounds, including reggae, doo wop, and gospel, as well as poetry and comedy, in a variety of formats—CDs, DVDs, and even cassettes, along with vinyl. 2928 Guadalupe St. www.antonesrecordshop.com. ✆ **512/322-0660.**

End of an Ear ★★ This place focuses on vinyl from all eras and genres, and a knowledgeable staff knows the stock inside out; describe the type of music you're interested in and odds are good you'll walk out with something you never heard of but instantly loved. Prices are reasonable, bands play in the corner of the store, and a back room carries music gear and stereos. 4304 Clawson Rd. www.endofanear.com. ✆ **512/462-6008.**

Waterloo Records and Video ★★★ Austin's best known music store, with good reason, this 6,400-square-foot emporium carries a huge selection of sounds. This is the place to come for new releases and old; if the store doesn't have something on hand, they'll order it for you, stat. Waterloo has a popular preview listening section, a vinyl section, a generous return policy, offers compilation tapes of Austin groups, and sells tickets to all major-label shows around town. It also hosts frequent CD-release performances by local bands. 600A N. Lamar Blvd. www.waterloorecords.com. ✆ **512/474-2500.**

Outdoor Gear

Austin has two branches of sporting goods chain **REI,** one downtown at 601 N. Lamar Blvd. (www.rei.com/stores/austin-downtown.html; ✆ **512/482-3357**), and one in the Gateway complex, 9901 N. Capital of Texas Hwy., Ste. 200 (www.rei.com/stores/austin-gateway.html; ✆ **512/343-5550**), both offering classes, outings, and events, in addition to gear. Half an hour away in Buda (p. 291), you'll find **Cabela's,** 15570 I-35 (www.cabelas.com; ✆ **512/295-1100**), a cavernous store with an indoor waterfall, large aquarium, and diorama of the African savanna. It's a major destination for local hunters, fishermen, campers, and kayakers.

See also p. 250 for the Lance Armstrong-owned **Mellow Johnny's Bike Shop.**

The Whole Earth Provision Co. ★★ Its original flagship store near the UT campus may have closed in 2016—space and parking limitations were part of the problem—but Austin's large population of outdoor enthusiasts still have two convenient spots in town to go to get outfitted in the latest gear and earth-friendly fashions. If you wouldn't think of hiking without a two-way radio or a Magellan positioning navigator, you can find them here. The Austin-based chain also carries gifts, housewares, educational toys, and travel books. 1014 N. Lamar Blvd. www.wholeearthprovision.com. ✆ **512/476-1414.** Also 4477 S. Lamar Blvd. (in Westgate Shopping Ctr.). ✆ **512/899-0992.**

Toys

Lions & Tigers & Toys ★★ It's a toss-up whether it'll be harder for you or any child you bring to leave this store; you're likely to find lots of toys and games that you grew up with, along with a great variety of the latest games and books, both mainstream and one of a kind. 4301 W. William Cannon Dr., Ste. E220. www.toystoreaustintx.com. ✆ **512/892-7627.**

Terra Toys ★★ It's hard to imagine any plaything you couldn't find here. The owner has brought together a vast array of beautiful and imaginative toys from around the world, including miniatures, train sets, games, and collectibles, along with a large selection of children's books. There's a separate department for children's clothing, and an affiliated art gallery/espresso bar next door. 2438 W. Anderson Lane. www.terratoys.com. ✆ **512/445-4498.**

Toy Joy ★★★ Not just for kids, this store carries a lot of toys and gadgets that are popular with a wide range of ages, from Fisher-Price, Disney, and Nintendo to such lesser-known brands as the Japanese Gunpla (a club for people who like to make Gunpla plastic models meets here). A partnership with Wild About Music (p. 263) enlarged the shop's inventory. A second location opened in Hyde Park, 4631 Airport Blvd. (✆ **512/904-0209**), in late 2017. 403 W. Second St. www.toyjoy.com. ✆ **512/320-0090.**

Western Wear

Allens Boots ★★★ Name notwithstanding, Allens sells a lot more than just boots, though heaven knows you'll have a hard enough time deciding on the footwear, given the number of colors and styles available. Come here too for Western hats, belts, and jewelry, and bring the young 'uns. This SoCo store has been around since 1977, well before the area got trendy. The newer, more spacious branch in Round Rock, 1051 I-35 Frontage Rd (✆ **512/310-7600**), has a larger selection of boot-scootin' accoutrements. 1522 S. Congress St. www.allensboots.com. ✆ **512/447-1413.**

Heritage Boots ★★ Handcrafted in León, Mexico—known for its long tradition of bootmaking—using only high-quality materials, the boots sold here are inspired by classic styles from the 1930s to 1960s. Prices start around $450 for the basics and vary in price depending on the amount of decorative stitching and detailed inlays you choose, or the exotic leather you opt for (think ostrich or shark). You can only buy these boots in the SoCo shop, where you will be carefully fitted, or online after consultation with the shop's resident "boot mavens." 1200 S. Congress St. www.heritageboot.com. ✆ **512/326-8577.**

Wine, Beer & Spirits

See also **Central Market** and **Whole Foods Market,** p. 258.

The Austin Wine Merchant ★★ The ultimate wine nerd destination, this downtown spot has held its own on a block that's seen a lot of turnover. The owner's devoted to hand-selecting bottles that give you a feel for the time and place where they were created. A small selection of spirits, regular tastings, and a super knowledgeable but friendly staff are other reasons this shop has stayed in business since 1991. 512 W. Sixth St. www.theaustinwinemerchant.com. ✆ **512/499-0512.**

Travis Heights Beverage World ★★ Featuring a terrific selection of wines and spirits of all varieties, including very esoteric ones, this shop off the freeway is known for its to-your-door (including hotel rooms) delivery service. It also hosts weekly wine and spirit tastings. Beverage World is an outgrowth of next door's **Whip In Wine and Beer,** 1950 I-35 S. (www.whipin.com; ✆ **512/442-5337**), once a convenience store known for its vast beer selection and now a gastropub that still sells beer and wine. 1948 I-35 S., Woodland Ave. exit on southbound service road. www.travisheightsbevworld.com. ✆ **512/440-7778.**

Wiggy's ★★ If liquor and tobacco are among your vices, Wiggy's can help you indulge in high style. In addition to its extensive selection of wines (more than 1,500 in stock) and single-malt scotches, this friendly West End store also carries a huge array of imported smokes, held in two walk-in humidors. Prices are reasonable, and the staff is very helpful. A second location at 1104 N. Lamar Blvd. (✆ **512/479-0045**) is smaller and doesn't have the same selection as the main store. 1130 W. Sixth St. www.wiggysliquor.com ✆ **512/474-9463.**

16 AUSTIN ARTS & NIGHTLIFE

Entertainment in Austin starts and ends with live music. You might get your first taste of it before you even pick up your bags at the airport, where eleven concerts serenade travelers each week. The scene is wonderfully fluid, mixing styles and genres. Musicians as different as Willie Nelson and Janis Joplin got their start in Austin, and today thousands of diverse bands and performers call the city home—though many are struggling to pay the rent.

Entertainment in Austin may start with live music, but it isn't the be-all and end-all of after-dark activities in town. For information about what's happening in the other performing arts, check out **Now Playing in Austin** (www.nowplayingaustin.com), a joint project of the Austin Creative Alliance and the city. Its comprehensive, well-organized calendar of events includes not only the symphony and theater, but also museum shows, poetry readings, film screenings, and more. It links to the sites themselves, so you can buy tickets directly from the venues.

In the midst of all the music and indie madness, you might forget that you're in Texas, where sports are taken very, very seriously. Information about where and when to root for the home team (that would be the UT Longhorns) is detailed here too.

For the best information about everything that's happening in town, check the events listings of the ***Austin Chronicle*** (www.austinchronicle.com) and the ***Austin American-Statesman*** (www.Austin360.com).

THE PERFORMING ARTS

Major Venues

The **Long Center for the Performing Arts** (www.thelongcenter.org; ✆ **512/457-5500**) is Austin's premier venue for the city's symphony, orchestra, opera, and ballet ensembles (80 percent of performances are local), and for visiting artists as well. The facility, set on the south shore of Lady Bird Lake, was designed to take advantage of its location, with a raised terrace framed by a circular colonnade looking out over the lake to the downtown skyline. The grand

THE LIMITLESS AUSTIN city limits

PBS's longest-running television program (it first aired in 1975), ***Austin City Limits*** has showcased such major talent as Lyle Lovett, Willie Nelson, Garth Brooks, the Dixie Chicks, and Phish. Originally pure country, it has evolved to embrace blues, zydeco, Cajun, Tejano—you name it. The show is taped live from August through December, and sometimes through February, at the state-of-the-art **Moody Theater,** 310 Willie Nelson Blvd./Second St. (✆ **512/225-7999**). Getting free tickets for the tapings is hit-and-miss. About a week before the show, KLRU producers set up an online form. Capacity is tight; passes are space-available only and don't guarantee admission. Log on to **www.acltv.com** for details on how to get tickets and for a more in-depth look at how the tapings work.

The Moody Theater is also a live music venue with a 2750-seat capacity; it showcases some 100 touring acts a year. Tickets for performances and for tours of the facility (tours run Mon–Fri 11am–noon) can be purchased in person at the ACL Live Box Office (✆ **877/435-9849**) or at the Austin Visitor Center (602 E. Fourth St.). To see what's playing when you're in town, click on **www.acl-live.com**. ***Note:*** You can't miss the theater. It's fronted by a life-size bronze **statue of Willie Nelson** sitting contempletively, smiling gently, guitar resting on his leg.

The **Austin City Limits Music Festival (www.aclfestival.com)** is an annual outdoor celebration held on consecutive 3-day weekends in early October, with multiple stages and many, many performers representing a mix of established artists and up-and-coming talent; check the website for details. This live music extravaganza debuted in September 2002 and its popularity keeps ballooning. Now, approximately 450,000 people attend the festival each year, with acts arriving early to make surprise appearances in clubs around town. In addition to music, there are seemingly countless food and drink vendors, a kids' area for families, large-scale art installations, and much more.

concert hall, named after Michael and Susan Dell, seats 2,400 people and is grand indeed. It's a modern version of the classic concert hall, using vertical space to accommodate seating. The acoustics are excellent here, as they are at the 229-seat Debra and Kevin Rollins studio theater, which hosts smaller performances. The HEB Terrace can accommodate some 2,000 people in its outdoor arena.

The University of Texas has five theaters—**Bass Concert Hall, McCullough Theatre, Payne Theatre, Brockett Theatre,** and the **Bates Recital Hall**—all of which are managed by Texas Performing Arts (www.texasperformingarts.org; ✆ **512/471-2787**). They attract major visiting shows, including Broadway musicals, pop singers, and classical music ensembles. Of the five theaters, the largest is Bass Concert Hall, which accommodates 2,900 people. ***Fun fact:*** Bass Hall boasts not only state-of-the-art acoustics but also the largest tracker organ in the United States. Linking contemporary computer technology with an 18th-century Dutch design, the Visser-Rowland organ has 5,315 pipes—some of them 16 feet tall—and weighs 24 tons. The university's **Harry**

Ransom Center (p. 229) features poetry readings and lectures by big literary names.

Also run by UT and often dedicated to sports (it's the home court for the Longhorns men's and women's basketball teams), the off-campus **Frank Erwin Center,** 1701 Red River (www.uterwincenter.com; ✆ **512/471-7744**) has hosted arena-worthy names from Prince to Radiohead and Paul McCartney. (In late 2018, plans were announced to replace the Erwin Center with an even bigger arena, to debut in 2021; UT alum actor Matthew McConaghey is among the investors behind it.) Also at UT but a bit of a drive from town, the open-air **Austin 360 Amphitheater** (www.austin360amphitheater.com), at the Circuit of the Americas racetrack in Del Valle, draws big crowds for its national acts.

Other venues are spread out across the city, including many small local theaters.

Opera & Classical Music

Austin Chamber Music Center ★ A local organization that includes members of the symphony orchestra and the university music school, the Austin Chamber Music Center performs a wide range of compositions in small ensembles, usually quartets. Venues include everything from churches, nursing homes, and public schools to private residences; performances might include works by anyone from Beethoven to Marvin Hamlisch. A black composers series called the African Diaspora debuted in the early 2000s. 7600 Burnet Rd. www.austinchambermusic.org. ✆ **512/454-0026.** Tickets $26–$80.

Austin Opera ★★ This professional opera company, founded in 1986 as the Austin Lyric Opera, draws international artists to performances ranging from the classical (Puccini's "La Boheme") to the modern ("La Curandera" by Robert Xavier Rodriguez). The company presents three productions a year at the Dell Hall of the Long Performing Arts Center. 3009 Industrial Terrace, Ste. 100. www.austinopera.org. ✆ **512/472-5992.** Tickets $25–$119 (boxes up to $260).

Austin Symphony ★★★ From September to May, the symphony orchestra performs a range of classic and modern works. A fall/winter Pops series features accessible classics as well as Broadway show tunes and light opera. Most performances are held at the Long Center, but a few of the Pops concerts are held at the **Palmer Events Center,** 900 Barton Springs Rd. (www.palmereventscenter.com; ✆ **512/404-4500**). The orchestra's administration operates out of **Symphony Square,** a complex comprising an outdoor amphitheater and four historic structures from the 1870s. Narrow Waller Creek runs between the seats and the stage of the amphitheater. 1101 Red River St. www.austinsymphony.org. ✆ **888/4-MAESTRO** (623-7876) or 512/476-6064. Tickets $19–$75.

Dance

Ballet Austin ★★★ One of the premier classical ballet companies in the country, Ballet Austin originates work as well as interprets it. The 22-member troupe performs such classics as *The Nutcracker* along with more avant-garde pieces, mostly at the Long Center (it's one of the center's founding resident companies) but also at the more intimate AustinVentures Studio Theater. Ballet Austin also cultivates home-grown talent at its downtown **Ballet Austin Academy.** 501 W. 3rd St. www.balletaustin.org. ✆ **512/476-2163** (box office) or 476-9151.

Theater

Founded in 1932, **Zach Theatre** (www.zachtheatre.org; ✆ **512/476-0541** [box office]) is the longest continuously running theater company in Texas, and one of the oldest in the country. It produces plays—everything from *Hedwig and the Angry Inch* to a family series for children—in three theaters in South Austin. Just off of Lamar Boulevard is the 130-seat (in the round) John E. Whisenhunt Arena at 1510 Toomey Rd.; directly behind it is the 225-seat Kleburg at 1421 W. Riverside Dr. The newest venue (built in 2012) is the 427-seat Topfer Theater, 202 S. Lamar Blvd.

Other theaters in town tend toward the smaller and, in some cases, more offbeat. These include the intimate **Hyde Park Theatre,** 511 W. 43rd St. (www.hydeparktheatre.org; ✆ **512/479-PLAY** [479-7529; box office] or 479-7530), which focuses on Austin writers, actors, and designers. It's the venue for Short Fringe performances at the annual 5-week-long **FronteraFest** (late January through February), the largest fringe theater/performance art festival in the Southwest. At the thriving theater department at St. Edward's University, the **Mary Moody Northen Theatre,** 3001 S. Congress Ave. (www.stedwards.edu/mary-moody-northen-theatre; ✆ **855/468-3768** or 512/448-8400), produces performances at its theater-in-the-round, augmenting student talent with a variety of professional directors and guest actors.

East Austin is a hub of experimental performance and film venues. The most established is the **Vortex,** 2307 Manor Rd. (www.vortexrep.org; ✆ **512/478-LAVA** [5282]), home to the Vortex Repertory Company. You can tell by the titles alone—*The Dark Poet's Binge,* say, or *St. Enid and the Black Hand*—that you're well into the fringe. **The North Door,** 501 Brushy St.

A Venerable Venue

The Marx Brothers, Sarah Bernhardt, Helen Hayes, and Katharine Hepburn all entertained at the **Paramount Theatre,** 713 Congress Ave. (www.austintheatre.org; ✆ **512/472-5470** [box office]), a former vaudeville house, which opened as the Majestic Theatre in 1915 and functioned as a movie palace for 50 years. Now restored to its original glory, the Paramount hosts a diverse roster of nationally touring plays, visiting celebrity performers and lecturers, film festivals and series, and local dance and theatrical productions.

(www.ndvenue.com; ✆ **512/710-9765**), hosts some of the city's edgiest theater performances, from *Sh! t-faced Shakespeare* to burlesque shows. **Salvage Vanguard Theater,** 2803 Manor Rd (www.salvagevanguard.org; ✆ **512/474-7886**), has its own company, which performs mostly contemporary works. Others in the area to look out for are **Off Center,** 2211 Hidalgo St. (www.rudemechs.com; ✆ **512/567-7833**), and the **Blue Theater,** 916 Springdale Rd. (www.bluetheater.org; ✆ **512/927-1118**). The Blue Theater does full-length FronteraFest performances and holds Flicker Fest film screenings.

Free Entertainment

The amount of free entertainment offered in Austin, including several performing arts and concert series, is mind-boggling.

MUSIC

Every Sunday evening from June through August, members of the symphony orchestra play classical and jazz pieces at the **Concerts in the Park** series (www.austinsymphony.org/education/community-concerts), held at 7:30pm at the Hartment Concert Park at the Long Center, 701 W. Riverside Dr. Every other Wednesday night from June through August, **Blues on the Green** is held at Zilker Park Rock Island, 2100 Barton Springs Rd., sponsored by radio station **KGSR** (www.kgsr.com). This series can attract some major bands. Every Thursday in the spring and summer at 7pm, popular local and touring bands play on the large shaded patio of Shady Grove, at Barton Springs Road (p. 209); for details on the **Unplugged at the Grove** series, check www.theshadygrove.com.

More places to hear free sounds while you eat include **Central Market** (www.centralmarket.com/Stores/Austin-Central.aspx) and the **Whole Foods Market** (www.wholefoodsmarket.com), at Fifth Street and Lamar Boulevard. There's often music too at **Fareground** (www.faregroundaustin.com), Austin's first food hall; see p. 203 for details.

On the last weekend of each month from April through September at 5 to 8pm, Charles Smith Wines presents **The Wine Down** at 3TEN Austin City Limits Live (www.3tenaustin.com/the-wine-down). Along with free music, the event includes food, shopping, and of course wine (not free) on downtown's Second Street. Bands always play at **First Thursdays** on South Congress Avenue (p. 254), a similar food- and shopfest.

PERFORMING ARTS

From ballet and Shakespeare to South Asian New Year celebrations, all performances at the city-run **Beverly F. Sheffield Zilker Hillside Theater,** 2206 William Barton Dr. across from Barton Springs Pool (www.austintexas.gov/zilkerhillsidetheater; ✆ **512/974-4000**), are free; check the website for the current schedule of events and for tips about viewing, parking, etc. More than 5,000 people can perch on the theater's grassy knoll to watch performances. If you can, take a blanket or a lawn chair to sit on.

From mid-July through late August, the venue hosts a summer musical mounted by Zilker Theater Productions (www.zilker.org; ✆ **512/479-9491**); started in 1959, this is the longest-running series of its type in the United States.

FILM

Every July and August, in partnership with Do512 and the Alamo Drafthouse, the Long Center holds **Sound & Cinema** (www.thelongcenter.org/event/sound-cinema), an outdoor movie screening paired with live music that complements the film's theme.

THE CLUB & MUSIC SCENE

Music was always important to life in Austin, but it really became a big deal in the early 1970s with the advent of "progressive country" (aka redneck rock). Local boy Willie Nelson became its principal proponent, along with several other Austin musicians. And the **Armadillo World Headquarters,** a music hall known for hosting all the 1960s rock bands, became the center of events and symbolized the marriage of country with counterculture. The city has since become an incubator for a wonderfully vital, crossbred alternative sound that mixes rock, country, folk, blues, punk, and Tejano.

Although the Armadillo is now gone, live music in Austin continues to thrive in bars all across Austin; see box p. 276 for a quick summary. Many popular venues don't fall inside these districts. All in all, there's a lot to explore. Have fun and poke around. You might come across the next Janis Joplin, Stevie Ray Vaughan, or Jimmie Dale Gilmore, to name just a few who were playing local gigs here before they hit the big time. When big events occur, such as SxSW (see box p. 279), the Republic of Texas Biker Rally (June), or the Lonestar Rod & Kustom Roundup (April), barhopping becomes a competitive sport.

The live music scene is inexpensive. Some really good bands play for tips on weekdays and for starving-artist pay at other times. This makes it hard for musicians to survive in this increasingly high-rent town—you get the sense that the city is getting a lot more from this arrangement than it's giving. Austin has made attempts to support its local talent through organizations like the **Health Alliance for Austin Musicians** (HAAM; MyHAAM.org), which provides insurance and runs an annual benefit concert. **Visit Austin** has a music division (www.austintexas.org/music-office) devoted to getting musicians paying gigs at the conventions, luncheons, and other receptions that come through town. Let's hope that it's not too little too late, and that Austin doesn't become a victim of its success in one of the arenas for which it's best known.

Note: Categories of clubs in a city known for crossover are often very rough approximations, so those that completely defy typecasting are dubbed "eclectic." When there is live music, both clubs and bars charge covers ranging from

$5 to $15 for well-liked local bands, more for national acts. That's the same on weekdays and weekends, the determining factor being who's on stage.

Eclectic

Carousel Lounge ★★ In spite of (or maybe because of) its out-of-the-way location and bizarre circus theme—complete with elephant and lion-tamer murals and an actual carousel behind the bar—the Carousel Lounge is a highly popular local watering hole. You never know what will turn up onstage; this place has hosted everything from fringey musical acts to belly dancers. 1110 E. 52nd St. www.carousellounge.net. ✆ **512/452-6790.**

Continental Club ★★★ This Austin institution (opened 1955) showcases rock, rockabilly, country, Latino, and new wave sounds. So many local acts have played here on their way to fame, and so many already famous acts will occasionally return, that it's worth your while to check out this small, dark club on South Congress. With high stools and a pool table in the back room, it feels much more like a neighborhood bar than a major venue—that's the lure of the place. (It's got the best happy hour music in town.) Next door, the club operates a small upstairs gallery featuring lesser known acts, often with no cover. 1315 S. Congress Ave. www.continentalclub.com. ✆ **512/441-2444.**

Emo's ★ Formerly one of Austin's top clubs, in its original Red River location, Emo's—now in a larger space on East Riverside—has been outpaced by other, newer establishments, but it's still a fine place to catch a show, with state-of-the-art sound quality. The music tends to be alternative forms of rock, pop, hip-hop, and anything that seems to be different and original. Emo's attracts a mostly young crowd and many off-duty musicians. 2015 E. Riverside Dr. www.emosaustin.com. ✆ **888/512-7469.**

The Parish ★★ This upstairs club on Sixth Street is known locally as a great place to hear live music in a range of genres—hip-hop, rock, funk, reggae, Latin, and electronic. You never know who'll be booked . . . even stand-ups like Aziz Ansari. 214 E. Sixth St., Ste. C. www.theparishaustin.com.

Saxon Pub ★★ Look for the oversize knight in a suit of armor on South Lamar Boulevard to find this iconic, yet comfortable club for country, rock, and blues performers, big and small. The crowd is older and more laid-back than at many clubs, and the music volume is lower. Check the calendar on the club's website; you'll find performers who rarely play in such a small venue. 1320 S. Lamar Blvd. www.thesaxonpub.com. ✆ **512/448-2552.**

Speakeasy ★★ The walk down a dark alley in the Warehouse District to reach this multilevel club is all part of the 1920s Prohibition theme, which, mercifully, is not taken to an obnoxious extreme. Lots of dark wood and red velvet drapes help create a swanky atmosphere on the ground floor. Walk up two flights of narrow stairs to enjoy a drink or dance on the rooftop Terrace59,

Downtown Austin Nightlife

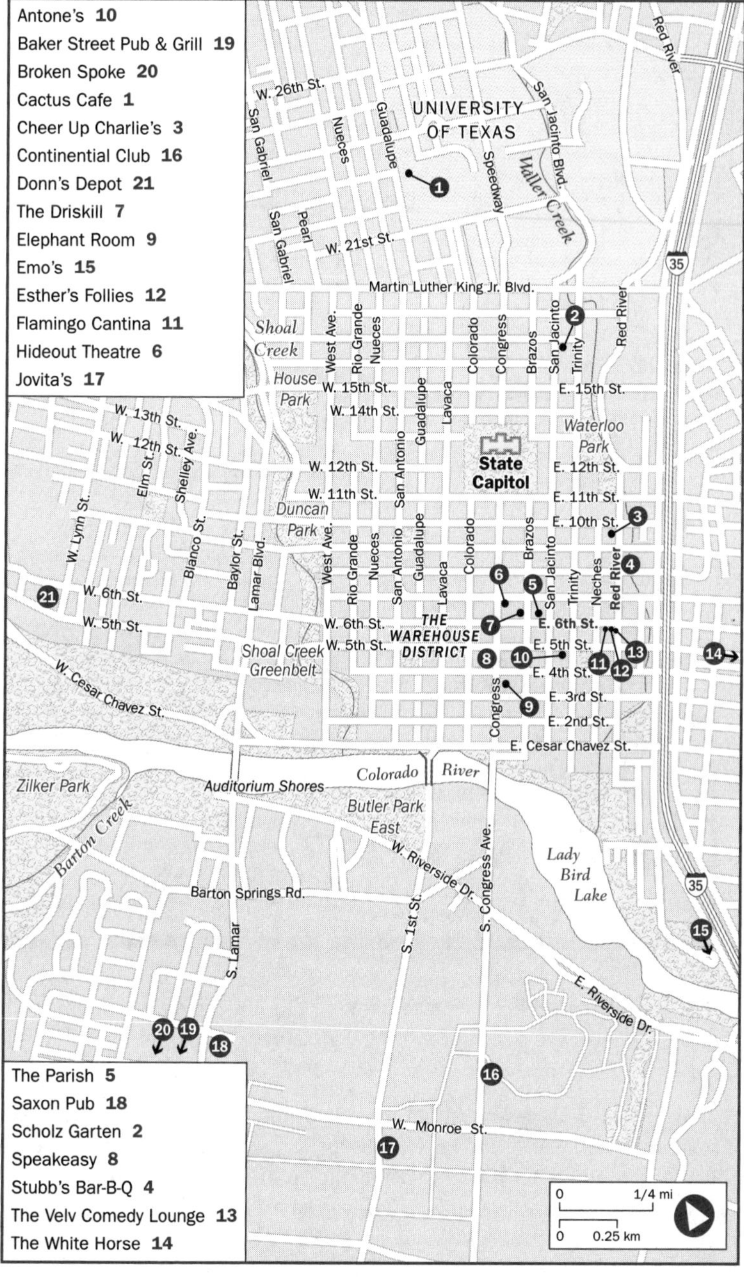

16 A BRIEF GUIDE TO AUSTIN'S bar scene

Austin's downtown bars are, for the most part, concentrated into six different areas: Sixth Street, the Warehouse District, the Market District, Red River, East Austin, and Rainey Street.

When locals talk about **Sixth Street,** they generally mean a 5-block portion of East Sixth from Congress Avenue to Red River; it's often referred to as Dirty Sixth for its blaring music, drunken crowds, and after-dark debauchery. This strip has all kinds of bars—from noisy saloons catering to college students, such as the **Library** (407 E. Sixth St.), to a fun piano bar, **Pete's Dueling Pianos** (421 E. Sixth St.; www.petesduelingpianobar.com), where the crowd is older and the volume of the music much lower. **Easy Tiger** (709 E. Sixth St.; www.easytigerusa.com), a German bakery and beer garden, provides a slight respite from the fray, and **Jackalope** (404 E. Sixth St.; www.jackalopebar.com) is usually the least crowded bar on the main strip.

Red River Street, between Sixth and 10th streets, is for those seeking out the local underground music scene. These less-commercial bars and nightclubs frankly don't look like much, but they're where Austinites and music aficionados, mostly in their 20s and 30s, go to hear local bands and dance the night away. **Empire Control Room & Garage** (606 E. Seventh St.; www.empireatx.com) is a fun, hip watering hole with warehouse-style parties and music events. **Beerland** (711 Red River St.; www.beerlandtexas.com) will usually have something "indie-garagey-punky." Farther down the street, the **Mohawk** (912 Red River St.; www.mohawkaustin.com) might have just about anything, including lounge music; and **Stubb's Bar-B-Q** (see below), a large venue with indoor and outdoor stages, hosts big-name touring acts as well as some of the most popular local bands. When it's time to get sweaty, **Barbarella + Swan Dive** (615 Red River St.) is where the locals like to sway to indie '80s and '90s tunes on an always-packed dance floor.

The **Warehouse District** lies west of Congress Avenue from Third to Seventh streets, and from Congress Avenue to Guadalupe. It's more of a social scene, with less emphasis on live music and fewer college crowds—ideal if you just want to have a drink and perhaps some food in attractive, vibrant surroundings. The best strategy is to stroll around until you see something that fits your mood. Vintage airport-themed **Hangar Lounge** (318 Colorado St.; www.thehangarlounge.com) has one of the best downtown rooftop views and buzzing crowds. On the tony side, the **Roosevelt Room** (307 W. Fifth St.; www.therooseveltroomatx.com) is a mixology mecca with

or bowl a few games in a vintage alley on the mezzanine, overlooking the stage. An impressive roster of A-listers sometimes drops into this club. 412 Congress Ave. www.speakeasyaustin.com. ✆ **512/476-8017.**

Stubb's Bar-B-Q ★★ Within the rough limestone walls of a renovated historic building, you'll find great barbecue and country Texas fare and three friendly bars—plus terrific music, ranging from singer-songwriter solos to hip-hop open mics to all-out country jams. Out back, the Waller Amphitheater hosts some of the bigger acts that come to Austin. The Sunday gospel brunch buffets ($29 with a view of the band, $23 without) are legendary. 801 Red River St. www.stubbsaustin.com. ✆ **512/480-8341.**

ultra-creative craft cocktails. Speaking of craft cocktails, **Garage Cocktail Bar** (503 Colorado St.; www.garagetx.com) is a nondescript gem, tucked away in the parking garage of the American National Bank building. **Cedar Street Courtyard** (208 W 4th St., Ste. C; www.cedarstreetaustin.com) is the perfect spot for a nightcap and live music.

The **Market District** encompasses the western part of downtown, from Guadalupe to Lamar, and Ninth Street to the bustling Seaholm District. There's an array of rooftop clubs and cool bars here, from **The Brew Exchange** (706 W. Sixth St.; www.brewexchangeaustin.com), a beer-heavy joint, to hometown fave **Mean Eyed Cat** (1621 W. Fifth St.; www.themeaneyedcat.com), a recently renovated "dive bar." **Boiler Nine Bar + Grill** (800 W. Cesar Chavez St.; www.boilernine.com) in the Seaholm District has a carefully curated drink selection, but its greatest asset is the stunning panorama of downtown Austin from its Deck Nine Observatory Bar.

Running adjacent to Lady Bird Lake, **Rainey Street** was previously a residential neighborhood, and most bars in its converted bungalows have a similar vibe—think lively crowds of young professionals, posh cocktails, twinkly-lit outdoor patios, and large-screen TVs showing live sports. If that's your scene, you can't go wrong with any of them. The bar at **Hotel Van Zandt** (605 Davis St.; p. 181) adds fancy city views; **Banger's Sausage House & Beer Garden** (79 Rainey St.; www.bangersausage.com) has 101 beers on tap; and **Clive Bar** (609 Davis St.; www.clivebar.com) offers great cocktails and a sizeable patio.

Though technically a mile from downtown, the **East Austin Entertainment District** (or the East Side, as it's known) is well worth a mention. The fastest growing neighborhood in Austin, this eclectic and somewhat gritty area is where the cool kids hang out. Stroll around past colorful graffiti murals, plentiful food trucks, and several hole-in-the-wall bars to find **The Yellow Jacket Social Club** (1704 E. Fifth St.; www.yellowjacketsocialclub.com), a downright cozy (albeit slightly grimy) watering hole that draws a hip crowd; relax poolside at the retro-fabulous **Kitty Cohen's** (2211 Webberville Rd.; www.kittycohens.com) with a tiki cocktail or glass of frozen rosé; enjoy the fancy vintage decor and solid drink selection at **Weather Up** (1808 E. Cesar Chavez St.; www.weatherupnyc.com/austin-1); and be sure to duck into **Whisler's** (1816 E. Sixth St.; www.whislersatx.com) to sip from a hidden mezcal menu.

Folk & Country

See also **Gruene Hall,** p. 299.

Broken Spoke ★★★ One of the great country music dance halls, Broken Spoke dates back to 1964, when people would come out here to two-step across the large wood-plank floor. It hasn't changed much, except for the occasional busload of tourists stopping by. You don't have to be all duded up for dancing here—bootscootin' is nice to do with real boots, but lots of people show up in sneakers and Hawaiian shirts. Photos of Hank Williams, Tex Ritter, and other country greats line the walls of the club's "museum." You can arge, open room out front (the chicken-fried steak can't be beat), or ır long necks back to a table overlooking the dance floor. 3201 S. Lamar /.brokenspokeaustintx.net. ✆ **512/442-6189.**

The White Horse ★★ For a rowdier, hipper honky-tonk experience, head to this endearingly gritty east side bar with reliably great (and often eclectic) live country and rockabilly tunes. Come for the free two-stepping, Cajun, and Zydeco dance lessons (every Thurs, Fri, and Sat at 7 pm); stay for the whiskey on tap. There's a Bomb Taco truck outside and a popcorn machine inside if you get a hankering for late-night bites; dogs are welcome on the patio. 500 Comal St. www.thewhitehorseaustin.com. ✆ **512/553-6756.**

Jazz & Blues

Antone's ★★★ While Willie Nelson and crossover country-and-western bands such as the Austin Lounge Lizards were known to turn up at Clifford Antone's place (opened in 1975), it didn't take long for the club to become synonymous with the blues. Stevie Ray Vaughan was a regular, and when major blues artists—say, Buddy Guy, Etta James, or Edgar Winter—ventured down to Austin, they'd either play Antone's or stop by for a surprise set. Clifford Antone died in 2006, but the club that bears his name remains, as one music critic described it, "a living shrine to all he created"—that is, THE place to hear great blues. Antone's also lends its name—and musicians—to a Jazz brunch Sundays at the Driskill Hotel (p. 178). 305 E. Fifth St. www.antonesnightclub.com.

Elephant Room ★★★ This downtown bar provides the ideal setting for listening to jazz—a cozy, softly lit chamber in the basement of one of Congress Avenue's old buildings. You have to keep your eyes peeled to find it: The club entrance is a small door with a tiny sign, and it isn't on Sixth or in the Warehouse District. The Elephant Room lines up first-class acts, mostly contemporary jazz. ***Tip:*** Go Sunday through Thursday, when the bar is less crowded. 315 Congress Ave. www.elephantroom.com. ✆ **512/473-2279.**

Latin & Reggae

Flamingo Cantina ★★ The Flamingo attracts local and touring acts in all genres of "good vibe" music—reggae, ska, rocksteady, dub, Latin, world beat, and so on. (Sometimes DJs fill in, too.) Lounge around one of several bars and open-air decks when you're not dancing, chowing down on jerk chicken, or sitting on comfy carpeted bleachers listening to the performers. 515 E. Sixth St. www.flamingocantina.com. ✆ **512/494-9336.**

Singer-Songwriter

Cactus Cafe ★★★ A small, dark cavern with great acoustics and a fully stocked bar, UT's Cactus Cafe is home-away-from-home for a lot of singer-songwriters. Robert Earl Keen, Lucinda Williams, and Lyle Lovett were frequent performers early on in their careers; countless others, including Alison

LABEL IT SUCCESSFUL—AUSTIN'S S×SW

Started in 1987 as a way to showcase unsigned Texas bands, **South by Southwest (S×SW)** has become one of the biggest creative gatherings in the world, celebrating the convergence of film, music, and interactive media. Headlining bands gain major cred; up-and-coming films can make or break it with a S×SW splash.

Typically held during the first 2 weeks of March, this all-encompassing 10-day festival takes over the entire city and features hundreds of notable speakers, musical acts, panels, film screenings, and more. Locals have taken to referring to it as just "the festival"—as if there's no other in town. The conference is so large that S×SW LLC purchased a building near the Capitol, at 1400 Lavaca St., with plans to install offices on the top three floors and rent out other space to retailers and restaurants.

S×SW is split into three portions: Interactive, Film, and Music. You can purchase badges for each, or opt for a Platinum badge to gain primary access to all three. Wristbands are also available for select events. Join the official e-mail list to be notified about wristbands, check the website at **www.sxsw.com**, or call ✆ **512/467-7979.** Those without badges or wristbands can take advantage of the seemingly endless lineup of free music shows; just be prepared to wait in line for (up to) hours at a time. One of the most popular venues for free parties is **Cheer Up Charlies** (p. 280).

Krauss, Jimmie Dale Gilmore, and Suzanne Vega, have taken the stage here too. The associated **Shirley Bird Perry Ballroom** and **Texas Union Theater** are used when already famous acts like the Dixie Chicks draw overflow crowds. Texas Union, University of Texas campus, 2247 Guadalupe St. (at 24th St.). www.cactuscafe.org. ✆ **512/475-6515.**

COMEDY CLUBS

Cap City Comedy ★★ Since it opened more than 3 decades ago, Cap City has hosted top acts on the stand-up circuit, nationally recognized comedians such as Dave Chappelle, Carlos Mencia, and Bobcat Goldthwait. But you'll also see up-and-coming talent in the Punch! improv series, and the annual Funniest Person in Austin laugh off. 8120 Research Blvd., Ste. 100. www.capcitycomedy.com. ✆ **512/467-2333.**

ColdTowne Theater ★★ A staple on the alternative comedy circuit, Coldtowne Theater is open 7 days per week and features a showstopping lineup of cutting-edge performers who tackle all forms of comedy, from sketch to stand-up to film. They also teach the art of improv to hundreds of students. ColdTowne is a little bit punk, a little bit intimate, and a whole lotta heartfelt. 4803 Airport Blvd. www.coldtownetheater.com. ✆ **512/814-8696.**

Esther's Follies ★★★ You might miss a couple punch lines if you're not in on the latest twists and turns of local politics, but the no-holds-barred

Esther's Follies doesn't spare Washington, either. It's satirical, irreverent, and very Austin. 525 E. Sixth St. www.esthersfollies.com. ✆ **512/320-0198.**

The Hideout Theatre ★★ What looks like a quaint coffeeshop is actually downtown Austin's premier improv theater. Every Thursday through Sunday, the Hideout hosts and produces improv shows that feature independent performers and regularly performing troupes. Expect everything from full-length, stylized plays to short interactive comedy bits. 617 Congress Ave. www.hideouttheatre.com. ✆ **512/443-3688.**

The Velv Comedy Lounge ★★ For one-stop comedy consumption, go straight from Esther's (see above) to the Velveeta Room next door, a deliberately cheesy club started by two humor-loving UT alums. Headliners vie with pop-up acts and open mics each week. 521 E. Sixth St. www.thevelveetaroom.com. ✆ **512/766-8358.**

BARS & PUBS

Baker Street Pub & Grill ★ Austin's version of a proper British pub, cozy Baker Street has a wide selection of hearty bar food, liquor, and craft beer, with happy hour specials to boot. Cover bands dominate the pub stage throughout the weekend, but you'll occasionally catch local musicians playing here as well. 3003 S. Lamar Blvd. www.bakerstreetpub.com/south-austin. ✆ **512/691-9140.**

Cheer Up Charlies ★★★ Inclusive, welcoming, and hipper than hip, Cheer Up Charlies is easily one of Austin's most cherished LGBTQ+-friendly bars. Glitter and rainbow art abounds, Kale-Lime Margaritas and kombucha are served alongside well whiskey and PBR, and the vibe feels more like a friend's backyard hangout than a bar scene. During S×SW, Cheer Ups (as it's affectionately known) is one of the best places to catch unofficial shows. 900 Red River St. www.cheerupcharlies.com. ✆ **512/431-2133.**

Donn's Depot ★★ A standout gem on the dive bar circuit, Donn's Depot is a bit of a local legend. If you go, you'd do well to wear your dancing boots. Live music fills the main room nearly every night (with owner Donn Adelman often at the piano), and the dance floor is always populated by white-haired regulars two-stepping the night away. Oh, and the "depot" thing is quite literal: Donn's is made up of an old train depot and rail cars. This is the real deal, a lesser known Austin original. 1600 W. Fifth St. www.donnsdepot.com. ✆ **512/478-0336.**

The Driskill ★★★ Sink into one of the plush leather chairs arrayed around a grand piano and enjoy everything from blues to classical music in the upper-lobby bar of this opulent historic hotel. A pianist accompanies happy hour hors d'oeuvres (nightly 5–7pm); major ensembles get going around 8pm Tuesday through Saturday. 604 Brazos St. www.driskillhotel.com/dining/driskill-bar. ✆ **512/439-1234**.

celluloid AUSTIN

Austin has long had an undercover Hollywood presence, and today the city is widely recognized as one of the biggest centers of indie filmmaking in the country. The cult classic *Texas Chainsaw Massacre* was shot by UT students in the 1970s, and during the past 3 decades, more than 90 films were made in the city and its vicinity. Yet you'd be hard-pressed to identify Texas's capital in most of them: With its wide range of landscapes, Austin has filled in for locations as far-flung as Canada and Vietnam.

The city has less of an identity crisis behind the camera. It first earned its cred as an indie director–friendly place in 1982, when the Coen brothers shot *Blood Simple* here. And when University of Texas graduate Richard Linklater captured some of Austin's loopier denizens in *Slackers*—adding a word to the national vocabulary in the process—Austin arrived on the *cinéaste* scene. Linklater, later known for *Dazed and Confused* and, most recently, *Boyhood,* is often spotted around town with Robert Rodriguez, who shot all or part of several of his films (including *El Mariachi, Desperado, The Faculty,* and the *Spy Kids* series); and with Quentin Tarantino, who owns property in town. Mike Judge, of *Beavis and Butthead* and *Silicon Valley* fame, lives on and off in Austin, too.

Of the many cinematic events held in town, October's **Austin Film Festival** is among the more interesting. Held in tandem with the Heart of Films Screenwriters Conference, it focuses on movies with great scripts. For current information, contact the Austin Film Festival, 1604 Nueces (www.austinfilmfestival.com; ✆ **800/310-FEST** [310-3378] or 512/478-4795). And the film component of S×SW (see box p. 279) gets larger every year. Panelists have included Linklater and John Sayles, whose film *Lone Star* had its world premiere here.

The Austin Gay & Lesbian International Film Festival, held in early September in several venues around town, was renamed in 2018 as the **All Genders, Lifestyles, and Identities Film Festival** (aGLIFF; www.agliff.org; ✆ **512/406-9699**). Founded in 1987, the 4-day event screens more than 100 films covering a wide range of issues. aGLIFF also collaborates with the Austin School of Film on the Queer Youth Media Project. Participants in the free progam, open to ages 12 to 20, create a short film that is screened at the film festival.

Scholz Garten ★★★ Since 1866, when councilman August Scholz first opened his tavern near the state capitol, every Texas governor has visited it at least once (and many quite a few more times). It's changed with the times, catering as much to students at nearby UT as to politicos. The extensive menu now combines vegan burgers, queso fries, and chicken-fried steak with such German standards as jagerschnitzel, bratwurst, and sauerkraut. It's packed during Longhorn football games or when any special university event happens; otherwise, it's a quiet spot to down a cold one and drink in some Austin history. 1607 San Jacinto Blvd. www.scholzgarten.com. ✆ **512/474-1958.**

The Skylark Lounge ★★ It looks like a shack from the outside and feels like an off-the-beaten-path neighborhood spot, but walk into this storied candle-lit haunt and you'll channel the ghosts of musicians past.

Impressions

There is a very remarkable number of drinking and gambling shops [in Austin], but not one bookstore.

—Frederick Law Olmsted, *A Journey Through Texas*, 1853

Nearly every evening, a diverse crowd of old and new Austinites congregates here to enjoy the consistently great live country, blues, and soul bands, both regionally known acts and hometown favorites. 2039 Airport Blvd. www.skylarkaustin.com. ✆ **512/730-0759.**

FILM

Not surprisingly, you can see more foreign films in Austin than anywhere else in the state. Founded in 1985 by director Richard Linklater, the **Austin Film Society** is the city's crown jewel of indie cinema. The Society's two-screen theater, 6406 N. I-35 Frontage Rd., #3100 (www.austinfilm.org; ✆ **520/322-0145**), curates a standout selection of films, from little-seen documentaries to new restorations to celebrated foreign cinema. On the UT campus, **Showtime** hosts weekly Blockbuster and Late Night film series at the Texas Union Theater, Texas Union Building, 2308 Whittis Ave. (www.universityunions.utexas.edu; ✆ **512/475-6636**). In 1997, **Alamo Drafthouse,** 1120 S. Lamar Blvd. (www.drafthouse.com; ✆ **512/707-8262**), started the national trend of making "dinner and a movie" into a one-stop affair; while it's a bit more mainstream than in the early days, the owners are still dedicated to providing a distinctive experience (for example, they might offer a Pakistani menu when filming *The Big Sick*). Other Austin locations of Alamo Drafthouse include one downtown in the old Ritz Theater at 320 E. Sixth St.

SPECTATOR SPORTS

Austin taps into its Texas roots when it come to team sports, particularly when the **University of Texas Longhorns** are playing. The most comprehensive source of information on the various teams is **www.texassports.com**, but you can get tickets through **TexasBoxOffice.com** and get hold of a real person at ✆ **512/477-6060** or 800/982-2386. See Baseball, Basketball, Football, and Soccer, below.

BASEBALL The **University of Texas** baseball team goes to bat February through May at Disch-Falk Field (east of I-35, at the corner of Martin Luther King, Jr., Blvd. and Comal). Many players have gone on to the pros.

Baseball Hall of Famer Nolan Ryan's **Round Rock Express,** a Texas Rangers farm club, competes in the Pacific Coast League. See them play at the Dell Diamond, 3400 E. Palm Valley Rd., in Round Rock (www.milb.com/round-rock; ✆ **512/255-2255**), an 8,688-seat stadium where you can choose from box seats or stadium seating. An additional 3,000 fans can sit on a grassy berm in the outfield.

BASKETBALL The **University of Texas** Longhorn and Lady Longhorn basketball teams, both former Southwest Conference champions, play in the Frank Erwin Center (just west of I-35 on Red River btw. Martin Luther King, Jr., Blvd. and 15th St.) November through March.

FOOTBALL Part of the Big 12 Conference, the University of Texas football team often fills the huge **Darrell K. Royal/Texas Memorial Stadium** (just west of I-35 btw. 23rd and 21st sts., E. Campus Dr., and San Jacinto Blvd.) during home games, played August through November. Those seeking to explore the inner workings of the stadium can take a behind-the-scenes tour: www.texassports.com/sports/2013/7/24/facilities_0724132616.aspx?path=general.

GOLF World Golf Championship excitement comes to Austin in March 2019 and 2020 for the **Dell Technologies Match Play** tournament (www.pgatour.com/tournaments/wgc-dell-technologies-match-play.html) at the **Austin Country Club** (www.austincountryclub.com).

HOCKEY The American Hockey League's **Texas Stars** take to the ice at the H.E.B. Center in Cedar Park, 2100 Avenue of the Stars (www.texasstars.com; ✆ **512/GO-STARS** [467-8277; team] or 512/600-5000 [stadium]); they're the primary affiliate of the NHL's Dallas Stars.

MOTOR SPORTS The highly celebrated 2012 opening of the **Circuit of the Americas** (www.circuitoftheamericas.com) racetrack and entertainment venue revved the engines of Texans and visitors from everywhere else who are mad for world-class motorsports. Set on 1,500 acres just southeast of the Austin-Bergstrom Airport, off Hwy. 130, the 3.41-mile Circuit of the

A (skating) LEAGUE OF THEIR OWN

If any sport embodies Austin's spirit, it's roller derby, a no-holds-barred free-for-all with ties to the punk scene. Long relegated to the halls of kitsch, the sport was resurrected in 2001 by the **SheEOs,** a group of music producers who realized just how much fun it could be to circle a banked track in roller skates while elbowing other women out of the way. The resulting **TXRD Lonestar Rollergirls** league (www.TXRD.com)—with teams named the Holy Rollers, Hellcats, Putas del Fuego, Cherry Bombs, and Rhinestone Cowgirls—spurred renewed interest in the sport around the country. You can watch the Lonestar Rollergirls January to October at the Palmer Event Center, 900 Barton Springs Rd.

The **Texas Rollergirls** (www.texasrollergirls.org), formed in Austin in 2003, compete in the slightly more rules-oriented flat track league. Their season lasts from March through August, with bouts taking place at the Austin Sports Center, 425 Woodward St.

For a sweetly humorous take on the scene, check out *Whip It* (2009), directed by Drew Barrymore (she also appears in it). The film stars Ellen Page as a misfit who finds her natural peer group among Austin's equally square-peg skaters.

Americas track is the only one in the U.S. that hosts both Formula 1 and MotoGP events, and the first one in the country built specifically for Formula 1. The biggest names in racing, action sports, and music turn up here year round, and rooms are hard to come by when the American Grand Prix is held (Nov 1–3 in 2019).

SOCCER From August through November, the University of Texas women's soccer team competes against other NCAA teams. Home games are played Friday or Sunday at the Mike A. Myers Stadium and Soccer Field, just northeast of the UT football stadium at Robert Dedman Drive and Mike Myers Drive. Money was allocated in 2018 to build a soccer stadium for a major league team north of town. Stay tuned.

DAY TRIPS FROM AUSTIN

17

In a short drive from Austin, you can find world-famous barbecue, explore the area's German past, kayak on a clear river, hike in a pine forest, shop in a Texas-size outlet mall—or mix and match these activities, depending on your interests. On a loop route from Austin to Lockhart, Luling, New Braunfels, and back, for example, you can enjoy barbecue and Teutonic history. Or you can just head back and forth down what's known as the Golden Corridor: the 80-mile stretch of I-35 between Austin and San Antonio that includes San Marcos and New Braunfels/Gruene.

Unfortunately, in the past several years, real-estate development has turned the I-35 Golden Corridor into more like the Stop-and-Go(lden) Corridor. Towns such as Buda and Kyle are being swallowed up as bedroom communities of Austin, while New Braunfels is edging closer to becoming a suburb of San Antonio.

Note: Because Austin and San Antonio are so close to each other, several of the side trips described in Chapter 9, especially the one to the LBJ parks and Fredericksburg, are as easy to do from Austin as from San Antonio.

EXPLORING TEXAS BARBECUE

Yes, chili con carne and chicken-fried steak have their champions, but when all is said and done, barbecue is the quintessential Texas food, deeply prized in all corners of the state. Just about every major culture and ethnic group that came to Texas—cowboys and Indians, Mexicans and Germans, Anglos and African Americans—have had their impact on Texas barbecue, perfecting the technique of combining meat, fire, and smoke into a sensory delight. Barbecue has a rich lore, lots of traditions, and, of course, endless debate over such important matters as wet or dry, direct or indirect heat, and sauce or no sauce.

No one would argue that Austin itself lacks good barbecue; several top spots are detailed in Chapter 13. But if you leave the city, you'll find towns where a slower rhythm of life and the importance of tradition add an essence to the experience that Austin can't provide. Small towns don't have the strict clean-air ordinances Austin

Exploring Texas Barbecue

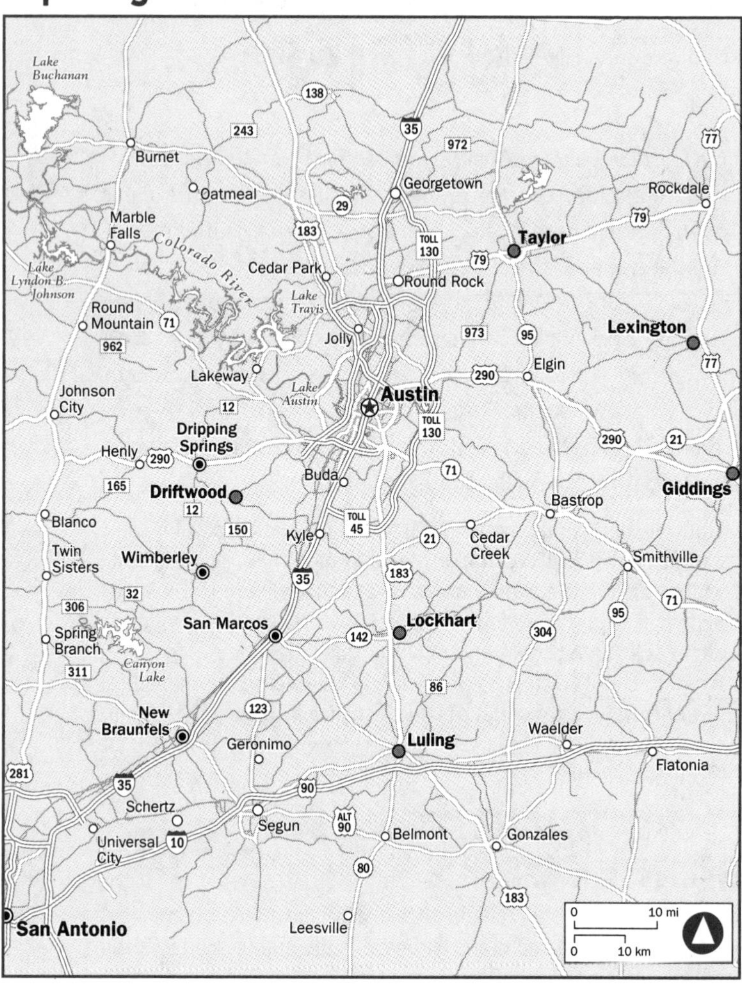

does—and to create old-time barbecue you need lots of smoke. City barbecue relies more and more on the use of commercial cookers, which just can't match the character of barbecue cooked using wood. Moisture and sap in the wood create the smoke that gives the meat its flavor, and the pink line just below the meat's surface is produced when nitrogen dioxide in the smoke mixes with myoglobin in the meat. Brisket cooked with a wood fire in a proper pit will have a line redder and deeper than brisket cooked in a commercial smoker.

South: Lockhart ★★★ and Luling ★★

LOCKHART If you have only one shot at trying "real" barbecue, Lockhart is the place to go. Texans flock to this little town (pop. 12,700), which boasts

EXPERIENCING CENTRAL TEXAS barbecue

In Texas, barbecue varies from region to region—and in central Texas, the traditional "dry" method is most often used: A dry rub is applied to the meat, which isn't marinated or basted; then the meat is cooked for many hours using indirect heat. This method produces a delicious crust. Barbecue joints in central Texas may cook a variety of meats, but there are three constants: brisket, spareribs (pork), and sausage. Beef ribs, pork chops, turkey, and chicken might be offered, but they are not considered essential. When ordering brisket, you'll often be asked if you want it lean or fatty: Try the fatty.

Another hallmark of Texas barbecue is the sauce—a sweet and spicy tomato-based concoction. There is a debate in Texas as to whether good barbecue needs sauce or not, to which there is no definitive answer. Almost all barbecue joints will offer sauce, letting you decide.

In Texas, barbecue is always served with plain white bread, onions, and pickles. Popular side dishes include chili beans, potato salad, and coleslaw. Often the barbecue is served on butcher paper (plates would be too highfalutin'). Most small towns sell barbecue by weight—prices run about $7 to $10 per pound for the mainstays, that is, ribs, sausage, and brisket.

It's important to note that barbecue is traditionally eaten early, to allow ample time for digestion. Many small-town barbecue joints close by 6pm, and many run out of meat long before then. And one more thing to remember when heading to these small towns for barbecue: **Bring cash.** Credit cards are often not accepted.

So where can you find the best 'cue in central Texas? That depends on the day, the time you arrive, perhaps the alignment of the stars—and of course, on your own taste. On some days, you might show up at a barbecue joint at just the right time: The smoky taste is at its height but the meat has not yet had a chance to dry out. On other days, you might miss the moment. But of the towns mentioned in this section, it's safe to say that Lockhart, Luling, and Lexington are the ones where that magical convergence is most likely to occur.

of being the "Barbecue Capital of Texas." From Austin, take Hwy. 183/Hwy. 130 south about 30 miles. Lockhart has three important barbecue joints. Perhaps the most famous is **Kreuz Market,** 619 N. Colorado St. (www.kreuzmarket.com; ✆ **512/398-2361**); it's open Monday to Saturday from 10:30am to 8pm. Go directly to the pit room in back, where a sign on the wall reads: NO SALAD. NO SAUCE. NO CREDIT CARDS. That's right, this is one of the few places that refuses to provide sauce. Once you buy your meat, head to the large dining room where you can buy drinks and what few side dishes are available.

If you want sauce with your barbecue, head to **Black's Barbecue,** 215 N. Main St (www.blacksbbq.com; ✆ **512/398-2712**), 3 blocks north of the town square; it opened in 1932 and is still run by the same family. In addition to excellent barbecue and a tangy sauce, Black's also offers well-prepared side dishes. Food is served daily from 10am to 8pm. ***Note:*** Black's also has branches in Austin and New Braunfels; check the website.

Your third option is **Smitty's Market,** 208 S. Commerce (www.smittysmarket.com; ✆ **512/398-9344**), a half-block south of the town square, open Monday to Saturday 7am to 6pm. Make a point of strolling into Smitty's just to see the smoke-caked pit room; you practically have to step over the open fire pits in the floor to get your meat. This is located on the original location of Kreuz Market (see above)—the family parted ways some years ago, with one side keeping the original location while the other side kept the name. The recipes are about the same in both places, but many argue that the quality of the meat might be a little better at the new(er) place.

Take a spin around Lockhart's town square to see the impressive **Caldwell County Courthouse.** Built in 1894 of uncolored sandstone with red sandstone trim, the three-story structure has mansard roofs on the corners and decorative towers in the center and on the north and south sides. The town also has a pretty little library and several antiques shops.

LULING From Lockhart, drive 16 miles south via Hwy. 183 to get to Luling. You'll *smell* the town before you get there: The many oil wells in the area have a rotten-egg sulfur odor that lingers in the air. Never mind: Luling (pop. 5,400) has some of the best barbecue in the state.

The town is divided down the middle by railroad tracks. Where Hwy. 183 crosses the tracks, look for **City Market,** 633 E. Davis St. (www.lulingcitymarket.com; ✆ **830/875-9019**), open Monday to Saturday from 7am to 6pm. As at other barbecue joints, you buy your barbecue in the pit room first, then get sauce, drinks, and sides (beans and potato salad only) in the dining room. ***Best bets:*** ribs or brisket. The dry rub on the ribs gives them a slightly crispy texture, and the brisket melts in your mouth.

Rockin' the Pumpjacks

While you're in Luling, pick up a brochure and map for the **Pumpjack Tour,** named after the rocking-horse-like machines that bob up and down in oil fields. Denizens of Luling started dressing them up for fun, and then the local chamber of commerce commissioned Texas sign artist George Kalesik to decorate some. The pumpjacks are located close enough together that you can see the majority on foot.

In the 1920s and '30s, Luling lay at the center of a central Texas oil boom. To earn more about that history, stop by the **Central Texas Oil Patch Museum,** 421 Davis St. (www.lulingoilmuseum.org; ✆ **830/875-1922**), in the historic Walker Brothers building. One large room is filled with artifacts of the early days of oil extraction. It's open Monday to Friday 9am to 4pm, closed noon to 1pm for lunch. Admission is $1 suggested donation. The museum doubles as the town visitor center.

Luling is also known for watermelon and celebrates with a late-June festival called the **Watermelon Thump.**

Southwest: Driftwood ★★

Thirteen miles southwest of Austin from the junction of U.S. 290 W. and FM 1826, the tiny rural town of Driftwood (pop. 144) is known primarily for one thing: the **Salt Lick,** 18001 FM 1826 (www.saltlickbbq.com; ✆ **512/858-4959**). You can't miss it—you'll start smelling the smoke at least 5 miles before you arrive in this pretty little rural town. Unlike many central Texas barbecue joints, the Salt Lick uses an open stone pit, direct heat, and basting; often called "cowboy style" in Texas, this preparation method is similar to Kansas City-style barbecue. The meat gets a good smoky flavor, but leans more heavily on sauce, which is rich and tangy here.

As you walk in the door of the original building (on the right as you enter the gate), you'll see an open pit heaving with juicy turkey and chicken, low-and-slow smoked beef, and pork. You can order individual portions or all-you-can-eat family-style platters of beef, sausage, and pork ribs, served with sides like slaw, potato salad, pinto beans, and homemade pickles. There are also chopped beef sandwiches, ribs, brisket, and sausage by the pound. But save room for the fresh-baked blackberry or peach cobbler or chocolate pecan pie. You can eat in one of a series of rustic dining rooms; on a screened porch, which is pleasant when the weather is mild; or on one of the outdoor picnic tables shaded by heritage oak trees. The Salt Lick is open daily 11am to 10pm; it's a cash-only place, but there's an ATM on-site.

The Salt Lick often gets crowded on weekends when Austinites come down with ice chests full of beer, which they drink while waiting for a table. It's a tradition: For years Driftwood was a "dry" community, and the restaurant still doesn't serve alcohol. But the liquor laws have changed, and now you can buy Texas wine or beer next door at **Salt Lick Cellars** (www.saltlickcellars.com; ✆ **512/829-4013**). It's ironic that a community that was dry for so long is now also home to several spots purveying potent potables; maybe Hays County is making up for lost time. Along with Salt Lick Cellars, several wineries in the area have formed the **Driftwood Wine Trail** group; see www.driftwoodwinetrail.com for details. In addition, **Stinson Distilling,** 18281 FM 150, #211 (https://stinson.business.site; ✆ **512/894-2009**), has won awards for its vodka, elderflower liqueur, and carajillo, a creamy rum and coffee combo. All are in a lovely section of the Texas Hill Country; it's a perfect fit with an excursion to Wimberley (p. 293).

Want another taste before flying home? You can pick up brisket and some of the signature sweet-tangy-sour barbecue sauce at the Salt Lick's Austin airport branch.

East: Taylor ★, Lexington ★ & Giddings ★

Taylor, Lexington, and Giddings aren't really en route to anywhere else, but they're close enough to each other to include all three in a day trip. Visiting them will give you a taste of rural Texas—as well as of smoked meat.

About 35 miles northeast of Austin—take I-35 north to Round Rock, then Hwy. 79 E.—**Taylor** is home to **Louie Mueller's,** 206 W. Second St. (www.louiemuellerbarbecue.com; ✆ **512/352-6206**). Here, the barbecue is cooked with the indirect heat method in an impressive pit. The rub uses a lot of black pepper, which, combined with the smoke, makes a wonderful black crust on the brisket. This large old-fashioned restaurant smells of the smoke that's been wafting through here since 1949. It's been in the same family from the beginning, and won a James Beard Foundation "American Classics" award. It's open Monday through Saturday from 10am to 6pm.

From Taylor, it's about a half hour's drive (head east on Hwy. 79 then south on Route 112) to **Lexington** (pop. 1100), home of **Snow's Barbecue,** 516 Main (www.snowsbbq.com; ✆ **979/542-8189**). Snow's is open only on Saturday, from 8am "'til sold out"—which might be as early as 10am. It became a foodie destination after *Texas Monthly* dubbed it the Best in Texas in 2017. Everything here is excellent, especially the brisket, and it's well worth the effort and timing needed to get here, although it is in the heart of barbecue country, which offers so many stellar options. If a trip to Lexington doesn't work out, you can order Snow's meat online.

It's only 19 miles south from Lexington via Hwy. 77 to downtown **Giddings,** where you'll find some excellent barbecue at **City Meat Market and BBQ,** 101 W. Austin St. (www.citymeatmarket.biz; ✆ **979/542-2740**). Opened in the early 1960s in an old-fashioned brick storefront at the intersection of Hwy. 77 (Austin St.) and Hwy. 290, this place sells fresh meat as well as barbecue. It's open Monday to Friday from 7:30am to 5:30pm and Saturday

LOST pines

Thirty-two miles southeast of Austin, just off Hwy. 71, lies an ecological anomaly—a pine forest surrounded on all sides by prairie. It is the last remnant of an extensive pine forest that once extended all the way from the Piney Woods of East Texas. This one piney patch has survived because its soil is rich in iron, which favors the growth of pine trees over grasslands. The area is also very hilly, which also marks a distinction from the surrounding flat prairieland. Located within the forest is **Bastrop State Park** (www.tpwd.texas.gov/state-parks/bastrop; ✆ **512/321-2101**), which offers plenty of hiking trails, a golf course, a swimming pool, campsites, and cabins (which must be reserved by phone well in advance: ✆ **512/389-8900**). Mountain biking is not permitted, but the park road, which extends to a nearby park, is one of the most popular bike routes in Texas.

Also located in this pine forest is **Hyatt Regency Lost Pines Resort and Spa** (www.lostpines.hyatt.com; www.lostpines.hyatt.com; ✆ **512/308-1234**), a family-oriented resort in the same style as the Hyatt Regency Hill Country Resort on the outskirts of San Antonio (see chapter 4, p. 50). It's located on the banks of the Colorado River and offers such activities as kayaking and canoeing, as well as horseback riding. Rates for a standard room run from $250 to $325, depending on the day of week and time of year. Promotional rates and packages are often available.

from 7:30am to 4pm, but most of the barbecue is gone by 1 or 2pm. You can call ahead to reserve meat; you can't miss with the pork shoulder.

While digesting your meal, stroll down Austin Street for a block to the Romanesque Revival-style **Lee County courthouse,** built in 1899 by J. Riely Gordon, who also built courthouses in San Antonio, New Braunfels, and Gonzales.

SAN MARCOS ★★

26 miles SW of Austin

The interstate highway connecting Austin and San Antonio roughly traces a boundary between the Hill Country to the west and the coastal prairie to the east. This relatively narrow strip of land is dotted with natural springs, formed when the upheaval that produced the Edwards Plateau and the Hill Country opened fissures in the limestone substrate along the Balcones fault line. Rainwater on the plateau seeps into these cracks and flows underground for many miles before bubbling back up to the surface at the lower elevation of this boundary zone.

Some of the largest of these springs are found in San Marcos. These springs and the wildlife they attracted were probably what brought the first human inhabitants to the region, some 12,000 years ago. Temporary home to two Spanish missions in the late 1700s, as well as to the Comanche and Apaches, this area was eventually inhabited by Anglo settlers in the middle of the 19th century. Now host to Texas State University–San Marcos (formerly Southwest Texas State), the alma mater of LBJ, San Marcos has the laid-back feel of a college town. It's also fast becoming a suburb of Austin, only half an hour away.

Exploring San Marcos

Before arriving in San Marcos, you pass through two small towns, **Buda,** a corruption of the Spanish word for widow, *viuda*), and **Kyle.** Both are almost entirely bedroom communities for Austin and have lost much of their distinctive character. Kyle, however, has a claim to literary fame—see box below.

To get oriented, stop at the excellent **San Marcos Tourist Information Center,** 617 I-35 (www.toursanmarcos.com; ✆ **512/393-5930**); take exit 204 B and travel ½ mile on the frontage road. It's open Monday to Saturday from 9am to 5pm and Sunday from 10am to 4pm.

San Marcos's entire downtown area is listed in the National Register of Historic Places. Start your exploration around **Courthouse Square.** San Marcos is the seat of Hays County, named after John Coffee Hays, one of the earliest members of the Texas Rangers; they fought many skirmishes with Mexicans, Apaches, and Comanche in the Hill Country and South Texas. A bronze statue of Hays stands by the 1909 courthouse.

Around the square, several old storefronts are in various stages of restoration, including the **State Bank and Trust Building,** dating back to the late

A Literary Aside

Pulitzer Prize–winning author Katherine Anne Porter, best known for her novel *Ship of Fools*, spent most of her childhood in the town of Kyle. In 2001, the **Katherine Anne Porter Literary Center,** 508 W. Center St. (www.kapliterarycenter.com; ✆ **512/268-6637**), was dedicated and opened to the public, as well as housing a visiting writer chosen by the Texas State University–San Marcos. The house, which was restored and furnished with period antiques, hosts Porter's works and a collection of her photographs. There's no admission charge, but you need to call ahead for an appointment.

1800s. It was robbed by the Newton Gang in 1924 and (most likely) by Machine Gun Kelly in 1933. Facing the square from across Guadalupe Street, the small **LBJ Museum of San Marcos,** 131 N. Guadalupe St. (www.lbjmuseum.com; ✆ **512/353-3300**), documents LBJ's early years, including those at Texas State University-San Marcos. The museum is open Thursday to Saturday 10am to 5pm. Admission is free.

Texas State University's Albert B. Alkek Library, at 601 University Dr., is home to the **Wittliff Collections,** on the library's seventh floor (www.thewittliffcollections.txstate.edu; ✆ **512/245-2313**). It showcases materials donated by the region's leading filmmakers, photographers, musicians, and wordsmiths. You might see anything from a 1555 printing of the journey of Spanish adventurer Cabeza de Vaca to a songbook created by an 11-year-old Willie Nelson, manuscripts by Sandra Cisneros, and photographs by Edward Curtis. The collection was founded by screenwriter Bill Wittliff, who wrote the script for *Lonesome Dove*—thus the display dedicated to that miniseries—as well as for *Legends of the Fall* and *A Perfect Storm.* Check the website for hours.

Just northwest of the Texas State campus, follow Aquarena Springs Drive to reach Spring Lake, which is filled entirely by natural springs. The waters are astonishingly clear and maintain a constant temperature of 72°F (22°C). On the lake's shore sits the **Meadows Center for Water and the Environment,** 201 San Marcos Springs Dr. (www.meadowscenter.txstate.edu; ✆ **512/245-9200**), an environmental research center (thus no swimming is permitted in the lake). Glass-bottom boat tours, which allow you to view the lake's rare flora and fauna, cost $9.75 for adults, $8 for seniors 65 and older, and $6 for children ages 3 to 12. Thirty-minute tours are available during the week; on weekends longer tours are offered, including guided tours via a boardwalk over the wetlands, where more than 100 species of birds have been spotted.

Spring Lake is the headwaters of the **San Marcos River,** which from here begins its winding course down to the Gulf of Mexico. If you want to get wet, the river is your best option; it's probably the cleanest river in Texas. (Log on to www.sanmarcosriver.org to find out about conservation measures taken by the San Marcos River Foundation.) Common activities on the river include tubing, kayaking, and canoeing. Tubing is possible in the warm months from May through mid-September, while the best time for kayaking is in September and October, after the summer vacation crowds are gone. The local **Lions Club** (www.tubesanmarcos.com; ✆ **512/396-LION** [396-5466]) rents inner tubes and operates a river shuttle at City Park, across the river from Texas State. **TG Canoes & Kayaks** (www.tgcanoe.com; ✆ **512/353-3946**) provides watercraft, gear, and transportation. If you would like to take a class before your trip, contact **Olympic Outdoor Center** (www.kayakinstruction.org; ✆ **512/203-0093**); the center offers a whitewater course at Rio Vista Park, which lies just north of I-35; it's also an attractive place to go swimming in a calm pool of water above the rapids.

When the Balcones Fault was active some 30 million years ago, an earthquake created the cave at the center of **Wonder World,** southwest of downtown at 1000 Prospect St., off Bishop Street (www.wonderworldpark.com; ✆ **877/492-4657** or 512/392-3760). The first commercial cave show in Texas, this attraction is a throwback to an era when natural phenomena had to be gussied up rather than let stand on their own—thus the rather tacky

Side Trip to Wimberley

From San Marcos, you can take a quick trip into rural Hill Country by driving to the town of Wimberley, on the banks of the Blanco River, some 15 miles northwest of San Marcos. Texans from around the state treat it as a weekend getaway, staying at a varied collection of bed-and-breakfasts—it's a favorite setting for family reunions. Shopping for antiques and art objects is one of the main activities here. From April through December, the first Saturday of each month is **Market Day,** a large crafts gathering on Lion's Field; it's the oldest outdoor market in the Hill Country. Check www.shopmarketdays.com for additional information. Most of the artsy-craftsy (and often overly cutesy) shops are on or near the town square. Head 1½ miles south of the town center to find the **Wimberley Glass Works,** 6469 R.R. 12 (www.wgw.com; ✆ **512/393-3316**), which stands out for its rainbow-like array of blown glassware, especially hanging light fixtures and lamps. You can watch glassblowers at work in the studio behind the showroom from Tuesday to Saturday. The nicest place to stay in Wimberley, the **Blair House Inn,** 100 Spoke Hill Rd. (www.blairhouseinn.com; ✆ **512/847-1111**), sits on 85 acres; it offers eight beautifully appointed rooms and three separate cottages in a Texas limestone ranch complex. There's a cooking school on the premises, so you know the breakfasts—and dinners, offered to outsiders as well as guests every Saturday night—are going to be good. Rates run $160–$209 for double rooms, $230–$270 for suites, $285–$310 for the cottages. The cooking classes and dinners are popular with Austinites (and others), so book in advance if you want to attend. For information about other places to stay, eat, or shop in Wimberley, contact the **Chamber of Commerce,** 14100 R.R. 12, just north of the town square (www.wimberley.org; ✆ **512/847-2201**), open Monday to Friday, 9am to 4pm.

Anti-Gravity House and petting farm, which is basically a tram ride through an enclosure of deer. It's not inexpensive either. That said, if you're traveling with kids, it's a good place to keep them entertained for a few hours. Check ahead for hours; Wonder World is generally open daily in summer, but only Friday through Sunday the rest of the year. Tickets for the entire park cost $25 for adults, $18 for kids 6 to 12, $17 seniors and military, and $9.50 for ages 3 to 5.

SAN MARCOS OUTLET SHOPPING

Some people bypass all the other tourist attractions in San Marcos and come solely for the outlet shopping. A couple of miles south of downtown, on the east side of the highway (exit 200), are two adjacent malls: **Tanger Outlets** (www.tangeroutlet.com/sanmarcos; ✆ **800/408-8424** or 512/396-7446) and the larger, more upscale **San Marcos Premium Outlets** (www.premium outlets.com/outlet/san-marcos; ✆ **512/396-2201**). Between them, they have almost 300 stores. You'll find the usual outlet mall suspects such as Famous Footwear, Bath & Body Works, and Sunglass Hut, along with such exclusives as Elizabeth Arden, Jimmy Choo, Kate Spade, Prada, and LaCoste. The food options are mostly kid-friendly chains, including Outback, Taco Bell, Johnny Rockets, and Auntie Anne's. Both malls also offer play areas for children.

Where to Stay & Eat in San Marcos

A few blocks from the courthouse, the **Crystal River Inn,** 326 W. Hopkins St. (www.crystalriverinnsanmarcostx.com; ✆ **512/396-3739**), offers something for every architectural preference. Nine rooms and three suites, beautifully decorated with antiques, occupy a large 1883 Victorian main house, a 1920s Mission-style house, and a 1930s rock bungalow. Rates run from about $115 to $170 for rooms and suites; there are sometimes 3-day minimums (or discounts during quiet periods). Day spa services are available, and sometimes murder mystery weekends are offered.

Closer to the courthouse, **Café on the Square,** 126 N. LBJ Dr. (www.facebook.com/CafeOnTheSquareSM; ✆ **512/396-9999**) serves burgers, sandwiches, Tex-Mex, and local standards like fried catfish at bargain prices. It's open for breakfast, lunch, and dinner. For something more upscale, try **Palmer's,** 216 W. Moore St. (www.palmerstexas.com, ✆ **512/353-3500**), just off Hopkins Street. Here you can dine on American standards with a Texas twist—for example, grilled pork chops topped with a habañero-honey sauce; eat outside in an attractive courtyard or inside in one of the wood-paneled dining rooms. Save room for the Key lime pie. The restaurant is open for lunch and dinner daily, and meals are moderate to expensive. Probably the prettiest place to eat in San Marcos is on the outdoor deck of the **Saltgrass Steakhouse,** 211 Sessoms Dr. (www.saltgrass.com; ✆ **512/396-5255**), just off Aquarena Drive. It's a one-of-a-kind setting, perched out over Spring Lake right where it feeds into the river. This is a chain, but if you stick to the steaks or chops, you'll be fine.

glamping AROUND AUSTIN

Travelers everywhere have discovered that glamour camping—aka glamping—can be more fun than the kind that involves discomfort. Less than an hour from Austin in all directions, you'll find high-end canvas tents and treetop yurts that allow you to enjoy nature's beauty from the comfort of a warm bed—and without having to go outdoors to use the bathroom. Expect to pay between $200 and $500 per night.

SOUTHEAST (NEAR SEGUIN)

Best Texas Travel (www.besttexastravel.com; ✆ **888-993-6772**) manages two properties near Seguin. The tipis and treehouse-style cabins at **Geronimo Creek Retreat** sit at the edge of the spring-fed creek for which they're named. With private access to the water, guests can spend the day paddleboarding, tubing, kayaking, or swinging from a rope swing. The property has four cabins (each sleeps up to six guests), and five fully furnished tipis, all with modern perks like air-conditioning and heat, satellite TVs, kitchenettes, queen-size beds, and living room areas. You can fulfill your Robinson Crusoe fantasies on nearby **Son's Island at Lake Placid,** where you can rent a thatched-hut cabana or glamping tent on a 4-acre island. Spend the day kayaking, paddleboarding, hydrobiking, and floating on this river-like long lake before the staff prepares a nighttime fire complete with all the fixin's for s'mores.

WEST (NEAR JOHNSON CITY)

Walden Retreats (www.waldenretreats.com; ✆ **830/321-0295**) is a top pick for a romantic getaway. Its luxury African safari-style tents have all the comforts of a five-star hotel with king-size bed, full bathroom, deck overlooking a high bluff, barbecue grill, and full kitchen. They sit on 96 acres with easy access to the Pedernales River; fishing poles and canoes are provided to help you enjoy it.

SOUTHWEST (NEAR WIMBERLY AND NEW BRAUNFELS)

Talk about authenticity: At the exclusive two-person **Sinya on Lone Man Creek** (www.hillcountrysinya.com; ✆ **713/502-3997**), you'll sleep in a safari tent imported from South Africa. True, on this luxury adventure you get Hill Country, not veldt, views, but you don't have to worry about getting eaten by a lion. At **Collective Retreats** (www.collectiveretreats.com; ✆ **970/445-2033**), 12 stylish wood-framed structures offer 1,500 thread-count linens, down comforters, and an in-room curated coffee bar that will have you forgetting you are supposed to be roughing it. The campsite sits along a ridgeline overlooking the 225-acre Montesino Ranch. The six luxurious treehouse-style cabins at **River Road Treehouses** (www.riverroadcabins.com; ✆ **888-993-6772**) overhang a creek that feeds into the Guadalupe River. Glampers have direct access to the river and can spend the day fly fishing, tubing, picnicking, or hanging in a hammock.

NORTHWEST (NEAR SPICEWOOD SPRINGS)

Four treehouses owned by a zip-lining outfitter, **Cypress Valley Canopy Tours** (www.cypressvalleycanopytours.com/lofthaven; ✆ **512/264-8880**), offer family-friendly fun about an hour northwest of Austin. This is not for those with a fear of heights: a zip-line canopy tour is required with your stay (if available), and wooden bridges, rope ladders, and rock staircases are used for getting around the property.

NEW BRAUNFELS ★★ & GRUENE ★★★

New Braunfels: 16 miles SW of San Marcos, 48 miles SW of Austin, 32 miles NE of San Antonio. Gruene: 4 miles NE of New Braunfels.

New Braunfels sits at the junction of the Comal and Guadalupe rivers—thus its current popularity as a watersports hub, and its original appeal as a spot to found a town. German settlers were brought here in 1845 by Prince Carl of Solms-Braunfels, the commissioner general of the *Adelsverein,* or the Society for the Protection of German Immigrants in Texas, the same group that later founded Fredericksburg (p. 143). Prince Carl returned to Germany within a year to marry his fiancée, who refused to join him in the wilderness, but his colony prospered without him. A flood of immigrants from Germany, spurred in particular by the revolution of 1848, made New Braunfels the fourth-largest city in Texas by the mid-1850s (after Houston, San Antonio, and Galveston).

Now a town of about 70,000 and growing fast—it gets a lot of overflow from nearby San Antonio—New Braunfels has lost much of its historic character, but its old downtown and nearby Gruene give you a taste of bygone days.

Tip: Keep in mind that some 100,000 people descend on New Braunfels during its 10-day annual Wurstfest (www.wurstfest.com), which starts at the end of October. If beer and brats and crowds—and, okay, a lot of fun—are up your alley, book a room far in advance.

Exploring New Braunfels & Gruene

NEW BRAUNFELS ★★

Take exit 187 from I-35 and turn left to get to the **Greater New Braunfels Convention and Visitors Bureau,** 390 S. Seguin St. (www.playinnewbraunfels.com; ✆ **800/572-2626** or 830/625-2385), open Monday to Friday 8am to 5pm. Here, you can pick up information about the area's water recreation as well as a pamphlet with tours of the Gruene Historic District and historic downtown New Braunfels.

This is one of the few towns in Texas that doesn't have a courthouse square; instead, it has a large traffic circle, with the Romanesque-Gothic **Comal County Courthouse** (1898) on one corner, surrounded by other buildings. Most of the old town lies within 5 blocks of this circle. In addition to the courthouse, downtown's highlights include the **Jacob Schmidt Building,** 193 W. San Antonio St., built on the site where William Gebhardt, of canned chili fame, perfected his formula for chili powder (see box p. 298). The 1928 **Faust Hotel,** 240 S. Seguin St. (p. 302), is believed by some to be haunted by its owner. Draughts pulled from the microbrewery on the Faust's premises help allay even the most haunting anxieties. **Henne Hardware,** 246 W. San Antonio St. (www.hennehardware.com; ✆ **830/606-6707**), established in 1857—it's said to be the oldest hardware store in Texas—sells modern bits and bobs,

New Braunfels

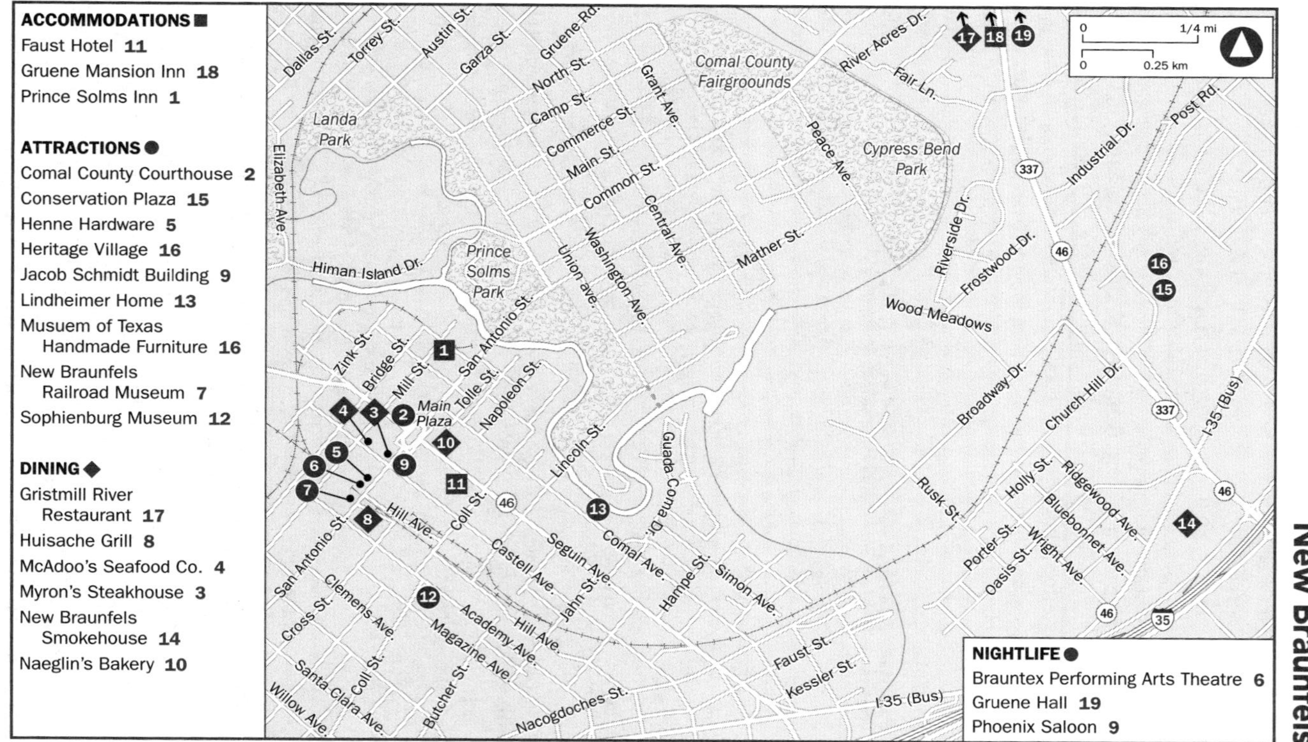

but maintains its original tin-roof ceiling, rings for hanging buggy whips, and an old pulley system for transporting cash and paperwork through the back office. **Naeglin's Bakery,** 129 S. Seguin Ave. (www.naegelins.com; ✆ **830/625-5722**), opened in 1868, stakes its claim as the state's longest-running bakery. It's the place to try *kolaches,* Czech pastries filled with cheese, fruit, poppy seeds, sausage, or ham, among other delicious fillings.

Several small historic museums are worth a visit. Set in a restored early 20th-century depot, the **New Braunfels Railroad Museum,** 302 W. San Antonio St. (www.newbraunfelsrailroadmuseum.org; ✆ **830/627-2447**), an all-volunteer effort, showcases a collection of train memorabilia, an elaborate model train set, and four antique rail cars: a locomotive, caboose, dining car, and boxcar. It's open Thursday through Monday from noon to 4pm. Admission is free.

CHILI POWDER, BADGERS & frito pies

Long before Taco Bell, William Gebhardt's Texas chili powder commercialized Mexican food on a national scale.

When Gebhardt, a German immigrant, moved to New Braunfels, he began taking an interest in the region's local cuisine. In 1892, he opened a cafe in what is now the Jacob Schmidt building and began experimenting with herbs and dried chile peppers. A few years later, satisfied with his "Tampico Dust," he began selling it around the state. In 1898, Gebhardt moved to San Antonio, where the Gebhardt Chili Powder Company became the largest purveyor of spices in the country. The company eventually branched out to produce canned chili (mostly meat) and canned tamales.

Gebhart's New Braunfels cafe occupied a space behind a bar called the **Phoenix Saloon** (193 W. San Antonio St.; www.thephoenixsaloon.com; ✆ **830/660-6000**), which is claimed to have been the first in Texas to serve women, albeit in a separate beer garden. Entertainment at the saloon included badger fights and an alligator pit. The Phoenix closed in 1918 and was not re-opened until 2010, when new owners Ross Fortune and Debbie Smith paid tribute to its venerable history by, among other things, exposing a brick wall from the original 1871 building; placing a stuffed badger above the bar; and putting several types of chili dishes on the menu, including Frito pies. For the uninitiated, a Frito pie is a bag of Fritos that is slit open and topped with chili. (Whether a Frito pie should include cheese and other toppings on the chili and whether it originated in Texas or New Mexico are subjects of heated debate that won't be covered here.) Co-owner Ross Fortune was a rock music critic for *Time Out* in his native England; when he decided to open a club in the U.S., he scoped out the Austin area until an old building in New Braunfels called out to him. So while craft beer and chili and an impeccable historic restoration set the scene, the reason for the Phoenix's existence is live music, from New Wave to dance, blues, and karaoke. You'll find live sounds here almost every night, usually without a cover charge. You can't miss the place—look for a stencil of the Gebhardt's Eagle Chili Powder logo on the side of the building.

Prince Carl never did build the castle he planned for his sweetheart, Sophia, but on that site today, the **Sophienburg Museum,** 401 W. Coll St. (www.sophienburg.org; ✆ **830/629-1572**), is a good spot to learn a bit about the history of New Braunfels and other Hill Country settlements. It's open Tuesday to Saturday 10am to 4pm; $5 general admission, $1 students.

Two other museums, next door to each other on the east side of New Braunfels, vividly evoke the life of early residents. In the 11-acre **Heritage Village** complex, 1370 Church Hill Dr. (www.nbheritagevillage.com; ✆ **830/629-6504**), the **Museum of Texas Handmade Furniture** sheds light on local 19th-century domestic life with its beautiful examples of Texas Biedermeier by master craftsmen, displayed in the gracious 1858 Breustedt-Dillen Haus. The complex also includes an 1848 log cabin and a barn with a replica of a cabinetmaker's workshop. Hours vary seasonally; the museum is closed August and December, though tours by appointment are still available then. Admission is $5 adults, $4 seniors, $1 children ages 6 to 12. To tour other historic structures, from a one-room schoolhouse to a barber shop with miniature circus figures, stop by **Conservation Plaza,** 1300 Church Hill Dr. (www.newbraunfelsconservation.org; ✆ **830/629-2943**). Most were moved onto this site from other places; the plaza centers around a gazebo and garden with more than 50 varieties of antique roses. Guided tours are offered from Tuesday to Friday from 10am to 2:30pm, and Saturday and Sunday 2 to 5pm; suggested donation is $2.50 per person.

Conservation Plaza is a project of the New Braunfels Conservation Society, which also manages the 1852 **Lindheimer Home** at 491 Comal Ave. (www.newbraunfelsconservation.org; ✆ **830/608-1512**); it's probably the best example of an early *fachwerk* house still standing. Ferdinand J. Lindheimer, one of the town's first settlers, was an internationally recognized botanist—41 species of plants were named for him—and editor of the town's German-language newspaper. Call ahead to request a tour, or to wander grounds planted with Texas native plants.

GRUENE ★★★

Get a more concentrated glimpse of the past at Gruene (pronounced "Green"), which sits high on a bluff overlooking the Guadalupe River, just 2 miles from I-35. First settled by German farmers in the 1840s, Gruene was virtually abandoned during the Great Depression. It remained a ghost town until the mid-1970s, when two investors realized the value of its intact historic buildings and sold them to businesses rather than raze them. These days, tiny Gruene is bursting at the seams, a place crowded with day-trippers browsing specialty shops—everything from smoked meat to antiques—in the wonderfully restored structures. Gruene is also home to potters and other artists with galleries here, as well as B&Bs, hotels, restaurants, and other tourist-friendly stops.

But Gruene is perhaps best known for **Gruene Hall ★★★,** 1281 Gruene Rd. at Hunter Road (www.gruenehall.com; ✆ **830/606-1281**). Built in 1878, it's the state's most famous and oldest continually operating dancehall. Everyone from Little Richard, Kris Kristofferson, and Merle Haggard to Garth Brooks and the Dixie Chicks has taken the stage here, and it's still one of the state's best places to hear live music. But it's also a down-home bar and beer garden, where you can sit out on a warm afternoon and soak in the old town atmosphere, even when there's no entertainment on tap.

OUTSIDE NEW BRAUNFELS

On the way from San Marcos to New Braunfels, you'll probably see a billboard or five advertising **Natural Bridge Caverns,** 26495 Natural Bridge Caverns Rd. (www.naturalbridgecaverns.com; ✆ **210/651-6101**). It's well worth a detour. Exit 175 off of I-35 and go under the freeway and head north about 8 miles on FM 3009. Named for the 60-foot limestone arch spanning the entryway, the caverns hold more than a mile of huge rooms and passages, some of which are filled with stunning, multihued formations—still being formed, as the dripping water attests. The daring—and physically fit—can opt to join one of the **Adventure Tours,** which involve crawling and, in some cases, rappelling, in an unlighted cave not open to the general public ($115–$140; age restrictions apply and advance reservations are required). The mild at heart might choose the **Discovery Tour,** which explores a half-mile of the cavern, or the **Illuminations Tour,** focusing on two chambers with lots of delicate formations. A variety of outdoor activities that involve climbing and swinging from ropes are available here too. The caverns are open 9am to 7pm June through Labor Day, 9am to 4pm the rest of the year; closed Thanksgiving Day, Christmas Day, and New Year's Day. Prices vary, depending on whether you book in advance. Generally, the Discovery and Illuminations tours are $22.50 for adults, $15 for kids ages 3 to 11; combination tickets are $30.50 and $20.

Just down the road, the 450-acre **Natural Bridge Wildlife Ranch,** 26515 Natural Bridge Caverns Rd (www.wildliferanchtexas.com; ✆ **830/438-7400**), is a drive-through safari park featuring some 50 species from around the world, including rhinos, camels, lemurs, and giraffes. You can either drive through or take a shorter (and equally safe) walking safari. Packets of food sold at the entryway inspire even some generally shy creatures to amble over to your vehicle. It's open daily 9am to 4pm, or until 6pm in summer; admission costs $22 adults, $20 seniors, and $13.50 for children ages 3 to 11.

Sports & Outdoor Activities

Tubing is a favorite summer pastime along the rapids of the Guadalupe River below Canyon Dam. Your experience here will depend on the Canyon Dam flow rate: When it's low, you hardly move on the water; when it's high—around 100 cubic feet per second or more—the ride is a lot more fun. The water here is fairly cold, which makes tubing fun during the summer, less so during spring and autumn. In addition, this area is sometimes subject to flooding. Contact the New Braunfels Visitors Bureau (p. 296) for up-to-date information. Outfitters who can help you ride the Guadalupe River on a tube, raft, canoe, or inflatable kayak include **Rockin' R River Rides** (www.rockinr.com; ✆ **800/553-5628** or 830/629-9999) and **Gruene River Company** (www.toobing.com; ✆ **830/625-2800**), both on Gruene Road just south of the Gruene Bridge.

You can go tubing too, at the original **Schlitterbahn ★**, 305 W. Austin St. (www.schlitterbahn.com/new-braunfels; ✆ **830/625-2351**), which now has several branches in Texas, and even one in Kansas City. At 70 acres, including two distinct sections separated by a free tram, Schlitterbahn has a lot more than tubing to offer (though there's an entire park section, named Tubenbach, devoted to that activity). Gigantic slides, wave pools, and rides, including a five-story water fun house and Dragon's Revenge water coaster, make for a day—or more—of fun; there's a resort on the property should you decide to stay overnight. The combination of a natural river-and-woods setting and high-tech attractions makes this splashy playland a standout. The park usually opens in late April and closes in mid-September; call or check the website for exact dates. All-day passes cost $65 for adults, $52 for children ages 3 to 11 and seniors 55+; significant discounts are available if you purchase tickets online.

Those who like their water play a bit more low-key might try New Braunfels' municipal **Landa Park Aquatic Complex,** 164 Landa Park Dr. (www.nbtexas.org/1434/Aquatic-Facilities; ✆ **830/221-4360**). Here you can swim in a pool that's fed by Comal Springs and maintains a constant 72°F (22°C) year round—it has a water slide and mushroom fountain—or at an Olympic-size pool. In the same park, the **City Tube Chute** (www.nbtexas.org/1438/City-Tube-Chute; ✆ **830-608-2165**), the world's longest water slide, gives tubers an exhilarating ride on the Comal River. If you're not prepared to immerse yourself, consider a paddleboat excursion on Landa Lake; see www.nbtexas.org/162/Landa-Park-Attractions or call ✆ **830/221-4350** for details.

Perhaps you want to buy your own toys—and learn how to use them. The 70-acre **Texas Ski Ranch,** 6700 I-35 N. (www.texasskiranch.com; ✆ **830/627-2843**), is paradise for those interested in wake, skate, and motor sports. Features of this expanding complex include a cable lake, boat lake, skate park, and motor track—at all of which you can test the equipment you want to purchase or rent (you can also bring your own). Training clinics and private lessons for a variety of sports are offered. Costs depend on the use of facilities and classes. The main building is open Monday 3pm to dark, Tuesday to Saturday 10am to dark, and Sunday 11am to 6pm. Various other facilities have different hours; check the website.

Where to Stay in New Braunfels & Gruene

See also the resort at the **Schlitterbahn,** above.

The **Prince Solms Inn,** 295 E. San Antonio St. (www.princesolmsinn.com; ✆ **830/312-5387**), was built in 1898 and has been in continuous operation as a hotel since then. A prime downtown location, tree-shaded courtyard, and eight "Texas Victorian" rooms—they're historic without being fussy—have made this inn popular. Many of the rooms are small and the location on a busy street—not to mention the piano bar downstairs—means that they're not overly quiet. Rates range from $125 to $195 double, including breakfast.

A classic 1929 hotel, the **Faust Hotel & Brewing Co.,** 240 S. Seguin St. (www.fausthotel.com; ✆ **830/625-7791**), has refurbished Art Deco–style standard rooms that average from $119 to $169, plus suites for $209. The cheery downstairs brewpub serves up such cross-cultural bar food as German nachos: Kartoffel chips topped with house-made bratwurst, sauerkraut, and beer cheese sauce.

In Gruene, the **Gruene Mansion Inn,** 1275 Gruene Rd. (www.gruenemansioninn.com; ✆ **830/629-2641**), offers 31 rustic-elegant rooms, some in the opulent 1875 plantation house, some in converted former barns, others in individual cottages; 2-night minimums apply in some cases. Accommodations range from $195 to $300 double per night, including buffet breakfast served in the plantation house.

Where to Eat in New Braunfels & Gruene

See also the **Faust Hotel & Brewing Co.** (above) and the **Phoenix Saloon** (p. 298).

At the stylish **Huisache Grill ★**, 303 W. San Antonio St. (www.huisache.com; ✆ **830/620-9001**), the American menu has both traditional and contemporary dishes. You can't go wrong with the pecan-crusted pork chop, the mixed grill, or the bleu-cheese steak. As might be expected from a dining room with a wine bar, there's a nice selection of bottles. Lunch and dinner are served daily. Prices are on the moderate side, with most dinner entrees ranging from $16 to $20, a bit higher for steak.

The **New Braunfels Smokehouse,** 1090 N. Business at I-35 (www.nbsmokehouse.com; ✆ **830/625-2416**), opened in 1951 as a tasting room for the meats it started hickory-smoking in 1943. Now in a smaller building around the corner from the original location, it's more of a deli with picnic tables and paper plates, along with a cold box where you can buy packaged meats. Hot dishes like chicken and dumplings are offered, too.

For classic surf-and-turf at classic prices, **Myron's Steakhouse,** 136 N. Castell Ave. (www.myronsprime.com; ✆ **830/624-1024**), offers clubby dining in a converted 1924 movie theater. The cocktail bar is a nice complement. Next door, **McAdoo's Seafood Company,** 196 N. Castell Ave. (www.mcadoos.com; ✆ **830/629-FISH** [629-3474]), serves well-prepared fish in a variety of styles—from Creole to fried and grilled—in a beautifully restored historic post office.

In Gruene, the **Gristmill River Restaurant & Bar,** 1287 Gruene Rd. (www.gristmillrestaurant.com; ✆ **830/625-0684**), a converted 100-year-old cotton gin, serves a Texas-casual menu of burgers and chicken-fried steak as well as healthful salads. Kick back on one of its multiple decks and gaze out at the Guadalupe River.

New Braunfels & Gruene Arts & Entertainment

See also **Gruene Hall ★★★**, p. 299, and the **Phoenix Saloon,** p. 298.

At the **Brauntex Performing Arts Theatre,** 290 W. San Antonio St. (www.brauntex.org; ✆ **830/627-0808**), a restored 1942 movie theater in midtown New Braunfels, you can expect to see anything from tribute shows to major talent like Travis Tritt.

PLANNING YOUR TRIP TO SAN ANTONIO & AUSTIN

18

Spontaneity is all well and good once you arrive at your destination, but to get the most out of your Texas adventure, a little planning goes a long way. In this chapter, you'll find a host of helpful tools, including information on how to get to San Antonio and Austin, how to get around once you're in each city, and how much you can expect things to cost. You'll also get the inside track on local resources, as well as more general trip planning information.

These details are all designed to ease your way after you make the first big decision: when to go. Although their climates are similar, San Antonio and Austin have different festivals, events, and major conferences that fill up hotel rooms—or that you might want to attend. For San Antonio's calendar of events, see p. 34; for Austin's, p. 174.

ARRIVING

Although San Antonio and Austin are only 80 miles from each other, they're very distinct in terms of sensibility and things to see and do. You might visit both if you have enough time, but as far as airfares and flight connections are concerned, there's no benefit to flying into the larger San Antonio airport if you want to visit Austin—especially since both cities are vying for, and often succeeding in getting, more and more direct/nonstop flights. Fly into the destination where you plan on staying primarily.

Arriving in San Antonio

BY PLANE

The two-terminal **San Antonio International Airport (SAT),** 8 miles north of downtown, is compact and easy to navigate.

After being a construction zone for several years, the airport completed new rental car and short-term public parking facilities at the end of 2017. For the most up-to-date information on new construction; added features, including a cell-phone waiting area; parking availability at the airport lots; and even the time it's likely to take you to get through TSA checking (Terminal A only), log on to **www.sanantonio.gov/SAT**. There's also a 24/7 information line, ✆ **210/207-3433**.

GETTING TO & FROM THE AIRPORT Loop 410 and U.S. 281 S. intersect just outside the airport. If you're renting a car here (see p. 307 for car rental information), it should take about 15 to 20 minutes to drive downtown via U.S. 281 S. Most hotels within a mile or two provide free shuttle service to and from the airport (check when you make your reservation). If you're staying downtown, however, you'll most likely have to pay your own way.

VIA Metropolitan Transit's bus no. 5 is the cheapest ($1.30) way to get downtown, but also the slowest; it'll take from 35 to 40 minutes. Pick it up at the far west end of Terminal B. **SuperShuttle** (www.supershuttle.com/locations/sanantonio-sat; ✆ **800/258-3826**), with a booth outside each of the terminals, offers shared van service from the airport to downtown hotels for $18 per person one way, $34 round-trip. If you download the mobile app, you can often get a discount. The drawback of this service is that you often share your ride with several others, who may be dropped off before you. You don't have to book in advance for pickups at the airport, but you must make an online reservation or phone 24 hours ahead to arrange a pickup when departing.

A series of **ride-share** stations line the lower level of Terminal A. **Uber.com** and **Lyft.com** are among the approved vendors; the police give extra vetting to the drivers in those companies who want to pick up passengers at the airport. Expect to pay about $24 to go from the airport to downtown.

There's also a **taxi** queue in front of each terminal, past all the ride-share stations. If you don't want to hassle with trying to find your Lyft or Uber driver among the waiting crowds when you arrive, it may be easier to take a cab, if more expensive: You'll pay approximately $35 to get downtown.

BY TRAIN

San Antonio's train station is located at 350 Hoefgen St., in St. Paul's Square, on the east side of downtown near the Alamodome and adjacent to the Sunset Station entertainment complex. Lockers are not available, but Amtrak will hold passengers' bags in a secure location. Information about the city is available at the main counter. For train schedules and fees, go to **Amtrak** (www.amtrak.com; ✆ **800/USA-RAIL** [872-7245]).

BY BUS

San Antonio's bustling **Greyhound** station, 500 N. St. Mary's St. (www.greyhound.com; ✆ **210/270-5868**), is located downtown about 2 blocks from the River Walk. The station, open 24 hours, is within walking distance of a number of hotels, and many public streetcar and bus lines run nearby.

BY CAR

As has been said of Rome, all roads lead to San Antonio. The city is fed by four interstates (I-35, I-10, I-37, and I-410), five U.S. highways (U.S. 281, U.S. 90, U.S. 87, U.S. 181, and U.S. 81), and five state highways (Hwy. 16, Hwy. 13, Hwy. 211, Hwy. 151, and Hwy. 1604). In San Antonio, I-410 and Hwy. 1604, which circle the city, are referred to as Loop 410 and Loop 1604. All freeways lead into the central business district; as noted before, U.S. 281 and Loop 410 are closest to the airport.

San Antonio is about a 4-hour drive from Dallas, a 3-hour drive from Houston, and an hour and a half from Austin.

Arriving in Austin

BY PLANE

The **Austin-Bergstrom International Airport (AUS)** is on the site of the former Bergstrom Air Force Base, just off Hwy. 71 (Ben White Blvd.), about 8 miles southwest of the Capitol. It has one main terminal, the Barbara Jordan Terminal, that serves most of the major airlines, as well as the newer South Terminal, for discount carriers.

For comprehensive information about the airport, including a map, list of food vendors, and schedule of live music performances, log on to www.austintexas.gov/department/airport. For all-day information, call ✆ **512/530-ABIA** [530-2242]).

GETTING TO & FROM THE AIRPORT Most of the major car-rental companies have outlets at the airport (see below). The trip from the airport to downtown by car can take anywhere from 20 to 45 minutes, much more if you're headed to north Austin. During rush hour, there are often backups along highways 290/71.

Bus No. 20 on CapMetro (www.capmetro.org; ✆ **512-474-1200**) is a high frequency route from the airport to downtown and the University of Texas, with many stops along the way for transfers to other parts of town. The fare is $1.25 for a single trip, $2.50 for limitless transfers in a single day. You'll recognize the bus stop in the ground transportation area: It's got a bright blue neon guitar. It should take about half an hour to get downtown. If you're not in a huge rush to get to your hotel, **SuperShuttle** (www.supershuttle.com/locations/austin-aus; ✆ **800/258-3826** or 512/258-3826) offers comfortable minivan service to hotels and residences. It costs $18 one-way ($34 round-trip) to a downtown hotel, with discounts for those who download the SuperShuttle app.

Ride-shares are by far the most popular way of getting from the airport to destinations in all parts of Austin. You'll find a series of designated waiting sections in the ground transportation area, coded to help your driver locate you (and vice versa). **Lyft.com**, **Uber.com**, and **RideAustin.com** (p. 311) all serve the airport. It'll cost about $22 to get downtown.

There's also a **taxi rank** outside the terminal, though occasionally you won't find any waiting. The cab companies that serve the airport include **ATX Co-op** (✆ **512/333-5555**) and **Yellow Cab** (✆ **512/452-9999**). The minimum fare is $12.30, which includes a $1 airport surcharge; expect to pay at least $30 (without tip) to get downtown. All taxis accept major credit cards.

BY TRAIN

Austin's **Amtrak** station, 250 N. Lamar Blvd. (www.amtrak.com, ✆ **800/872-7245** or 512/476-5684), is in the southwest part of downtown. The city is on the Texas Eagle route; see www.texaseagle.com/station/AUS.php for details about the train station. A ride-share to any downtown destination shouldn't cost more than $6.50; several CapMetro bus routes stop here too.

BY BUS

Austin's **Greyhound** station, 916 E. Koenig Lane (www.greyhound.com; ✆ **800/231-2222** or 512/458-4463), located near the city's old Robert Mueller Airport, is convenient for the Mueller/North Loop area but not much else. That said, it's on several CapMetro bus routes and only about 15 minutes from downtown by ride-share.

BY CAR

Austin is about 2½ to 3 hours from Houston and 3 to 4 hours from Dallas/Fort Worth; it's about a 90-minute drive from San Antonio. **I-35,** the north-south approach to Austin, intersects with **Hwy. 290,** a major east-west thoroughfare, and **Hwy. 183,** which also runs roughly north-south through town. For those staying on the west side of Austin, **Loop 1** (known as MoPac) is helpful. **Hwy 130,** a toll road, is a faster alternative to I-35, bypassing traffic on the east side of town.

CAR RENTALS

Both San Antonio and Austin have compact downtowns that are not generally easy to navigate by car. Many of the streets are narrow and one-way, and it can be tough to find a parking spot; in Austin, streets are also constantly being closed off for festivals. Overnight parking at hotels in both cities is expensive. ***Bottom line:*** If you're planning to stay downtown for all or part of your stay, it makes sense not to rent a car, or rent one only when you're ready to do some touring outside the city. (Downtown San Antonio in particular is a treat for walkers, who can stroll from one tourist attraction to another or amble along a beautifully landscaped river.)

If you're staying on the outskirts or in an area where parking isn't a problem, it might be convenient to rent a car at the airport, but remember that airports may tack on facility charges or have higher tax rates than city offices. Also be sure to check if there's an extra charge for returning your car to a different location.

Austin is one of only seven cities in the U.S. to have a **Car2Go** (www.car2go.com/US/en/austin) car-sharing program. It's a bit like short-term car rental only with more flexibility: You use the app to locate a car near you and drop it off at a parking spot near your destination. In Austin, the car fleet consists of two types of Mercedes Benz, so you get the extra kick of driving a luxury car. Note that you have to plan in advance to get vetted; the FAQ section of the website has more details.

All the national car rental companies operate in both San Antonio and Austin and have desks at the airports. Companies include **Alamo** (www.alamo.com; ✆ **800/651-1223**), **Avis** (www.avis.com; ✆ **800/352-7900**), **Budget** (www.budget.com; ✆ **800/218-7992**), **Dollar** (www.dollar.com; ✆ **800/800-5252**), **Enterprise** (www.enterprise.com; ✆ **855/266-9289**), **Hertz** (www.hertz.com; ✆ **800/654-4173**), **National** (www.nationalcar.com; ✆ **800/227-7368**), and **Thrifty** (www.thrifty.com; ✆ **800/367-2277**). Most car rental agencies have a minimum age requirement—usually age 25. Some also have a maximum age limit. If you're concerned that these limits might affect you, ask about rental requirements at the time of booking to avoid problems later.

Instead of going to the car rental companies directly, we recommend using **AutoSlash.com**. This nifty website applies every discount code around to your rental, finding you rates you won't find elsewhere at all of the usual car rental outlets. But the savings don't end there: Between the time you make your reservation and pick up your car, the company tracks the rental rate, and if it drops, AutoSlash automatically rebooks you at the lower rate. It's miraculous.

INSURANCE Make sure you're insured. Hasty assumptions about your personal auto insurance or a rental agency's additional coverage could end up costing you tens of thousands of dollars, even if you are involved in an accident that is clearly the fault of another driver.

If you already have your own car insurance, you are most likely covered in the United States for loss of or damage to a rental car and liability in case of injury to any other party involved in an accident. Be sure to check your policy before you spend extra money (around $15 or more per day) on the **collision damage waiver (CDW)** offered by all agencies.

If you use a major credit card (especially gold and platinum cards) to pay for the rental, it may provide some coverage as well. Terms vary widely, so call your credit card company directly before you rent, to learn if you can rely on the card for coverage. If you are uninsured, your credit card may provide primary coverage as long as you decline the rental agency's insurance. If you already have insurance, your credit card may provide secondary coverage, which basically covers your deductible. However, note that *credit cards will not cover liability,* which is the cost of injury to an outside party and/or damage to an outside party's vehicle. If you don't hold an insurance policy, seriously consider buying the rental company's additional liability insurance, even if you decline the CDW.

GETTING AROUND SAN ANTONIO

By Public Transportation

BUS **VIA Metropolitan Transit Service** (www.viainfo.net; ✆ **210/362-2020**) offers regular bus service for $1.30, with an additional 15¢ charge for transfers. Express buses cost $2.60. You'll need exact change if you don't download the **VIA goMobile app.** You can also buy a pass online (www.viaonlinestore.net) or pick one up at a VIA service center. A single day pass is $2.75 for unlimited use; 7-day passes cost $12.

Via has three VIVA routes designed to streamline visits for tourists. The **VIVA Culture Route** (buses 11, 11a, 11b) travels from downtown to the San Antonio Museum of Art, Japanese Tea Garden, San Antonio Zoo, Witte Museum, Brackenridge Park, and the Botanical Garden; the **VIVA Missions** (bus 40) goes from downtown to the four historic missions in the south; and the **VIVA Centro** (bus 301) takes you all around downtown, east side and west side. You can catch all of these VIVA buses at Alamo Plaza. ***Tip:*** During large festivals such as Fiesta and the Texas Folklife Festival, VIA offers many Park & Ride lots that allow you to leave your car and take a bus downtown.

RIVER TAXI **GO RIO river-taxi shuttles** (www.goriocruises.com; ✆ **210/227-4746**) stop at locations along the Downtown Reach and Museum Reach sections of the River Walk; they run daily from 10am to 9pm. Tickets ($12 for unlimited rides for one day on either the Downtown Reach or Museum Reach sections, $16 for a dual ticket) are available from boat drivers—just wave from one of the marked stops—or at various hotels along the River Walk.

By Ride-share and Taxi

Uber.com and **Lyft.com** are both popular in San Antonio. Cabs are available outside the airport, near the Greyhound and Amtrak terminals (only when a train is due, though), and at major downtown hotels, but they're next to impossible to hail on the street; most of the time, you'll need to phone for one in advance. The best of the taxi companies in town and also the largest is **Yellow Cab** (www.yellowcabsa.com; ✆ **210/222-2222**), which has an excellent record of turning up when promised. There's also an app for the company, which provides such services as wheelchair-accessible taxis (see "Disabled Travelers," p. 316).

By Bicycle

San Antonio has a public bike-share program, **SWell Cycle** (formerly San Antonio Bcycle and still part of the Bcycle city network), with bikes available throughout the city at B-stations. Get the details, plus B-station locations and bike routes at **https://sanantonio.bcycle.com** or download the SWell Cycle app. Purchase passes at B-stations for 30-minute rides ($3). A 24-hour pass is $12, and monthly membership is $18 ($100 for entire year).

By Car

San Antonio's weekday rush hour (generally 7:30 to 9am and 4:30 to 6pm Mon–Fri) may not be bad compared with that of Houston or Dallas, but it's getting worse. The city's rapid growth means you can expect to find major highway construction or repairs going on anywhere at any given time.

SAN ANTONIO PARKING You'll find plenty of parking lots scattered around the north and east sides of downtown. These run about $5 to $10 per day. Parking meters are not plentiful in the heart of downtown, but you can find some on the streets near the River Walk and on Broadway. The cost is $1.80 per hour (with a 1-hr. time limit) in many downtown spots. Parking is free after 5pm on Tuesdays as a part of the Downtown Tuesday (www.downtowntuesday.com) program. There's also free on-street parking after 6pm daily and all day Sunday; and $5 parking at select city-run facilities after 5pm on weeknights. A full list of city-owned garages, lots, and meters can be found at www.sanantonio.gov/CCDO/parking/parkingmap. For non-city owned lots and garages, click on www.downtownsanantonio.org/discover. A San Antonio parking app is in development; for updates, check www.sanantonio.gov/CCDO/parking/ParkingLocatorApp.

GETTING AROUND AUSTIN

By Public Transportation

Austin is eco-friendly, youth-oriented, and tech crazy, so even though it has as much of an entrenched car culture as most western cities, it's trying to move toward solutions to its increasing traffic. Public transportation is widely used by the young and the middle-class (partly because they're too broke paying rent to keep cars). The city's **Capital Metropolitan Transportation Authority** (www.capmetro.org; ✆ **800/474-1201,** 512/474-1200, or TTY 512/385-5872), operates more than 50 bus routes. A single ride on the standard MetroBus costs $1.25; a day pass $2.50; a week pass $11.25. MetroExpress routes that take advantage of MoPac express lanes cost $3.50 for a single ride, $7 for a full-day pass, and $27.50 for a week of unlimited rides.

There are several ways to get tickets and passes. You can buy them on board the bus with exact change; purchase them at various retail outlets, including H-E-B and Ralph supermarkets; get them from kiosks at any MetroRail (see below) station; get them online at https://marketplace.bytemark.co/marketplace/cmta; or—the easiest way—download the Capital Metro app and use your smart phone to board. The app will also help you plan your route and let you know how long you'll have to wait for rides and connections.

From Monday to Saturday, CapMetro also offers MetroRail **light-rail service** between downtown and the bedroom community of Lakeline, with a few stops in between, including one near the UT campus at Martin Luther King Blvd. The price is the same as the MetroExpress routes and tickets may be purchased the same way. Bikes are welcome aboard MetroRail, too.

By Ride-share & Taxi

For a while, **Uber.com** and **Lyft.com** were not available in Austin; as a result, several other ride-share companies vied to take their place. Uber and Lyft are back and the only ride-share app that gives them any competition is the non-profit **RideAustin.com**. It's a great local company with fair rates, a high percentage of which are shared with the drivers. The only hitch is that the app can't be used outside of Austin.

Austin's most reliable taxi company, with the largest fleet, is **Yellow Cab** (www.yellowcabaustin.com; ✆ **512/452-9999**).

By Bicycle

Austin's bike-share program, **Austin BCycle,** has bikes available throughout the city at B-stations. Get the details, plus B-station locations and bike routes at **https://austin.bcycle.com**. Purchase passes at B-stations for unlimited 60-minute rides ($4 for each additional half-hour). A 24-hour pass is $12, a weekender pass is $18, and monthly membership is $11 (plus a $15 enrollment fee).

By Car

Driving in Austin can be a challenge for visitors. Highways are rife with signs that suddenly insist LEFT LANE MUST TURN LEFT or RIGHT LANE MUST TURN RIGHT—generally positioned so they're noticeable only when it's too late to switch. I-35 is mined with tricky on-and-off ramps and, around downtown, a confusing complex of upper and lower levels. The rapidly developing area to the northwest, where Hwy. 183 connects I-35 with MoPac and the Capital of Texas Highway, requires particular vigilance, as the connections occur very rapidly. A number of major downtown streets are one-way; many don't have street signs or have signs so covered with foliage they're impossible to read. Driving is particularly confusing in the university area, where streets like "32½" suddenly turn up. Multiply the difficulties at night, when you need super vision to read the ill-lit street indicators. Even GPS can't help you when a jerk cuts you off when you're quickly trying to change lanes. All this to say it's a good idea to check your route before you hit the road, so you'll know where to anticipate exiting the freeway, or where those street signs you can't read are likely to be.

AUSTIN PARKING Unless you have legislative plates, you're likely to find the selection of parking spots in downtown Austin extremely limited during the week; as a result, many downtown restaurants offer valet parking (hourly rates $4–$6). There are several lots around the area, costing from $6 to $10 per hour, but the most convenient ones fill up quickly; use the **Park Me**

Texas Driving Rules

Texas has a reputation for frontier lawlessness, but in fact has fairly strict driving regulations. See the Texas Department of Transportation's Safety and Laws section for additional information: www.txdot.gov/driver/laws.html. For current road conditions, check the constantly updated site www.drivetexas.org, or phone ✆ **800/452-9292.** The **Waze Navigation & Live Traffic app** can also help with current road conditions and can alert you if you're exceeding the speed limit.

Speed limit: The maximum speed limit is **70 mph** for the most part, but the Texas Transportation Commission is permitted to establish a higher one if a traffic or engineering study determines it to be safe. The only road in the state that has a maximum speed of **85 mph** is the 40-mile stretch of Hwy. 130 toll road from Austin to Seguin, just north of San Antonio. If you don't see a speed limit posted in a busy urban area, you can assume that it's no higher than **30 mph.**

Turning right on a red light: You are allowed to make a right turn on red after stopping at a designated place (including both lanes of dual right turn lanes) unless it is prohibited by a specific sign.

Seat Belts: Seat belts are mandatory for both passengers and drivers. If you're caught without buckling up, you might have to pay up to $200 in fines.

Messaging: There's a **statewide ban on the use of cell phones for reading or writing text messages or emails while driving**. Additionally, the use of handheld cell phones is **not allowed** under state law for drivers under 18 years of age.

Child safety seats: Children under 8 years old must use a safety seat unless they are taller than 4 ft. 9 in.

app (www.parkme.com/austin-parking) to save yourself time and gas. If you're lucky enough to find a metered spot, it'll run you $1 per hour, with a 3-hour limit; most meters have card readers or accept payment via the **Park X app** (https://austin.getparkx.com). There is a free Capitol visitor garage on 15th and San Jacinto (2-hr. time limit). After 5pm, some garages charge a flat fee of $10 to $12.

In the university area, trying to find a spot near the shopping strip known as "the Drag" can be just that. However, cruise the side streets and you'll eventually find a pay lot that's not filled. The two most convenient on-campus parking garages are located near San Jacinto and East 26th streets and off 25th Street between San Antonio and Nueces. There's also a (free!) parking lot near the LBJ Library. Check **www.utexas.edu/parking** for additional places to park your car.

BEFORE YOU GO

What to Bring

Pack for weather contingencies, even in summer. You never know when an unexpected cool front or storm system will blow in. And you can depend on

WHAT THINGS COST IN SAN ANTONIO & AUSTIN	US$
Ride-share from airport to city center (both cities)	24.00
Adult fare day pass on bus San Antonio/Austin	2.75/2.50
Gallon of gas (Texas average)	2.60
Double at St. Anthony Hotel, San Antonio (expensive)	300.00
Double at The InterContinental Stephen F. Austin (moderate)	159.00
Double at Holiday Inn Express—San Antonio Riverwalk (inexpensive)	89.00
Lunch for one at Guero's Taco Bar, Austin (moderate)	11.00
Dinner for one, without wine, at Bliss in San Antonio (expensive)	65.00
Dinner for one, without beer, at Eastside Cafe Austin (moderate)	23.00
Dinner for one, without beer, at Schilo's, San Antonio (inexpensive)	12.00
Long-neck beer, bar	5.00
Soft drink at restaurant	2.00
Cup of espresso	3.50
Adult admission to LBJ Library & Museum (Austin)	19.00–90.00
Movie ticket, adult (average)	11.00

needing a sweater or light jacket when you go out to eat. Air-conditioning in many San Antonio and Austin restaurants is cranked up to frigid levels—maybe to compensate for how many warm bodies they pack in, maybe to keep patrons from lingering too long.

Pack **prescription medications** in your carry-on luggage, and carry them in their original containers, with pharmacy labels—otherwise they won't make it through airport security. Visitors from outside the U.S. should carry generic names of prescription drugs.

Don't forget to bring your health insurance card along, whether it be for a private plan or government-issued Medicare or Medicaid. It's essential to check beforehand what doctors, dentists, and emergency services in your destination are covered by your health plan.

For more helpful information on packing for your trip, go to Frommers.com and click on the "Tips & News" section, which has packing tips and information.

What It Will Cost

Things in San Antonio tend to be moderately priced, especially for a large city that's a major tourist hub. You can drop a lot of money here, but you'll also find plenty of hotel and restaurant bargains. In Austin, room scarcity and soaring real estate prices keep hotel prices high. Despite a thriving culinary scene, however, restaurant meals aren't nearly as expensive in Austin as in places like

FOR international VISITORS

If you plan to **rent a car** in the U.S., your foreign driver's license will probably suffice, but to be safe you may want to obtain an international driver's license. Also note that insurance and taxes are almost never included in quoted rental car rates in the U.S. Ask your rental agency about these fees—they can add significantly to your rental car cost.

You should also check with your credit or debit card issuer to see what fees, if any, will be charged for **overseas transactions.** Fees can amount to 3 percent or more of the purchase price. ATM fees are often higher for international transactions (up to $5 or more) than for domestic ones (where they're rarely more than $3).

Mobile phones: Outside of the U.S., most mobile phones use the GSM (Global System for Mobile Communications) wireless network; be advised that GSM has poor reach in much of the U.S. Your phone will probably work in major cities, but it may not work in rural areas, and you may not be able to text back home. If you plan to cover a lot of territory, consider buying a cheap American phone for the duration of your stay.

Currency: The most common bills in the U.S. are $1 (a "buck"), $5, $10, and $20 denominations. There are also $2 bills (seldom encountered), $50 bills, and $100 bills. (The last two are usually not welcome as payment for small purchases.) Coins come in seven denominations: 1¢ (1 cent, or a penny); 5¢ (5 cents, or a nickel); 10¢ (10 cents, or a dime); 25¢ (25 cents, or a quarter); 50¢ (50 cents, or a half dollar); the gold-colored Sacagawea coin, worth $1; and the rare silver dollar. Note that the U.S. has no **value-added tax** (VAT) at the national level, but every state, county, and city may levy its own local taxes on purchases, hotels, air travel, and other line items.

Electricity: Like Canada, the United States uses 110 to 120 volts AC (60 cycles), compared to 220 to 240 volts AC (50 cycles) in most of Europe, Australia, and New Zealand. Converters that change 220–240 volts to 110–120 volts are difficult to find in the United States, so bring one with you.

Time Zones: The continental United States is divided into four time zones: Eastern Standard Time (EST), Central Standard Time (CST), Mountain Standard Time (MST), and Pacific Standard Time (PST). Most of Texas is in Central Standard Time, which means that when it's 9am in San Antonio (CST), it's 10am in New York City (EST), 3pm in London (GMT), and 2am the next day in Sydney.

Tipping: In the U.S., most service personnel are paid lower wages with the expectation that they'll make it up in tips. Don't stiff the people whose job is to make your trip a success. In hotels, tip **bellhops** $5 and tip the **chamber staff** $5 per day. Tip the **doorman** or **concierge** only if he or she has provided you with some specific service. Tip **valet-parking attendants** $2–$5 every time you get your car. In restaurants, bars, and nightclubs, tip **service staff** and **bartenders** 15 to 20 percent of the check. (American restaurants usually don't include a service fee in the bill.) Tip **cabdrivers** 15 to 20 percent of the fare, and tip **skycaps** at airports at least $2 per bag.

Embassies: All embassies are in the nation's capital, Washington, D.C. To find where your embassy is, go to **www.embassy.org/embassies**.

New York or San Francisco. In both cities, museums and other indoor attractions won't break the bank, and there are so many free outdoor activities in Austin, they (almost) compensate for the high hotel rates.

It's always advisable to bring money in a variety of forms on a vacation: a mix of cash, credit cards, and ATM cards. Credit and debit cards are the most widely used form of payment: You must have a credit card (not a debit card) to rent a car, and hotels usually require a credit card imprint as a deposit against expenses. Increasingly, however, people are using smart phones linked to bank accounts instead of credit or debit cards: Apple Pay for iPhones and other devices with iOS platforms (www.apple.com/apple-pay/where-to-use) and Google Pay for Android devices (https://pay.google.com/about/where-to-use).

Frommer's lists prices in the local currency. The currency conversion rates we list here were correct at press time, but rates fluctuate—before you leave on your trip, consult a currency-exchange website such as www.xe.com to get up-to-the-minute rates.

THE VALUE OF THE U.S. DOLLAR VS. OTHER POPULAR CURRENCIES

US$	Can$	UK£	Euro (€)	Aus$	NZ$
1	1.33	0.77	0.88	1.41	1.48

[FastFACTS] SAN ANTONIO & AUSTIN

Area Code The telephone area code in San Antonio is **210.** In Austin it is **512.** The area code for most of the Hill Country towns, including Fredericksburg, Kerrville, and New Braunfels, is **830.**

Business Hours Banks are usually open Monday to Friday 9am–5pm, Saturday 9am–1pm. Many banks have 24-hr. ATMs in lobbies or via drive-through windows. Shops tend to be open from 9 or 10am until 5:30 or 6pm Monday through Saturday, with shorter hours on Sunday. Most malls are open Monday to Saturday 10am–9pm, Sunday noon–6pm.

Crime and Safety The crime rate for both property and violent crime in **San Antonio** has risen in recent years, so there's a strong police presence downtown; as a result, muggings, pickpockets, and purse snatchings in the area are rare. Use common sense as you would anywhere else: Walk only on well-lit, well-populated streets.

Austin's rate of property crimes is above the national average, but it's at a 20-year low in comparison to past years—thanks in good part to a special police task force created in 2016. Violent crimes are lower than the national average, but sexual assaults on the hike-and-bike trail in 2017 and a series of bombings in 2018 shook the city. Exercise caution. Most crimes have occurred when people return late to their cars in quiet areas or are too inebriated to pay attention to their surroundings.

Dentists To find a dentist, contact the **San Antonio District Dental Society,** 14603 Huebner Rd., Ste. 2403 (www.sadds.org; ✆ **210/732-1264**), or in Austin, the **Texas Dental Association,** 1946 S. IH-35, Ste. 400 (www.tda.org; ✆ **512-443-3675**), which should be able to help with referrals. Your hotel should be able to provide good referrals, too.

Disabled Travelers In San Antonio, the **Disability Access Office,** Municipal Plaza Building, 114 W. Commerce St., 9th fl. (www.sanantonio.gov/DAO; ✆ **210/207-7135**), is a good resource for travelers with disabilities. Among the resources on its website are a map of places that offer wheelchair access to the River Walk, and details on where to find Audible Pedestrian Signals for the Visually Impaired. Public transportation in San Antonio is not accessible to all, but the VIAtrans Paratransit service (www.viainfo.net/viatrans-paratransit; ✆ **210/362-2140**) provides shared-ride door-to-door service for those requesting it at least a day in advance. As this service is primarily for residents, an application must be provided and approved in advance. **Yellow Cab** vehicles for wheelchair users can be booked through the company's website (www.yellowcabsa.com/wheelchair-taxi-service) or app, or by phoning ✆ **210/222-2222** and specifying that you require a wheelchair-accessible taxi.

Austin is one of the most accessible cities in the U.S., with an active **Americans with Disabilities Act (ADA)** office, 505 Barton Springs Rd., # 600 (www.austintexas.gov/department/americans-disabilities-act-office; ✆ **512/974-3256** or 512/974-1897). The website has lots of useful links, and you can phone to check whether specific hotels or other facilities are in compliance with the Act. All the large downtown hotels maintain accessible rooms and parking, as do most large hotels in outlying areas. All of Austin's public buses are equipped with lifts, and CapMetro maintains paratransit service (for details call ✆ **512/369-6083** or go to the website www.capmetro.org/accessibility). For taxi service for wheelchair users, call **Yellow Cab**'s service line (✆ **512/452-9999**), and make it clear that you need a wheelchair-accessible cab, or order a cab through the website (www.yellowcabaustin.com/wheelchair-taxi-service/) or app.

Doctors Check your medical insurance plan in advance to see if there are physicians in your network in the city you're visiting. For a referral in San Antonio, contact **the Bexar County Medical Society** at 4334 N. Loop 1604 W. (www.bcms.org; ✆ **210/301-4391**), Monday through Friday 8am–5pm. In Austin, the **Travis County Medical Society,** 4300 North Lamar Blvd. (www.tcms.com; ✆ **512-206-1249**), and **Seton Medical Center** (www.seton.net; ✆ **512/324-1000**) both have physician referral services. Another option is **Urgent Care** facilities—found either through your insurance network, or an online search—if you need to see a physician quickly and don't want to pay emergency room prices.

Drugstores **CVS** (www.cvs.com; ✆ **800/746-7287**) and **Walgreens** (www.walgreens.com; ✆ **800/925-4733**) are the major chains in both San Antonio and Austin. Most are open late every day; some Walgreens are open 24 hours. Call the 800 number or log onto the website to find the nearest location to you. You'll find several branches of **Randalls** drugstores in Austin, and most **H-E-B grocery stores** in both cities also have pharmacies. In Austin, the **Medsavers** pharmacy, 1800 W. 35th St. (www.medsaverspharmacy.com; ✆ **512/465-9292**), provides affordable medications for everyone, even the uninsured.

Emergencies In both cities, call ✆ **911** for police, the fire department, or an ambulance.

Family Travel With its three major theme parks and museums galore for kids to enjoy, San Antonio is one of the family friendliest places to visit in the country. A good online resource for up-to-date happenings is https://sanantonio.kidsoutandabout.com. See p. 103 for more suggestions.

Austin is perfect for outdoorsy and eco-conscious families, though there are fewer places to play indoors than there are in some cities. A good resource for things to see and do around town is https://austin.kidsoutandabout.com; another is Austin Family (www.austinfamily.com; ✆ **512/733-0038**), though it's geared more to residents than visitors. See p. 245 for more suggestions.

Hospitals The main downtown hospital in San Antonio is **Baptist Medical Center,** 111 Dallas St. (www.baptisthealthsystem.com; ✆ **210/297-7000**). The **Children's Hospital of San Antonio,** 333 N. Santa Rosa St. (www.chofsa.org; ✆ **210/704-2011**), is also downtown.

In Austin, **Dell Seton Medical Center** at the University of Texas, 1500 Red River St. (www.seton.net/locations/dell-seton; ✆ **512/324-7000**); **St. David's,** 3801 N. Lamar Blvd. (www.stdavids.com; ✆ **512/407-7000**); and **Seton Medical Center Austin,** 1201 W. 38th St. (www.seton.net/locations/smc; ✆ **512/324-1000**), have good and convenient emergency-care facilities.

Internet & Wi-Fi Most hotels, inns, and Airbnbs in both San Antonio and Austin offer access to Wi-Fi; although there's often an extra charge in the rooms, where it's secure, many hotels have (nonsecure) signals in their lobbies. Most coffee shops also offer free Wi-Fi. Public libraries in both cities are a great place to plug in to free Wi-Fi networks or even work on a library computer. See the **San Antonio Public Library** site (www.mysapl.org/Services/Additional-ServicesPublic-Computers-Wifi) or the **Austin Public Library** site (https://library.austintexas.gov/computers-and-wifi) for information.

Liquor Laws Texas liquor laws are complicated, with many arcane regulations on the books. What you need to know: In both Austin and San Antonio packaged **liquor** may be sold between 10am and 9pm Monday through Saturday, but not on Sunday, though you can buy **beer and wine** on Sunday after noon. On Sunday, alcoholic beverages may not be served in bars and restaurants until noon. Last call in Texas is at 2am (some restaurants and bars have licenses that permit them to sell alcohol until later.) The legal age to buy and consume alcohol in Texas is 21, but anyone over age 5 is permitted to drink under a parent's supervision.

LGBT Travelers San Antonio has a large, but not exceedingly visible, lesbian, gay, bisexual, and transgender population. The top info resources are the **San Antonio LGBT Chamber of Commerce** (www.salgbtchamber.org; ✆ **210/504-9429**); and **Out In SA** (www.outinsa.com), a lifestyle site with comprehensive listings of LGBT-friendly events and activities, along with news, food and nightlife reviews, health and fitness tips, and more. The **Esperanza Peace & Justice Center,** 922 San Pedro (www.esperanzacenter.org; ✆ **210/228-0201**), often screens films or has lectures on topics of interest to LGBT travelers. See p. 127 for nightlife suggestions.

A university town and the most left-leaning enclave in Texas, Austin has the third largest LBGTQ community in the U.S. The premier online resource for events, programs, and political action is the **Austin LGBT Chamber of Commerce** (www.austinlgbtchamber.com; ✆ **512/761-5428**). **Book Woman,** 5501 North Lamar, #A-105 (www.ebookwoman.com; ✆ **512/472-2785**) is the best place to find gay and lesbian books and magazines. Established in 1987, the annual **Austin Gay and Lesbian International Film Festival,** held in September, debuts works by gay, lesbian, bisexual, and transgender filmmakers from throughout the world. Log on to www.agliff.org for additional information, or call ✆ **512/302-9889.** See p. 280 for details on the popular bar **Cheer Up Charlie's.**

Newspapers & Magazines The ***San Antonio Express-News*** (www.mysantonio.com) is the city's daily newspaper; San Antonio also has a free alternative weekly, ***The Current*** (www.thecurrent.com), which has a skimpy print version but a good online presence. The daily ***Austin American-Statesman*** (www.austin360.com) is Austin's daily newspaper; the free alternative weekly ***Austin Chronicle*** (www.auschron.com) focuses on the arts, entertainment, and politics. Monday through Friday, the University of Texas in Austin publishes the ***Daily Texan*** (www.dailytexanonline.com) newspaper, covering everything from on-campus news to international events.

Police In both cities, call ✆ **911** in an emergency, ✆ **311** if the call is not urgent. The stranded/ disabled motorists line for the Texas Highway Patrol is **800/525-5555.**

Postal Services To find the closest **United States Postal Service** office to you, go to www.usps.com. **UPS** (www.ups.com) and **FedEx** (www.fedex.com) have several offices in both cities if you need to send packages.

Senior Travel In both San Antonio and Austin, seniors can expect to get $1 or $2 off the price of admission to museums and attractions. Golf resorts in the San Antonio area attract a lot of retirees. Senior travel isn't as highly promoted in youth-oriented Austin as it is in many other destinations, and the city doesn't get many "winter Texans," part-time residents from Canada or the northern U.S. Austin's **Old Bakery and Emporium,** 1006 Congress Ave. (www.austintexas.gov/ obemporium; ✆ **512/974-1300**), which sells art and crafts made by seniors, is a good place to find out about senior activities in town.

Smoking Smoking is prohibited in all public buildings and common public areas (that includes hotel lobbies, museums, bars, restaurants, enclosed malls, and so on) in both San Antonio and Austin. It is also prohibited in the following outdoor places in San Antonio: the San Antonio Zoo, all sports arenas and amphitheaters; within 20 feet of public transportation stations and shelters; and in all pavilions and playgrounds in city-owned parks. In Austin, smoking is not allowed within 15 feet of any pedestrian entrance. As of October, 2018, you need to be 21 years old to purchase cigarettes in San Antonio; in Austin, the legal age for buying smokes is 18.

Taxes The sales tax in both San Antonio and Austin is 8.25%. In San Antonio, a city surcharge on hotel rooms raises the tax to a whopping 16.75%; in Austin, the tax on hotel rooms is 9%.

Visitor Information The main office of the **Official San Antonio Visitor Information Center** is across the street from the Alamo, 317 Alamo Plaza (www.visitsanantonio.com/ location/visitor-information-center; ✆ **210/244-2000**). Hours are daily 9am–5pm; it's closed New Year's Day, April 24, September 30, Thanksgiving Day, and Christmas Day. The **Austin Visitor Information Center,** 602 E. Fourth St. (www. austintexas.org/plan-a-trip/visitor-center; ✆ **866/ GO-AUSTIN** [462-8784] or 512/478-0098), is open Monday through Saturday 9am–5pm, Sunday 10am–5pm; it's closed on major holidays.

Index

See also Accommodations and Restaurant indexes, below.

General Index

A

B

X–Y–Z

Accommodations

Restaurants

Photo Credits

cover: © Andrew Olscher / Shutterstock.com; p. i: © Courtesy of Fredricksburg Tourism / Blake Mistich; p. ii: © Courtesy of Visitsanantonio.com; p. iii: © Courtesy of Bob Howen / VisitSanAntonio; p. iv: © Courtesy of Visitsanantonio.com; p. v, top: © Courtesy of Bob Howen / VisitSanAntonio; p. v, bottom left: © Courtesy of Visitsanantonio.com; p. v, bottom right: © Courtesy of Visitsanantonio.com; p. vi, top left: © Courtesy of Visitsanantonio.com / Bernadette Heath; p. vi, top right: © Courtesy of Visitsanantonio.com; p. vi, bottom: © Courtesy of Visitsanantonio.com; p. vii, top left: © Joshua Rainey Photography / Shutterstock.com; p. vii, top right: © Courtesy of Visitsanantonio.com / Marks Moore; p. vii, bottom left: © Courtesy of Visitsanantonio.com / Donald Nausbaum; p. vii, bottom right: © Courtesy of Visitsanantonio.com; p. viii, top left: © Courtesy of Visitsanantonio.com / Al-Rendon1; p. viii, top right: © Courtesy of Visitsanantonio.com; p. viii, bottom: © Courtesy of Visitsanantonio.com / Mark Menjivar; p. ix, top: © Fotoluminate LLC / Shutterstock.com; p. ix, bottom left: © LBJ Library photo by Jay Godwin; p. ix, bottom right: © Brandon Seidel / Shutterstock.com; p. x, top: © amy gizienski; p. x, middle: © Alizada Studios / Shutterstock.com; p. x, bottom: © Austin Convention & Visitors Bureau; p. xi, top left: © Fotoluminate LLC / Shutterstock.com; p. xi, top right: © Earl McGehee; p. xi, bottom: © evan bench; p. xii, top left: © Austin Convention & Visitors Bureau; p. xii, top right: © Roberto Cipriano; p. xii, bottom left: © Ralph Arvesen; p. xii, bottom right: © MarkScottAustinTX; p. xiii, top: © Djmaschek ; p. xiii, bottom left: © Barna Tanko / Shutterstock.com; p. xiii, bottom right: © Courtesy of Dixi Dude Ranch / 1881 Western Photography Co.; p. xiv, top left: © sbmeaper1; p. xiv, top right: © Fredsrickburg Tourism / Blake Mistich; p. xiv, bottom left: © Courtesy of Fredericksburg CVB; p. xiv, bottom right: © Courtesy of Fredericksburg CVB / Steve Rawls; p. xv, top: © Reuben Strayer; p. xv, bottom left: © Anthony Quintano; p. xv, bottom right: © Jason Squyres; p. xvi, top: © Todd Dwyer; p. xvi, middle: © Dustin Larimer; p. xvi, bottom: © Mark Bonica.

Map List

Frommer's EasyGuide to San Antonio & Austin, 1st Edition

Published by
FROMMER MEDIA LLC

Copyright © 2019 by Frommer Media LLC. All rights reserved. No part of this publication may be reproduced, stored in a retrieval system, or transmitted in any form or by any means, electronic, mechanical, photocopying, recording, scanning or otherwise, except as permitted under Sections 107 or 108 of the 1976 United States Copyright Act, without the prior written permission of the Publisher. Requests to the Publisher for permission should be addressed to the support@frommermedia.com.

Frommer's is a registered trademark of Arthur Frommer. Frommer Media LLC is not associated with any product or vendor mentioned in this book.

ISBN 978-1-62887-484-6 (paper), 978-1-62887-485-3 (e-book)

Editorial Director: Pauline Frommer
Editor: Holly Hughes
Production Editor: Cheryl Lenser
Cartographer: Roberta Stockwell
Photo Editor: Meghan Lamb
Assistant Photo Editor: Phil Vinke
Indexer: Cheryl Lenser
Cover Design: Dave Riedy

For information on our other products or services, see www.frommers.com.

Frommer Media LLC also publishes its books in a variety of electronic formats. Some content that appears in print may not be available in electronic formats.

Manufactured in the United States of America

5 4 3 2 1

ABOUT THE AUTHOR

Edie Jarolim has worn many hats, including a sombrero on one-margarita-too-many nights. She got a Ph.D. in American literature from NYU and was an editor at Frommer's in New York before she indulged her warm weather—and large living space—fantasies and moved to Tucson, Arizona. She has written about the Southwest and Mexico for a variety of major publications, including *National Geographic Traveler*, *Sunset*, *The Wall Street Journal*, and USAToday.com. She's the author of three travel guides, one dog guide, and one memoir. See www.ediejarolim.com for more details.

ABOUT THE FROMMER TRAVEL GUIDES

For most of the past 50 years, Frommer's has been the leading series of travel guides in North America, accounting for as many as 24% of all guidebooks sold. I think I know why.

Though we hope our books are entertaining, we nevertheless deal with travel in a serious fashion. Our guidebooks have never looked on such journeys as a mere recreation, but as a far more important human function, a time of learning and introspection, an essential part of a civilized life. We stress the culture, lifestyle, history, and beliefs of the destinations we cover, and urge our readers to seek out people and new ideas as the chief rewards of travel.

We have never shied from controversy. We have, from the beginning, encouraged our authors to be intensely judgmental, critical—both pro and con—in their comments, and wholly independent. Our only clients are our readers, and we have triggered the ire of countless prominent sorts, from a tourist newspaper we called "practically worthless" (it unsuccessfully sued us) to the many rip-offs we've condemned.

And because we believe that travel should be available to everyone regardless of their incomes, we have always been cost-conscious at every level of expenditure. Though we have broadened our recommendations beyond the budget category, we insist that every lodging we include be sensibly priced. We use every form of media to assist our readers, and are particularly proud of our feisty daily website, the award-winning Frommers.com.

I have high hopes for the future of Frommer's. May these guidebooks, in all the years ahead, continue to reflect the joy of travel and the freedom that travel represents. May they always pursue a cost-conscious path, so that people of all incomes can enjoy the rewards of travel. And may they create, for both the traveler and the persons among whom we travel, a community of friends, where all human beings live in harmony and peace.

Arthur Frommer

NOTES